Every Product Tells a Story

Index 1/2

Droog Lighting

Droog Furniture & Objects

Droog Table Top

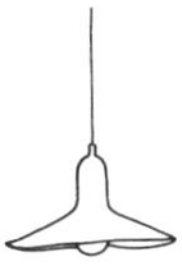

page 116
Flexlamp
Sam Hecht

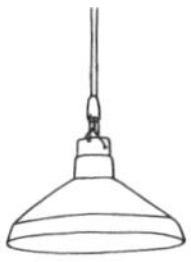

page 134
Porcelain lamp
Dick van Hoff

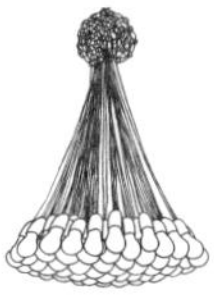

page 158
85 Lamps
Rody Graumans

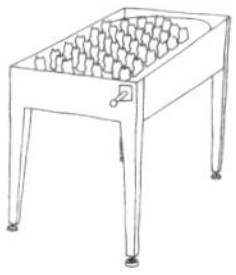

page 82
Lucky cat
Tadaaki Narita

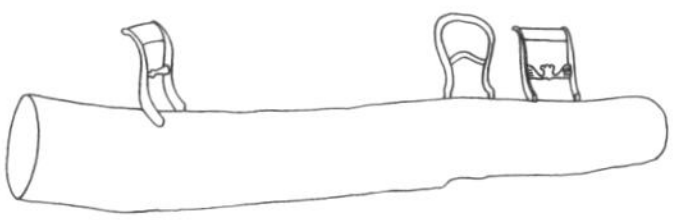

page 86
Tree-trunk bench
Jurgen Bey
• produced by
Jurgen Bey

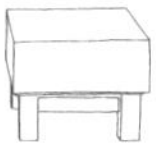

page 94
Stool
Richard Hutten
• produced by
Richard Hutten

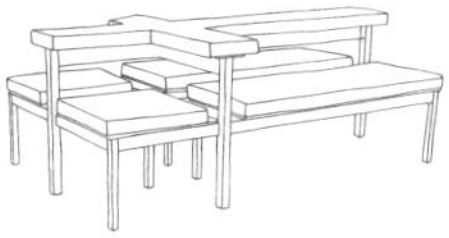

page 96
The cross
bench
Richard Hutten
• produced by
Richard Hutten

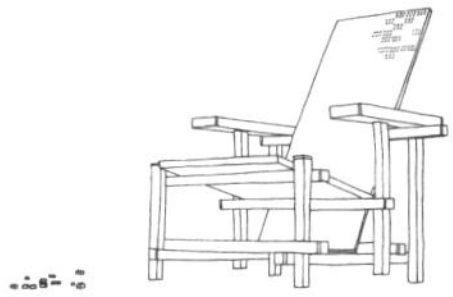

page 100
Red blue lego chair
Mario Minale

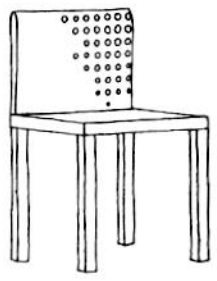

page 136
Chair with holes
Gijs Bakker

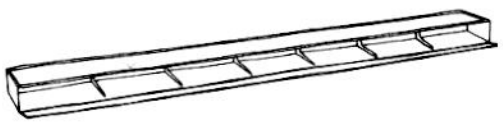

page 138
Extended cigar box
cupboard
Wieki Somers,
Dylan van den Berg

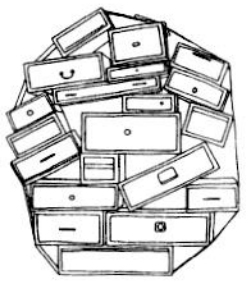

page 144
Chest of drawers
Tejo Remy

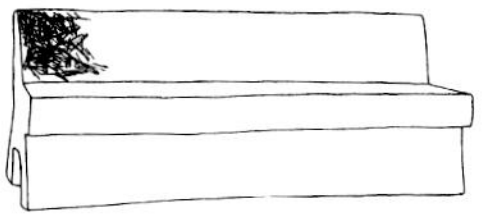

page 146
Gardening bench
Jurgen Bey
• produced by
Jurgen Bey

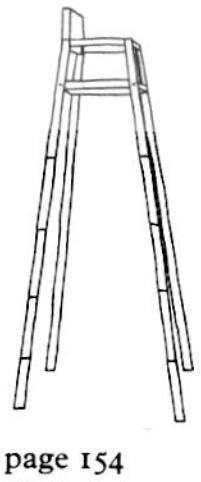

page 154
Highchair
Maartje
Steenkamp

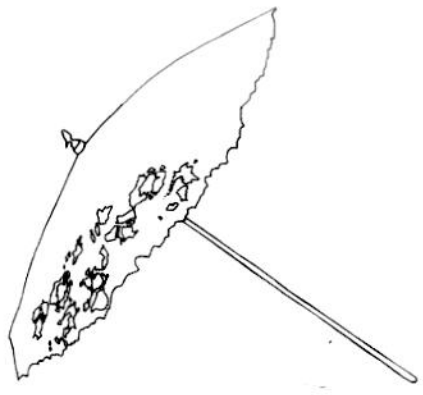

page 148
Shadylace
parasol
Chris Kabel

page 150
Shadylace XL
parasol
Chris Kabel

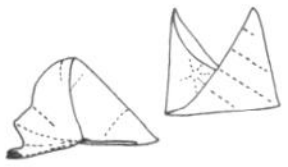

page 92
Twofold
napkin
Chris Kabel

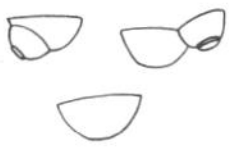

page 102
Bowls plus
Michelle Huang

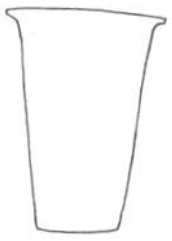

page 110
Soft vase
Hella Jongerius

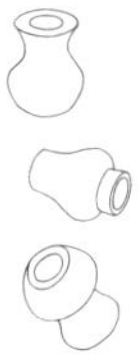

page 112
Monte Azul
vase
Nadine Sterk,
Lonny van
Rijswijck

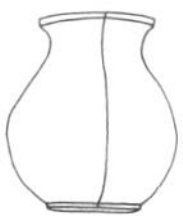

page 114
Urn vase
Hella Jongerius
• produced by
Hella Jongerius

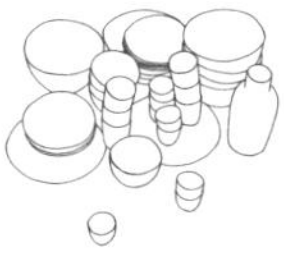

page 128
B-set service
Hella Jongerius
• produced by
Koninklijke
Tichelaar

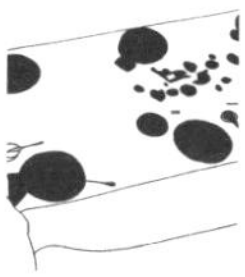

page 156
Tableau
tablecloth
Maurice
Scheltens

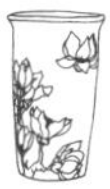

page 160
Blooming
over cup
Mina Wu,
Jan B.

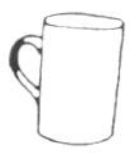

page 162
Perfect
cuppa cup
Onkar Singh
Kular

Index 2/2

Droog Bathroom

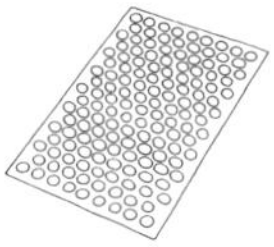
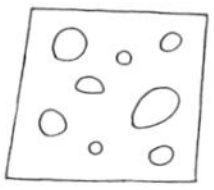
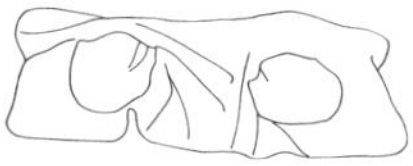
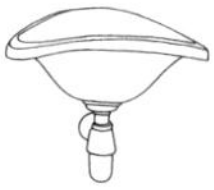
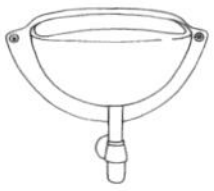

Droog Accessories

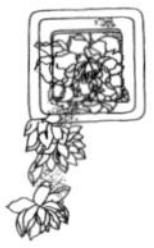

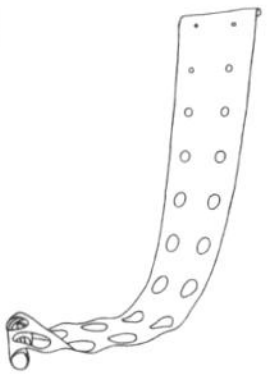
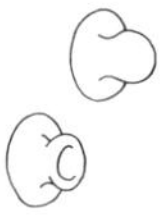
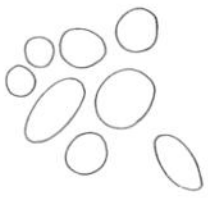
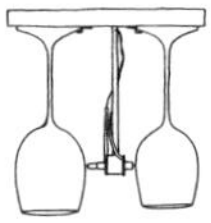
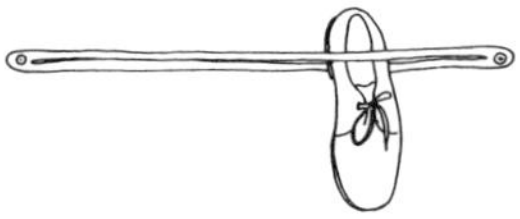

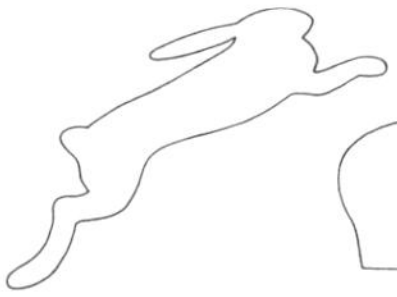
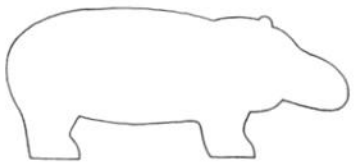
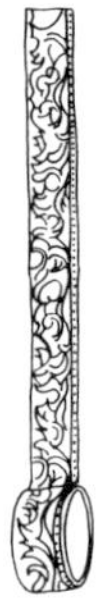
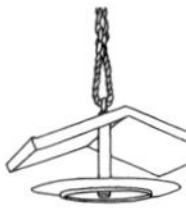
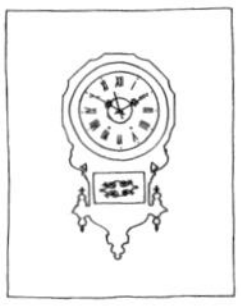
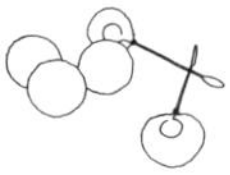
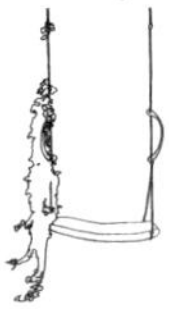

Droog Apparel

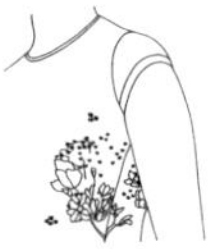
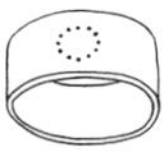
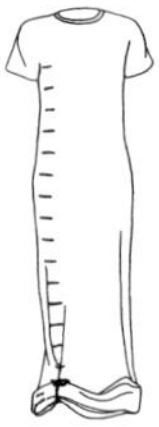

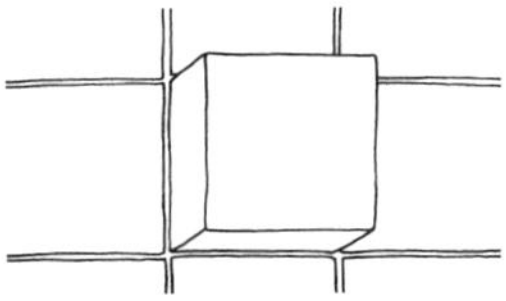

cube

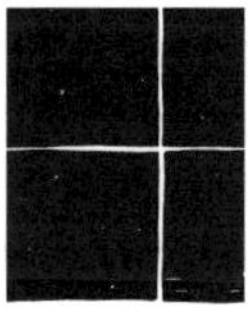

blackboard

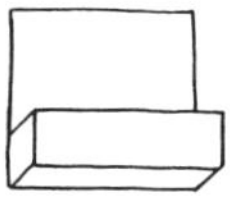

bookshelf

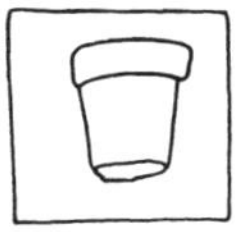

herbpot

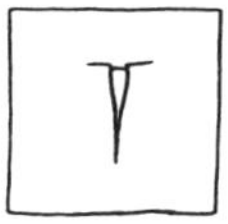

towelhook

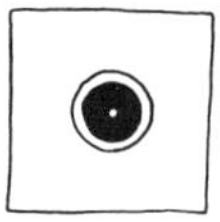

tub stop

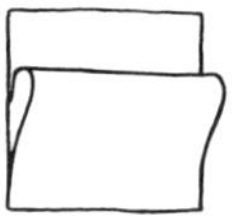

cutlery

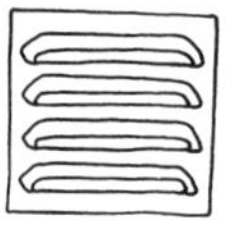

ventilation grid

page 74
Function tiles
Arnout Visser, Erik Jan Kwakkel,
Peter van der Jagt
• produced by Visser, Kwakkel,
Van der Jagt

What is Droog

Many people know Droog. From publications, from our lectures, via the website, by word of mouth. It is difficult to explain Droog in a few sentences, for our activities are quite diverse: we organise exhibitions and events, manage a collection, promote young designers, carry out design commissions for companies and institutions, initiate debate, publish books, produce and distribute, direct a masters course at the Design Academy Eindhoven and we have also opened a gallery and shop in Amsterdam where not only exhibitions are held but from time to time even dinners are organised. Actually we see no limits to our activities. That can appear confusing. Yet there is a clear line.

How it started

We started our activities in 1993. We had seen how a new design mentality was arising in the Netherlands. The work of a number of young designers who had graduated from various design schools stood out because of an emphasis on the concept. They were notable for a simple, clear execution of their designs and an aversion to Design with a capital D, that is to say, Design that wants to look designed: smooth styling, perfect construction, form practiced for its own sake. It was a clear break from the past, a genuinely new approach to design.

One very radical product was certainly Tejo Remy's Chest of drawers: twenty second-hand drawers around which twenty boxes have been built and bound together by a jute strap. This chest, which has become world famous and is included in numerous museum collections, caused a commotion in the design world at the time.

The designer had declared that he didn't want to design, but to improvise. He accepted the drawers as he found them, the user can remove or combine other things at will. How the chest is constructed is completely left to the user. One owner has placed a television set in it, while we ourselves added a wine rack for one of our exhibitions.

We decided to show the work of the new generation of designers during the International Furniture Fair in Milan. Before we did so, we agreed: 'If we've made a mistake and they think it's worth nothing we'll shut up shop. If it catches on, we'll keep going'. The fourteen objects we showed in Milan ranged from Remy's bundle of found wooden drawers, his Rag chair and Milk bottle lamp to Marcel Wanders' set up shades stack of ready-made lamps, Richard Hutten's Table chair and the oil and vinegar set and letter-scales by Arnout Visser, both of which were based on physics and executed in laboratory glass. We called our presentation after the Dutch word 'droog' since, in our opinion, the designs were executed very 'dryly', that is to say without frills. The word 'droog' could be connected to 'dry' in the sense of dry wit, or wry, subtle sense of humour. This first presentation was an overwhelming success. The French newspaper Liberation suggested that the 'unknowns' called Droog should be given a medal for spiritual 'savoir vivre'.

Droog Lab

Cheered by the response to the Milan exhibition we established the Droog Design foundation with the goal to stimulate innovative design. We therefore began initiating experimental projects, which would stimulate designers to be innovative and would introduce coherence to our activities. The first project was Dry Tech, carried out in collaboration with the Aviation and Aerospace Laboratory at the University of Technology in Delft. The starting point was a craftsman's approach to high-tech fibres. Marcel Wanders' famous 'knotted' chair, which is now being marketed by the Italian company Cappellini, was one of the products that came out of this project. Dry Tech marked the beginning of an ongoing series of diverse projects: from creating visionary concepts for a New York Times millennium competition and designing a flagship store in Paris for Mandarina Duck, the Italian producer of luggage and clothing, the coffee bar for the European Union Council building in Brussels to the annual thematic projects during the furniture fair in Milan, with such titles as Go Slow, Value for Money, Hotel Droog and Do Create. All these projects can be found on our website. We have since developed the Droog concept not by repeating and refining the original formula but by experimenting with new concepts, new products, new materials, new designers and new partners. The core of our work is the Droog collection with more than 150 products, prototypes and concepts, which are either resulting from Droog's many projects or designer's work that has been selected by us.

Droog Label

From the beginning we have acknowledged the importance of production and distribution of the products in our collection. But we found at the time that it did not suit our objectives to start doing this ourselves. For this reason we have always delegated this to others, which is why one comes across Droog products produced by other companies such as Cappellini and Moooi. To have more control on demands of quality and price, we decided two years ago to take charge of the production and distribution of the Droog collection. For this we established Droog as a limited company, which now produces more than fifty products from the Droog collection and a lot of new products are on the way. All the products included in this book are available. Of course we have also included the products that historically are produced by other parties because they are part of the collection and will remain so. Designs are not included in the collection for purely commercial reasons. The concept and the execution are always the deciding factors. We then look to see whether the product can be produced at a good price/quality ratio. Should it prove impossible to produce a design for a reasonable price, technical reasons or because of the concept, then it is supplied in a small edition, numbered and signed. This has resulted in a range that varies from Tejo Remy's handmade Chest of drawers to Martí Guixé's mass produced Do frame tape, which can be used to frame photos and posters in a simple way.

droog@home

In order to increase our visibility, we opened a gallery and shop in Amsterdam in 2004. Here a part of our collection is on permanent display and for sale. We also organize exhibitions by young designers who have come to our notice. People can watch our videos and now and then dinners are held. Sometimes these are private dinners for organizations and companies, sometimes we make them open to the public. Naturally these are no ordinary dinners. They are linked to the Droog mentality; they have a conceptual slant, with a lot of attention paid to the content, presentation and interaction with the public.

Droog Mentality

All Droog projects reflect the Droog mentality. What this mentality implies has been described by the press in all kinds of ways in the last 12 years: gutsy, intelligently provocative, quirky, hip, funky, fashionable, the rock and roll of design and so on. For us, it's always a question of original ideas, clear, up-to-date concepts which have been shaped in a wry, no-nonsense manner and that product usability is a must. Within this framework literally everything goes.
When we started in 1993 conceptual design was hardly an issue. Droog's activities have partly contributed to the situation whereby young designers all over the world have started to work in tune with the Droog mentality. You could say that Droog has unleashed a whole movement. Some of the pieces unveiled in the first Droog exhibitions are now regarded iconic objects of the early nineties. Many young designers featured in our first shows, such as Marcel Wanders, Hella Jongerius,

Richard Hutten and Jurgen Bey, have since emerged as pivotal figures in contemporary design. We no longer work only with Dutch designers.
Our network has gradually expanded to all corners of the world and currently embraces around 150 independent designers. The products in the collection cut across the usual categories: furniture, lamps, wall tiles, wallpaper, tablecloths, a birdhouse, a parasol.... What they have in common is that they are made for people. Hence the title of this book 'A Human Touch'.
For the product photography by Joke Robaard and Maarten Theuwkens, we asked staff, friends and visitors at droog@home to be our models as an example that the products are designed for everyone. The products in the Droog collection are special and at the same time accessible. They are far from what is normally meant by design – a style. They are very close to man. Because of the way they can be caressed and the way they are used, through a certain degree of imperfection, because they have something familiar, evoke memories, because they produce an experience and allow the user to participate, or through their simplicity, through their function, through their meaning, through their poetry and their humour. The products tell stories that are understood all over the world and are passed on. They are products that are meant to be used. This is why the stories are also about the user. And the users are us.

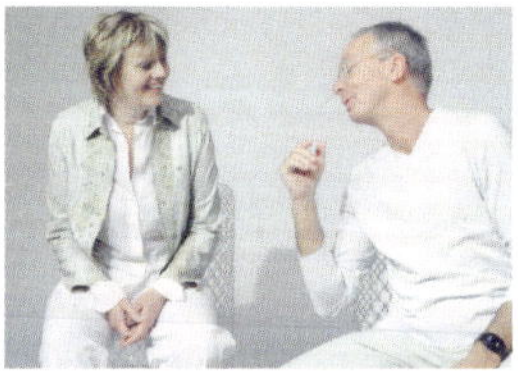

Renny Ramakers, Gijs Bakker
Founders of Droog

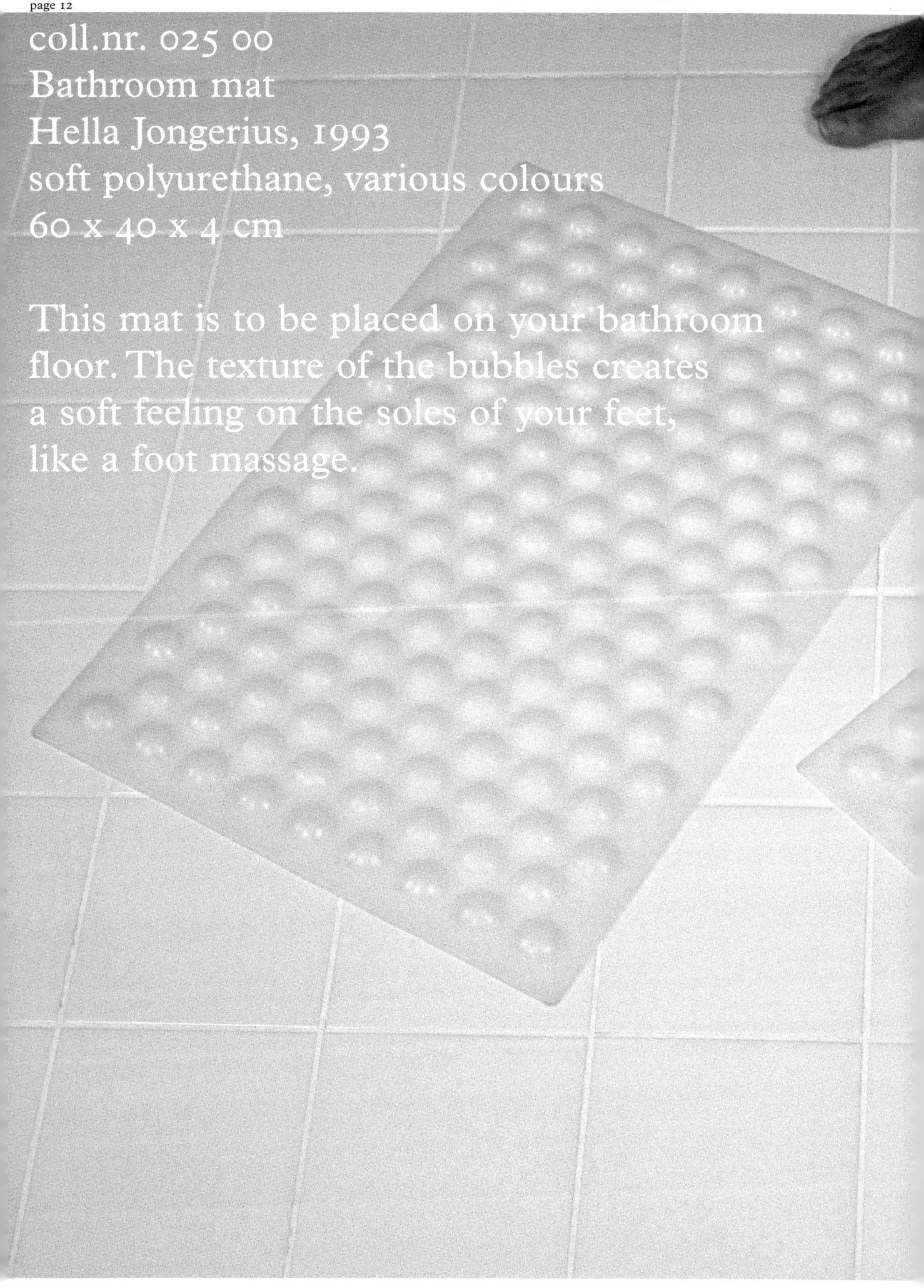

coll.nr. 025 00
Bathroom mat
Hella Jongerius, 1993
soft polyurethane, various colours
60 x 40 x 4 cm

This mat is to be placed on your bathroom floor. The texture of the bubbles creates a soft feeling on the soles of your feet, like a foot massage.

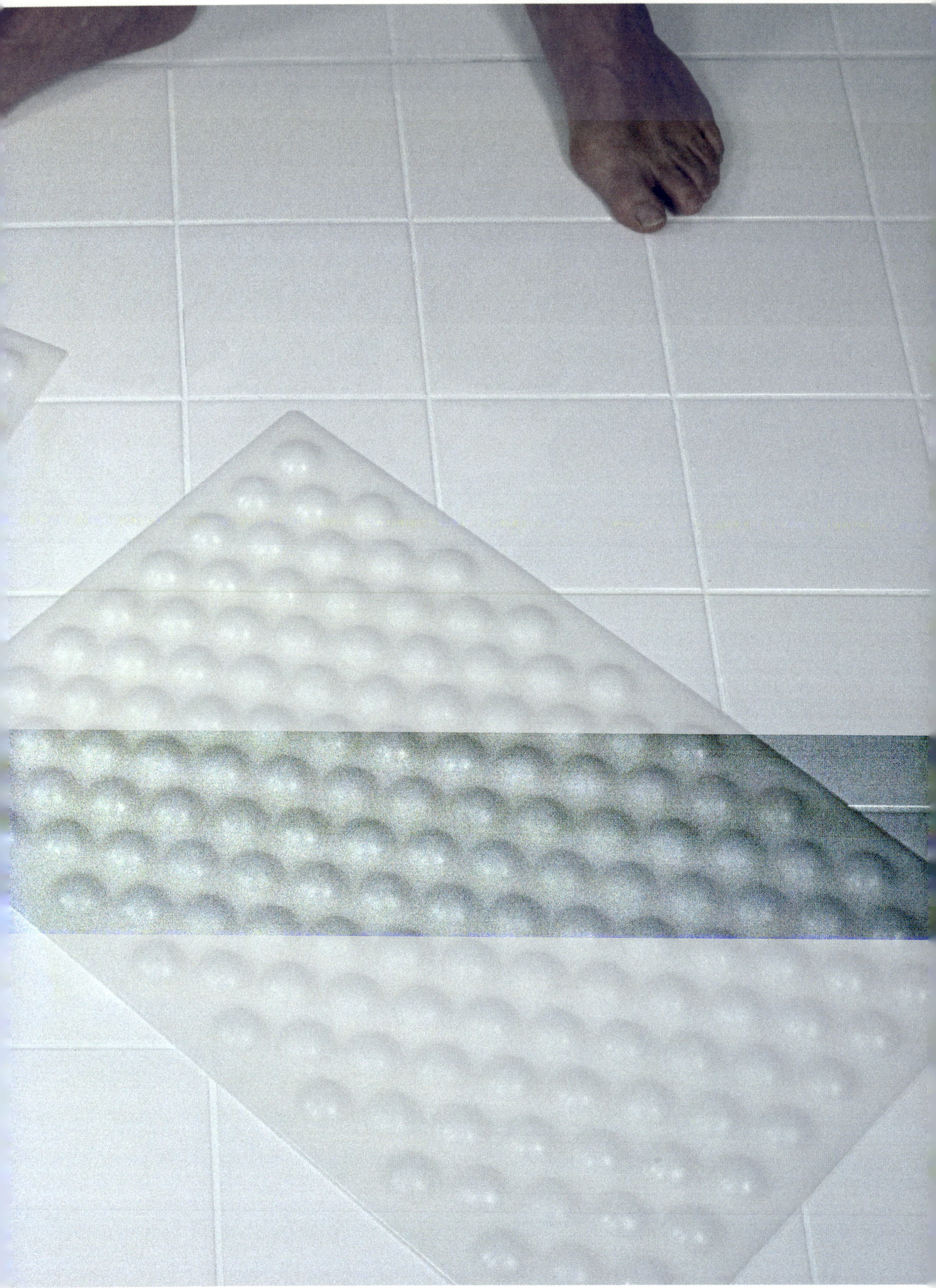

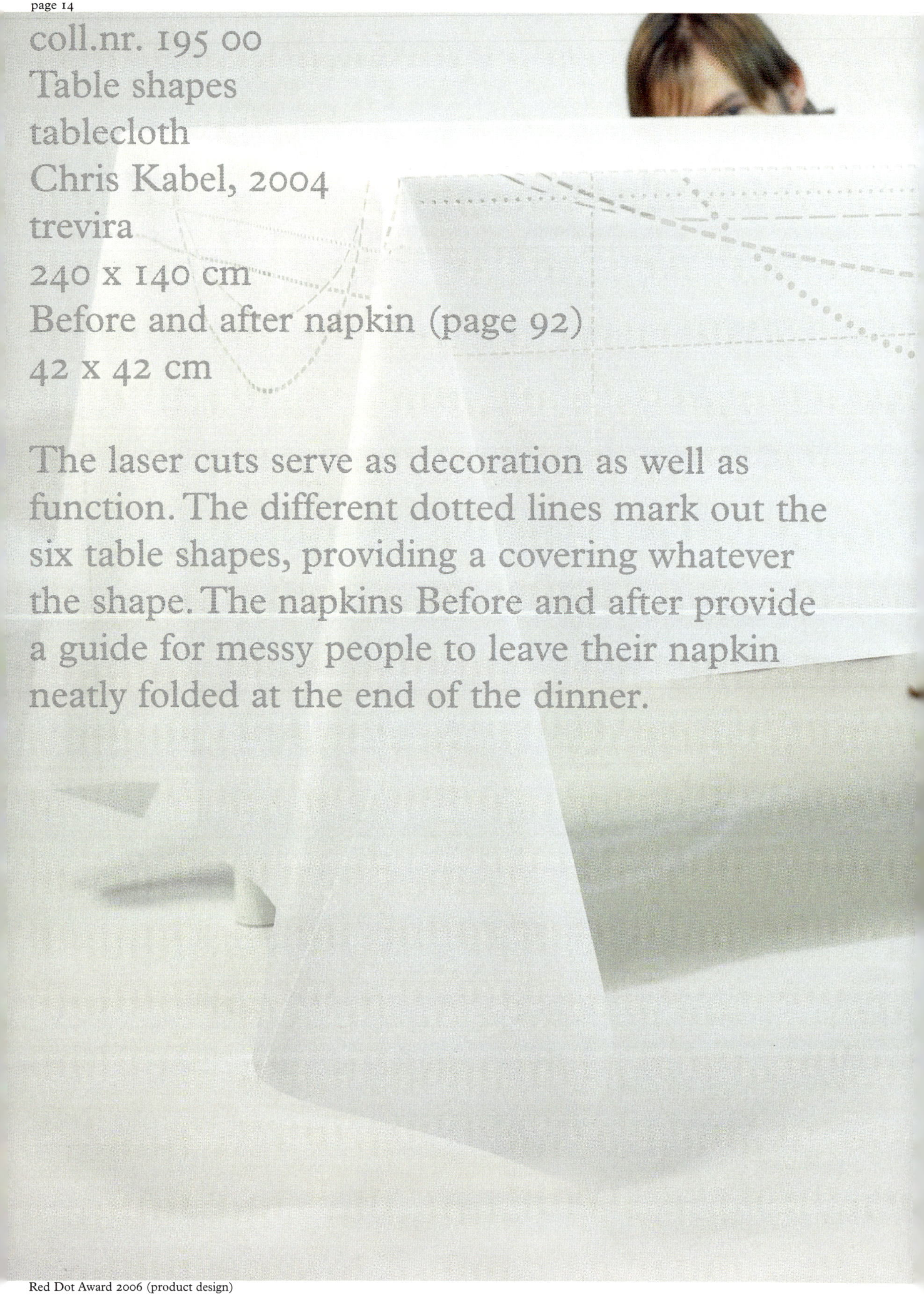

coll.nr. 195 00
Table shapes
tablecloth
Chris Kabel, 2004
trevira
240 x 140 cm
Before and after napkin (page 92)
42 x 42 cm

The laser cuts serve as decoration as well as function. The different dotted lines mark out the six table shapes, providing a covering whatever the shape. The napkins Before and after provide a guide for messy people to leave their napkin neatly folded at the end of the dinner.

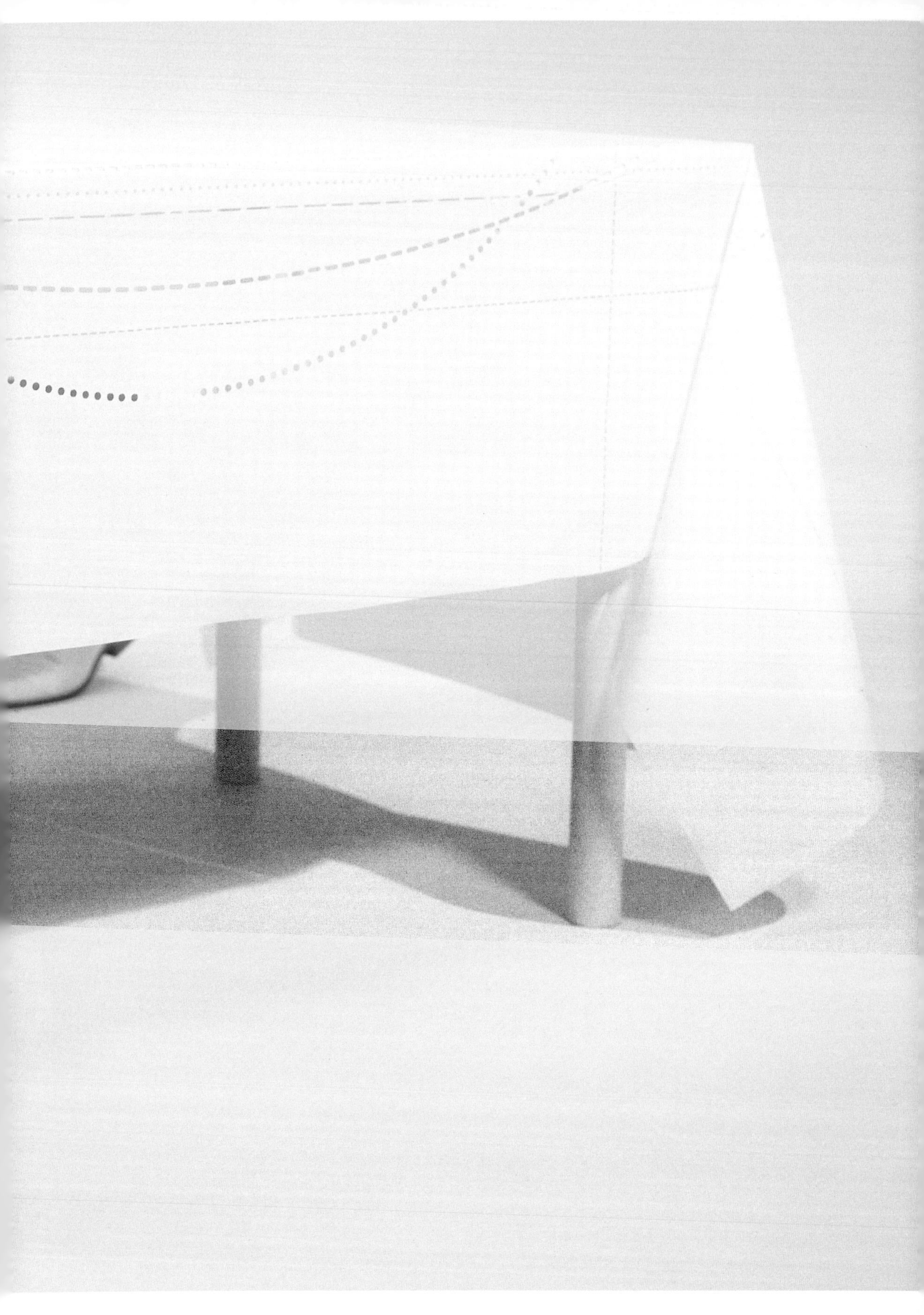

coll.nr. 173 00
Bloom switch
Mina Wu, 2004
hand painted, transfer print, various colours
10 x 3 x 20 cm
limited edition of 50 pieces per year

You can order this hand-painted transfer to make an unusual but beautiful feature of your light switch or socket.

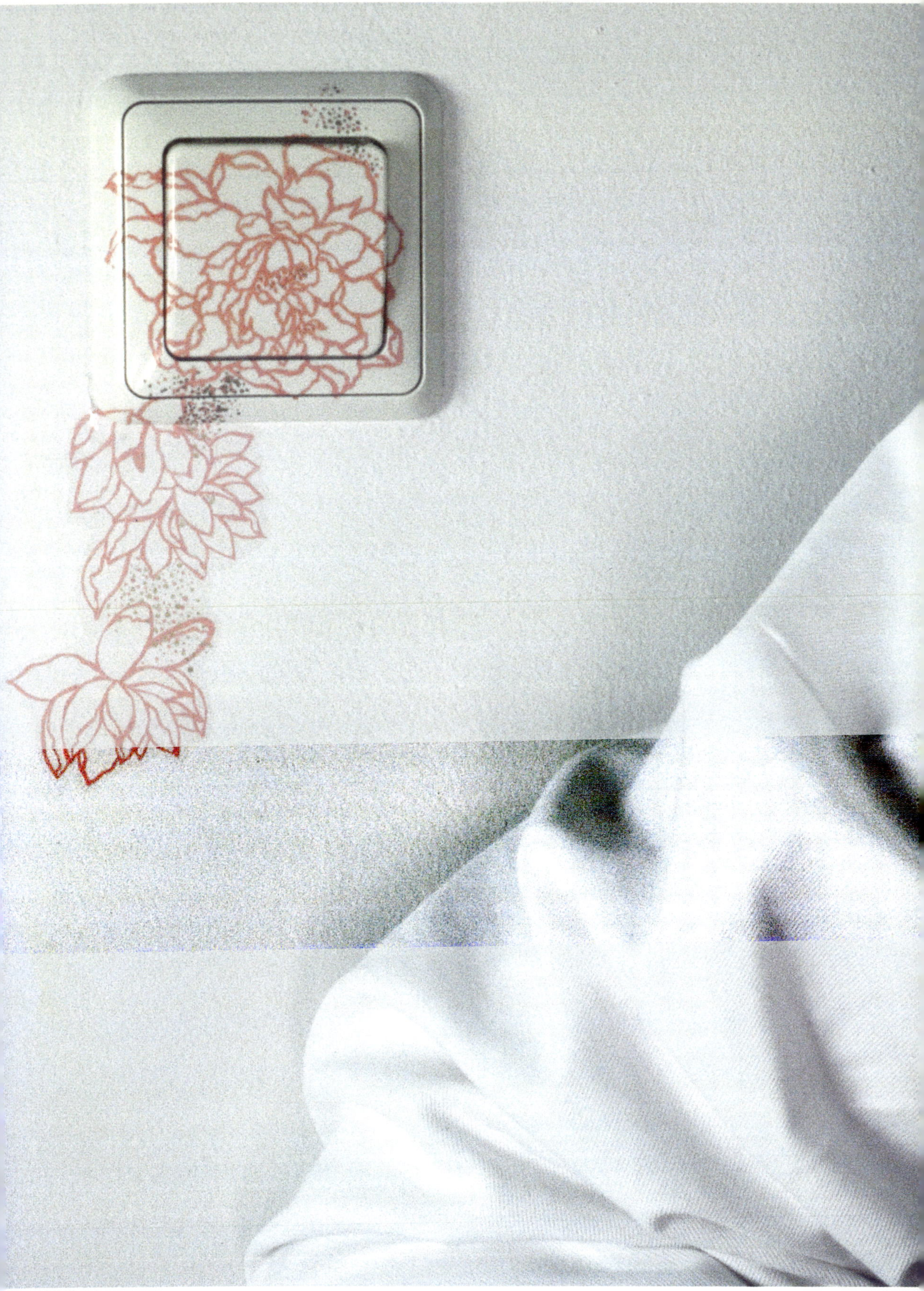

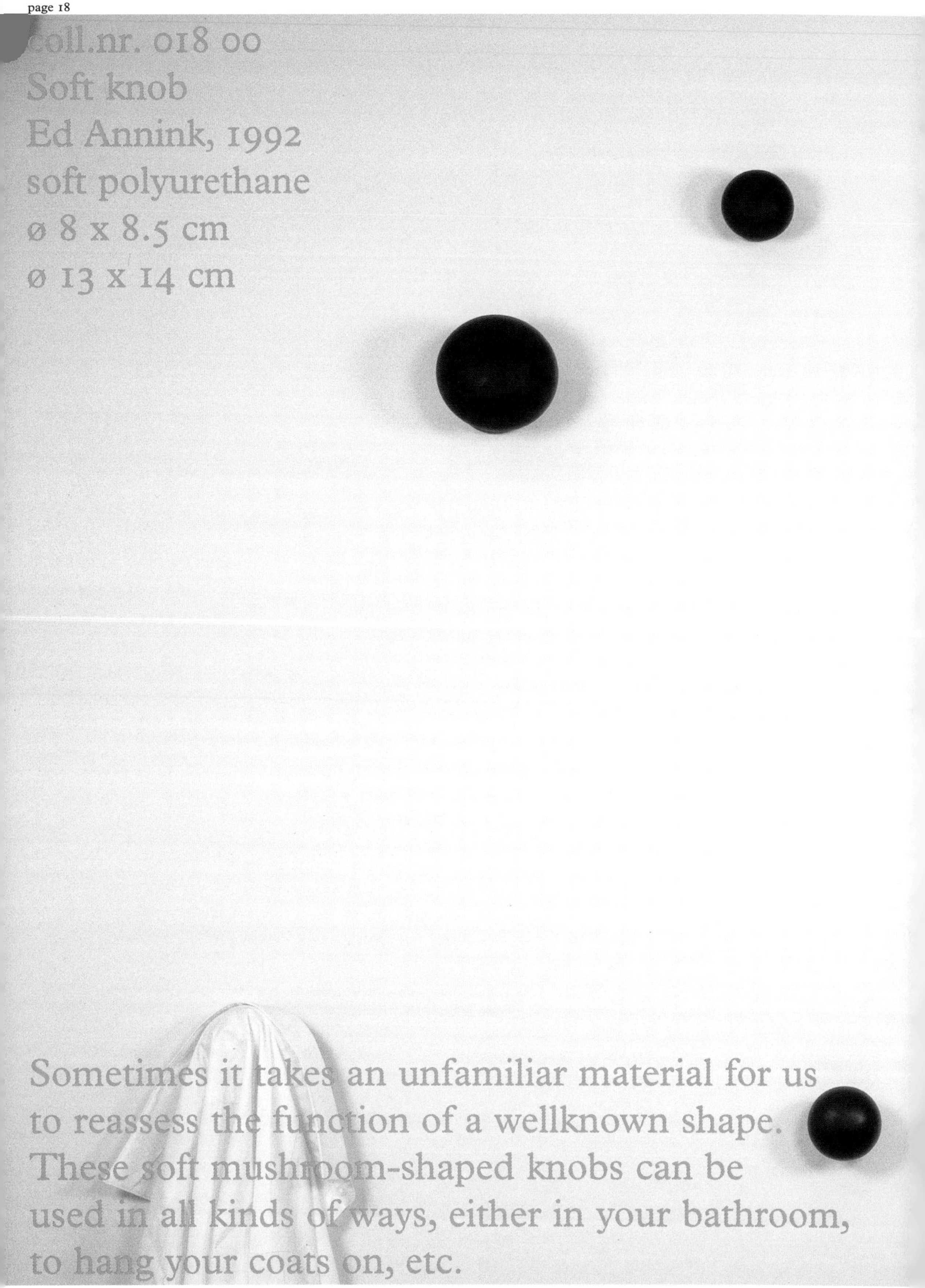

coll.nr. 018 00
Soft knob
Ed Annink, 1992
soft polyurethane
ø 8 x 8.5 cm
ø 13 x 14 cm

Sometimes it takes an unfamiliar material for us to reassess the function of a wellknown shape. These soft mushroom-shaped knobs can be used in all kinds of ways, either in your bathroom, to hang your coats on, etc.

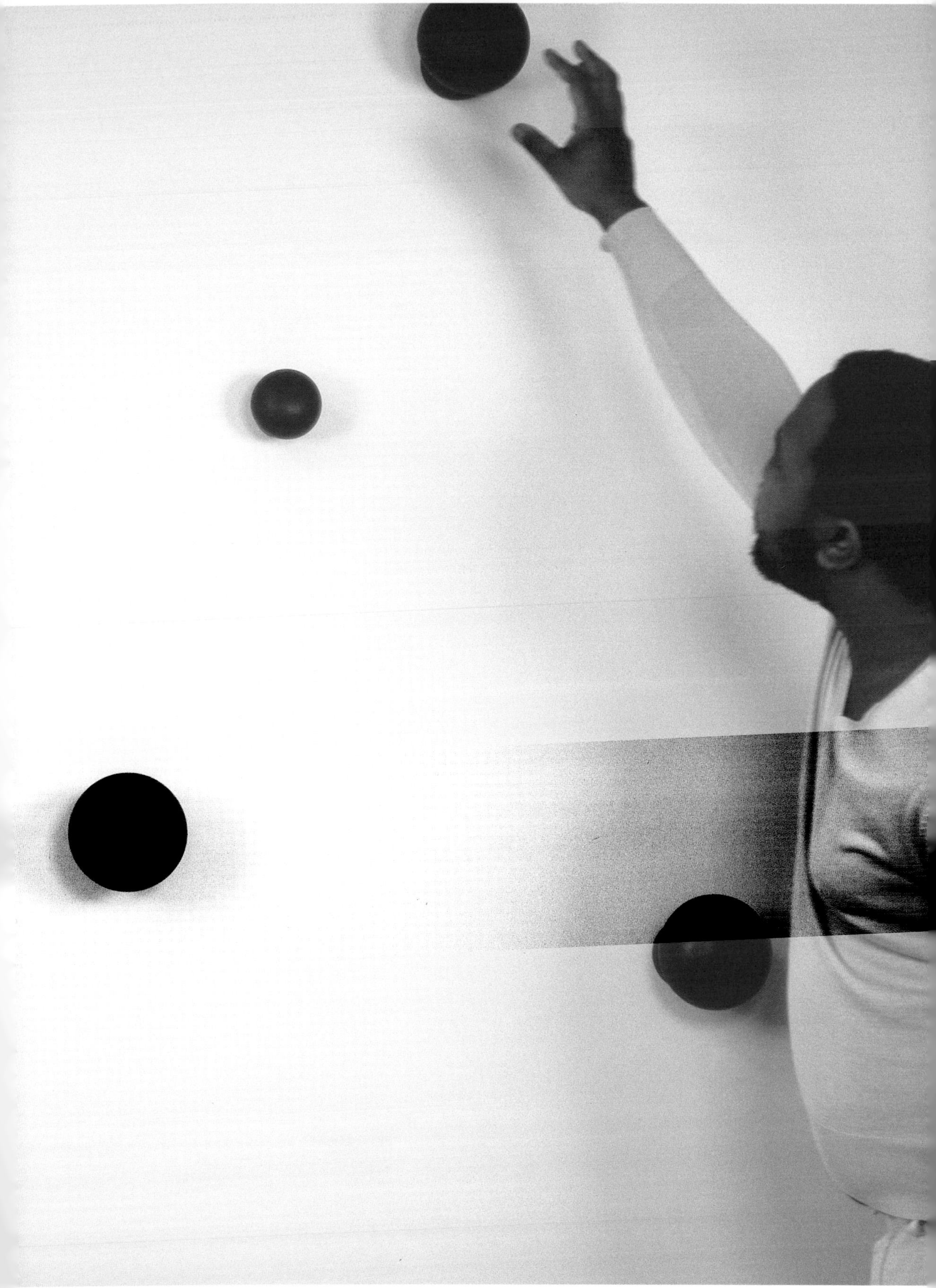

coll.nr. 019 00
Peepshow
wallpaper
Gijs Bakker, 1992
high quality craft paper
53 x 320 cm

This simple design of plain paper with cu
circles can be put directly on top of exis
decoration. The wallpaper gives a new l
with windows to look back on past me

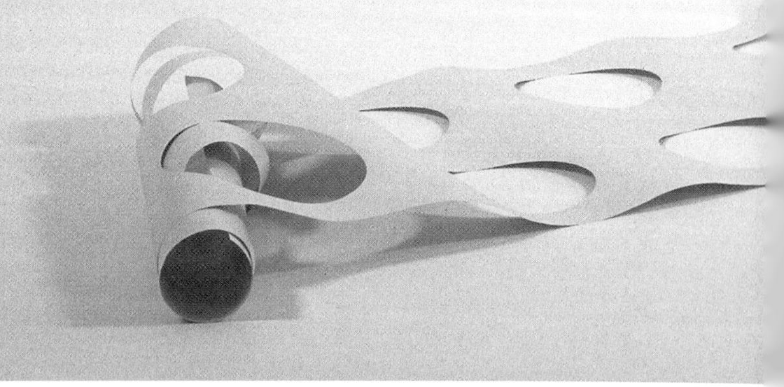

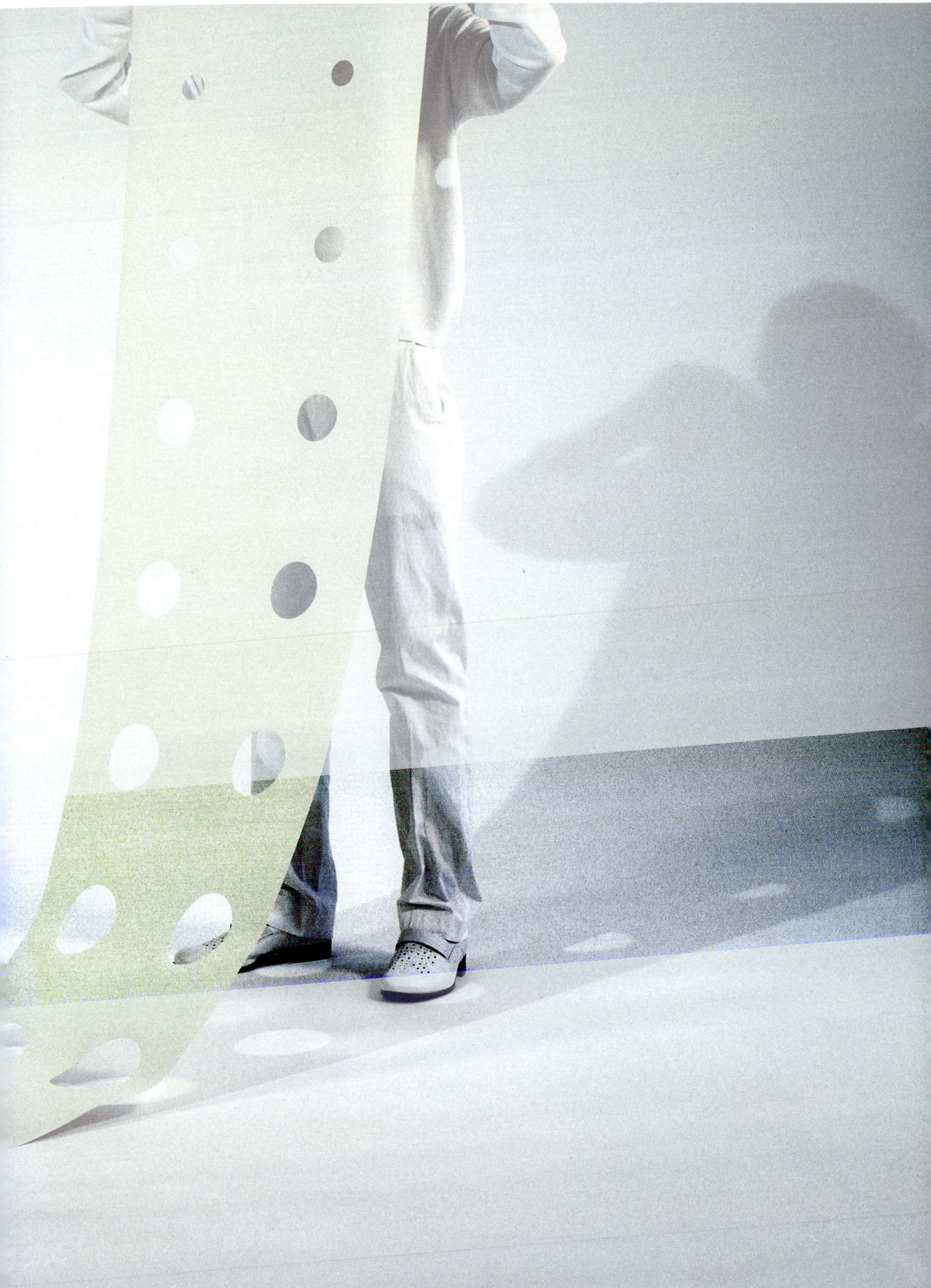

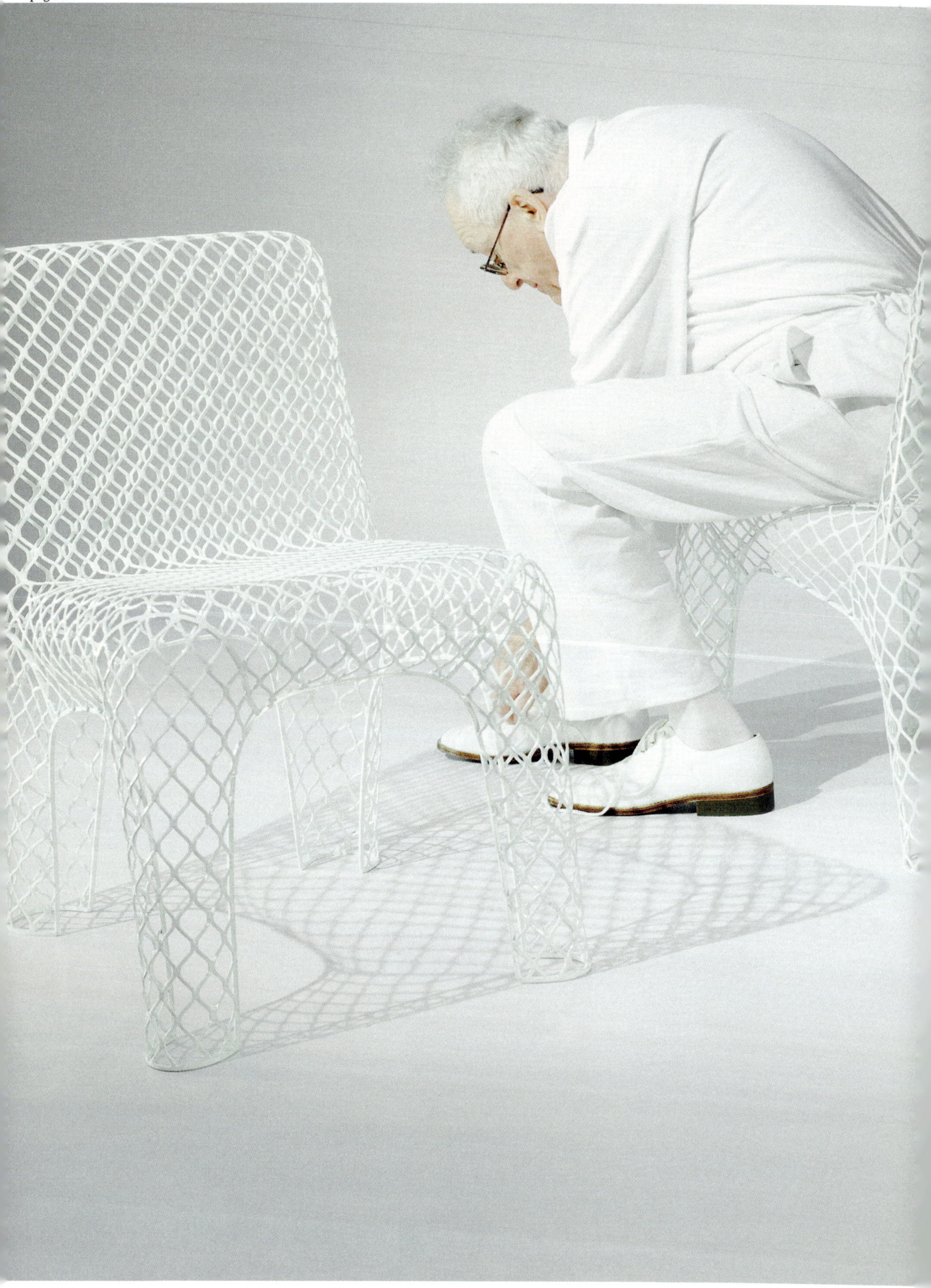

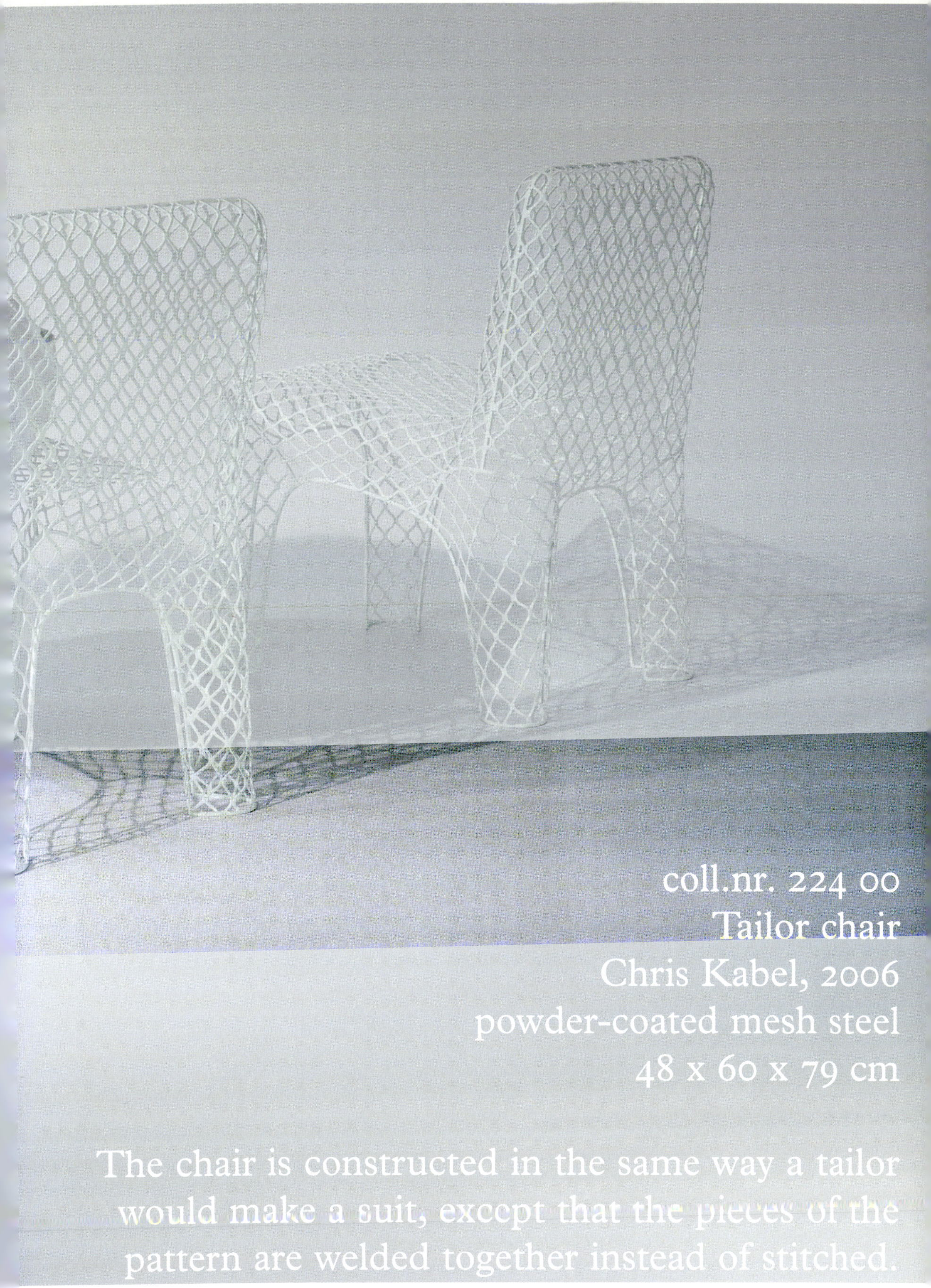

coll.nr. 224 00
Tailor chair
Chris Kabel, 2006
powder-coated mesh steel
48 x 60 x 79 cm

The chair is constructed in the same way a tailor would make a suit, except that the pieces of the pattern are welded together instead of stitched.

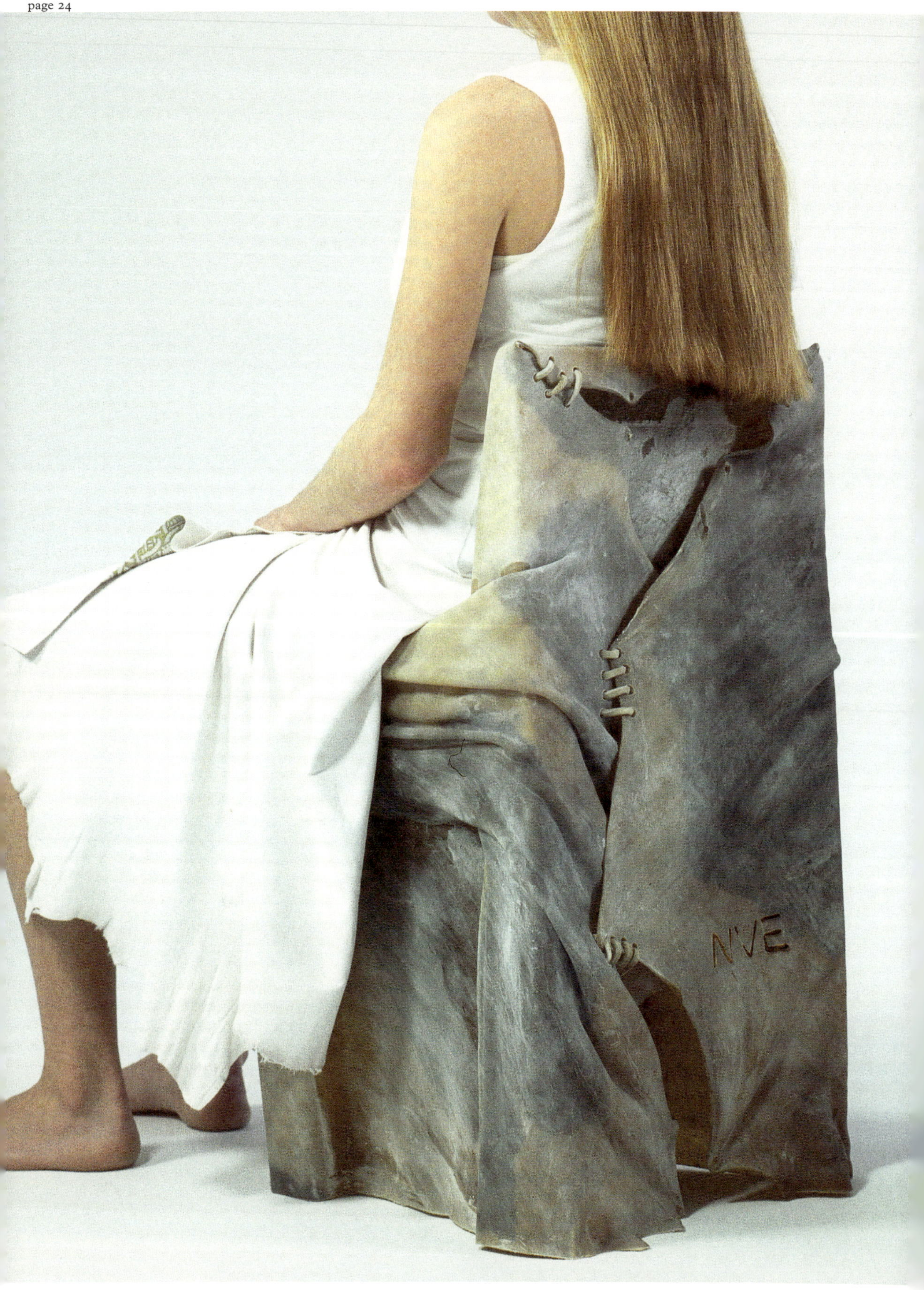
N'VE

coll.nr. 057 00
Cow chair
Niels van Eijk, 1997
cowhide
44 x 38 x 72 cm

Each chair is naturally unique, consisting of nothing more than a single cowhide. The untreated cowhide is stretched around a form when soaking wet and then left for one week until it has dried into a solid form.

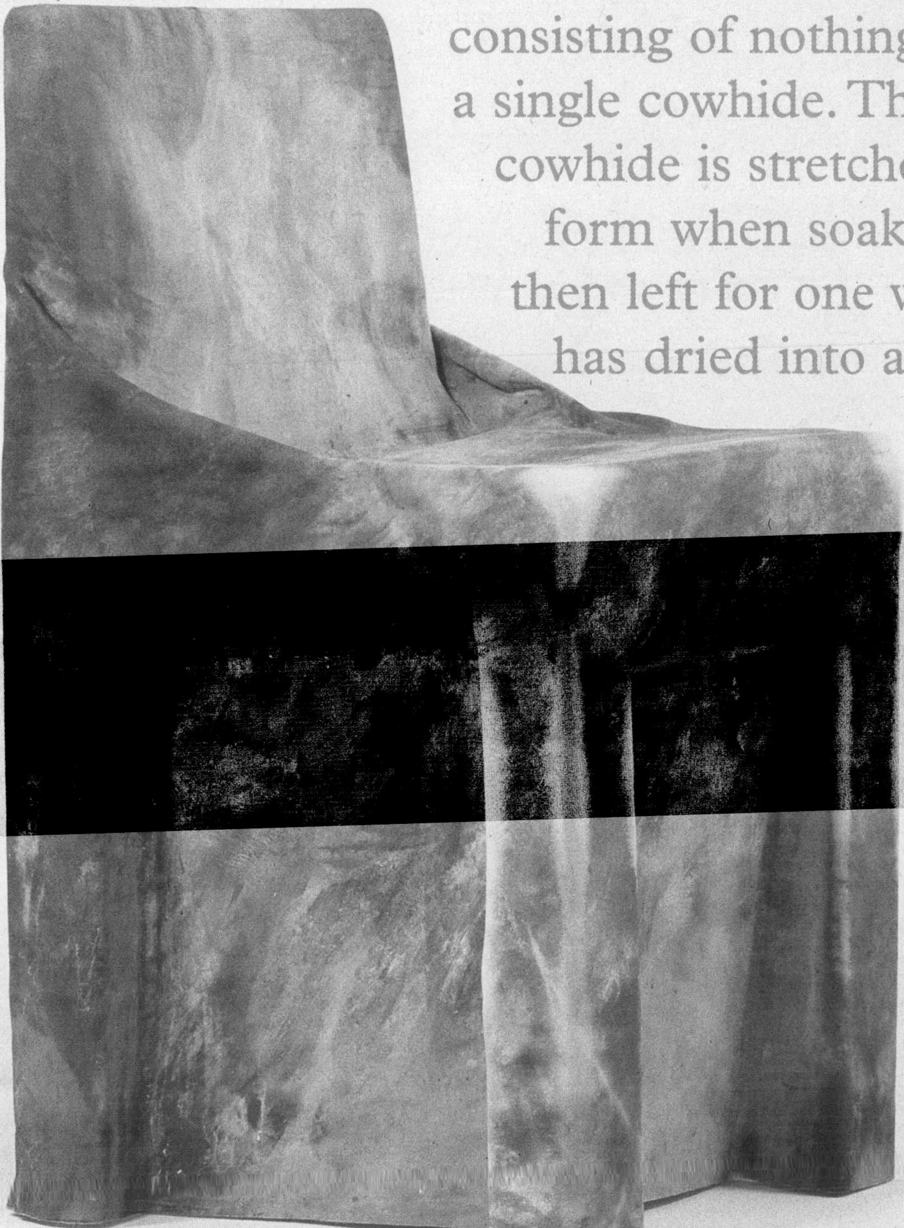

coll.nr. 015 00
Rag chair
Tejo Remy, 1991
rags, metal strips
60 x 60 x 100 cm

This chair is layered from the contents of 15 bags of rags. It arrives ready made but the user has the option to recycle their own discarded clothes to be included in the design. Each piece is unique, but it can also become a treasured chest of memories.

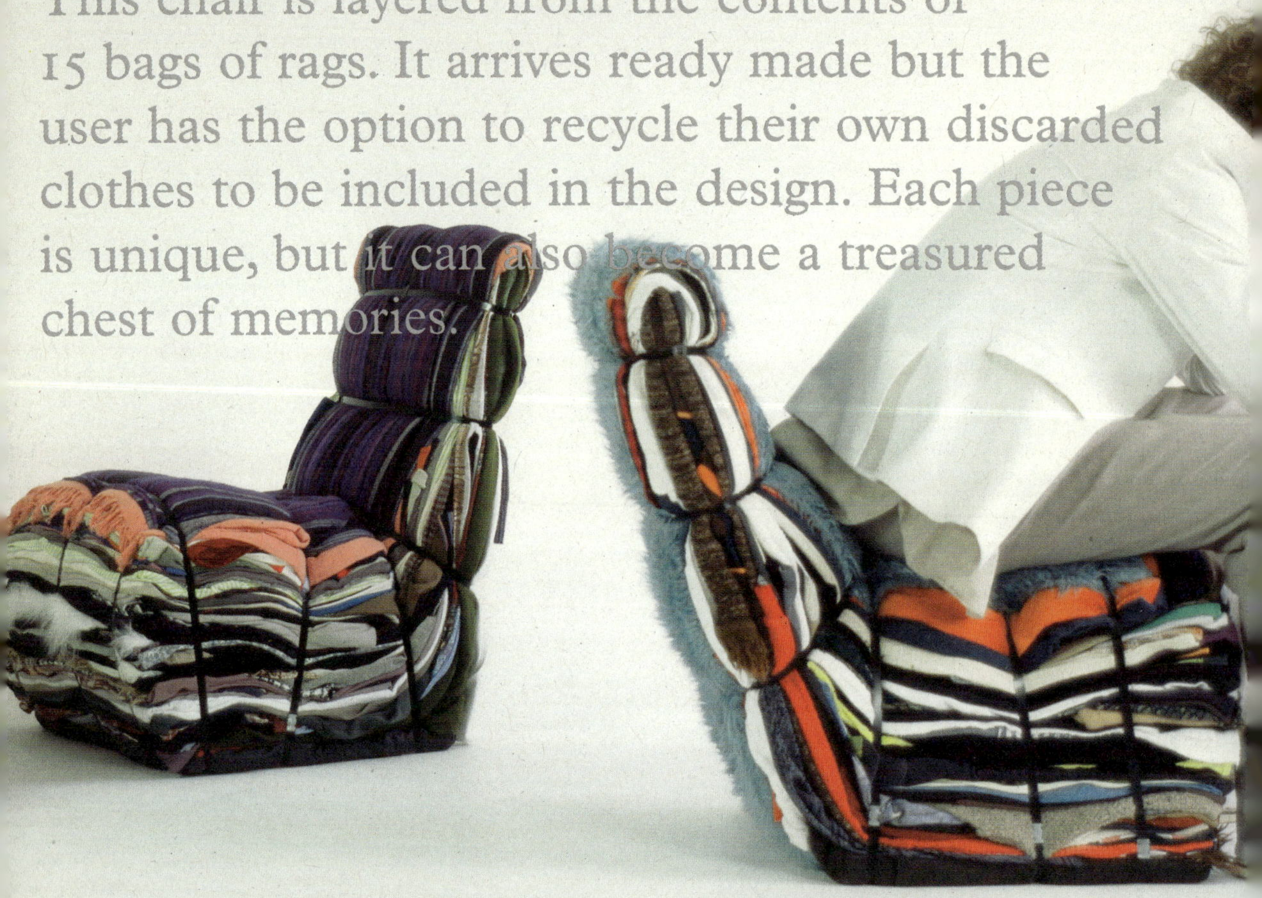

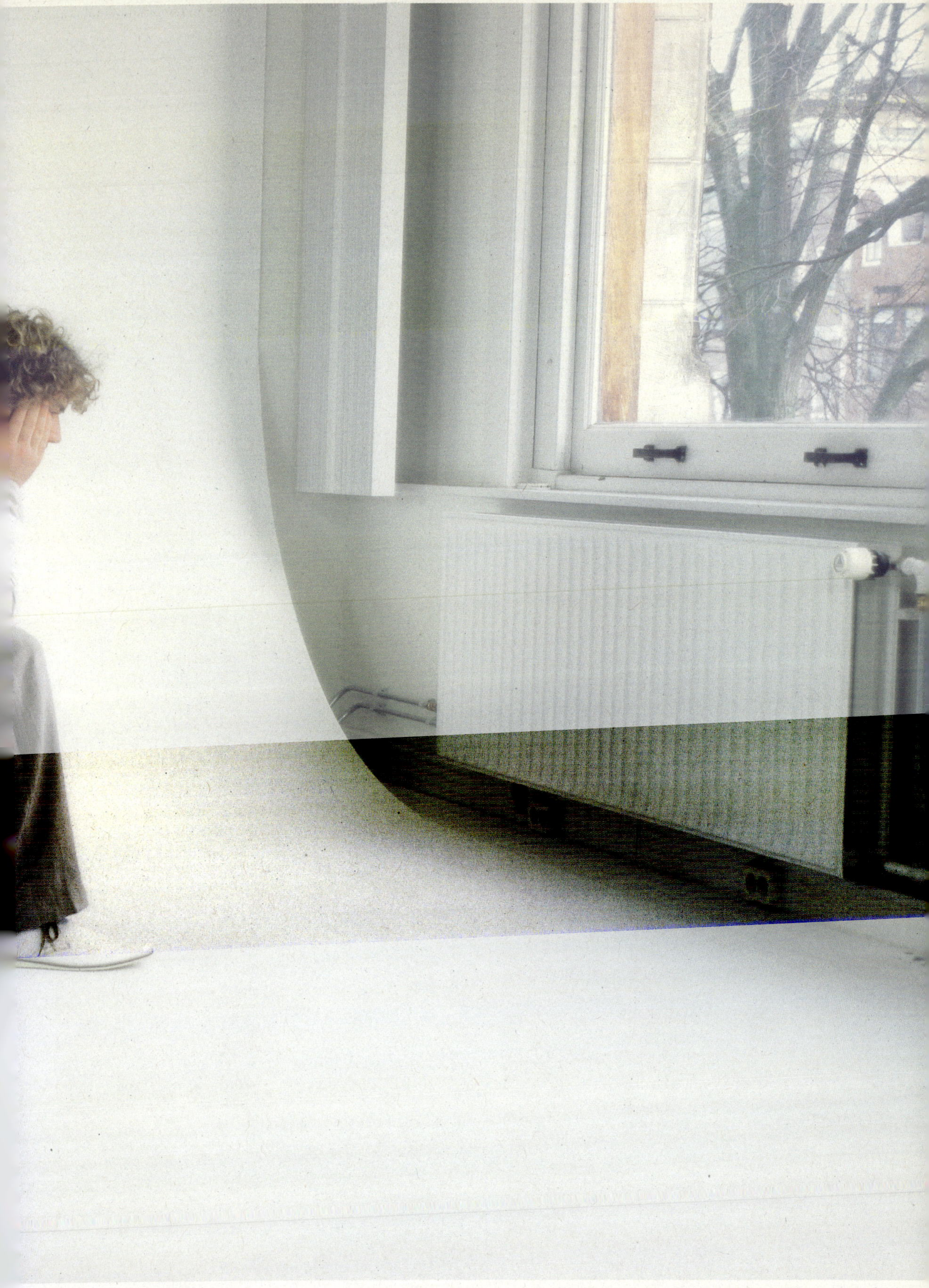

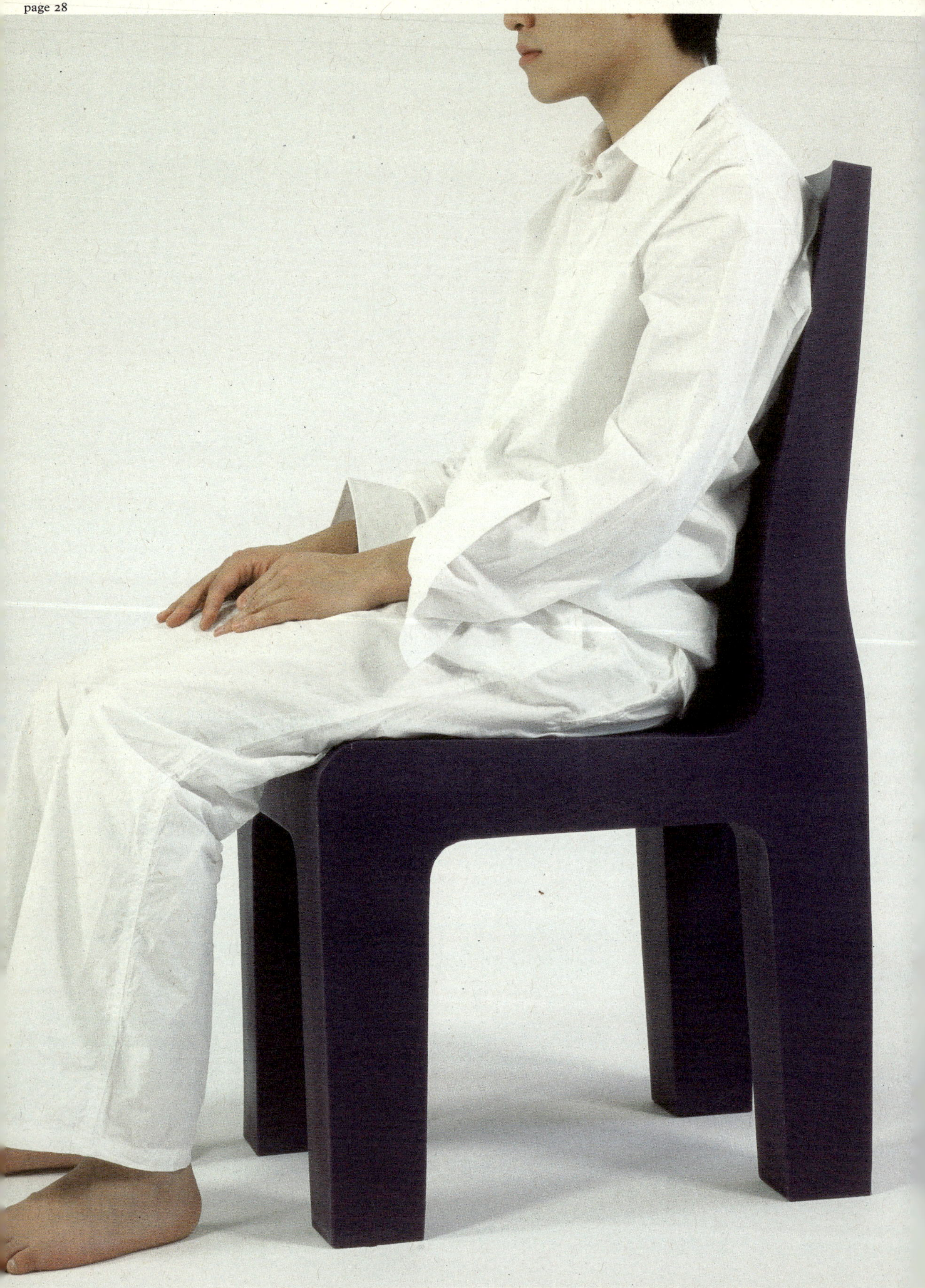

coll.nr. 083 00
CM chair
Richard Hutten, 1999
rotation moulded PE, dark grey, purple, red
45 x 55 x 100 cm

Named after the Centraal Museum in Utrecht after they commissioned Richard Hutten to design a chair for their restaurant. He took inspiration from the museum's history as a former monastery, with the restaurant situated in the refectory. The chair is designed as if it were a 21st century refectory chair. With its high back and square legs it looks heavy, but in reality it is light due to its hollow construction and the use of polyethylene as a construction material.

coll.nr. 058 00
Bronto child's chair
Richard Hutten, 1997
rotation moulded PE, various colours
55 x 28 x 35 cm

A colour coded chair. Combining a hard and soft polyurethane of different colours in a rotation mould technique results in uniquely decorated chairs. Where strain on the construction is greater this part is made from the harder material. The corners are soft making it an ideal child's chair.

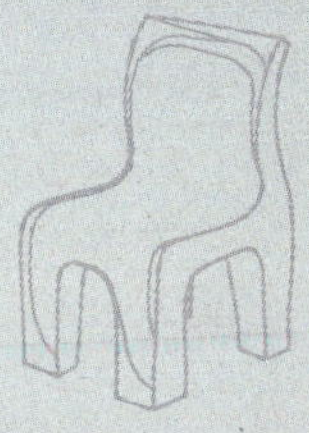

coll.nr. 112 00
Private rocking chair
Martí Guixé, 2001
birch plywood, textile, paint
150 x 140 x 84 cm

The integrated walls in the chair provide a hideaway to exclude yourself, even when in hectic surroundings.

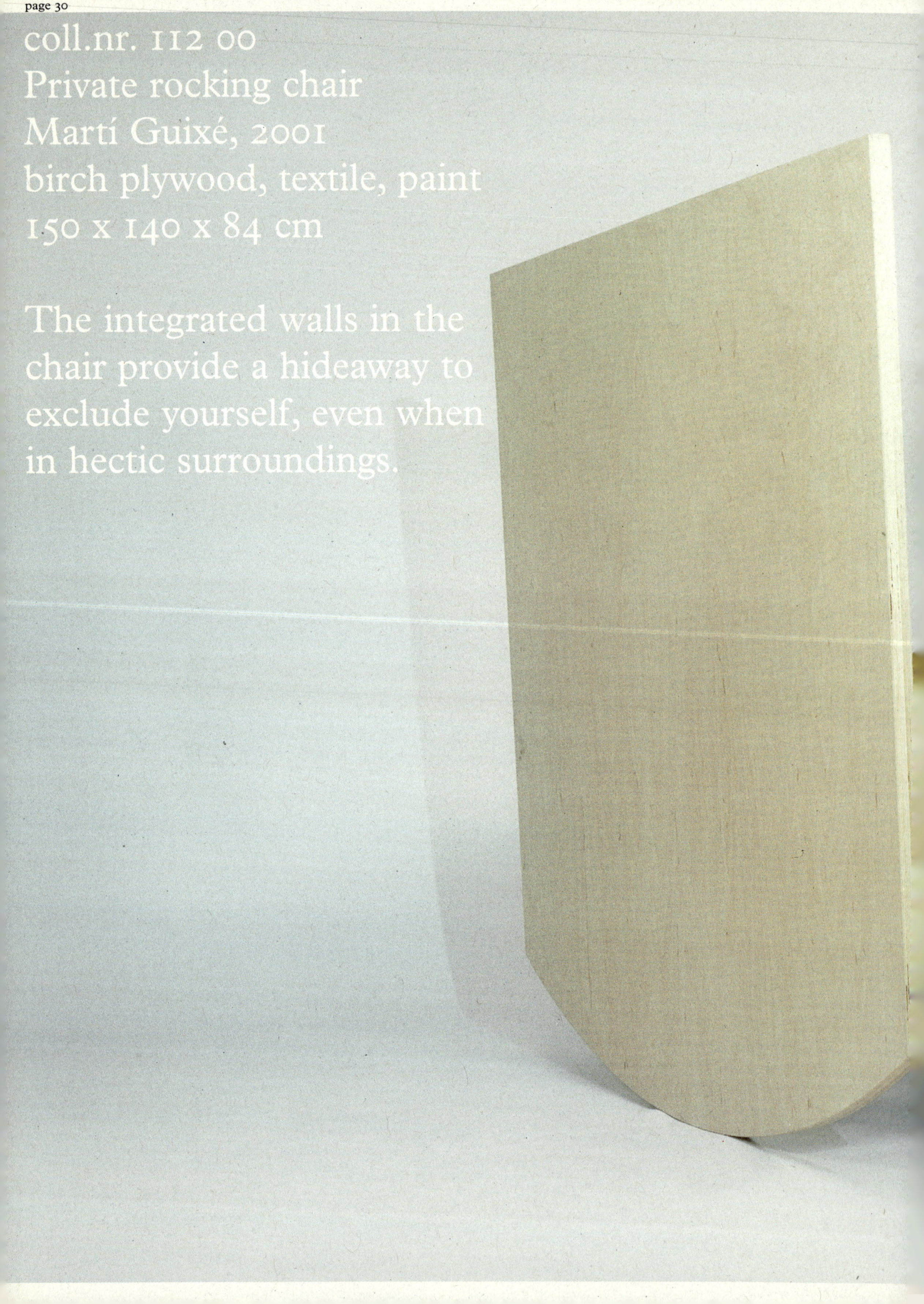

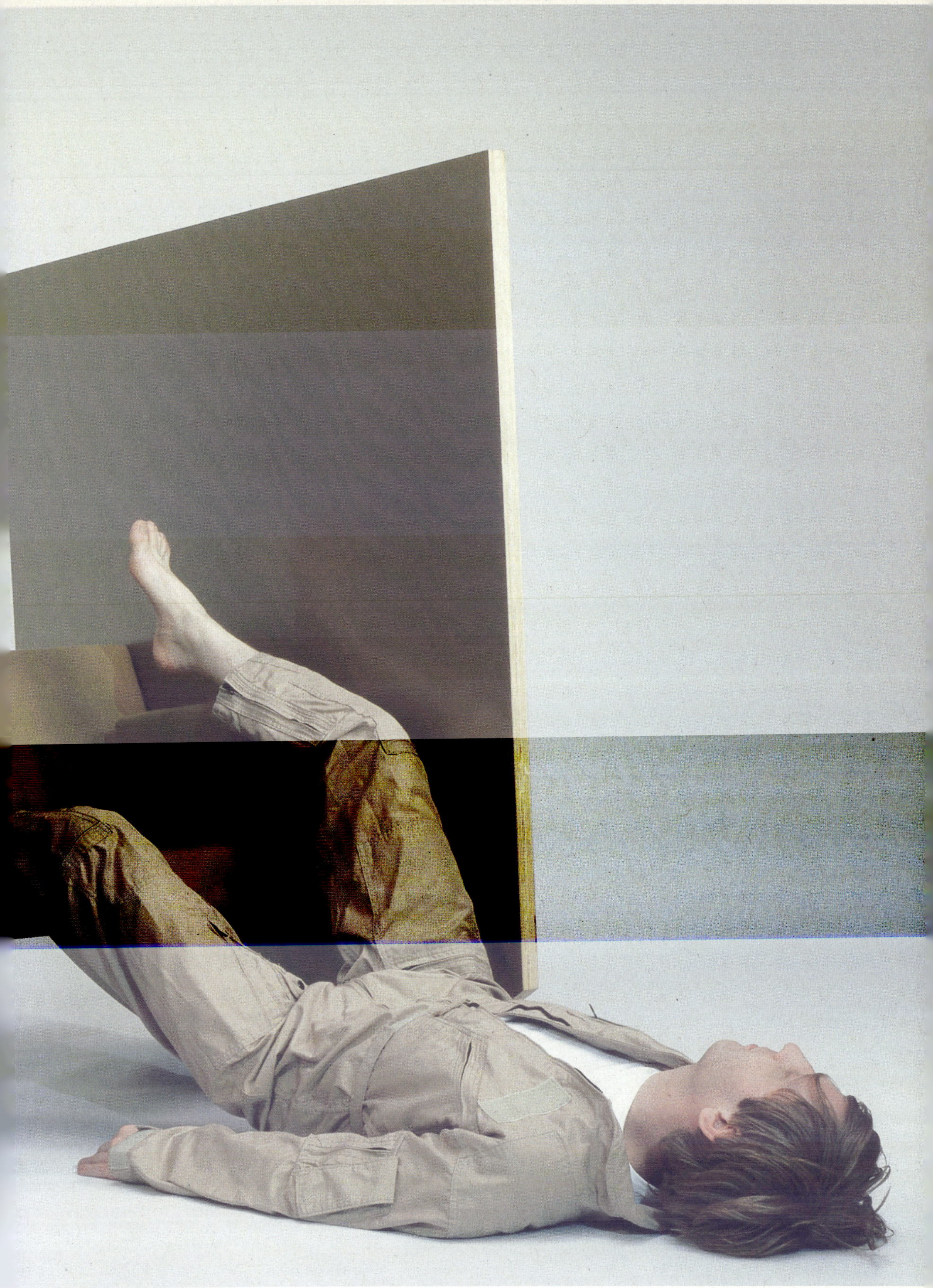

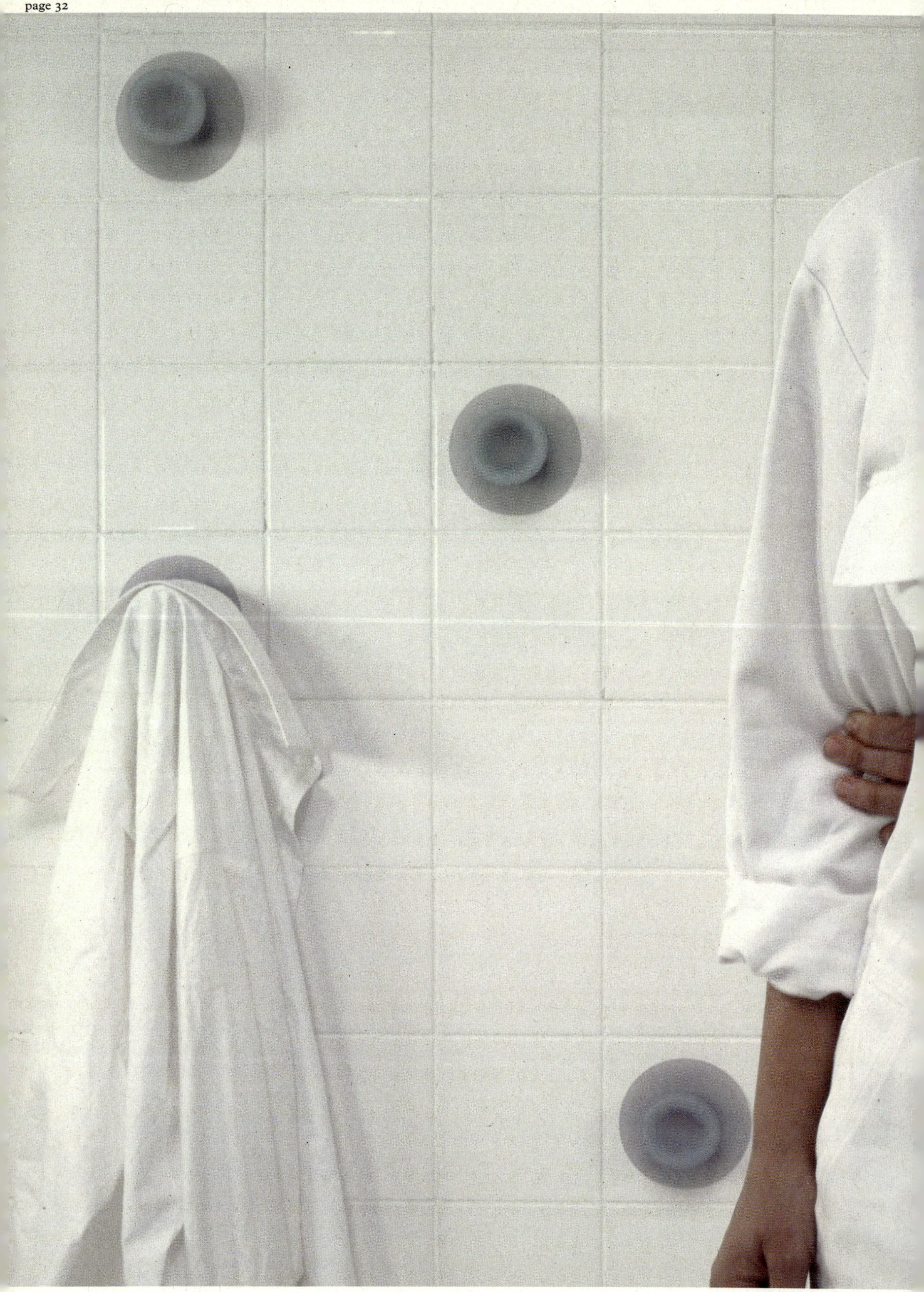

coll.nr. 208 00
Sucker
Jan Hoekstra, Leon Ramakers, 2005
silicone, white, purple, aquamarine
ø 12 x 8.5 cm

The sucker solves the problem of having to drill holes in tiles, glass or any other smooth surface. Its beauty is in its simplicity and the experience of attaching it to the wall: it literally sucks itself onto the surface.

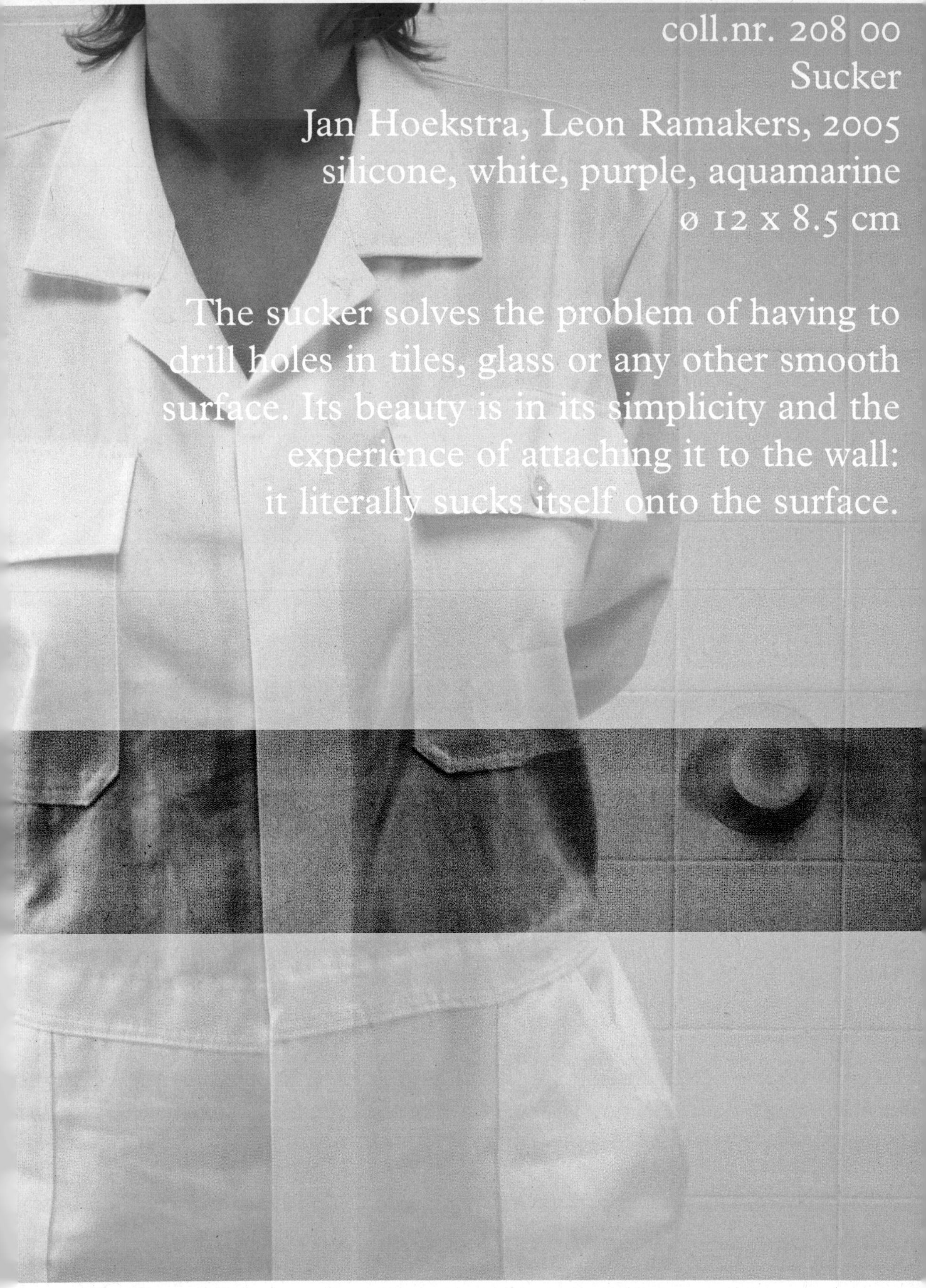

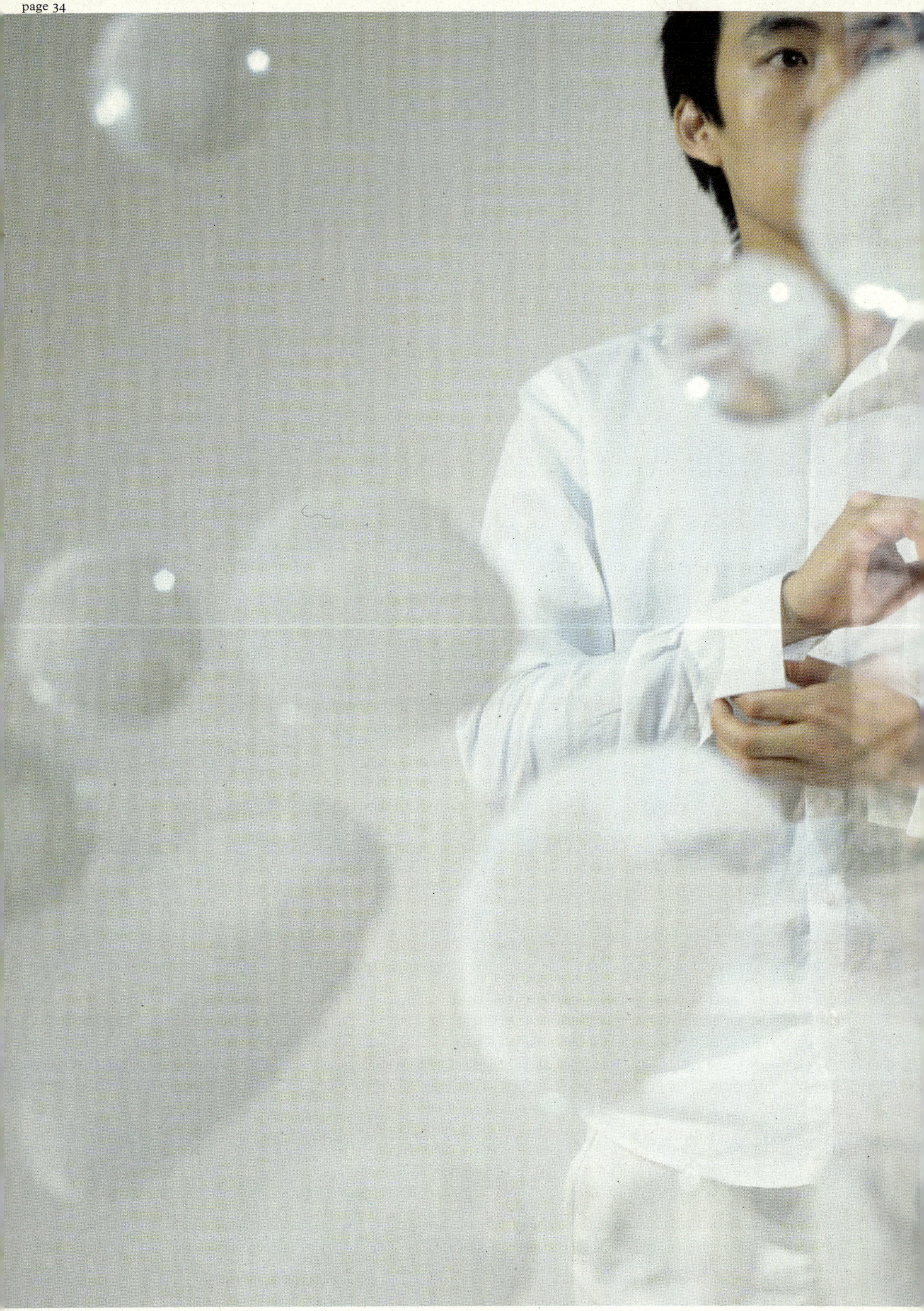

coll.nr. 133 00
Window drops
Arnout Visser, Bas van Tol, 2002
PVC
set of 8 ‘drops’ of various sizes

These self-adhesive transparent ‘water drops’ can be stuck on windows and mirrors. They morph the users view and create interesting reflections.

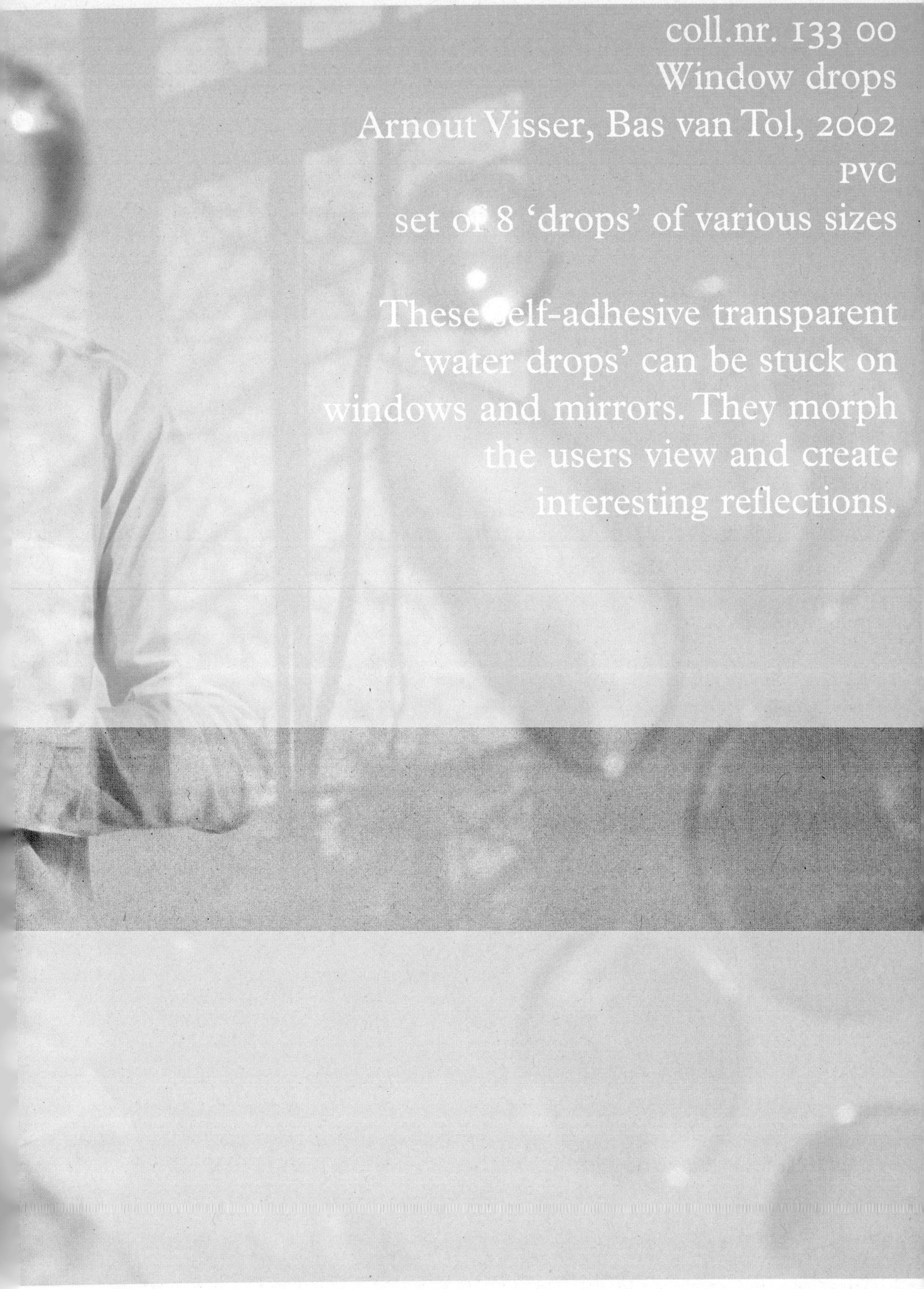

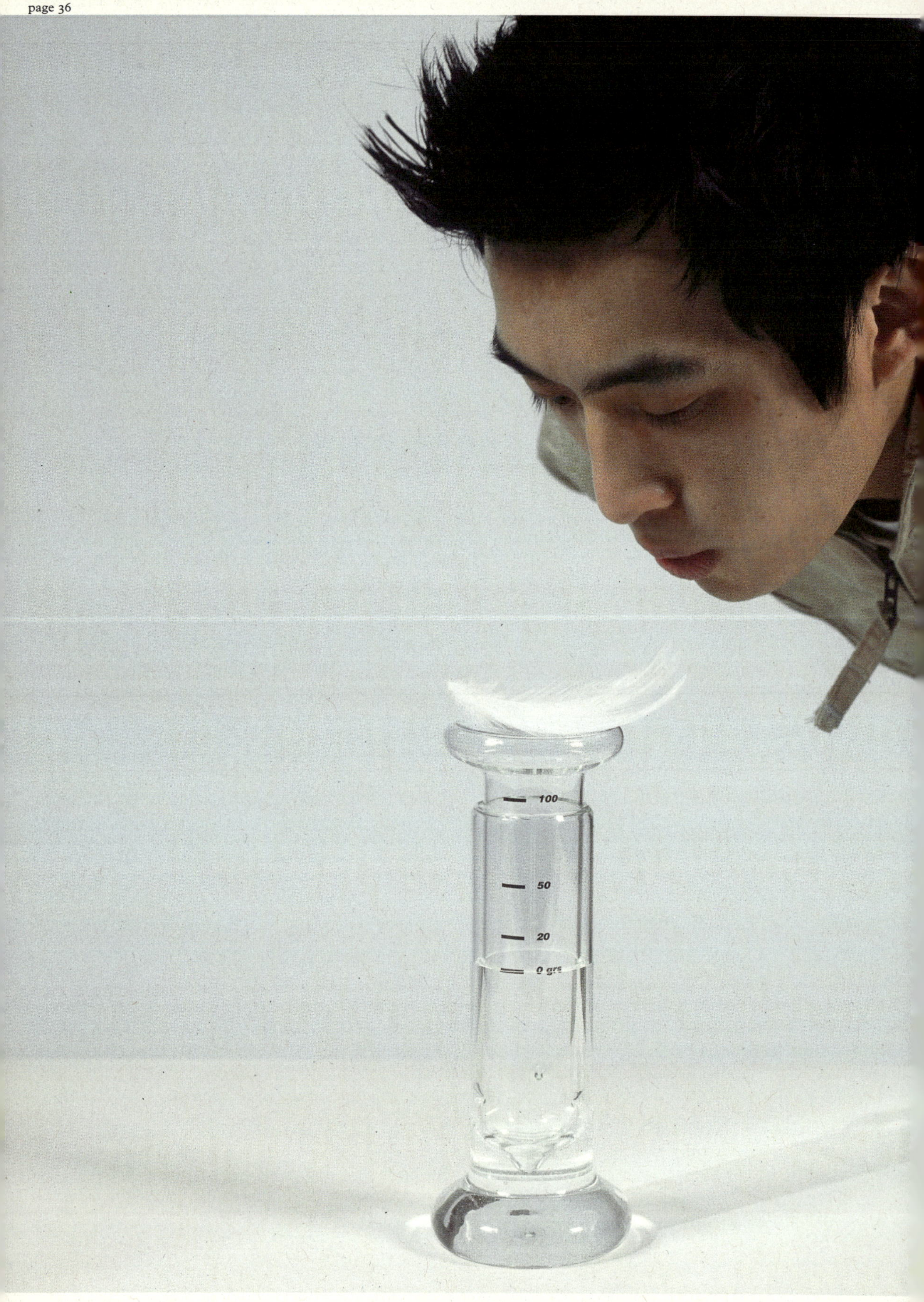
100
50
20
0 grs

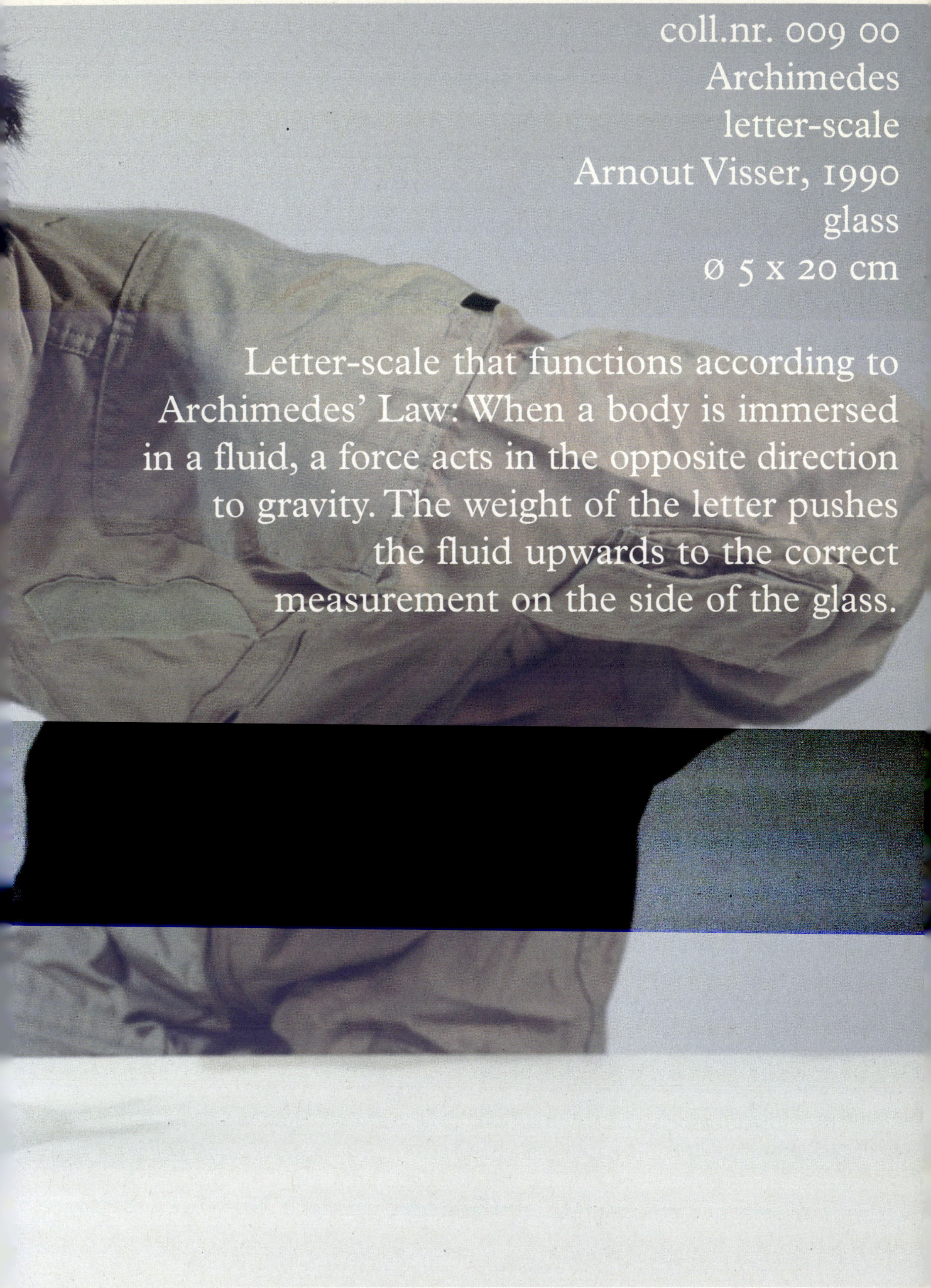

coll.nr. 009 00
Archimedes
letter-scale
Arnout Visser, 1990
glass
ø 5 x 20 cm

Letter-scale that functions according to Archimedes' Law: When a body is immersed in a fluid, a force acts in the opposite direction to gravity. The weight of the letter pushes the fluid upwards to the correct measurement on the side of the glass.

coll.nr. 004 00
Salad sunrise
oil and vinegar set
Arnout Visser, 1990
pyrex glass
ø 6 x 18 cm

This vessel highlights the natural properties of oil and vinegar. The physics of the two liquids mean that the oil will always float on top of the vinegar, so there is no need for separate containers. One vessel with two tubes. Start by pouring in the vinegar, followed by the oil and watch how they part.

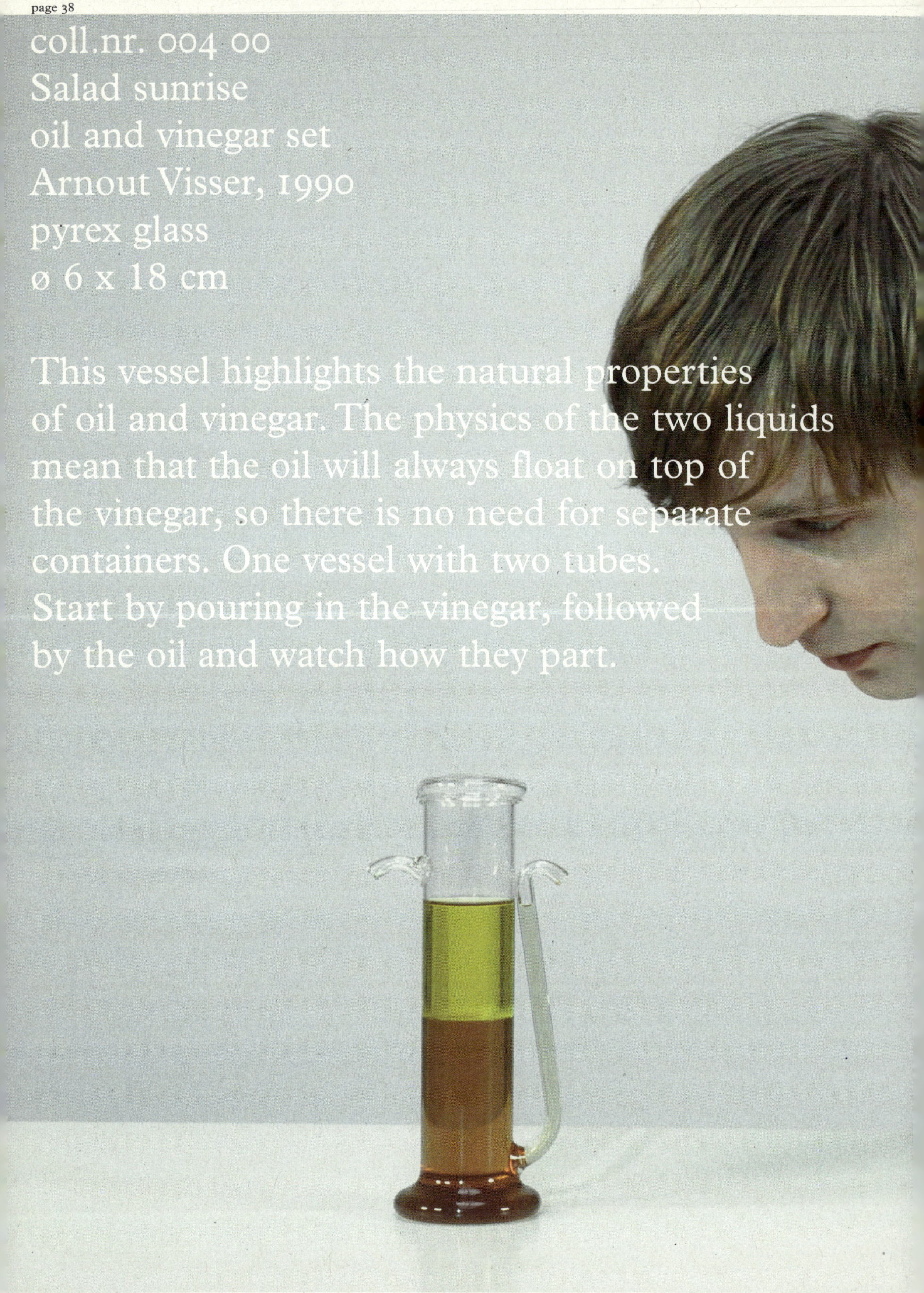

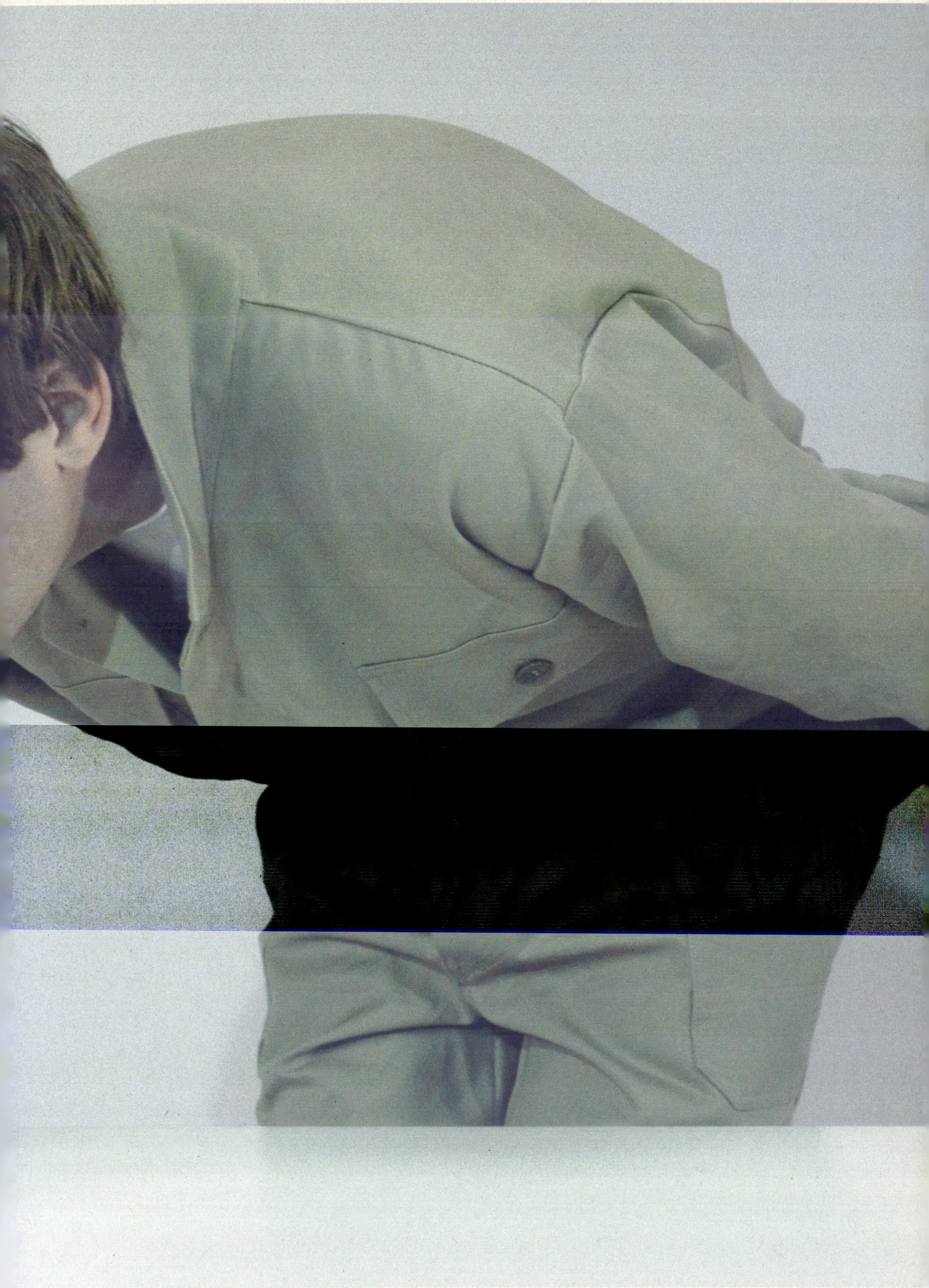

coll.nr. 034 00
Saltglass
Arnout Visser, 1995
glass
ø 7 x 28 cm

This saltcellar works on the principle of an hourglass. When it is placed on the table after use, the salt slowly trickles back.

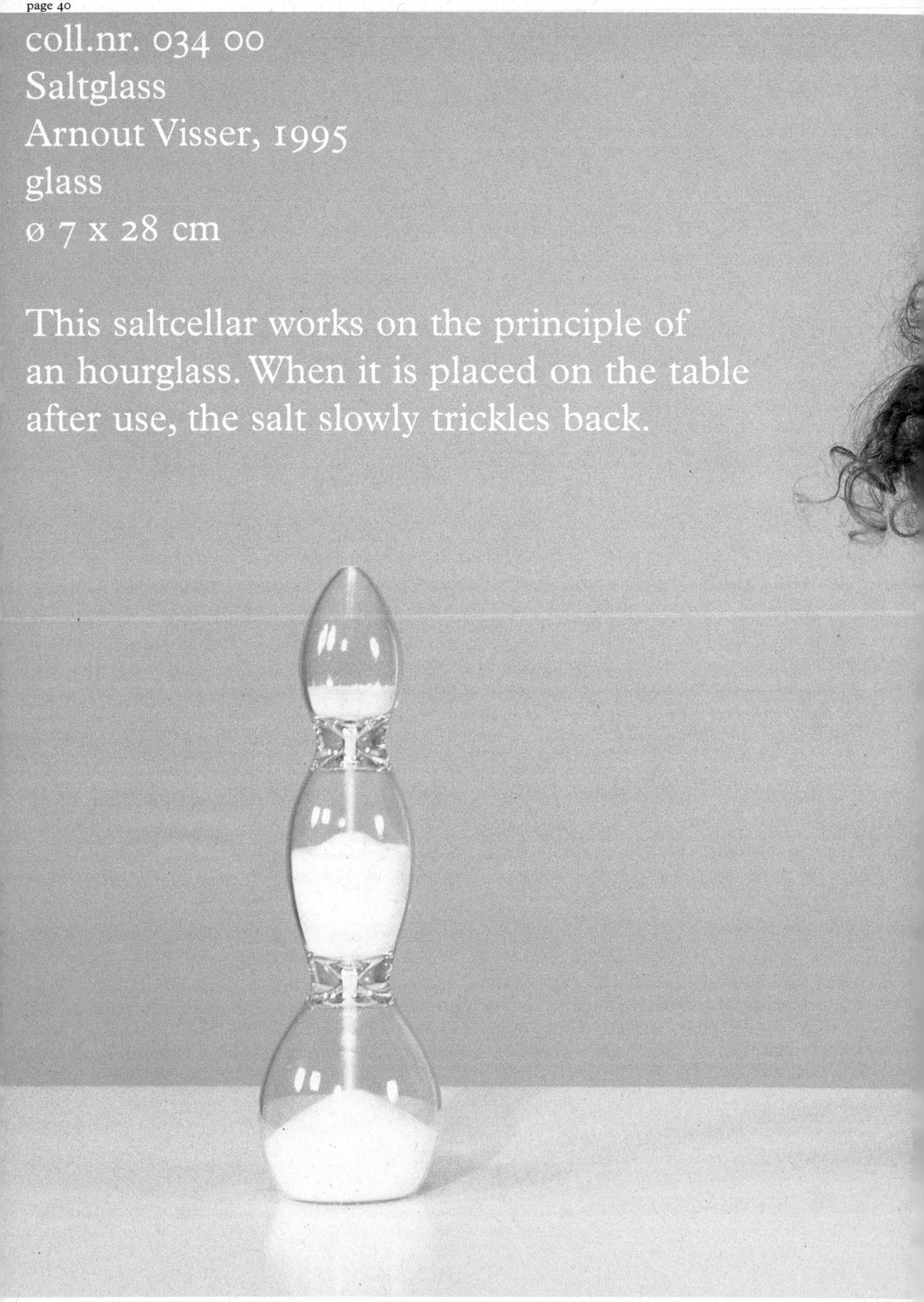

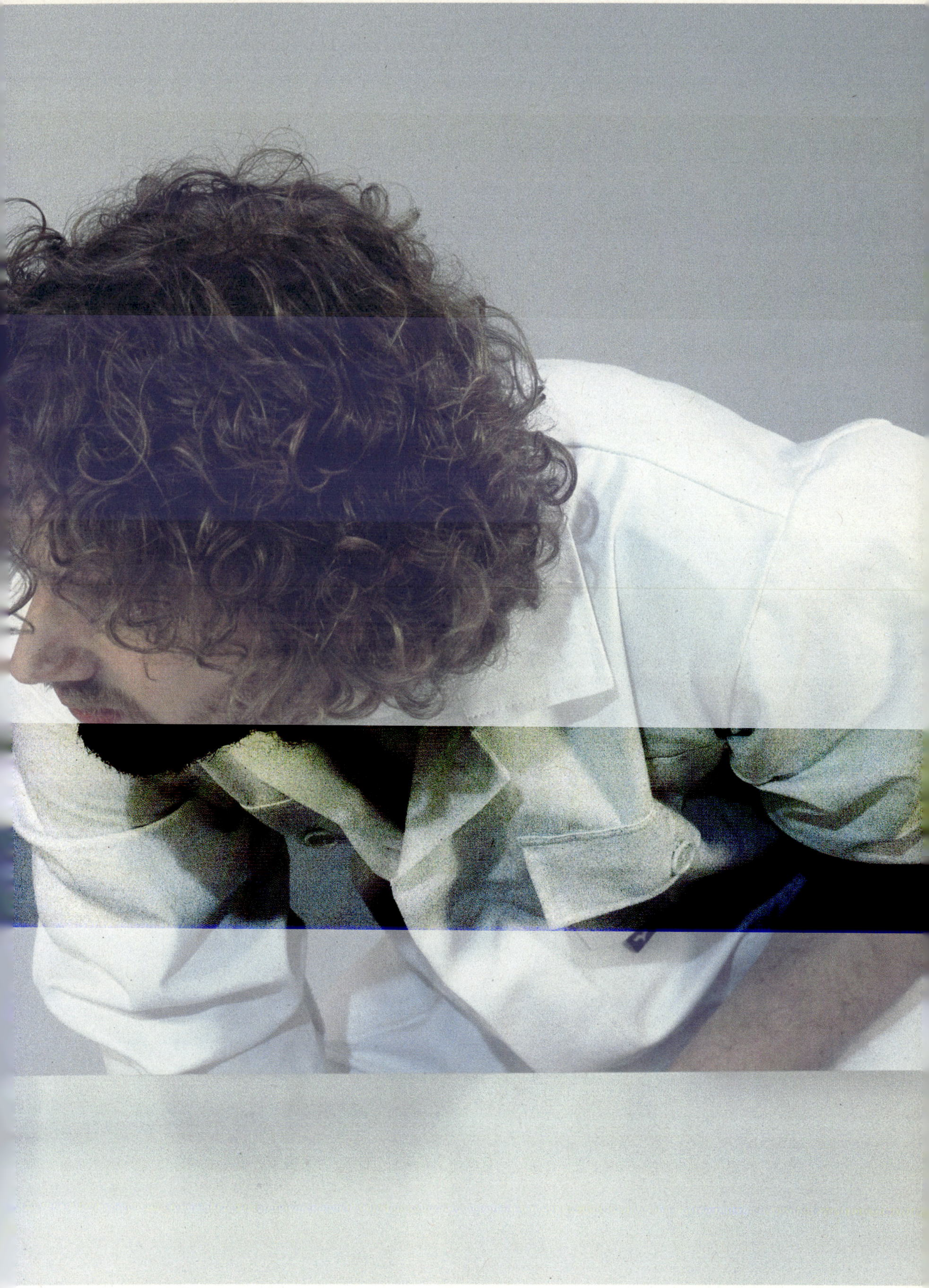

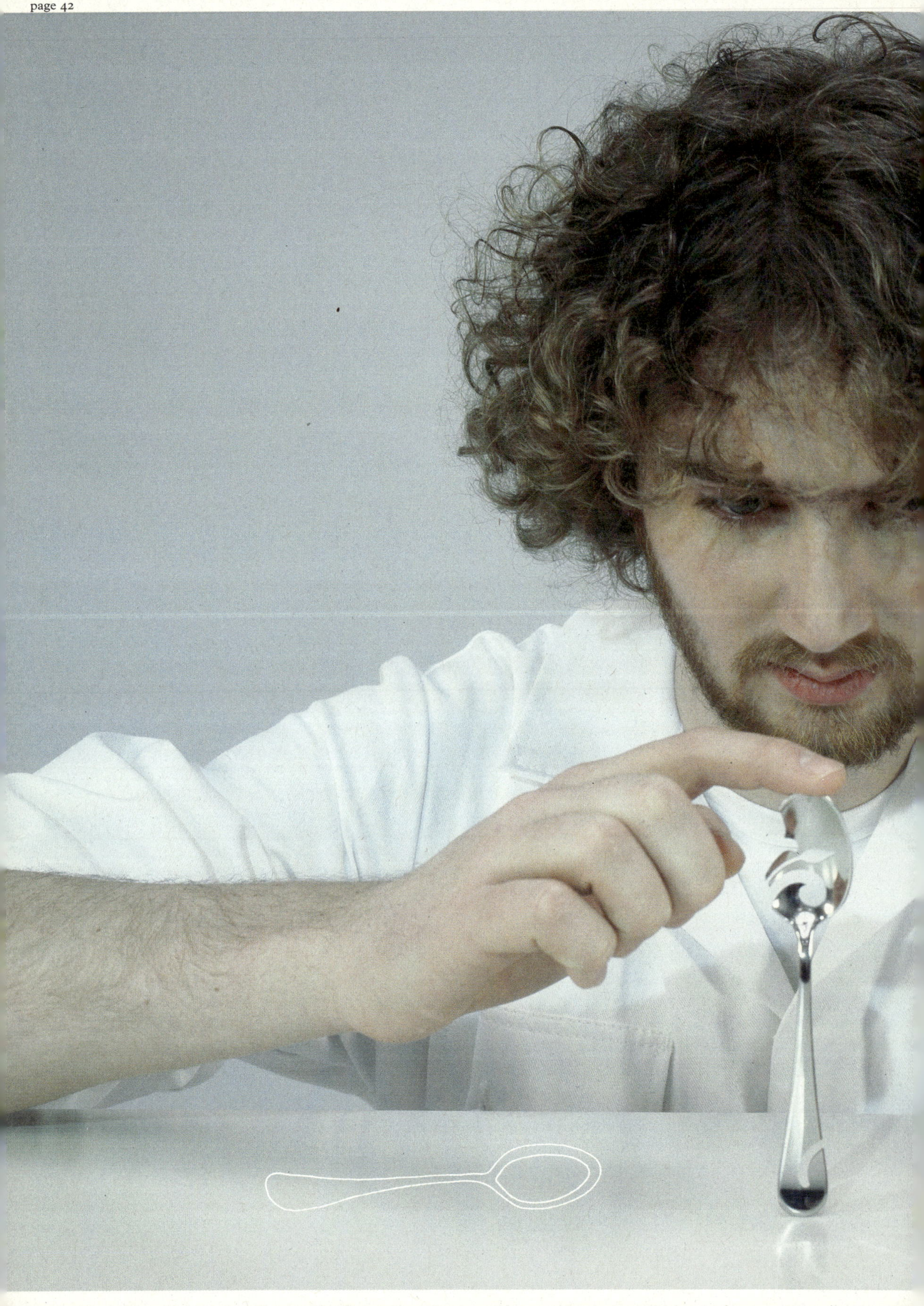

coll.nr. 192 00

MP, DB

sugar spoon

Ed Annink, 2005

stainless steel

13 x 2.5 cm

This design takes a classic Dutch spoon and highlights how the art of tea making has changed. Where cubes have replaced loose sugar, the spoon's main duty is stirring. Therefore Ed Annink has taken advantage of this and opened up the spoon with a laser cut floral pattern inspired by Delft Blue decoration (DB), and another version (MP) of which the middle has been removed.

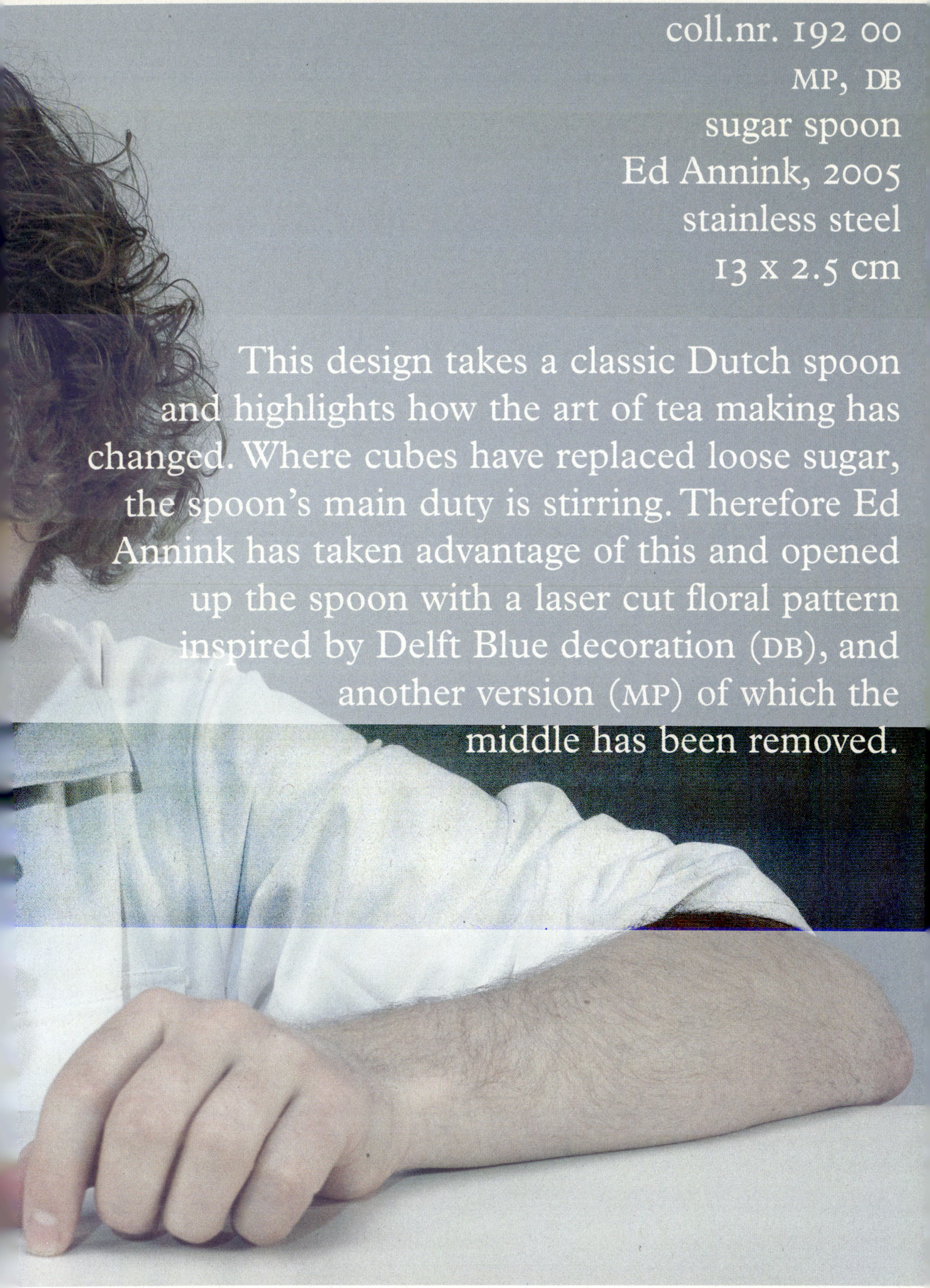

coll.nr. 127 00
Clothes hanger lamp
Hector Serrano, 2002
acrylic, 11W energy saving bulb
37 x 23 x 5.5 cm

By hanging the garment of your choice on the hanger you create a personalized lamp.

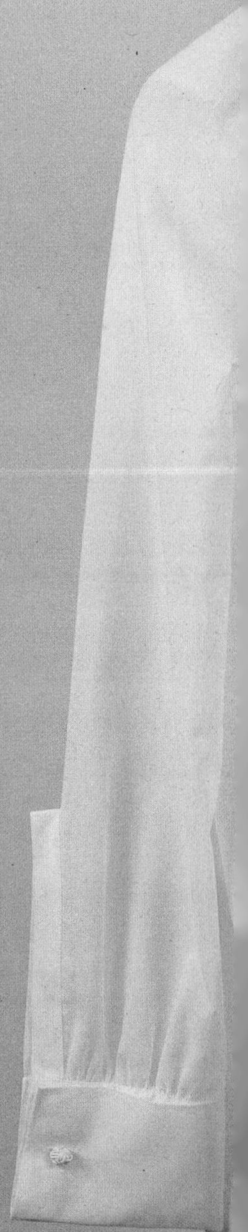

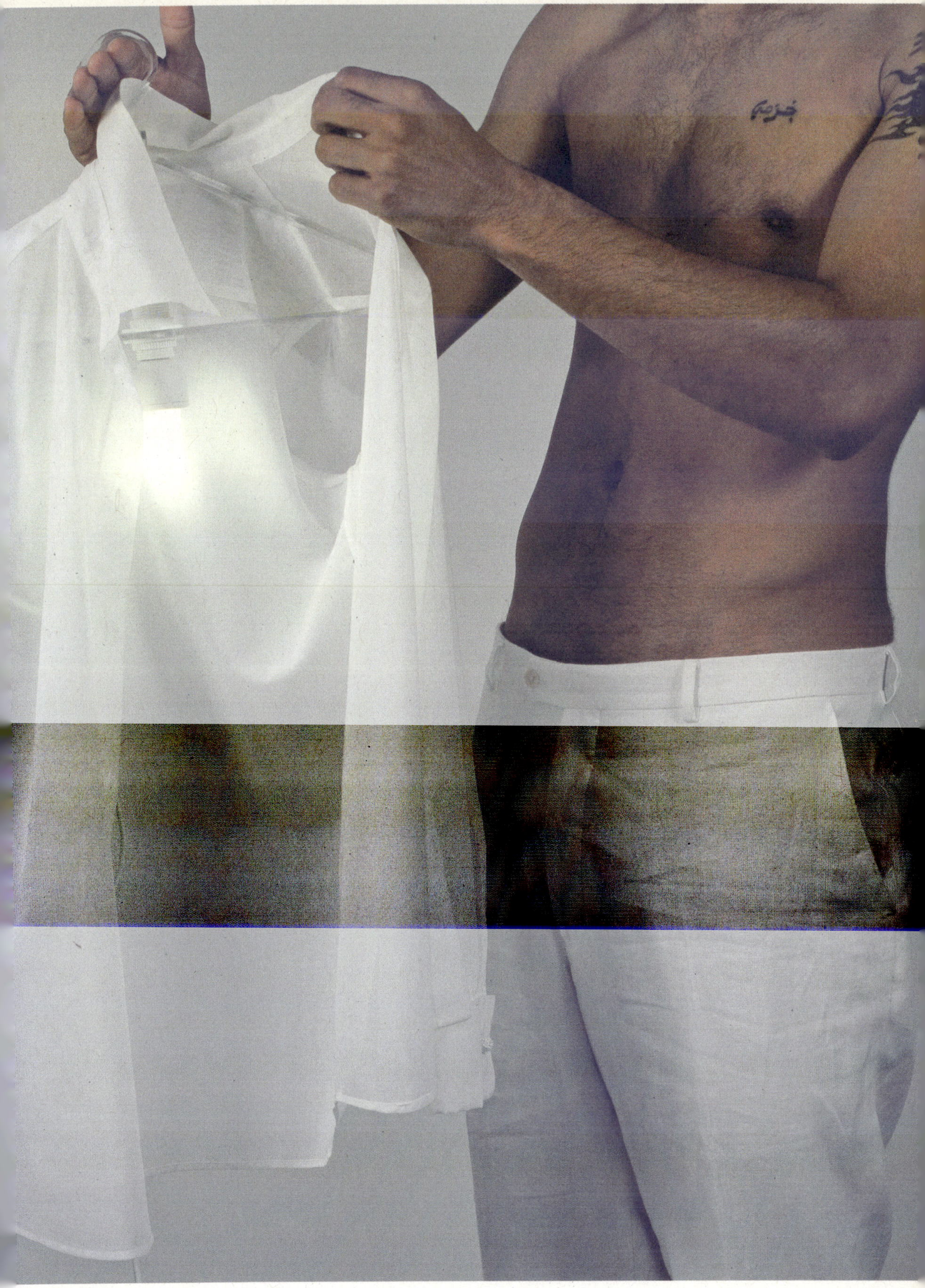

coll.nr. 164 00

Slow glow lamp

NEXT Architects, Aura Luz Melis, 2004

glass, vegetable fat, cork, 25W/G9 bulb

ø 16 x 31 cm

The light source is immersed in fat. As the heat from the light slowly melts the substance, an intriguing process gradually unravels before your eyes. The light glows brighter and brighter and the lamp becomes warmer and warmer in a comforting way.

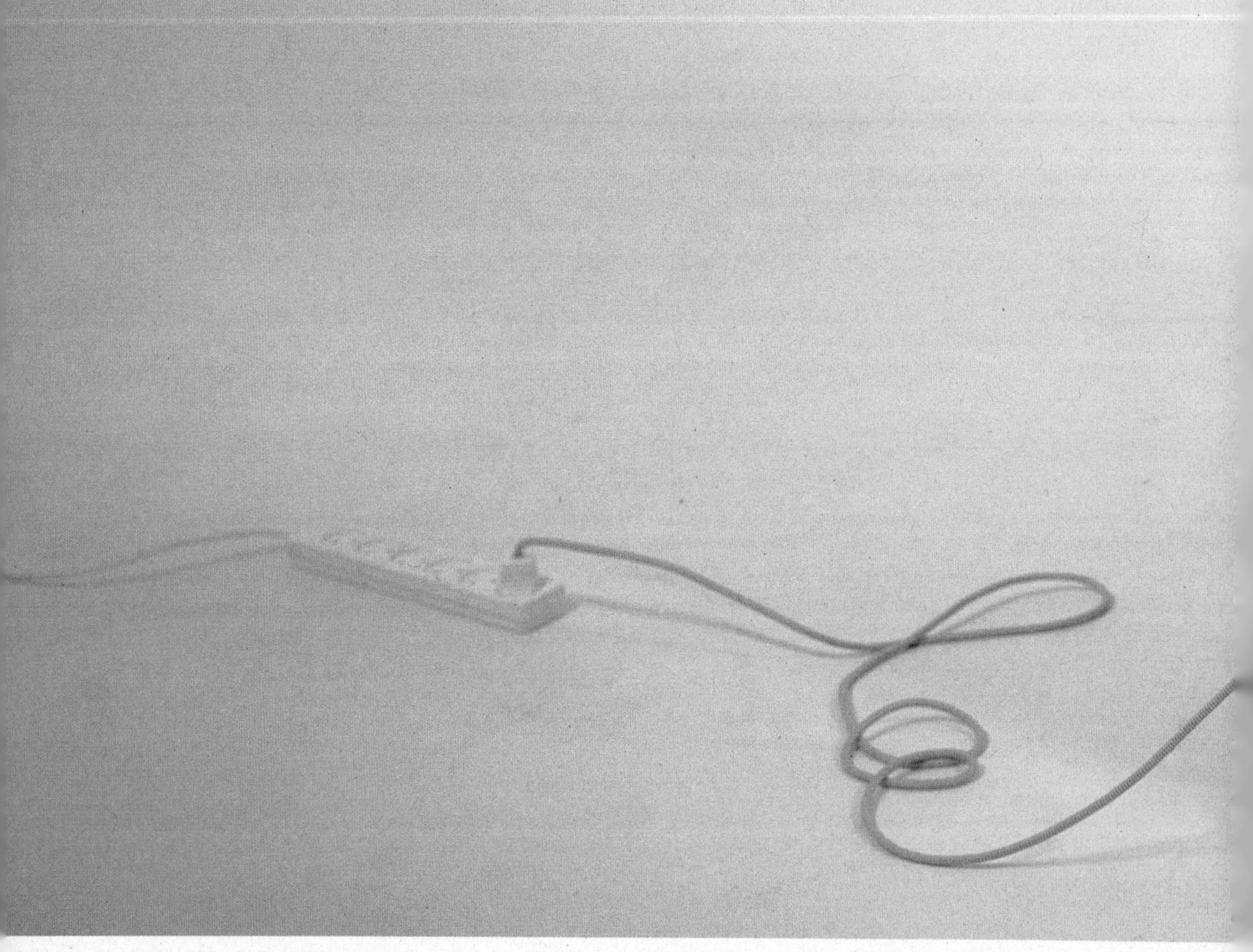

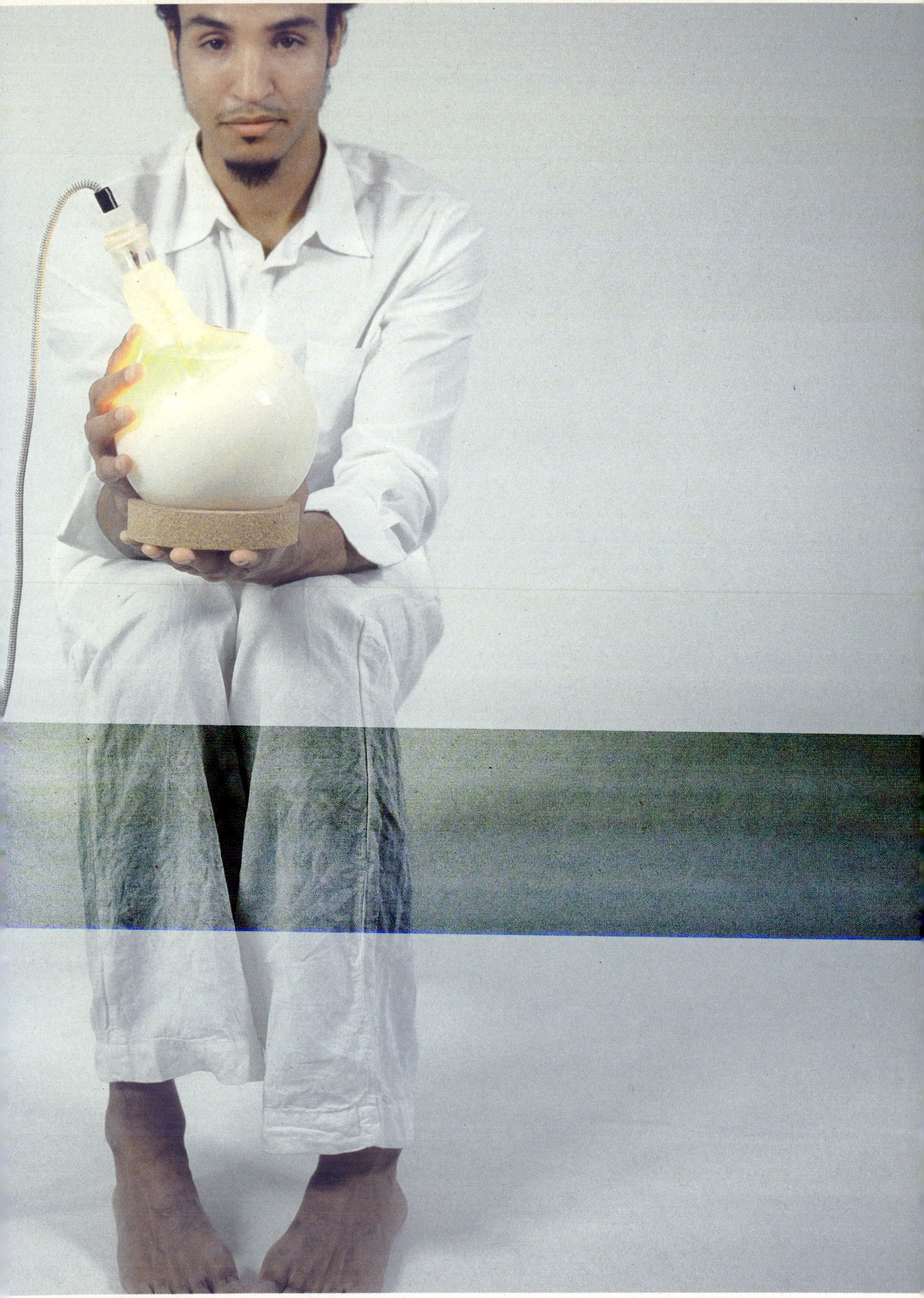

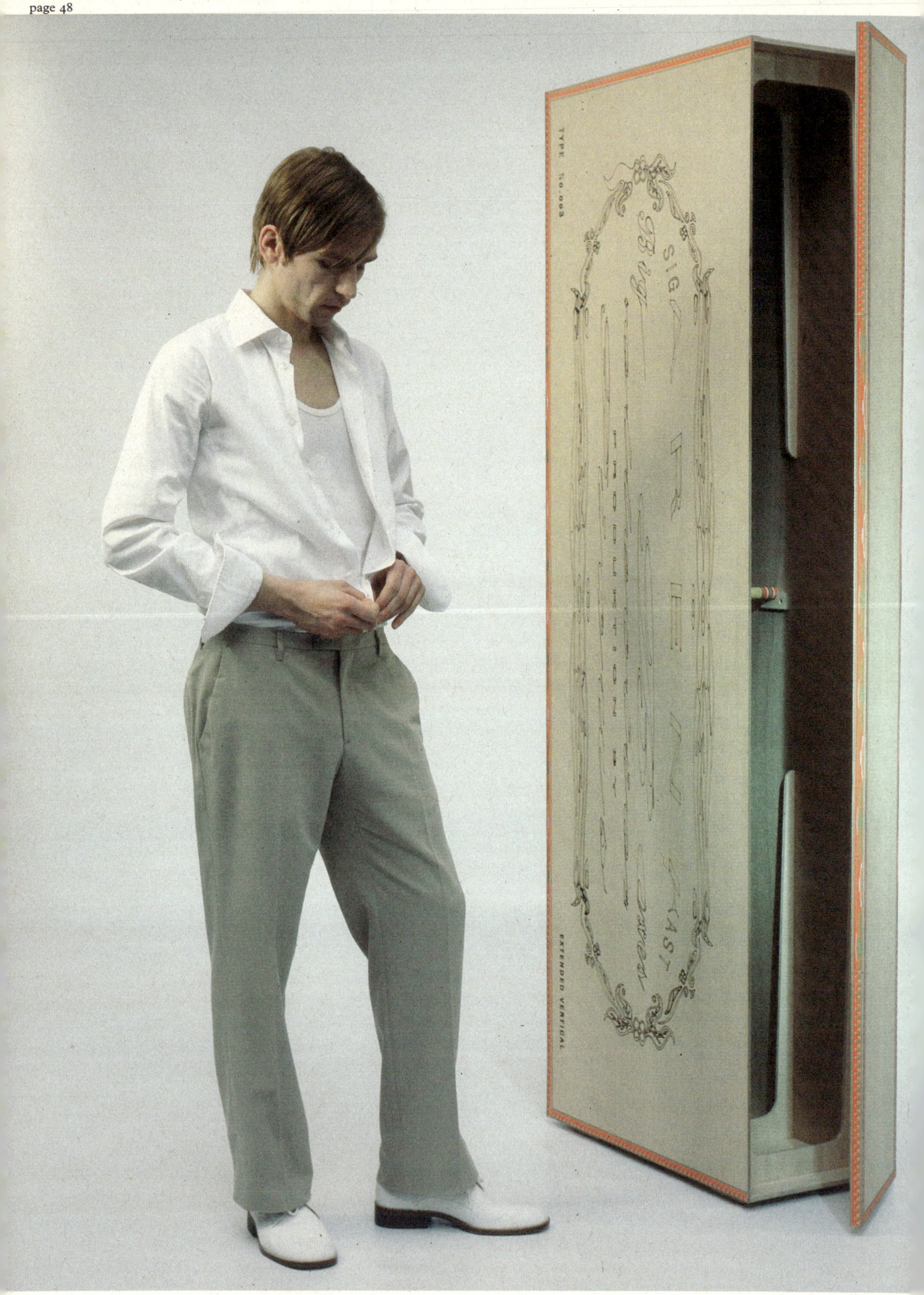
PRODUCTION BY
EXTENDED VERTICAL

coll.nr. 104 00
Extended cigar box
wardrobe
Wieki Somers and
Dylan van den Berg, 2001
okoumé plywood, hinges
sealing paper, laser imprint
70 x 30 x 201 cm
numbered edition

In this design Wieki Somers and Dylan van den Berg play with ideas of proportion and imagination. They have radically stretched a cigar box to the size of a wardrobe, including the hinges, locks and even the sealing paper along the edges. The wardrobe's cross section is not much bigger than a normal cigar box but standing at two metres high it functions as a free-standing cupboard.

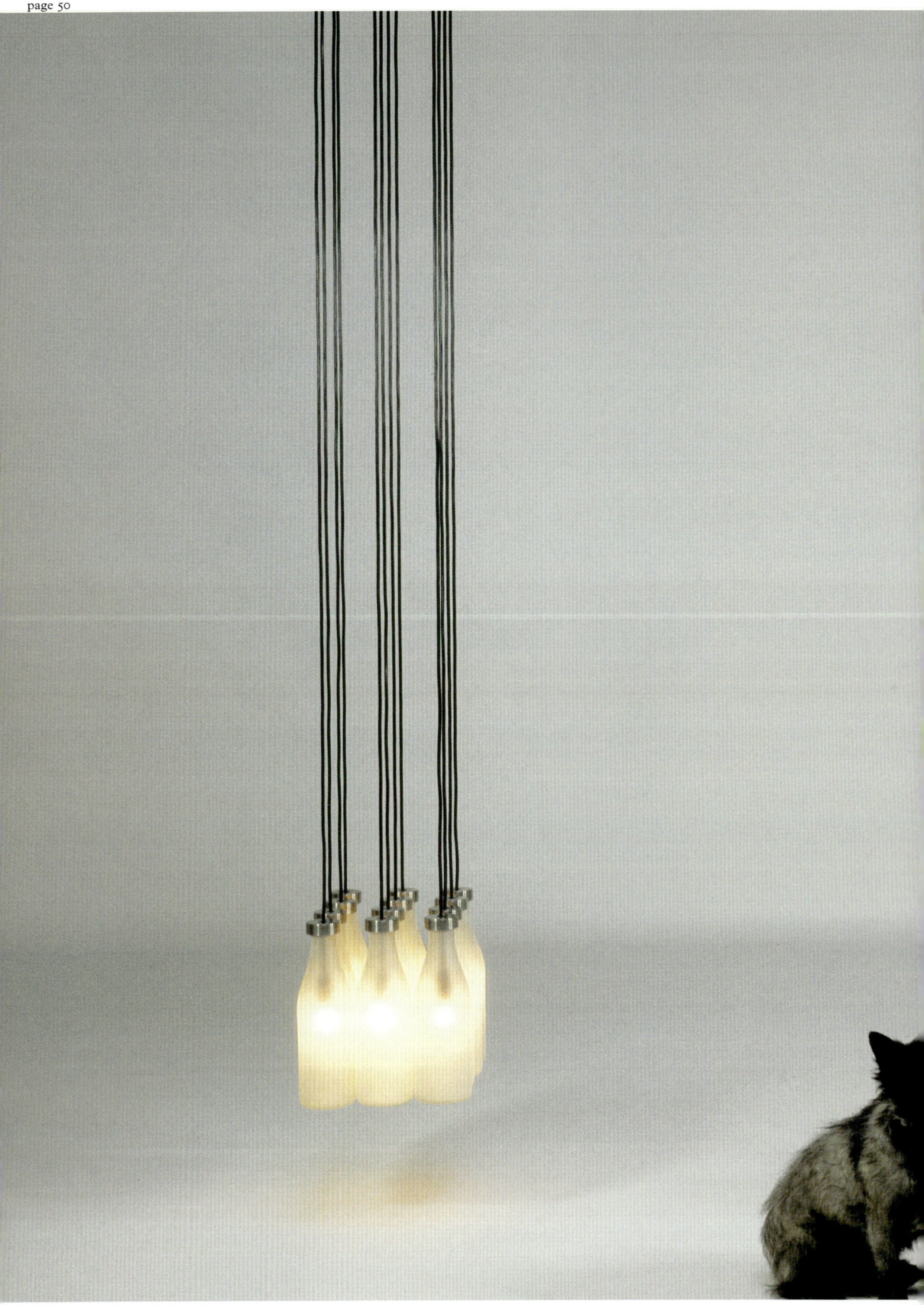

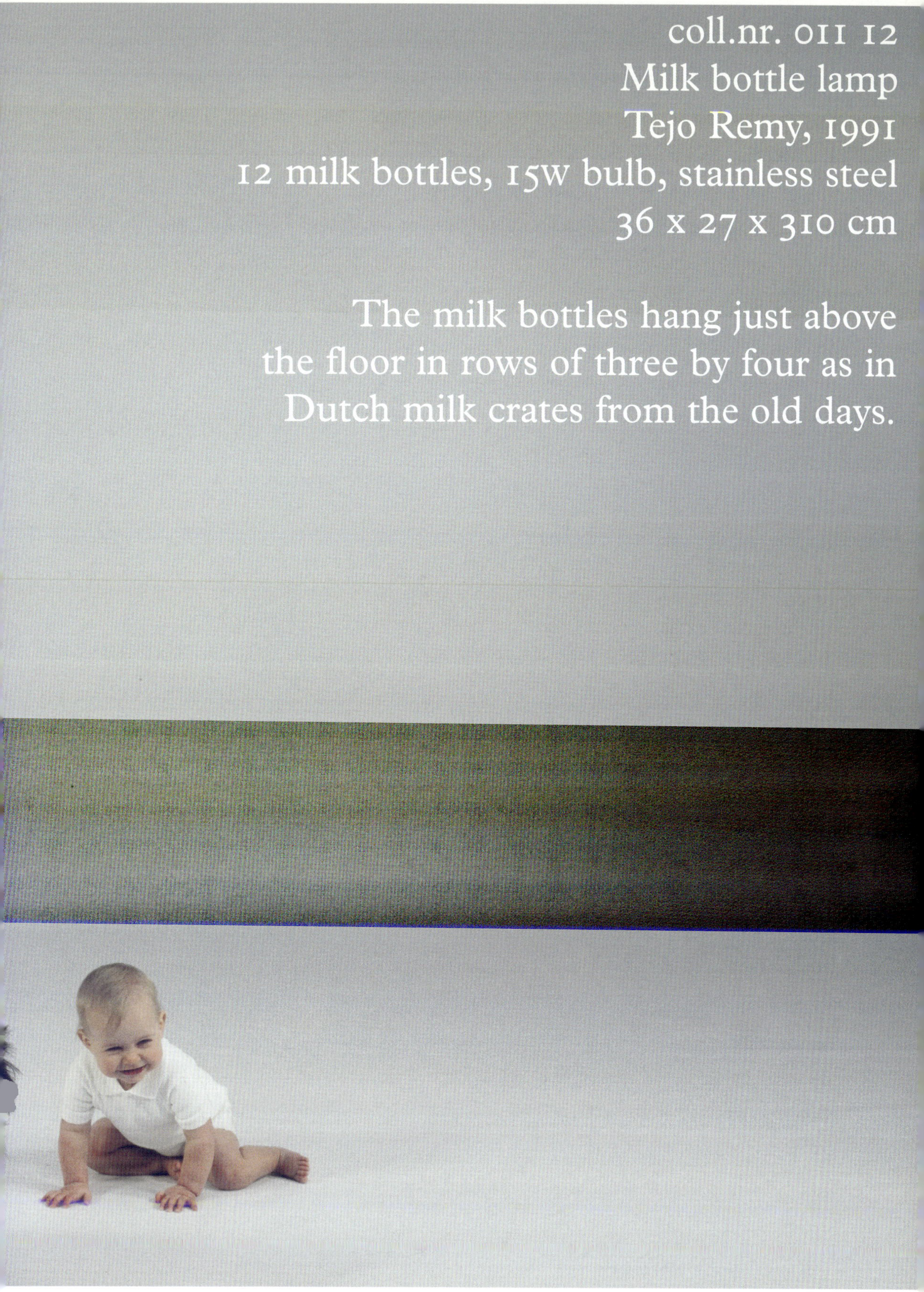

coll.nr. 011 12
Milk bottle lamp
Tejo Remy, 1991
12 milk bottles, 15w bulb, stainless steel
36 x 27 x 310 cm

The milk bottles hang just above the floor in rows of three by four as in Dutch milk crates from the old days.

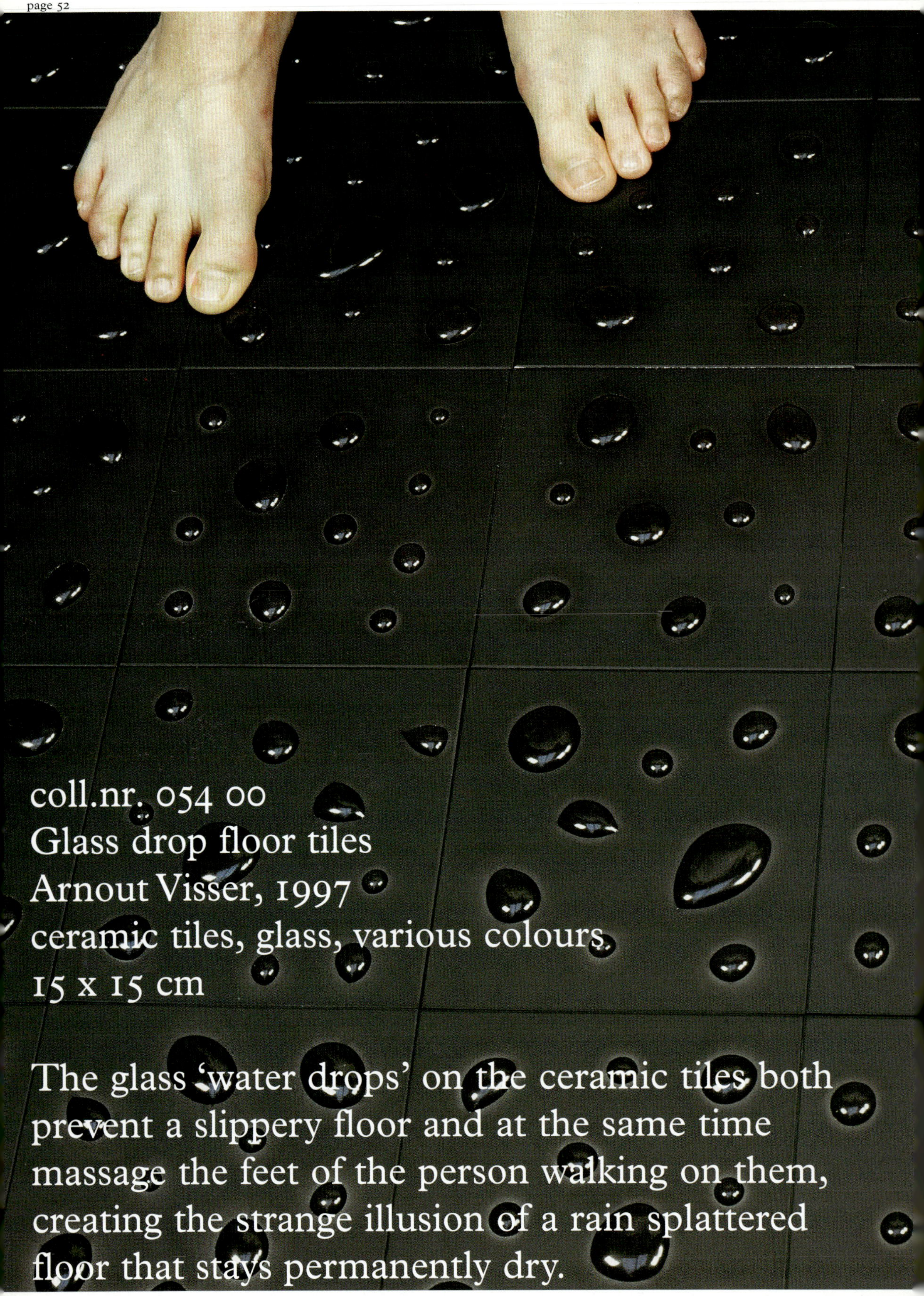

coll.nr. 054 00
Glass drop floor tiles
Arnout Visser, 1997
ceramic tiles, glass, various colours
15 x 15 cm

The glass 'water drops' on the ceramic tiles both prevent a slippery floor and at the same time massage the feet of the person walking on them, creating the strange illusion of a rain splattered floor that stays permanently dry.

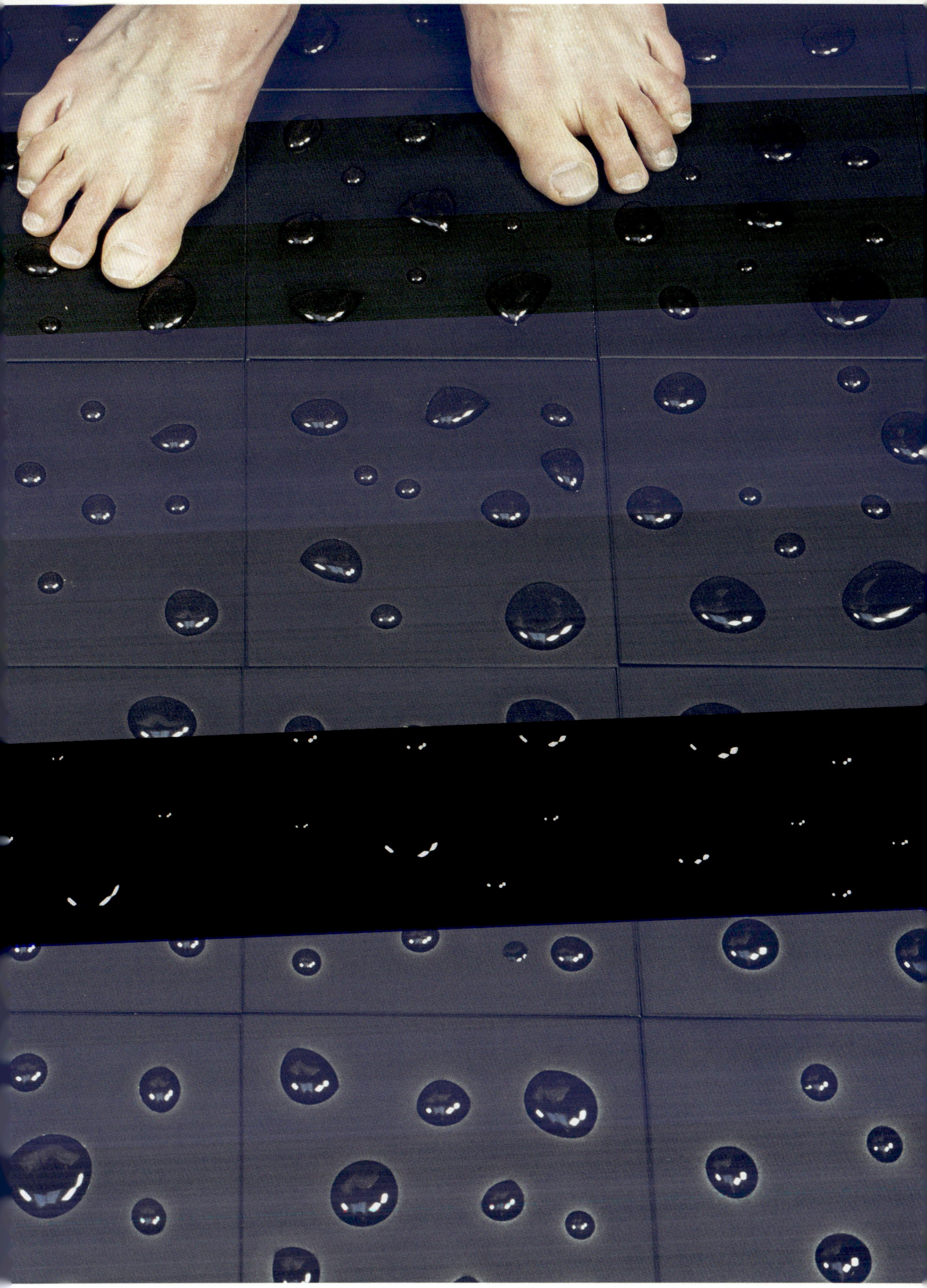

coll.nr. 129 24
Mat walk
bathroom mat
Paolo Ulian, 2002
cotton
59 x 95 cm

Slippers are integrated into the mat, allowing you to walk comfortably and without slipping on dirty or wet floors.

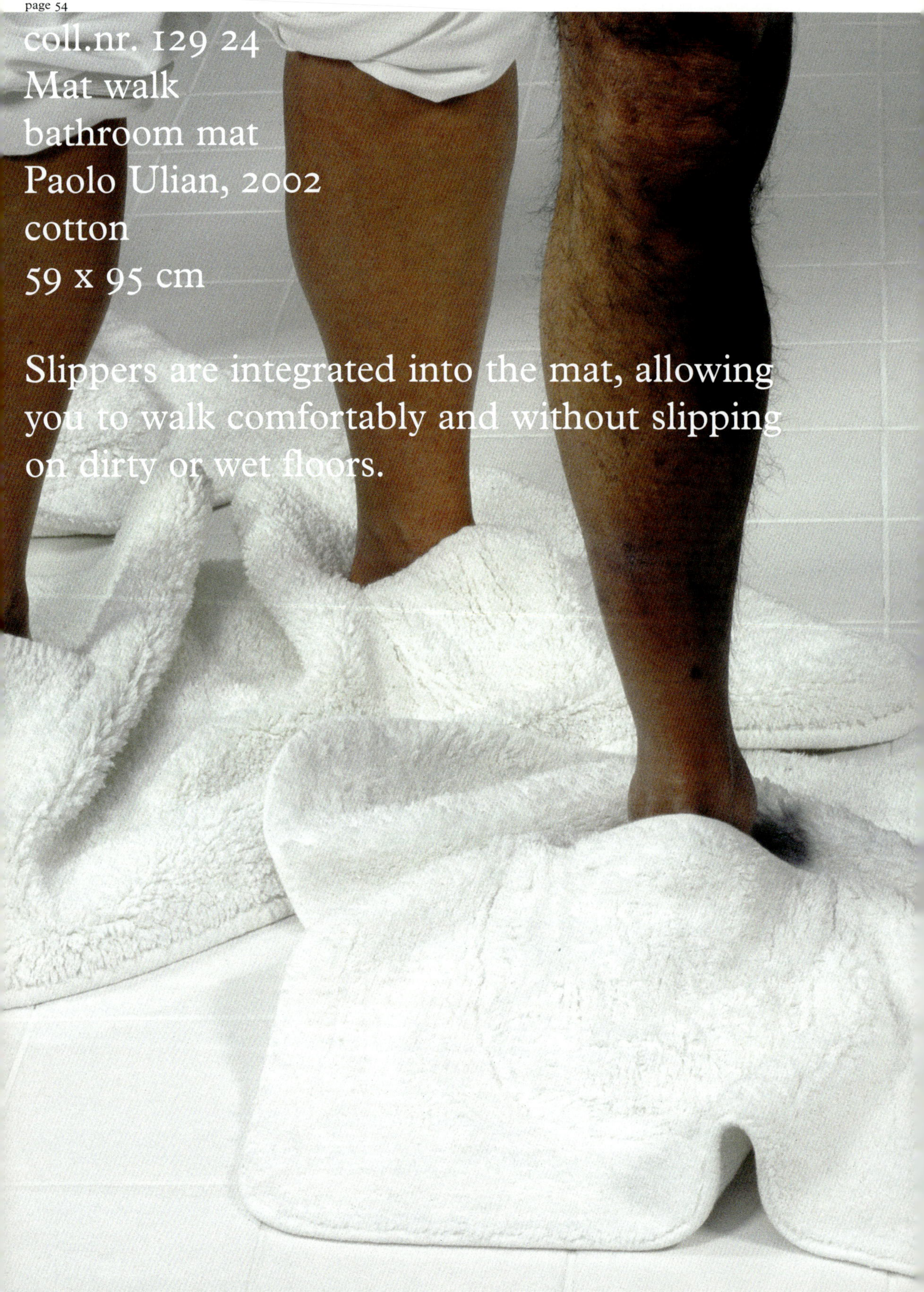

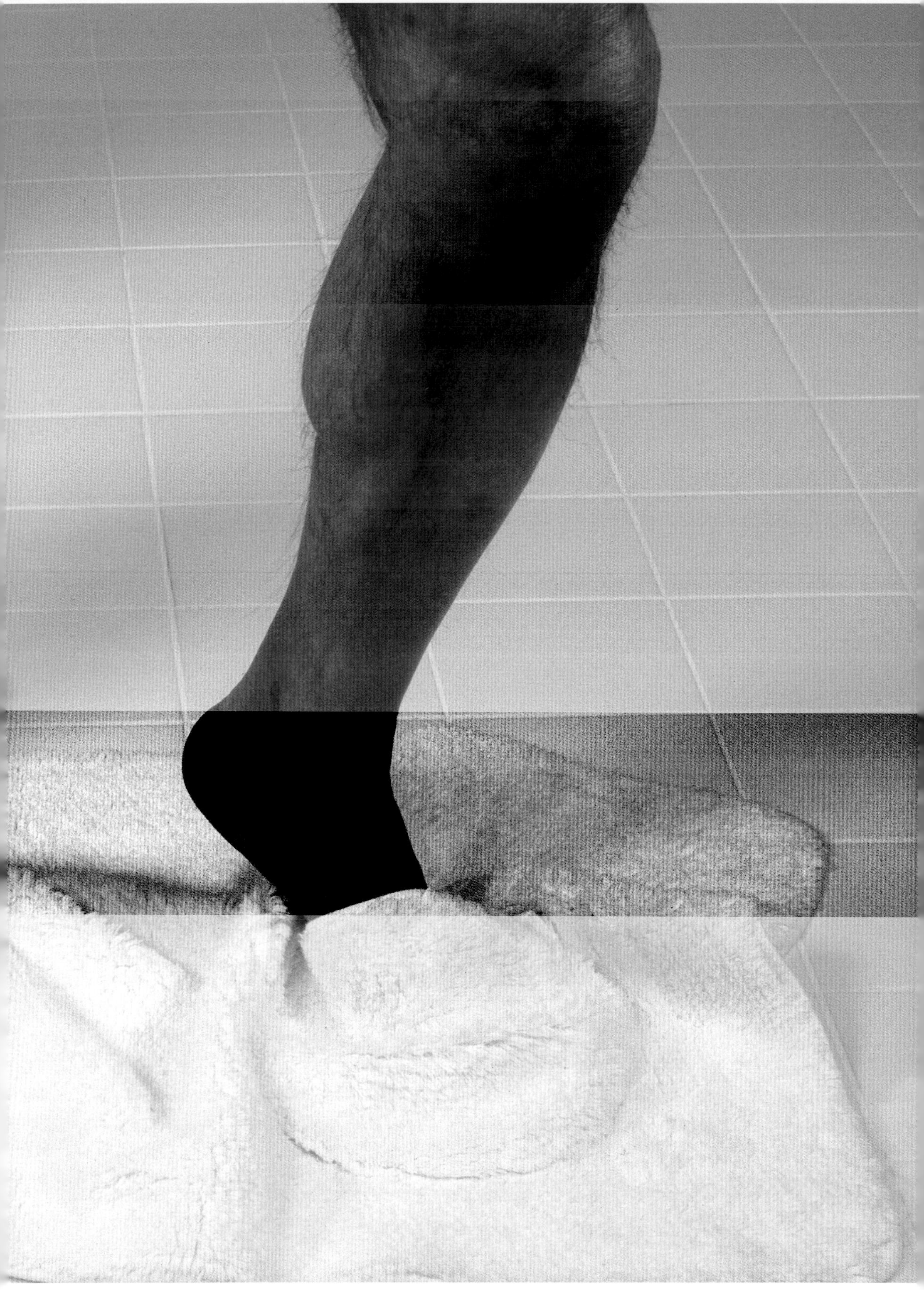

coll.nr. 069 00
Optic glasses
Arnout Visser, 1998
glass
ø 6 x 11 cm

The glass comes to life when it is filled with water. The concave and convex lenses create a new view of the world. The structure feels really good in the hand.

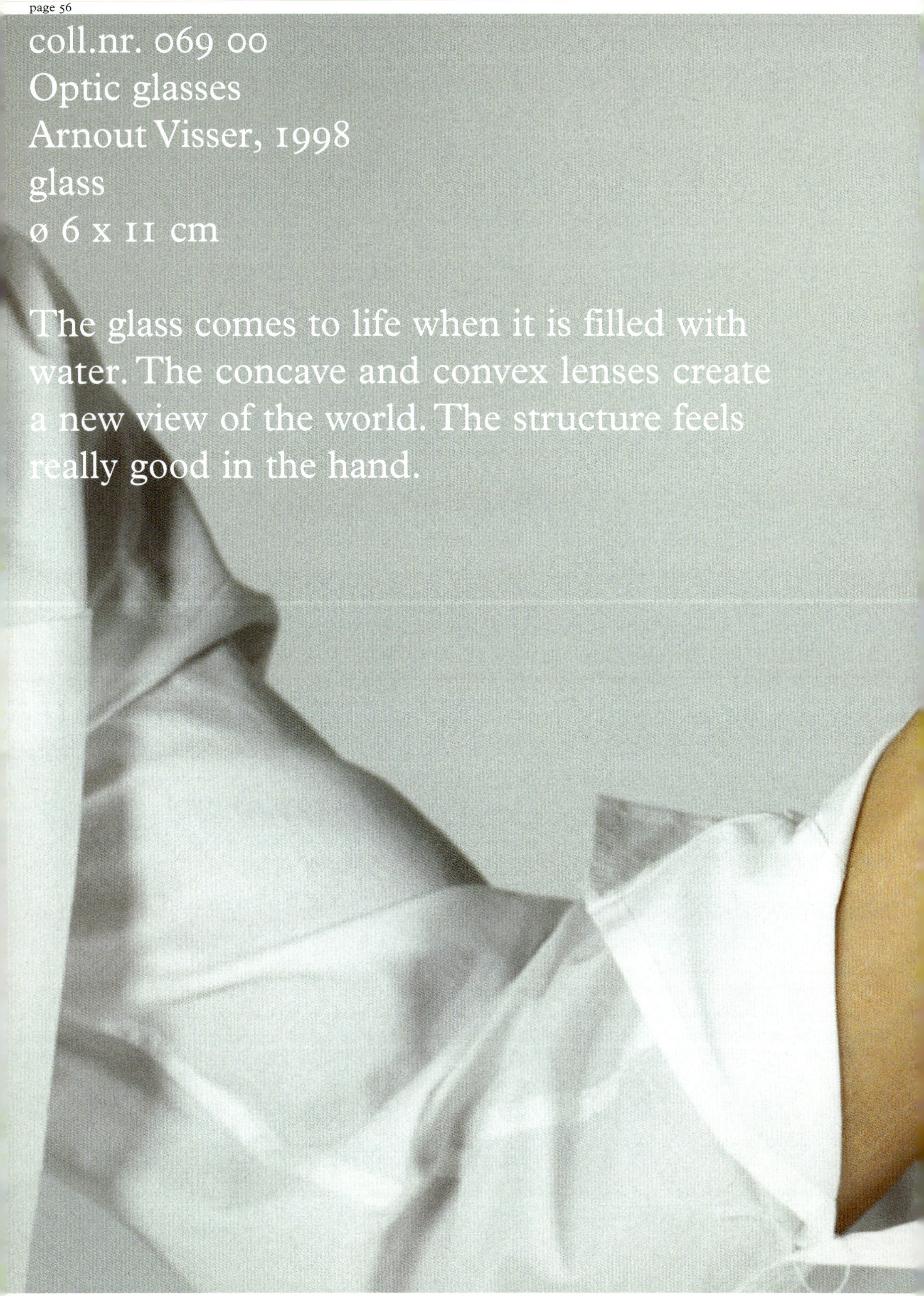

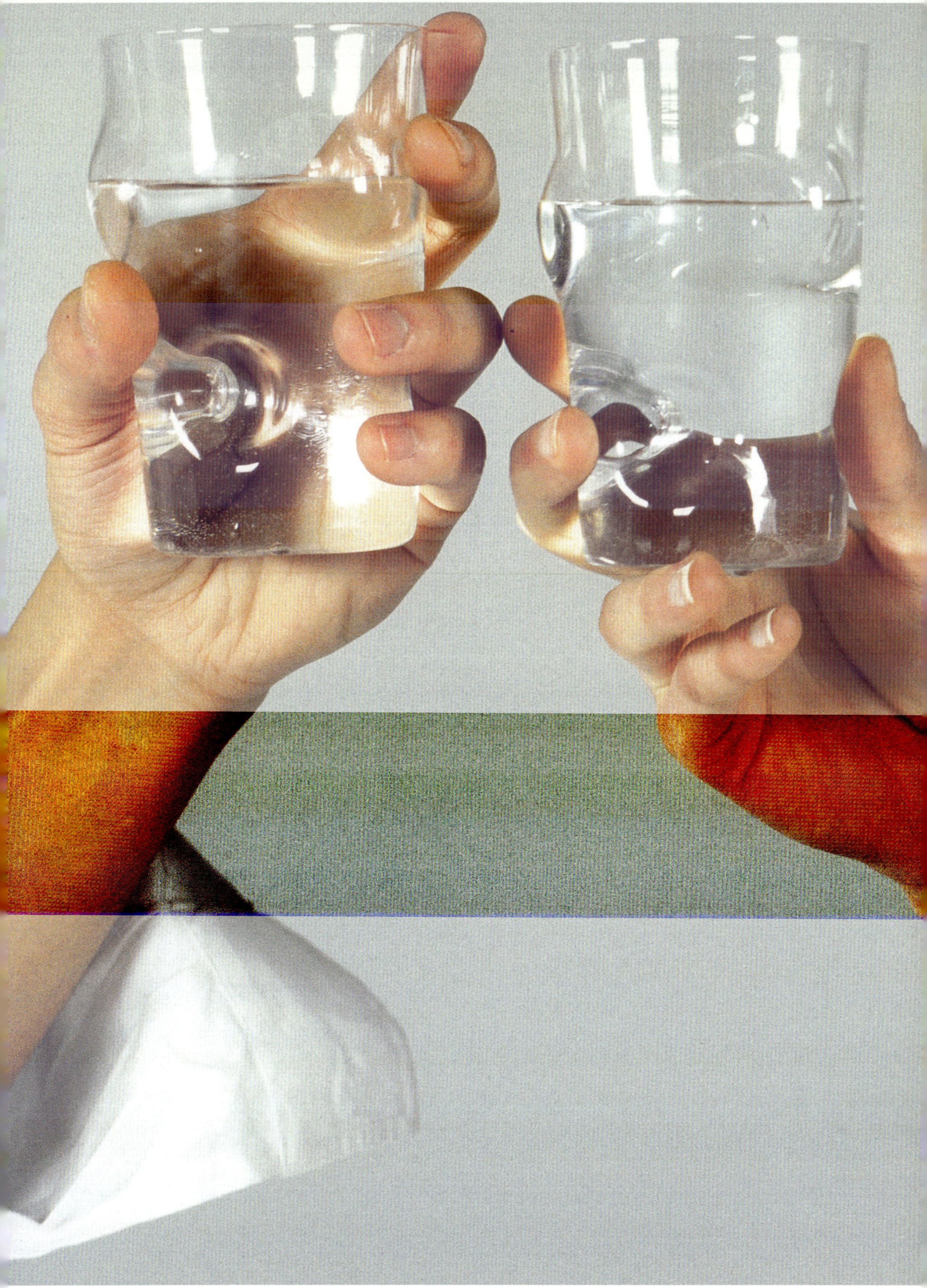

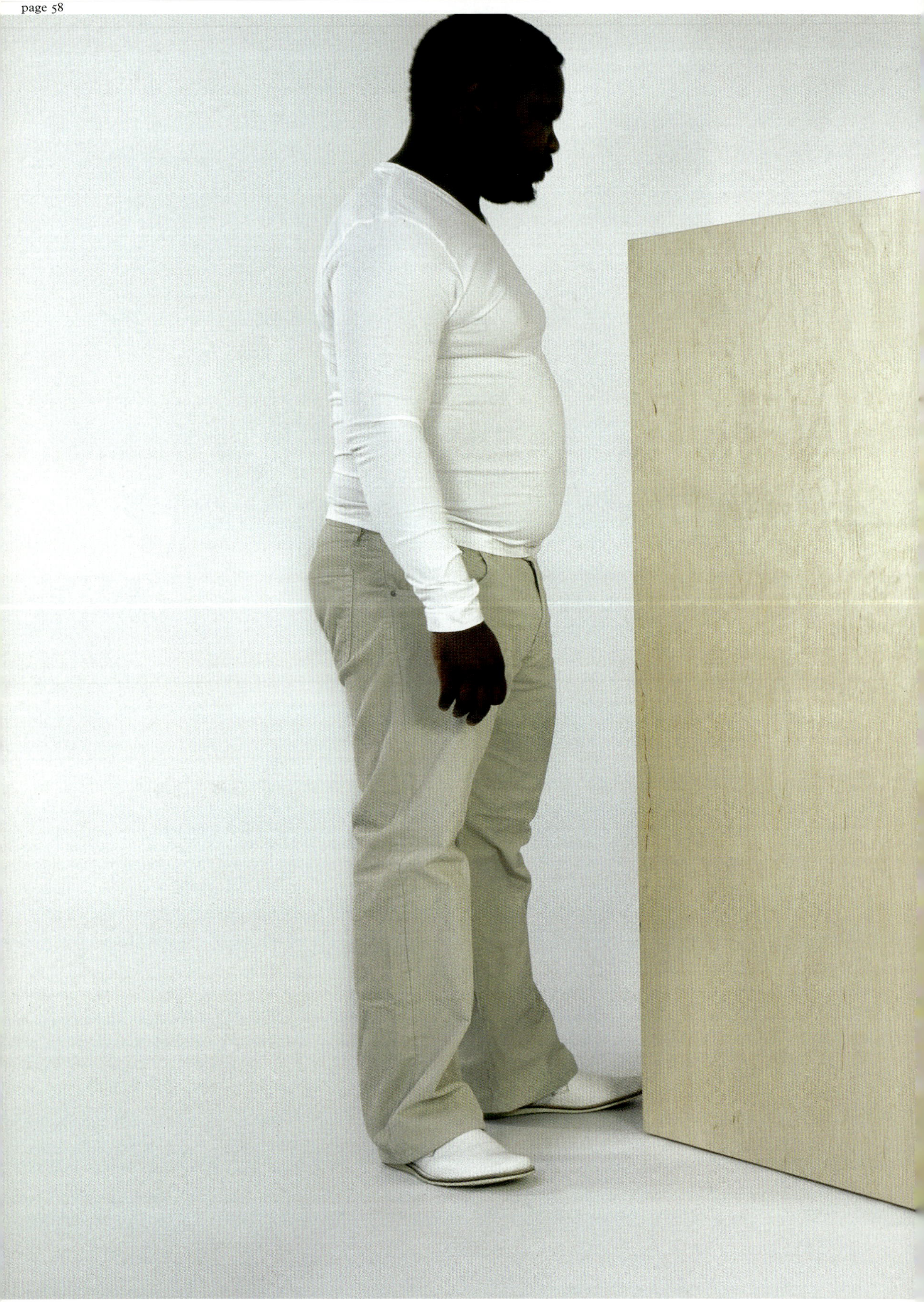

coll.nr. 111 00
Private chair
Martí Guixé, 2001
birch plywood
100 x 140 x 57.5 cm
numbered edition

The integrated walls in the chair provide a hide away to exclude yourself, even when in hectic surroundings.

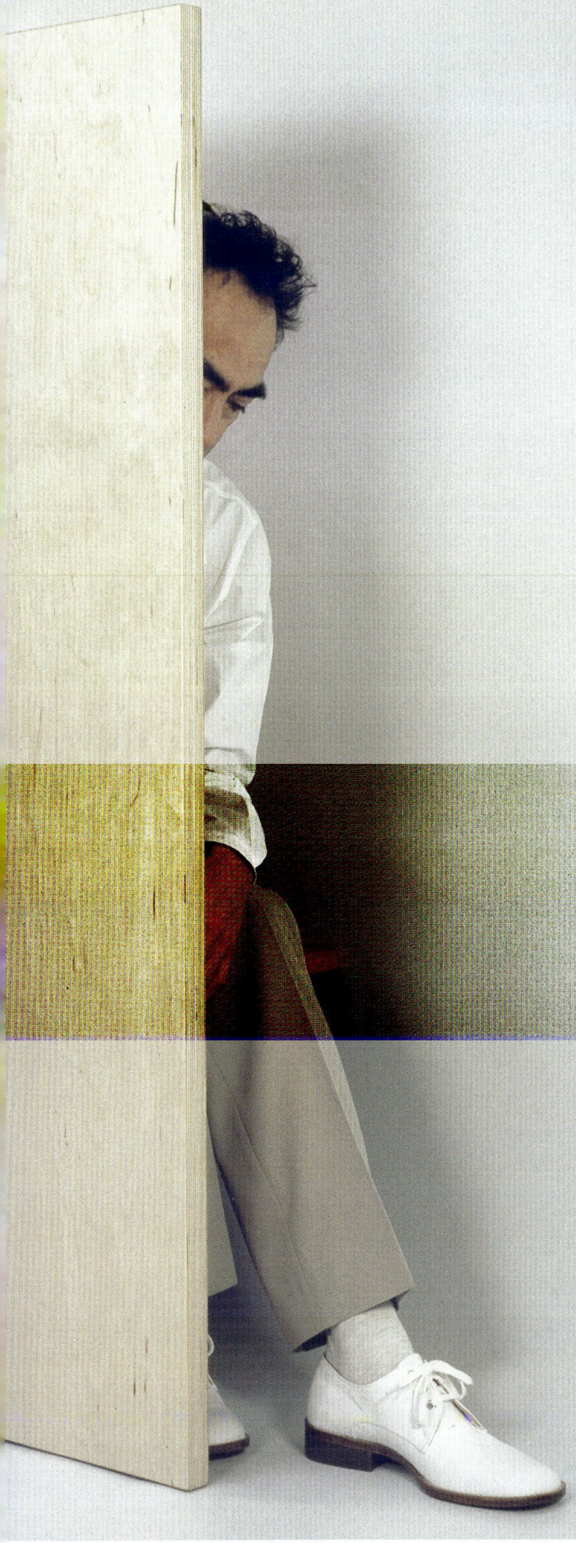

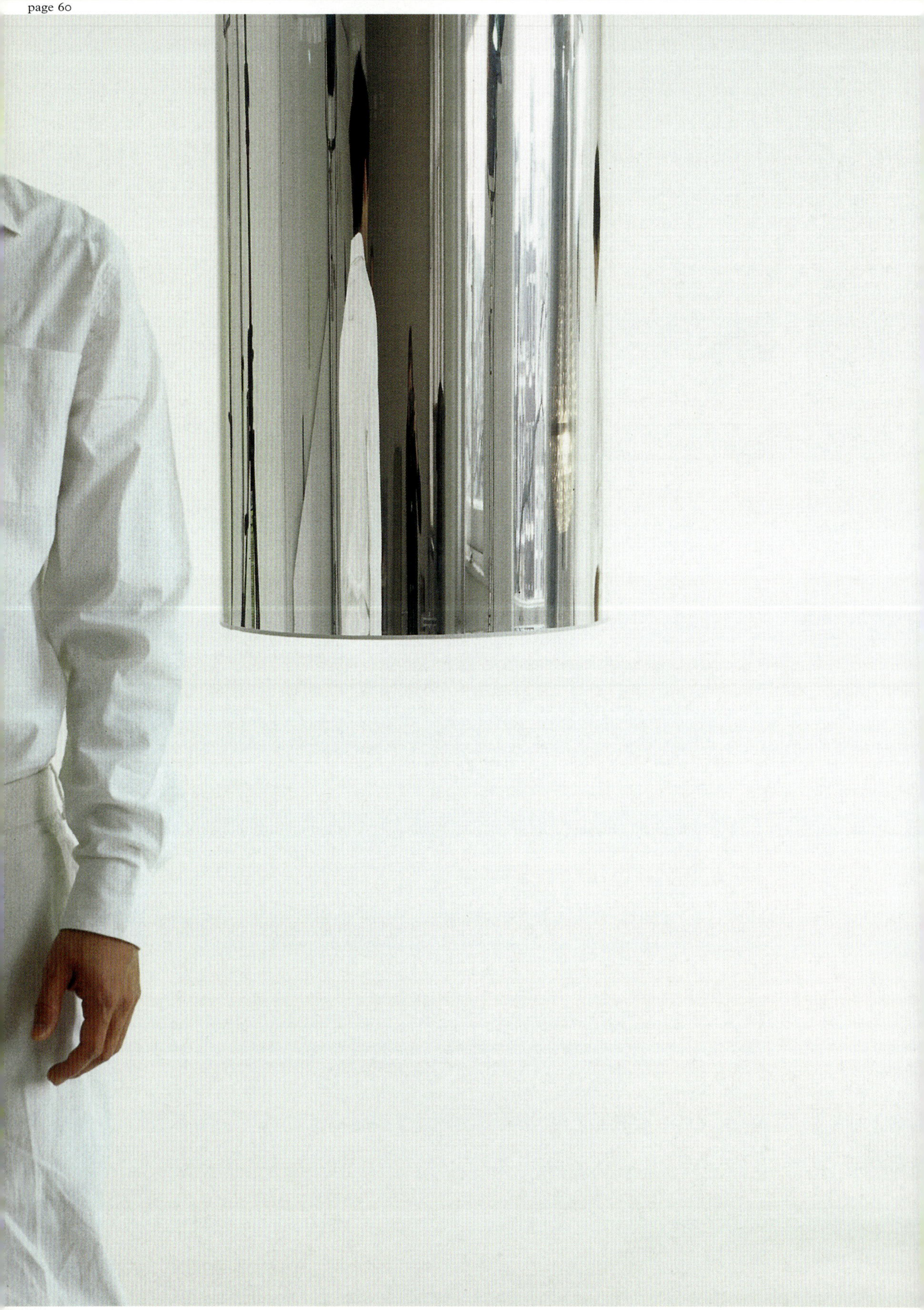

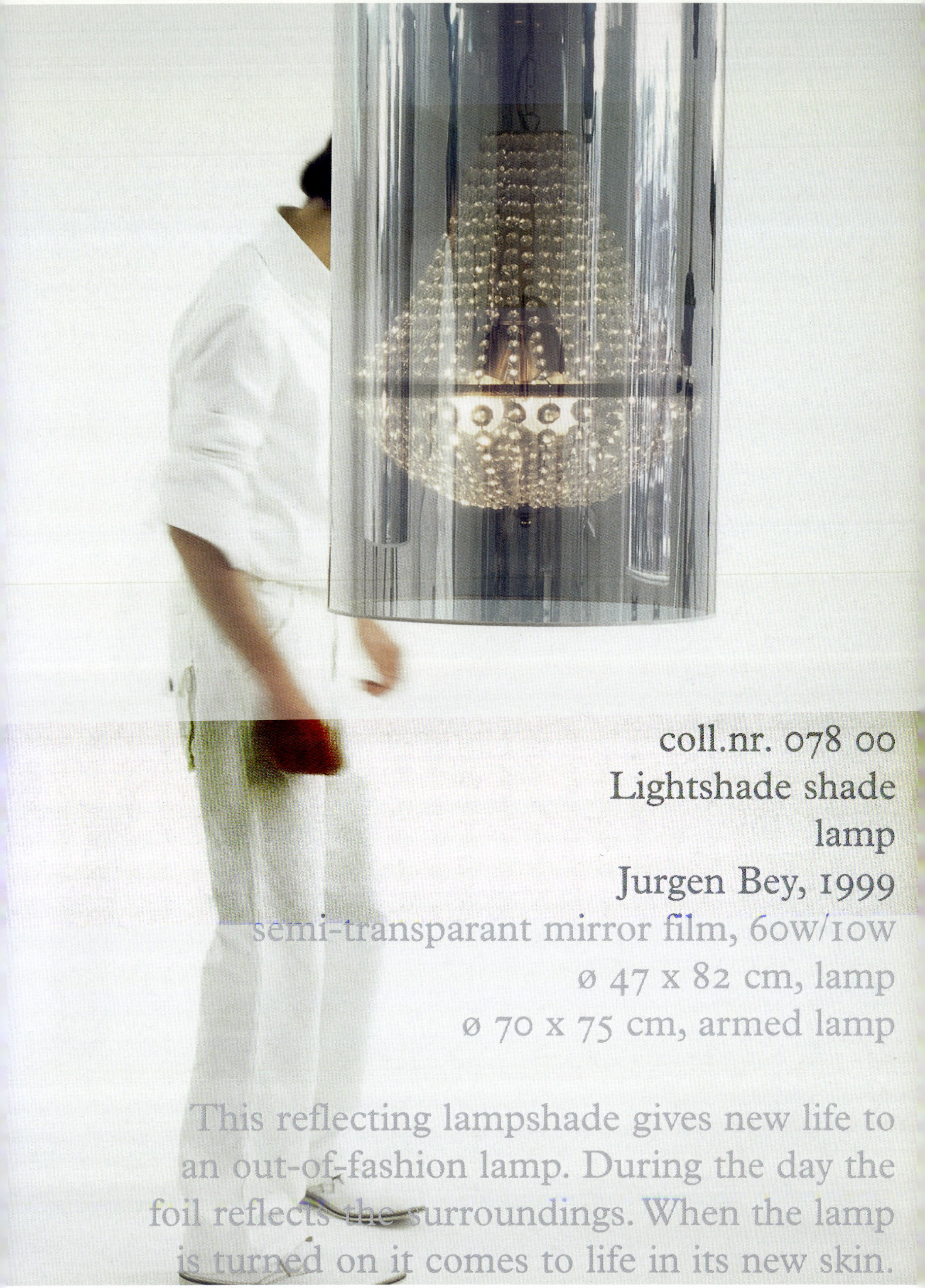

coll.nr. 078 00
Lightshade shade
lamp
Jurgen Bey, 1999
semi-transparant mirror film, 60W/10W
ø 47 x 82 cm, lamp
ø 70 x 75 cm, armed lamp

This reflecting lampshade gives new life to an out-of-fashion lamp. During the day the foil reflects the surroundings. When the lamp is turned on it comes to life in its new skin.

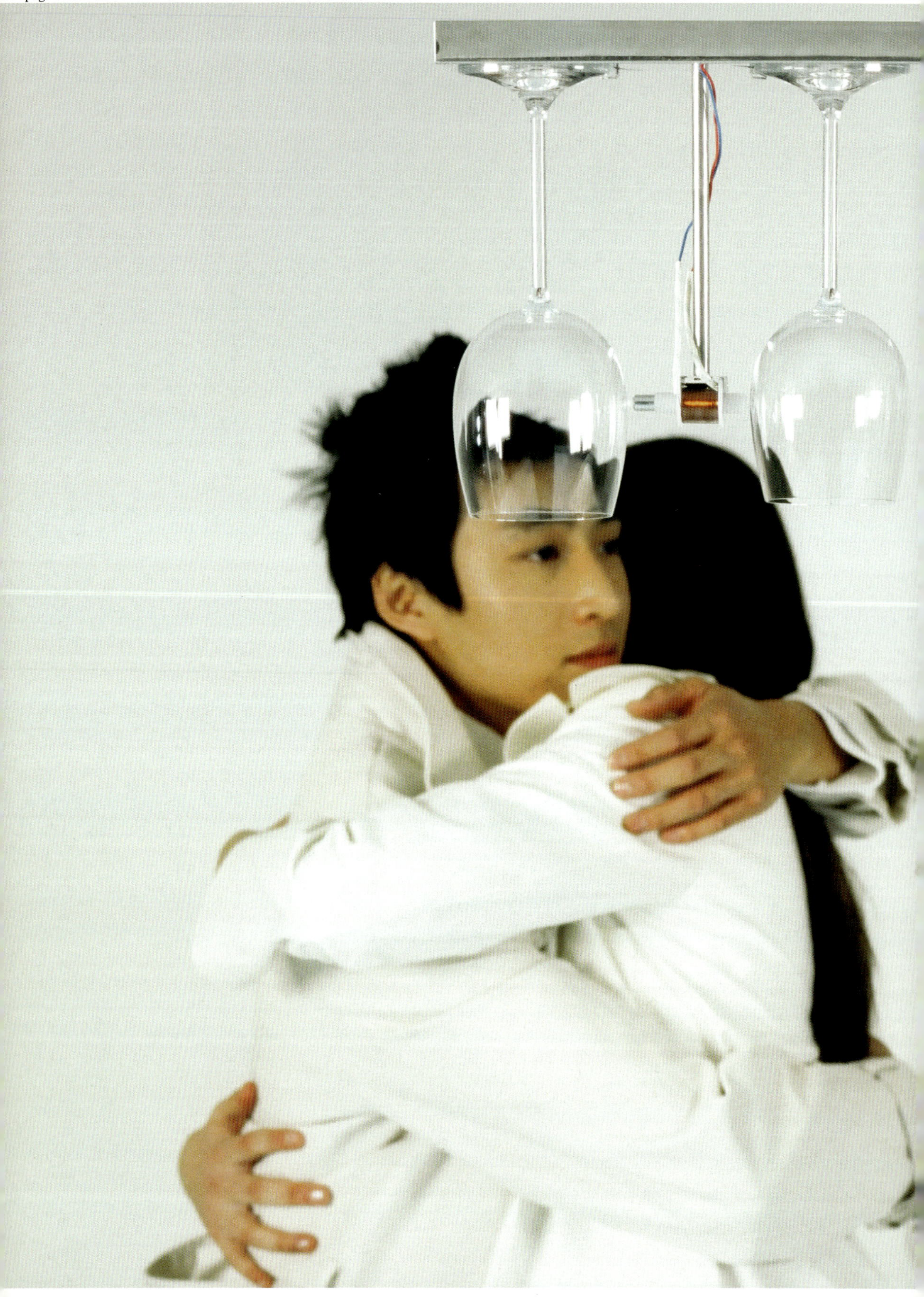

coll.nr. 031 00
Bottoms up
doorbell
Peter van der Jagt, 1994
wineglasses, electromagnet, stainless steel
25 x 9 x 24 cm

What we know as a doorbell, a square box, does not actually indicate its function. In Bottoms up nothing is hidden. The sound is created and symbolised by the crystal wineglasses. This doorbell announces guests with a musical toast.

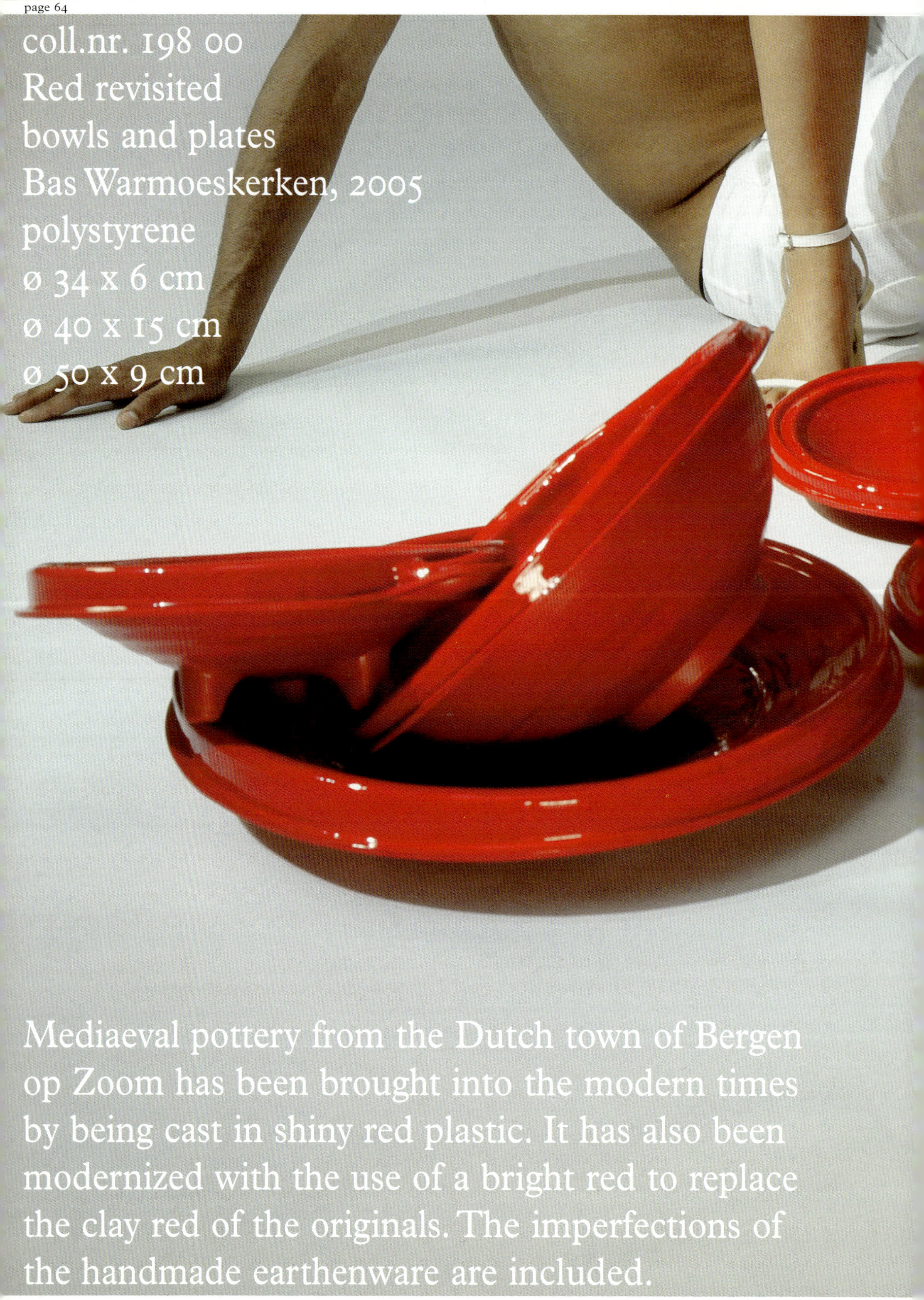

coll.nr. 198 00
Red revisited
bowls and plates
Bas Warmoeskerken, 2005
polystyrene
ø 34 x 6 cm
ø 40 x 15 cm
ø 50 x 9 cm

Mediaeval pottery from the Dutch town of Bergen op Zoom has been brought into the modern times by being cast in shiny red plastic. It has also been modernized with the use of a bright red to replace the clay red of the originals. The imperfections of the handmade earthenware are included.

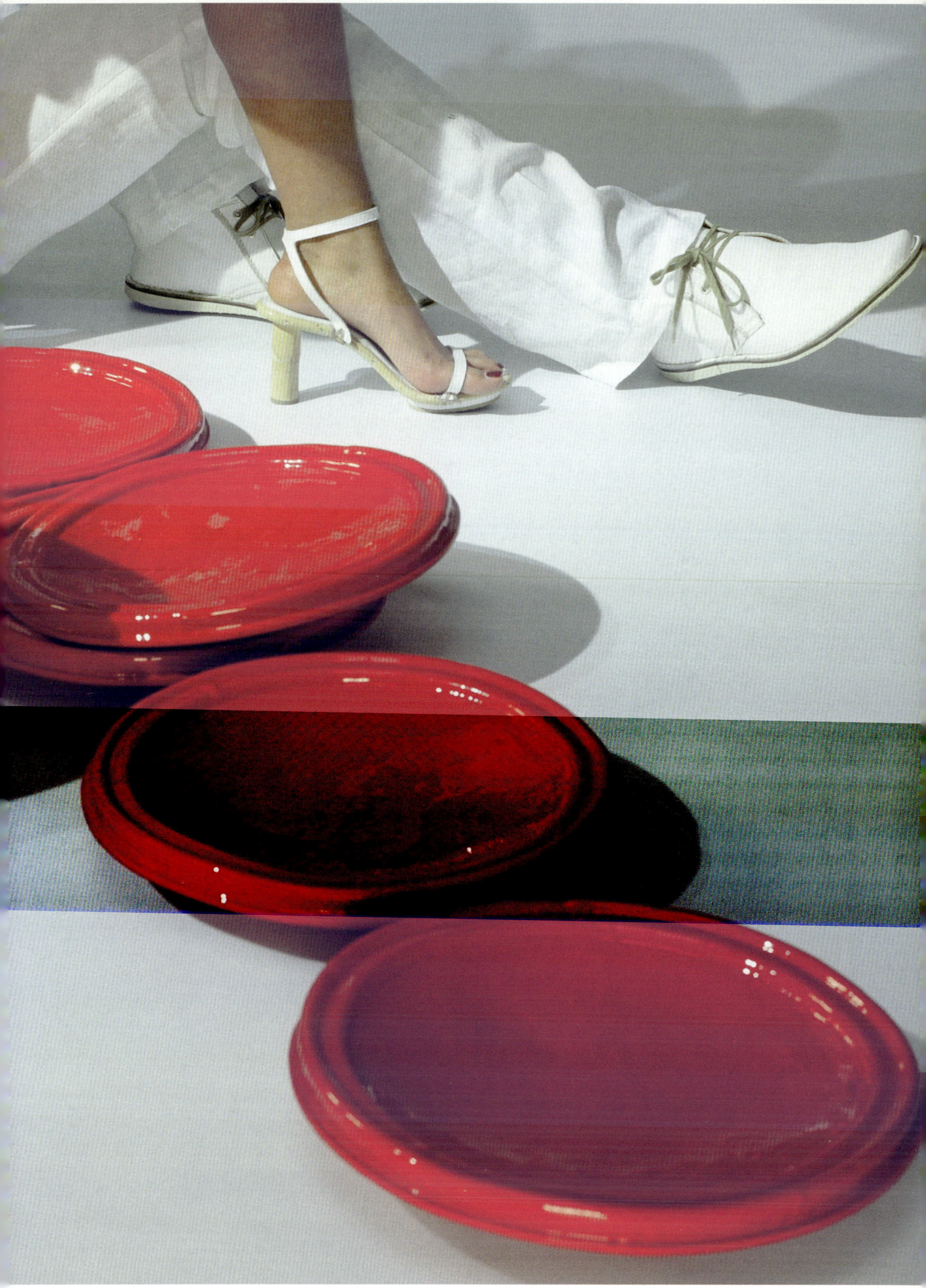

coll.nr. 087 01
Do hit
chair
Marijn van der Poll, 2000
1.25 mm stainless steel, hammer
100 x 70 x 75 cm

With the hammer provided and your own resources you shape the metal box into whatever you choose it to be. After a few minutes or hours of hard work you become the co-designer of Do hit.

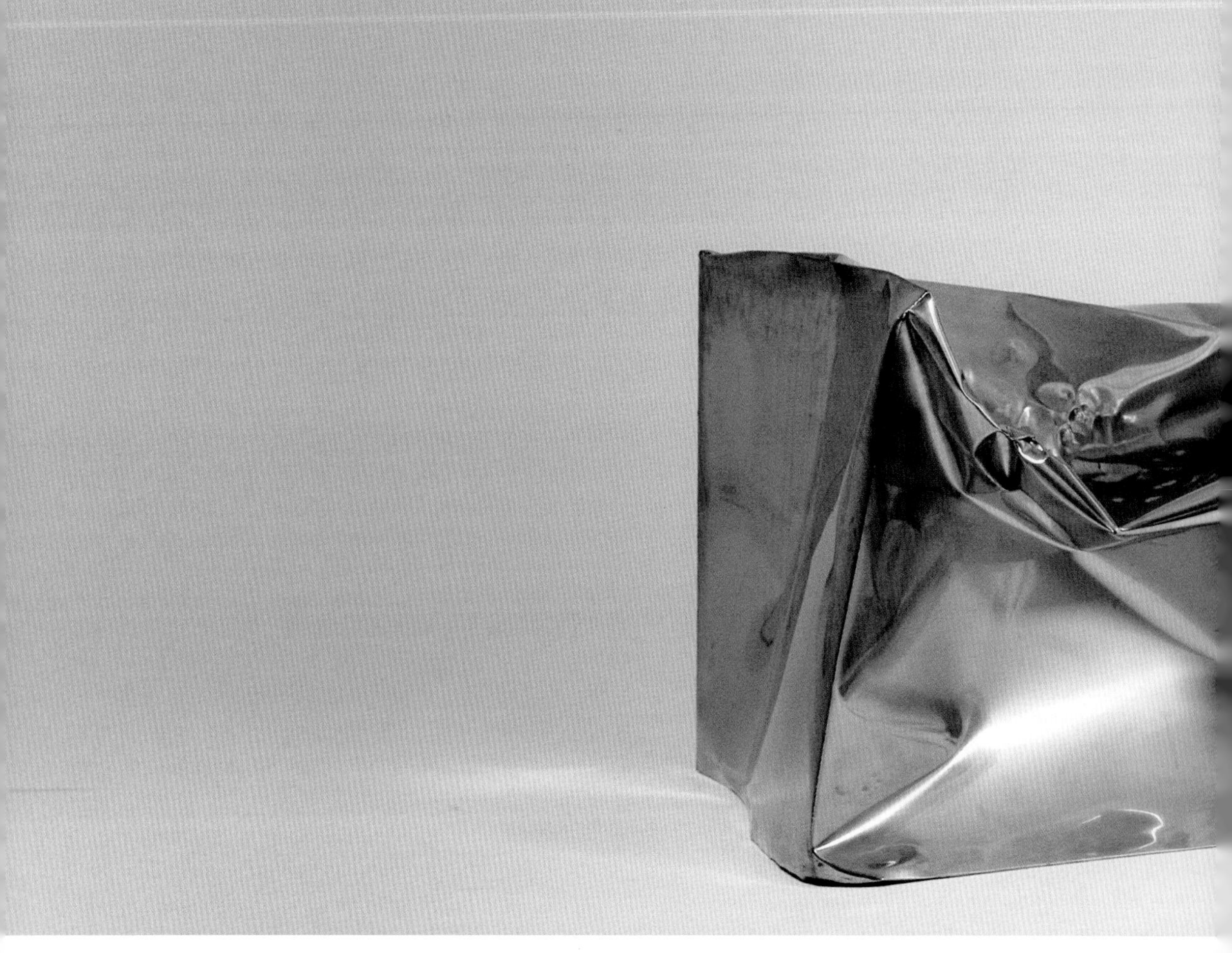

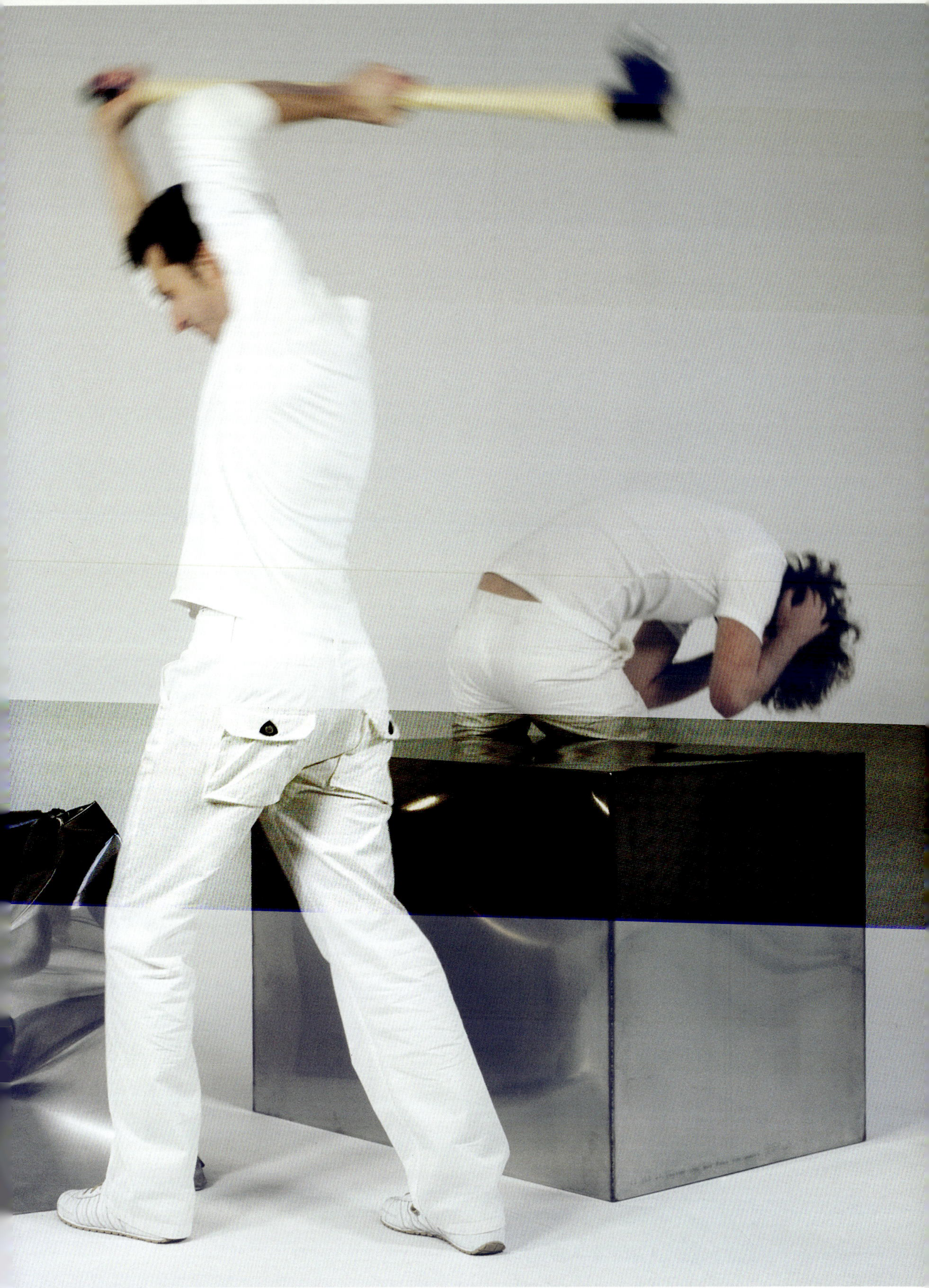

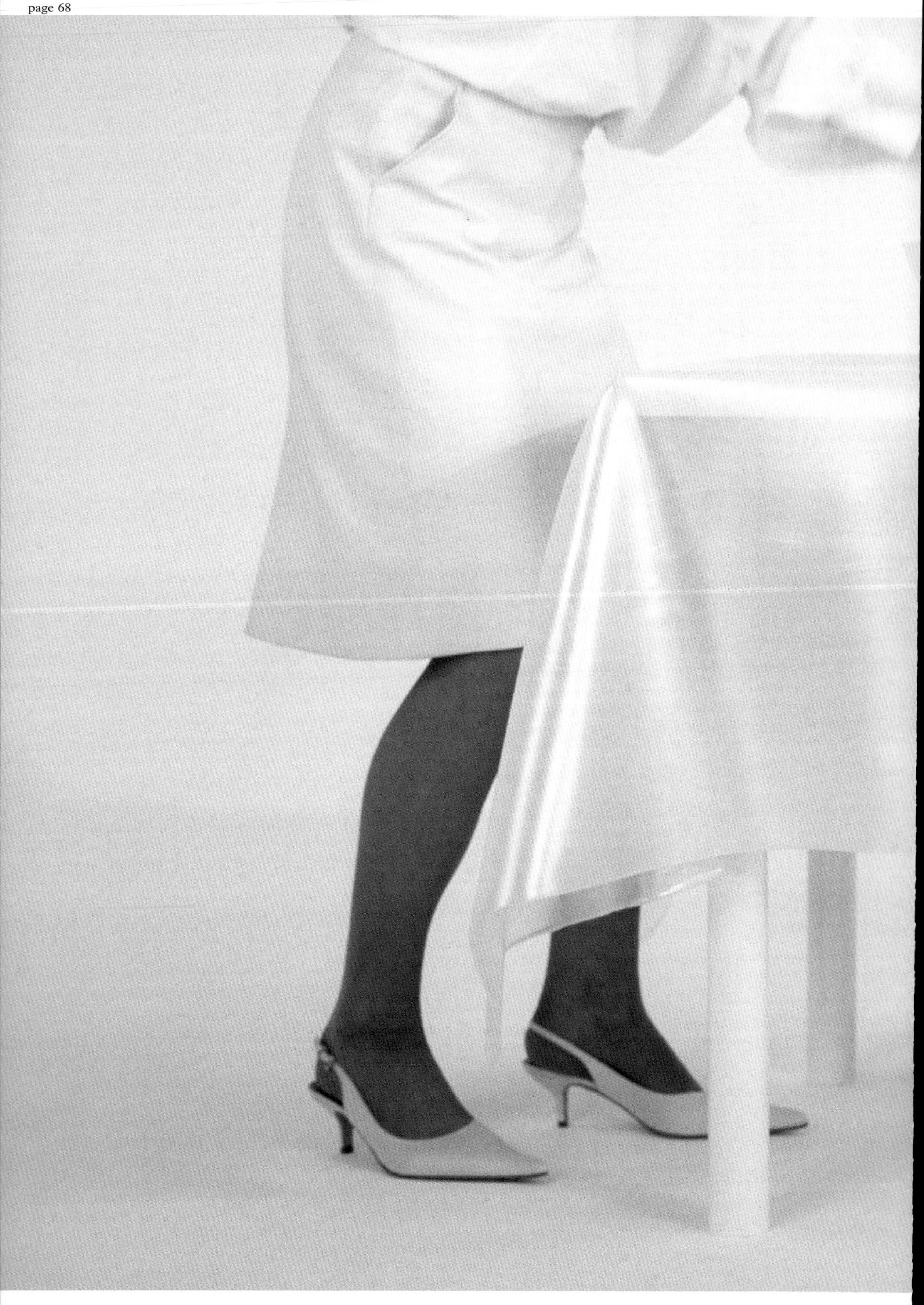

coll.nr. 068 00
Tablecloth with bowl
Saar Oosterhof, 1998
silicone, various colours
160 x 160 x 14 cm

Here objects which are normally seen on the table become one product. The bowl literally fuses with the tablecloth. This reinvents the traditional table setting.

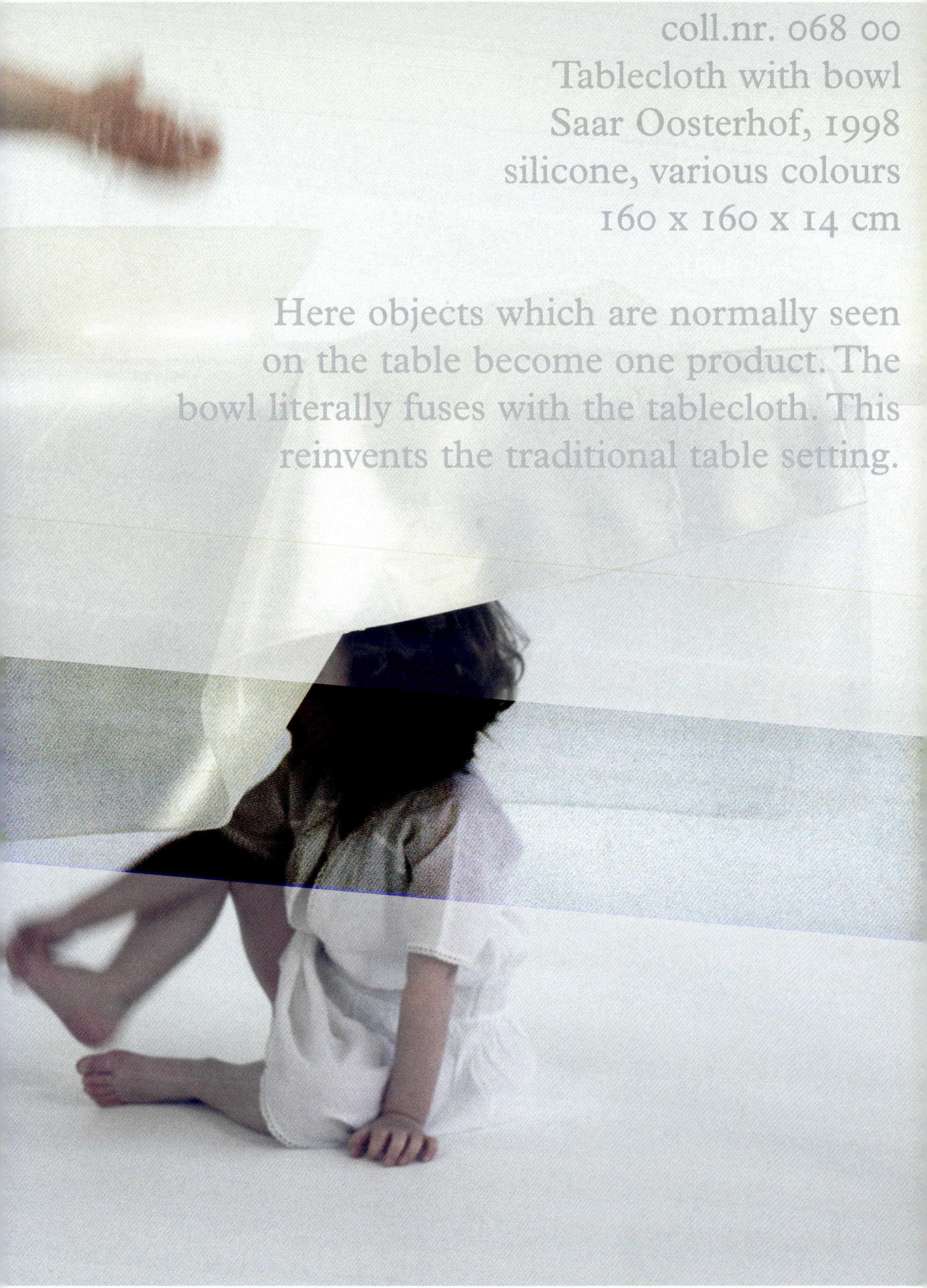

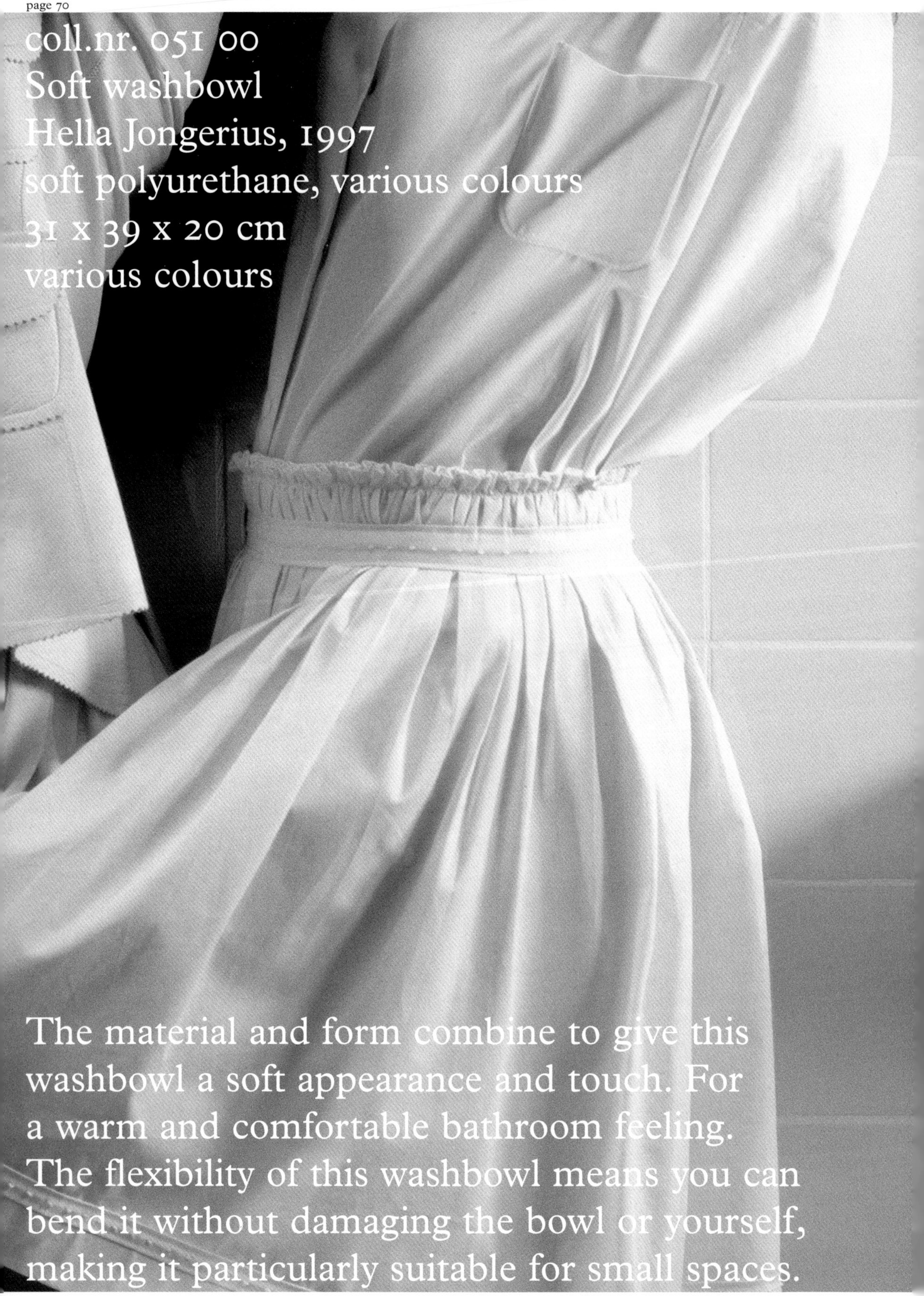

coll.nr. 051 00
Soft washbowl
Hella Jongerius, 1997
soft polyurethane, various colours
31 x 39 x 20 cm
various colours

The material and form combine to give this washbowl a soft appearance and touch. For a warm and comfortable bathroom feeling. The flexibility of this washbowl means you can bend it without damaging the bowl or yourself, making it particularly suitable for small spaces.

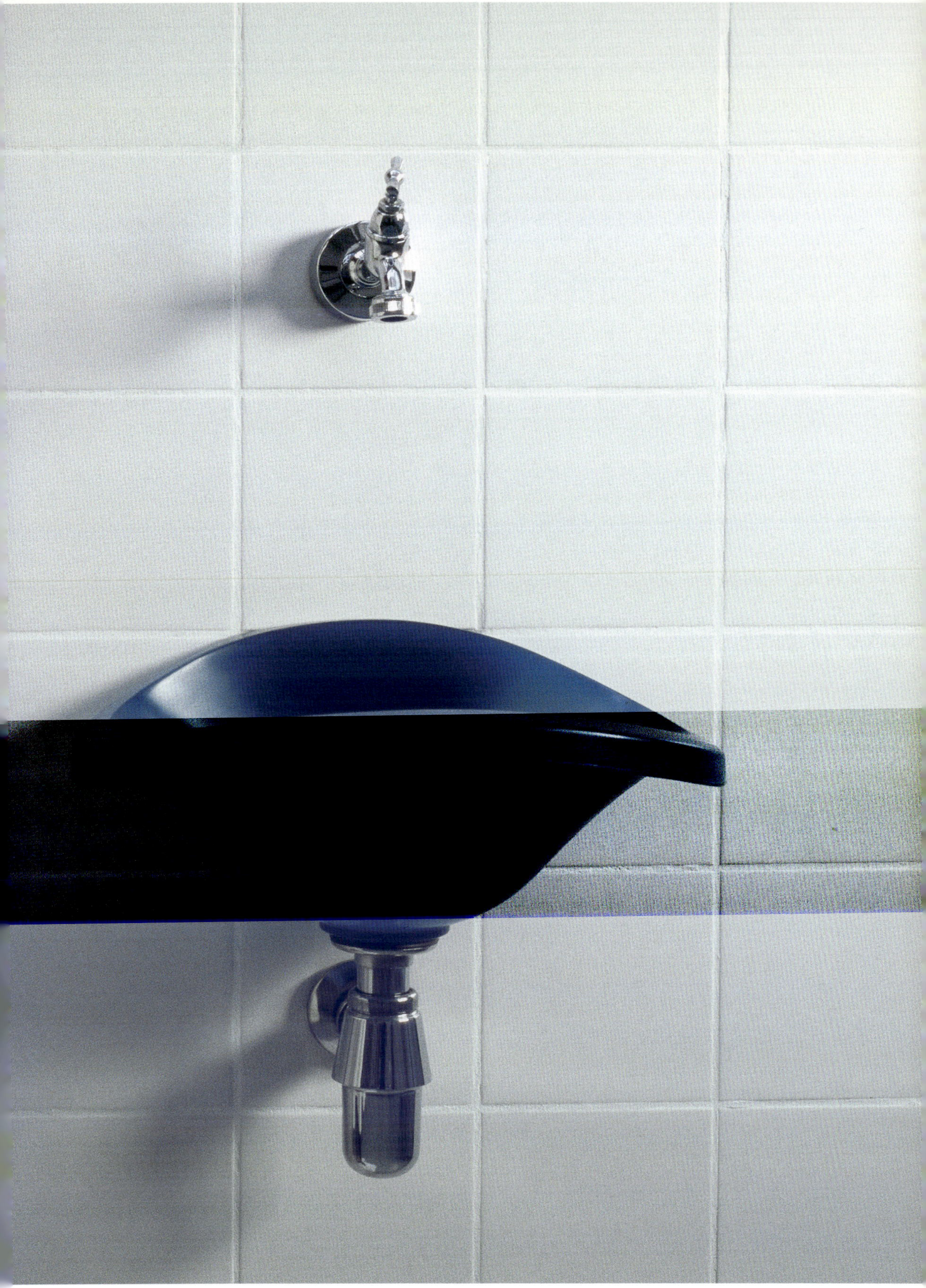

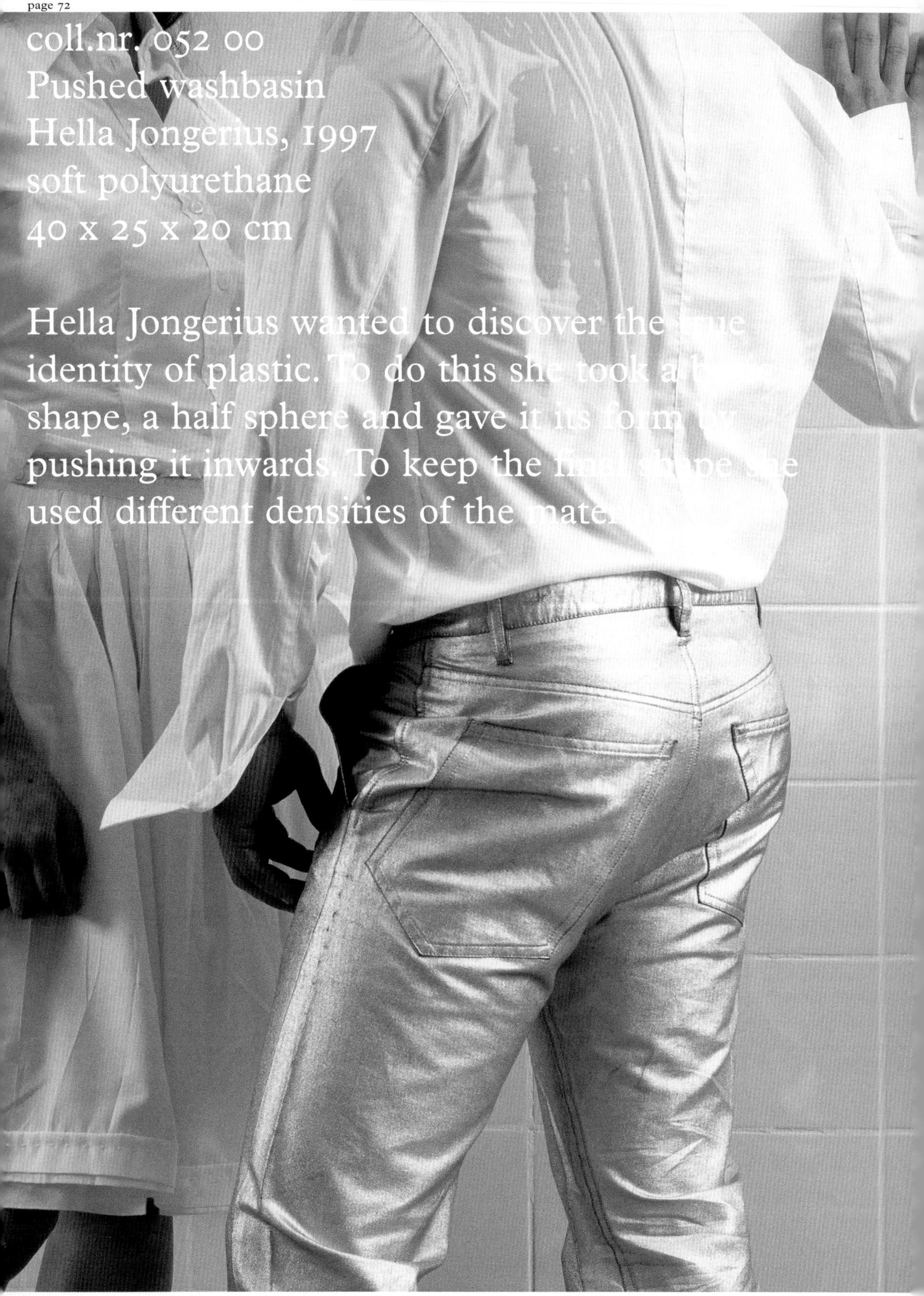

coll.nr. 052 00
Pushed washbasin
Hella Jongerius, 1997
soft polyurethane
40 x 25 x 20 cm

Hella Jongerius wanted to discover the true identity of plastic. To do this she took a basic shape, a half sphere and gave it its form by pushing it inwards. To keep the final shape she used different densities of the material.

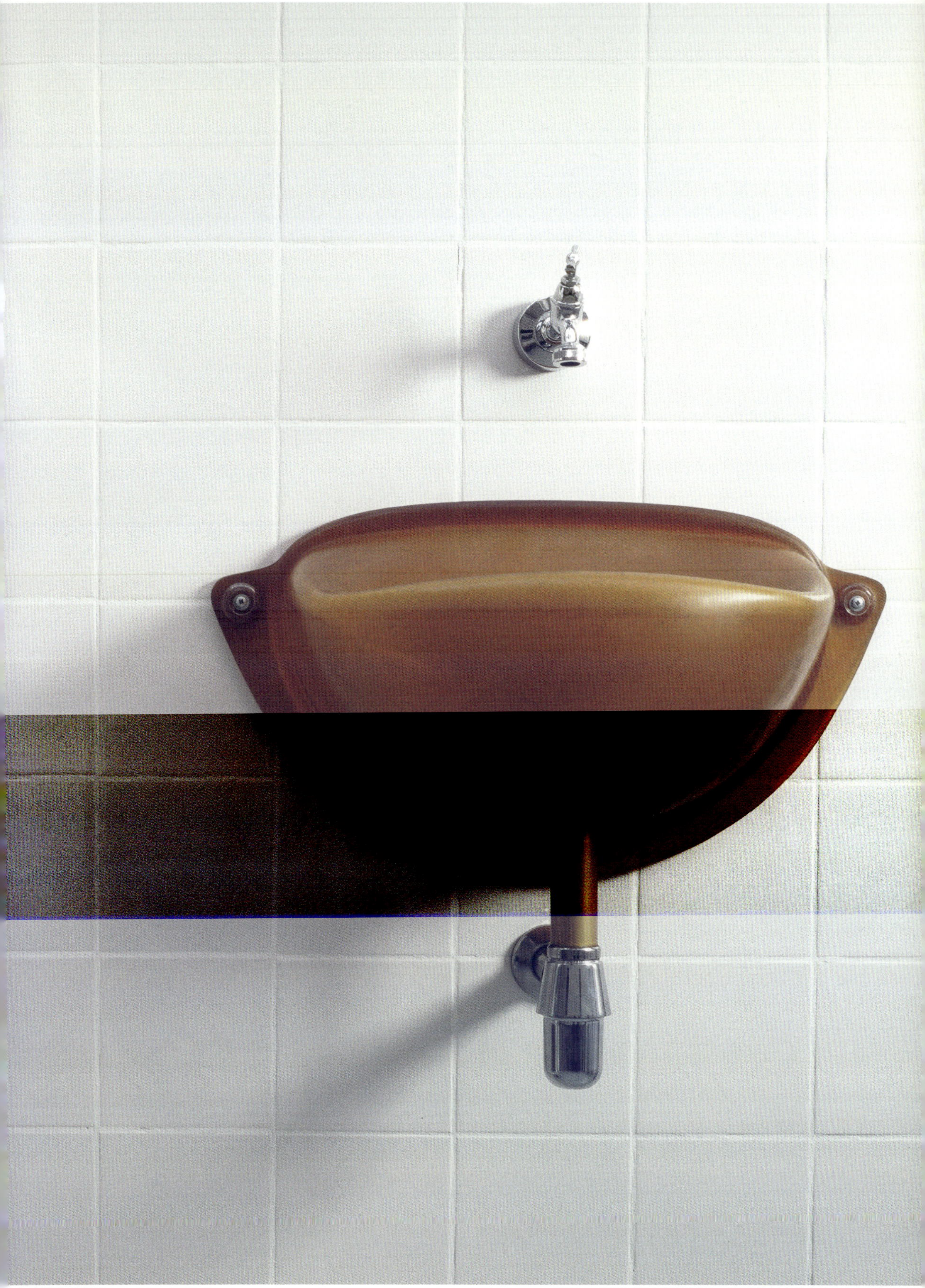

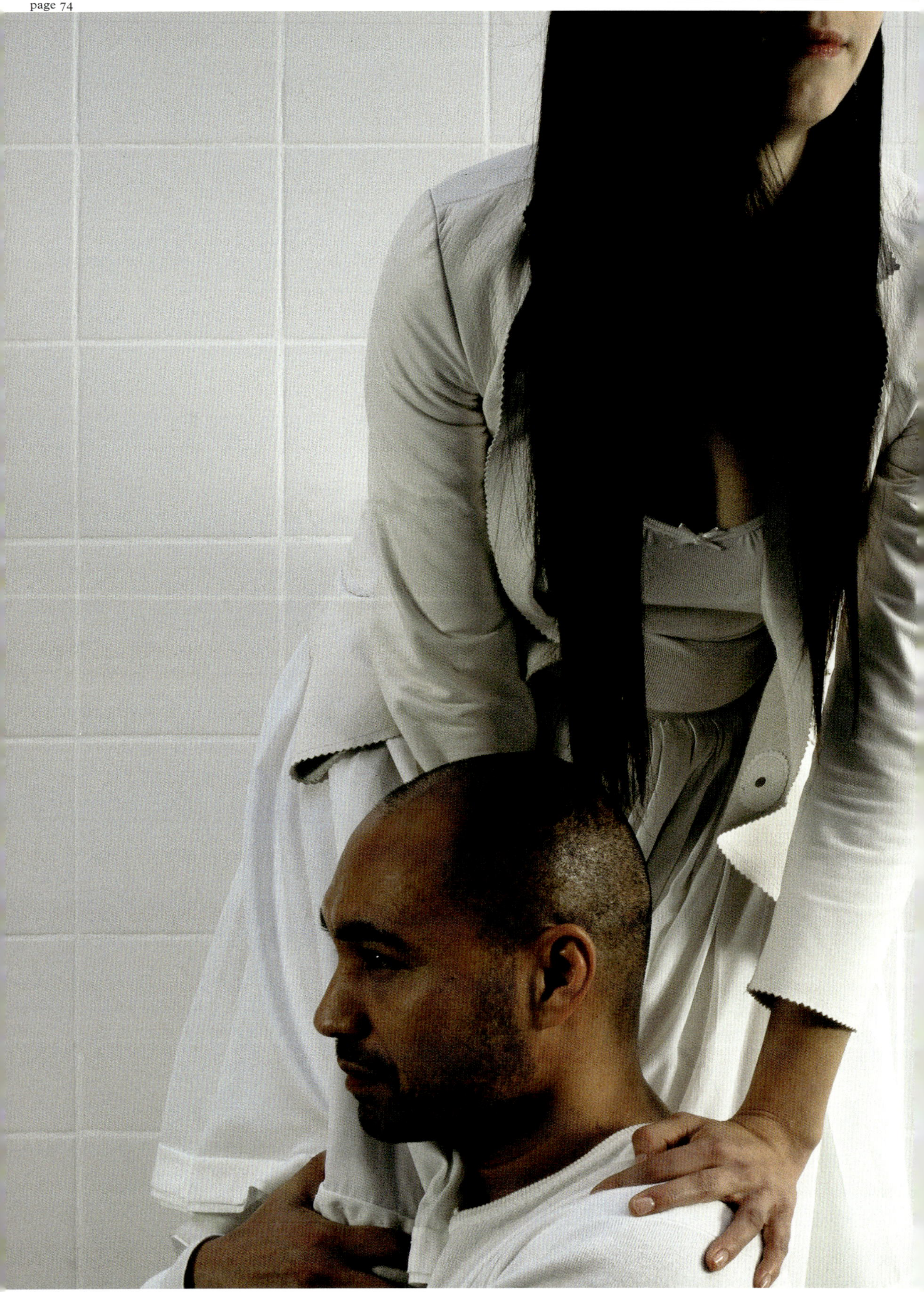

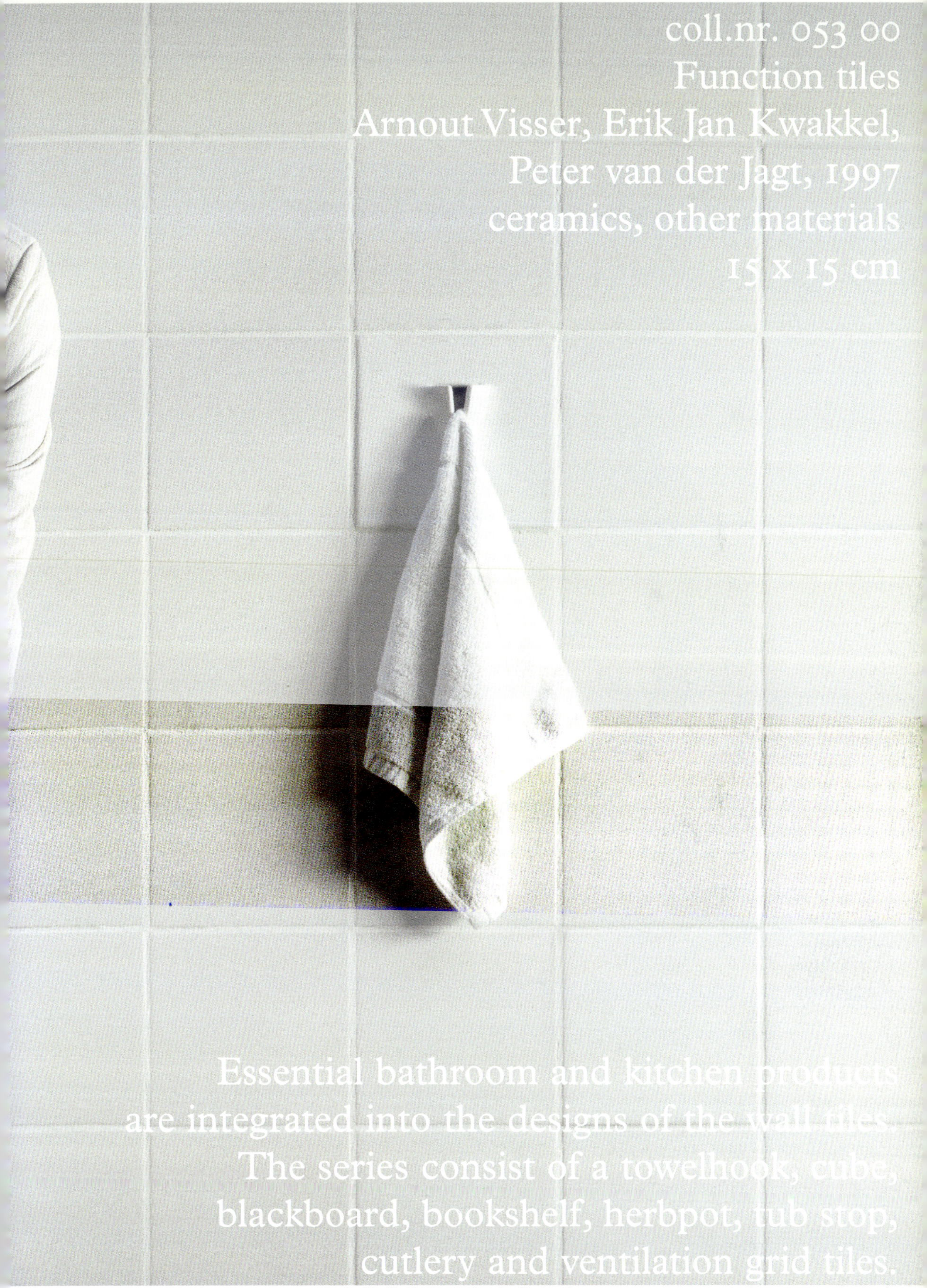

coll.nr. 053 00
Function tiles
Arnout Visser, Erik Jan Kwakkel,
Peter van der Jagt, 1997
ceramics, other materials
15 x 15 cm

Essential bathroom and kitchen products are integrated into the designs of the wall tiles. The series consist of a towelhook, cube, blackboard, bookshelf, herbpot, tub stop, cutlery and ventilation grid tiles.

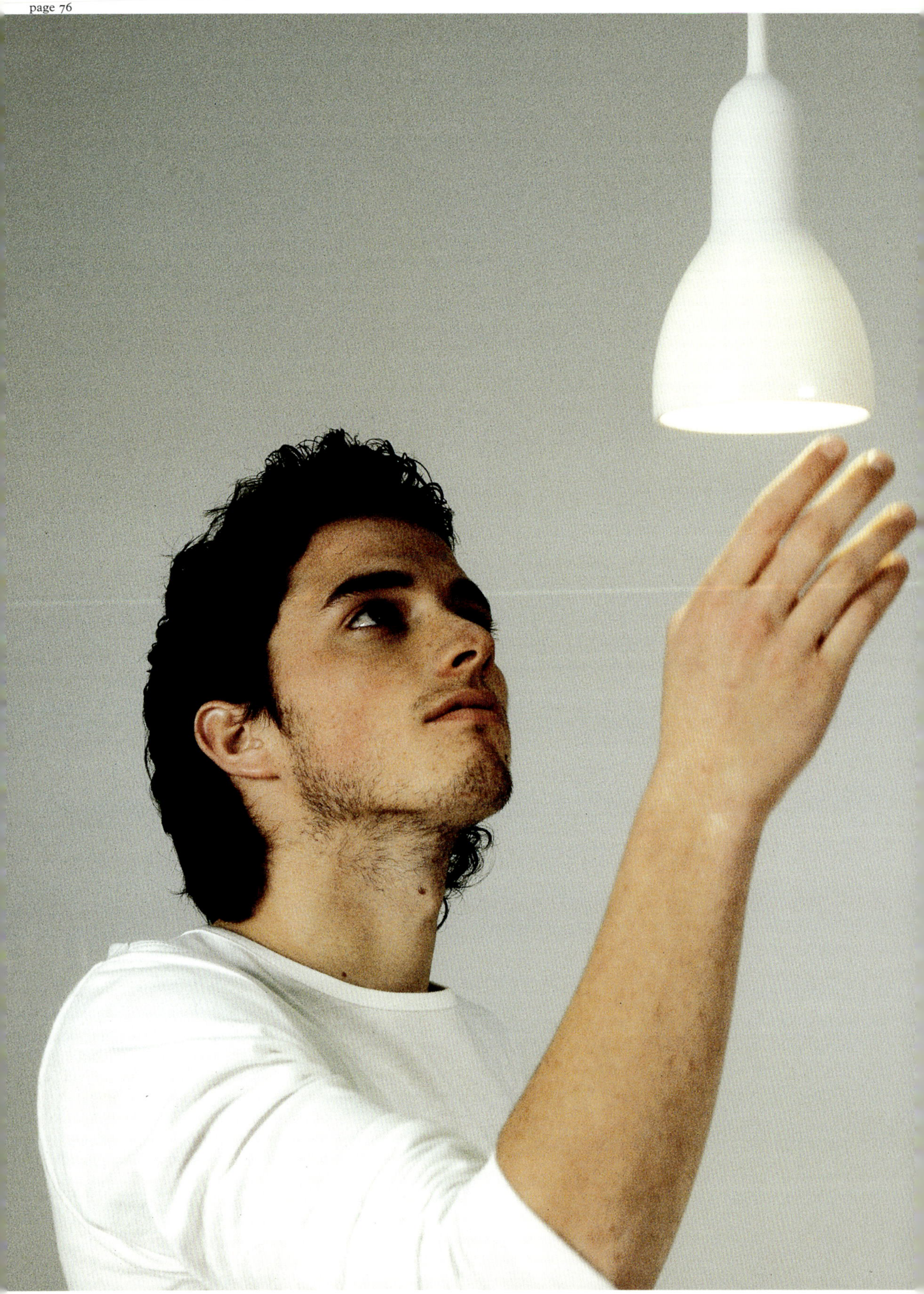

coll.nr. 035 24

Soft lamp

Arian Brekveld, 1995

soft PVC, 7W energy saving bulb

ø 10.5 x 22 cm

This lamp gives a new use to the old PVC dip technique. The material of the soft lampshade gives the impression that the cord is melting into the shade. When the light is turned on the seemingly opaque material radiates a warm glow.

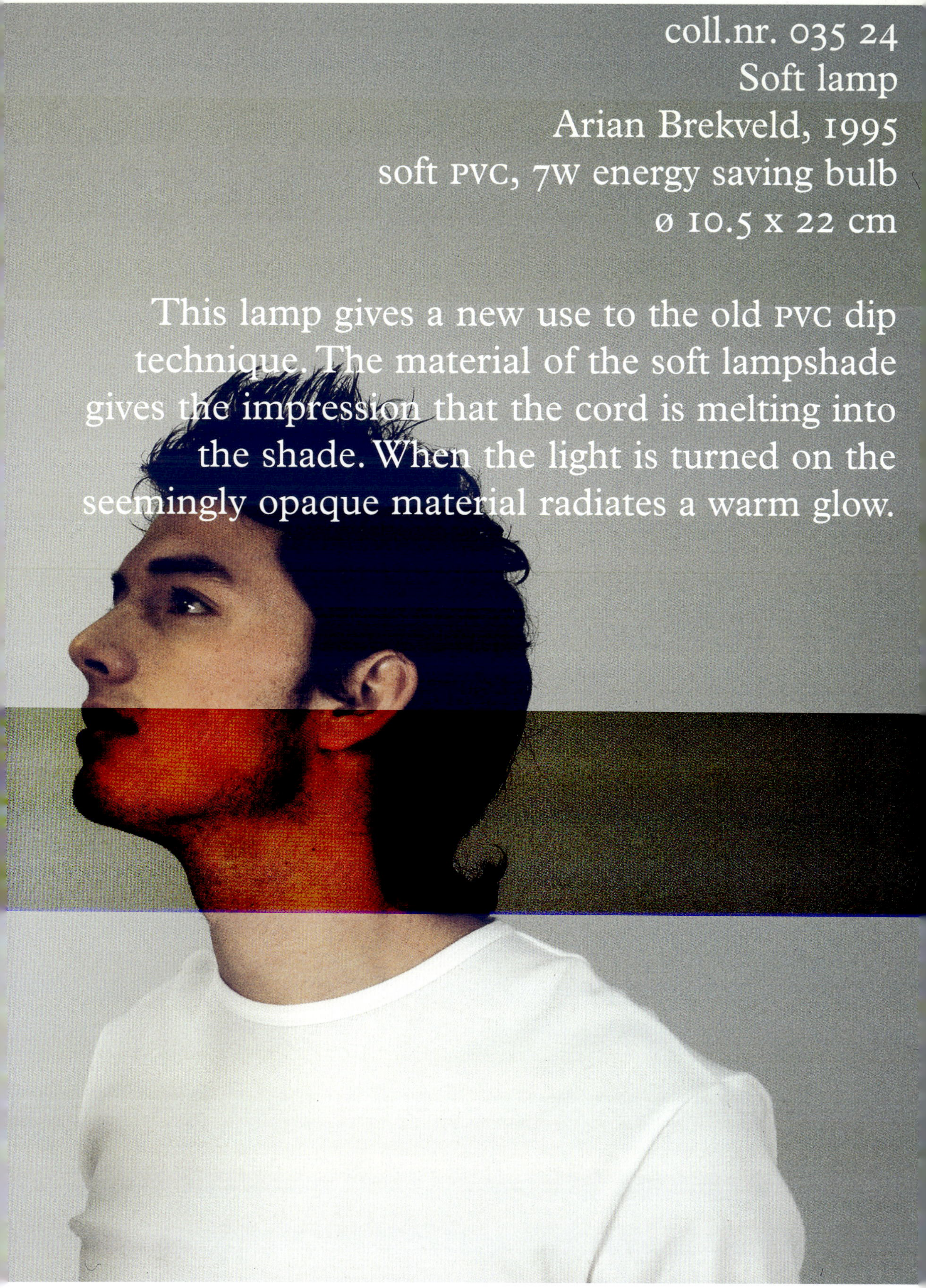

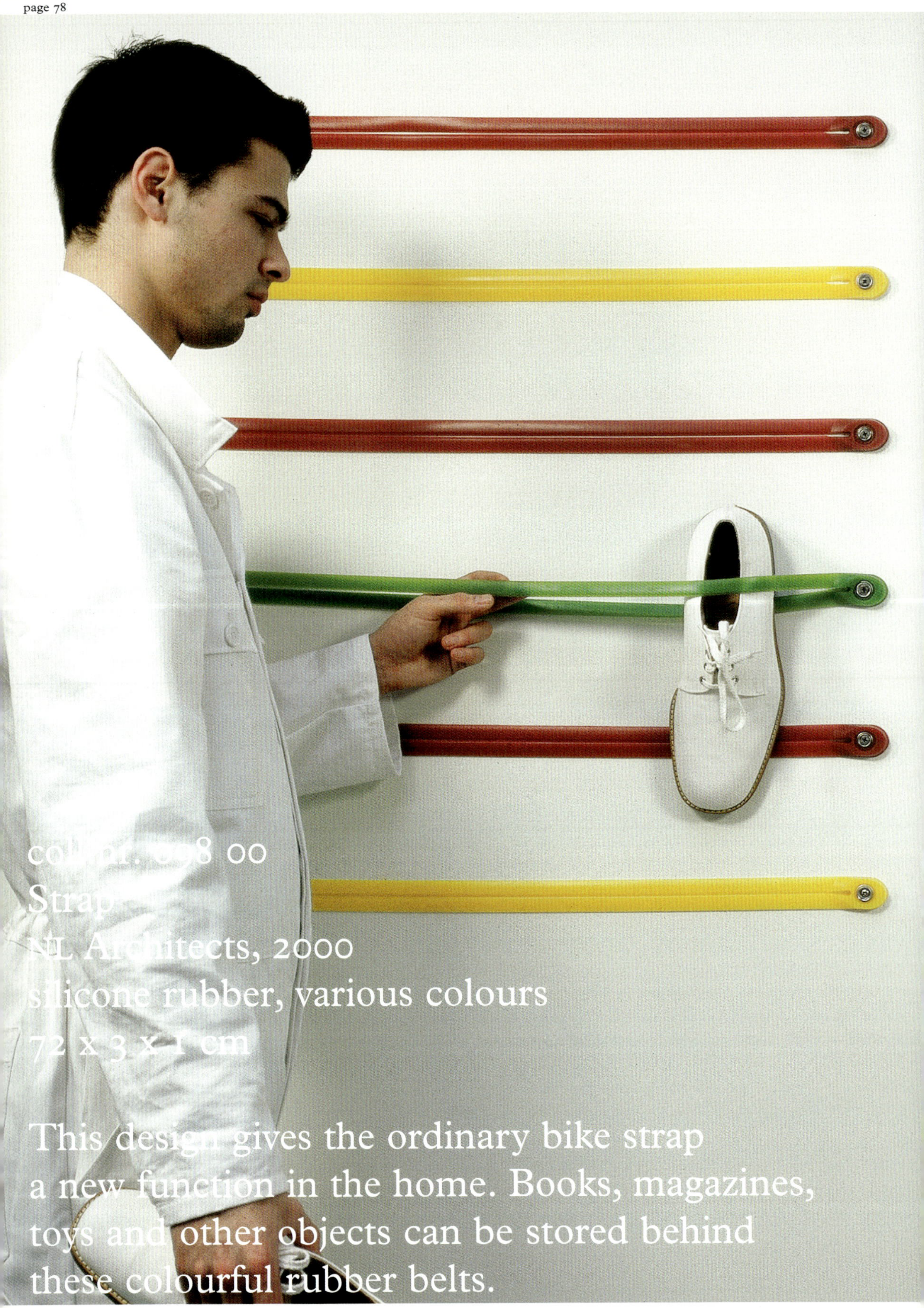

coll. nr. 098 00
Strap
NL Architects, 2000
silicone rubber, various colours
72 x 3 x 1 cm

This design gives the ordinary bike strap a new function in the home. Books, magazines, toys and other objects can be stored behind these colourful rubber belts.

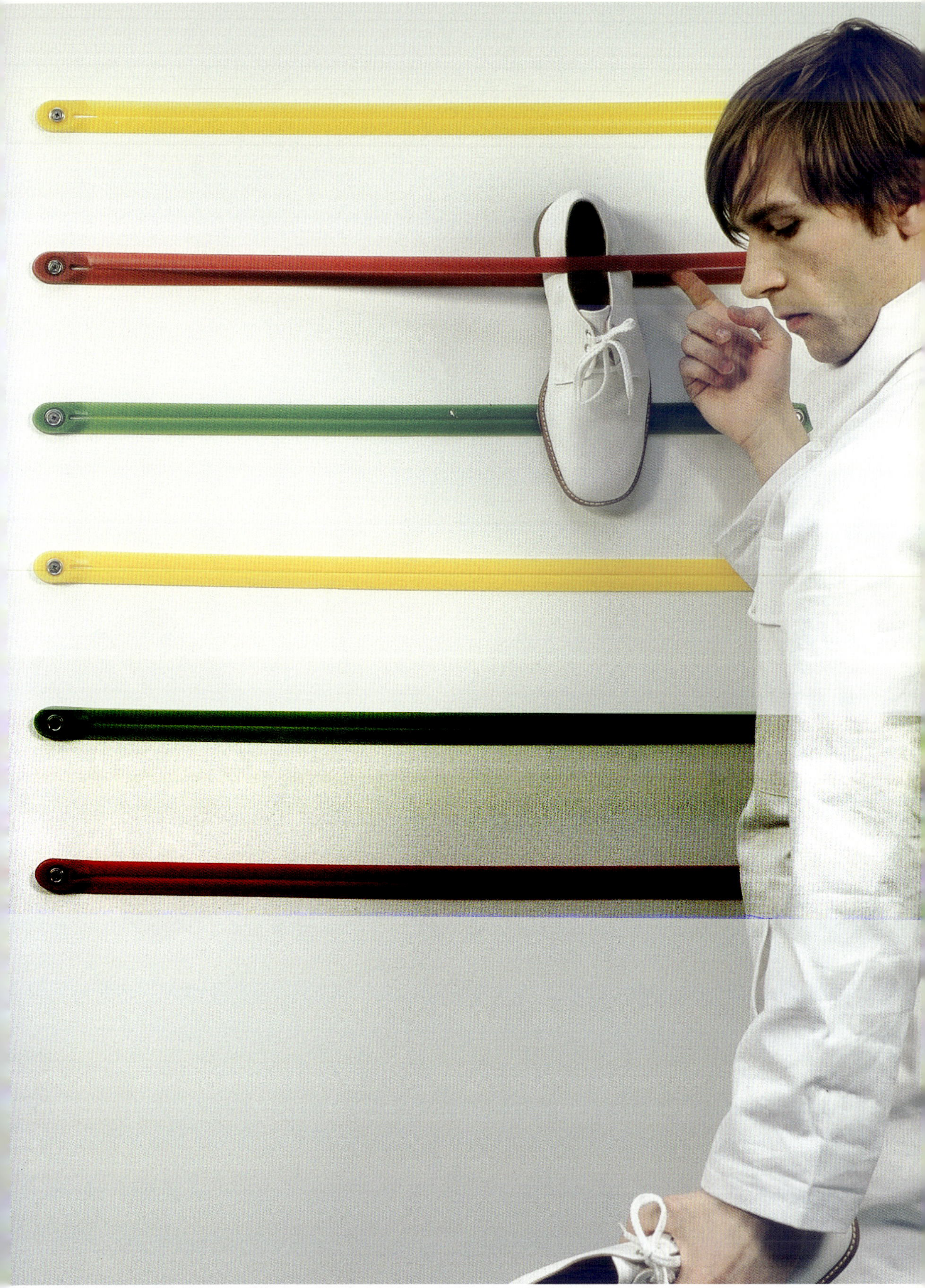

coll.nr. 091 00
Do scratch
lamp
Martí Guixé, 2000
wall lamp, black coating
27 x 27 x 5 cm

Let the light escape where you choose to scratch the surface. You make it as creative as you want it to be through your personal graffiti.

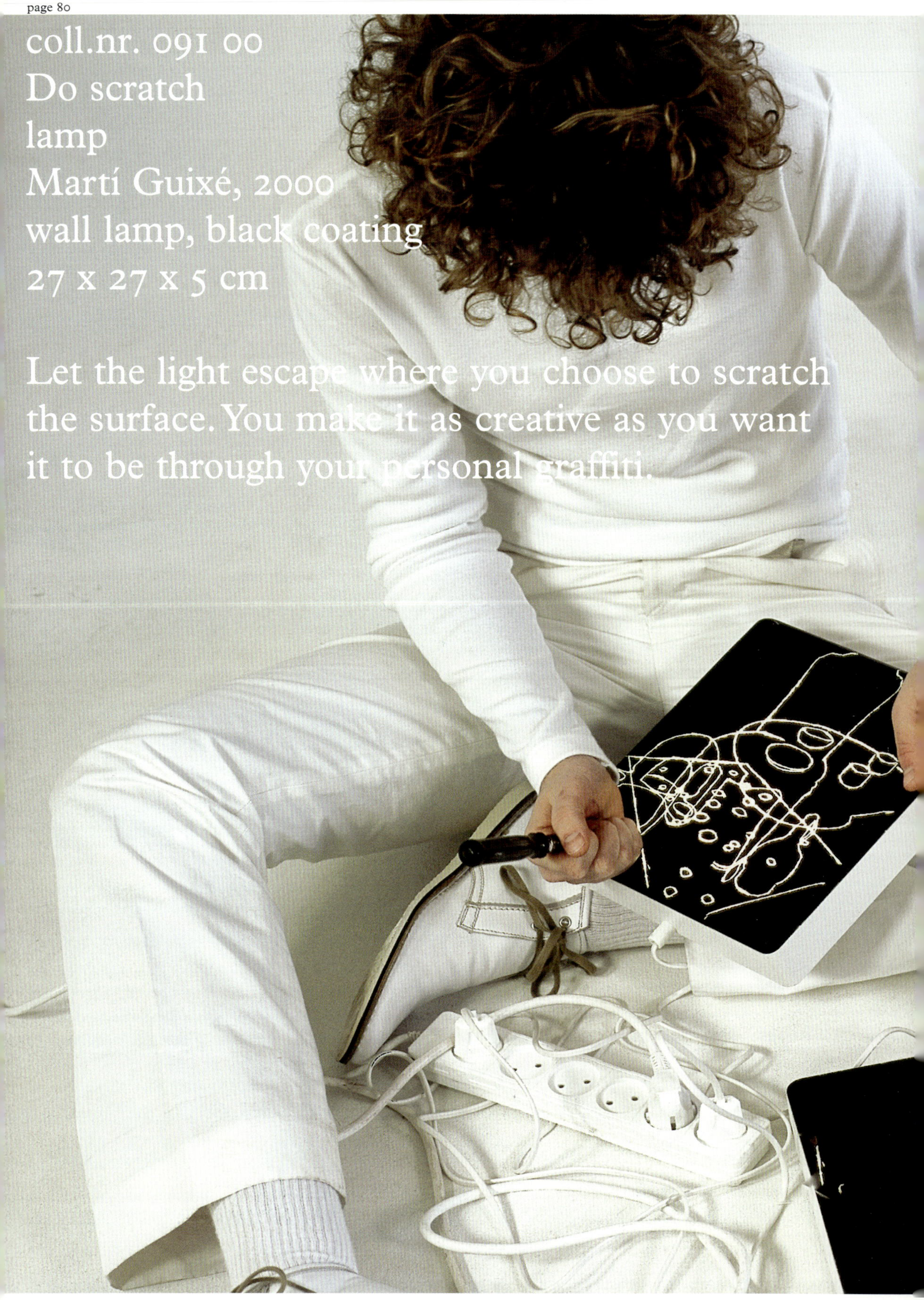

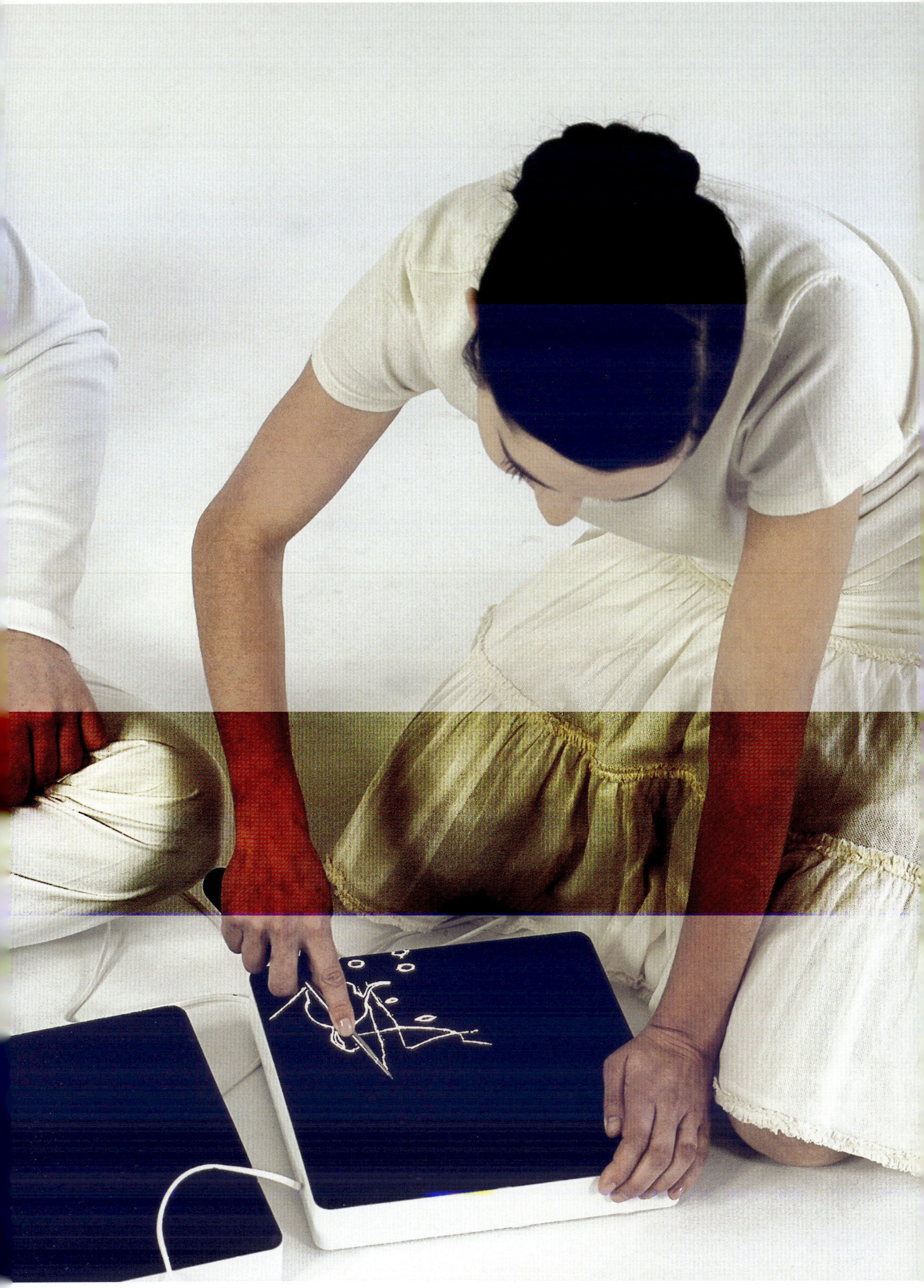

coll.nr. 159 00
Lucky cat
Tadaaki Narita, 2003
ceramics, wood, metal
84 x 104 x 130 cm

In Japanese culture when the lucky cat waves at you, you are showered with good fortune. With this pinball machine you can win nothing but good luck. As the balls interact with the cats, each one having its own chime, you become the conductor of the lucky cat orchestra.

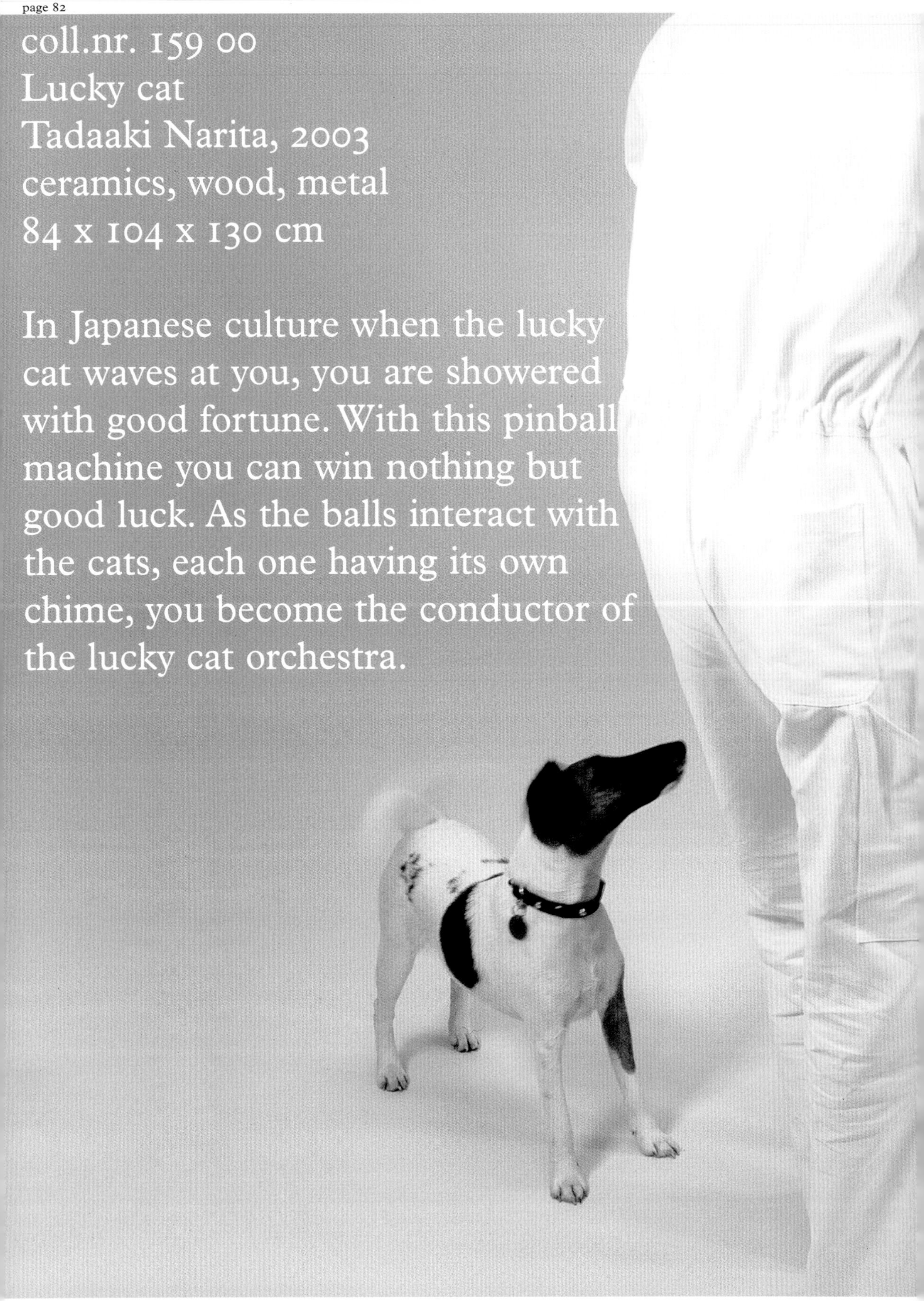

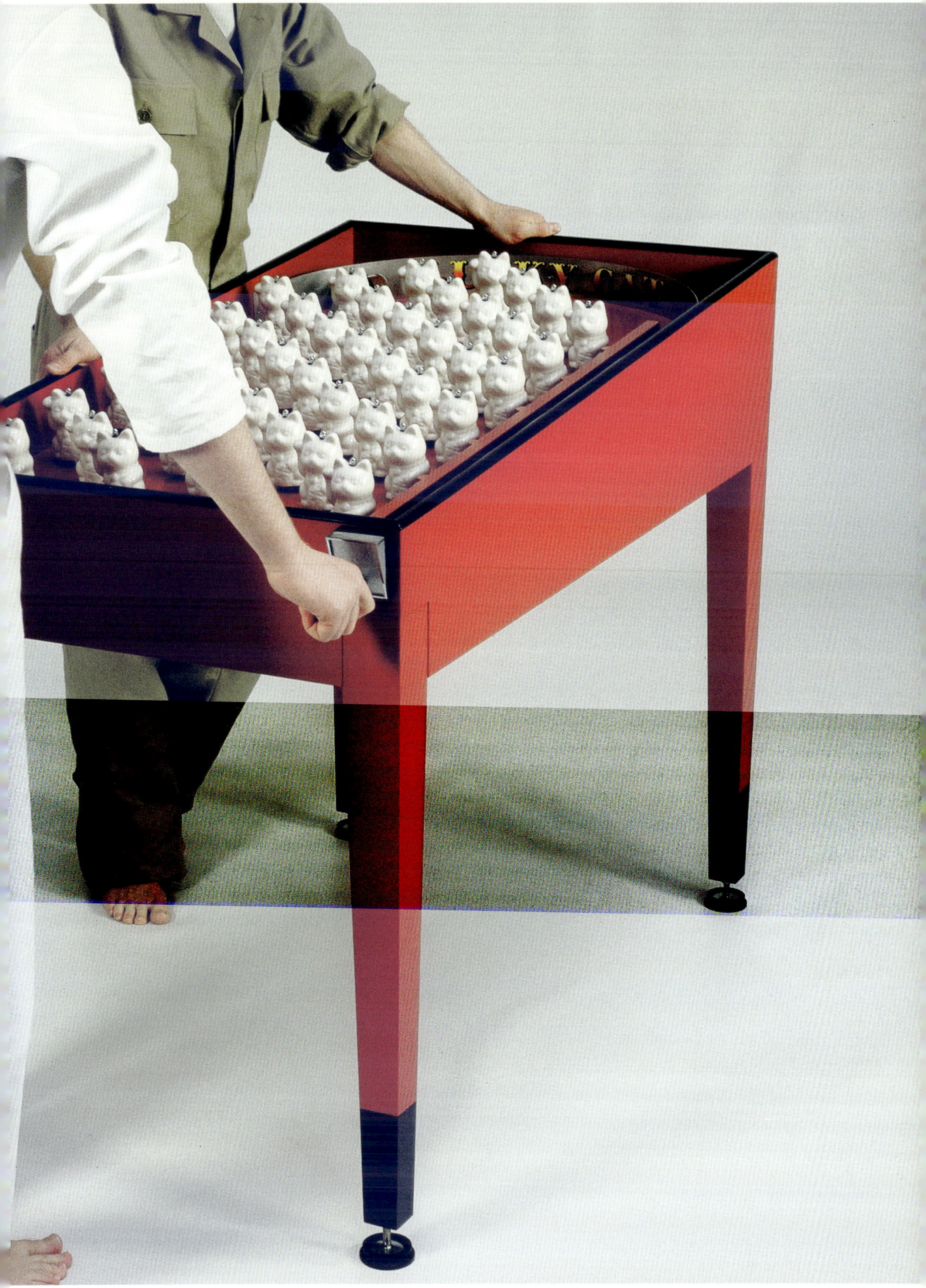

coll.nr. 001 00
Set up shades
lamp
Marcel Wanders, 1988
lampshades
ø 15 x 55 cm

In this design Marcel Wanders takes a number of basic lampshades. By stacking them they become the structure of the lamp and perform the role they were designed to fulfil, as a shade.

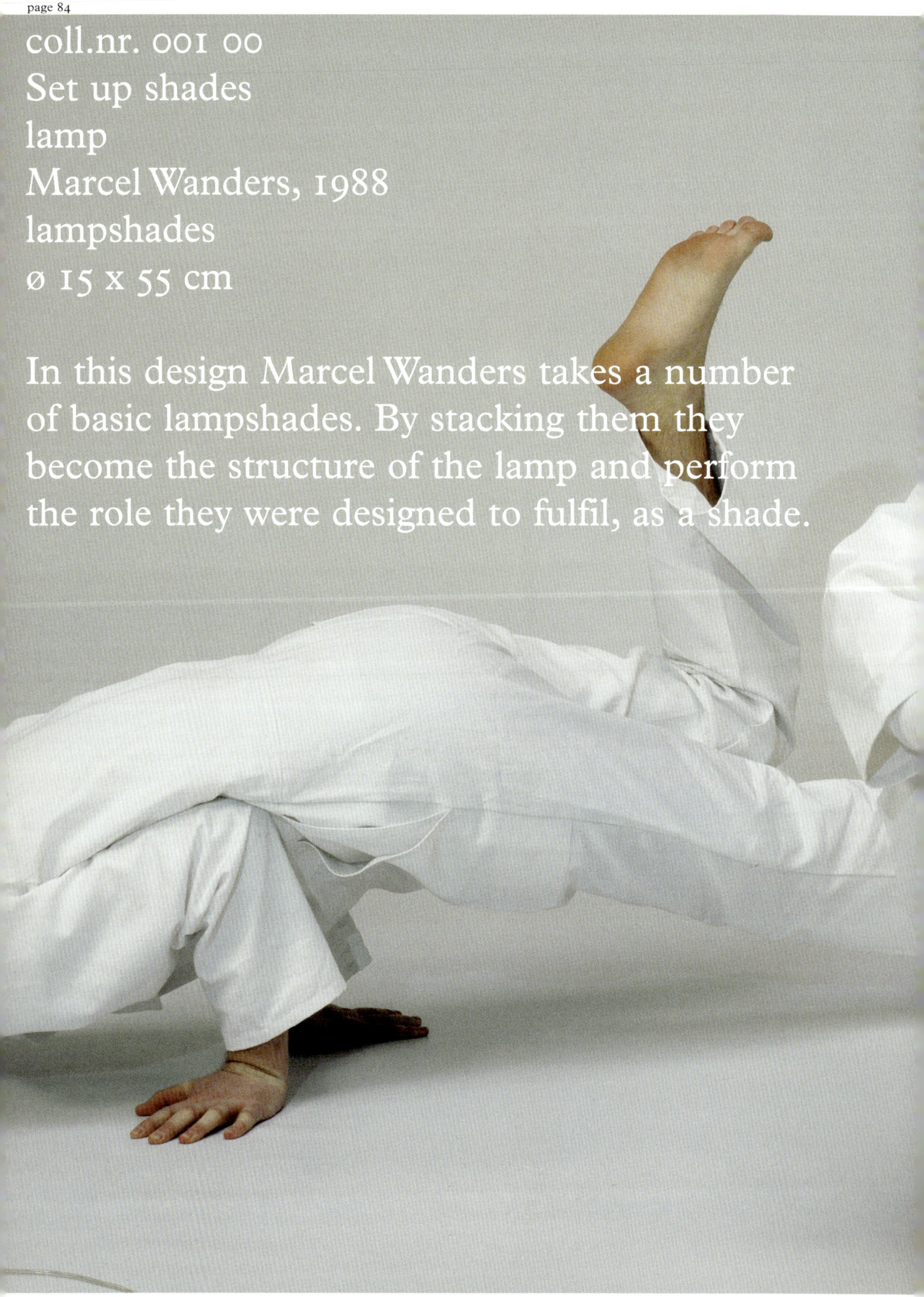

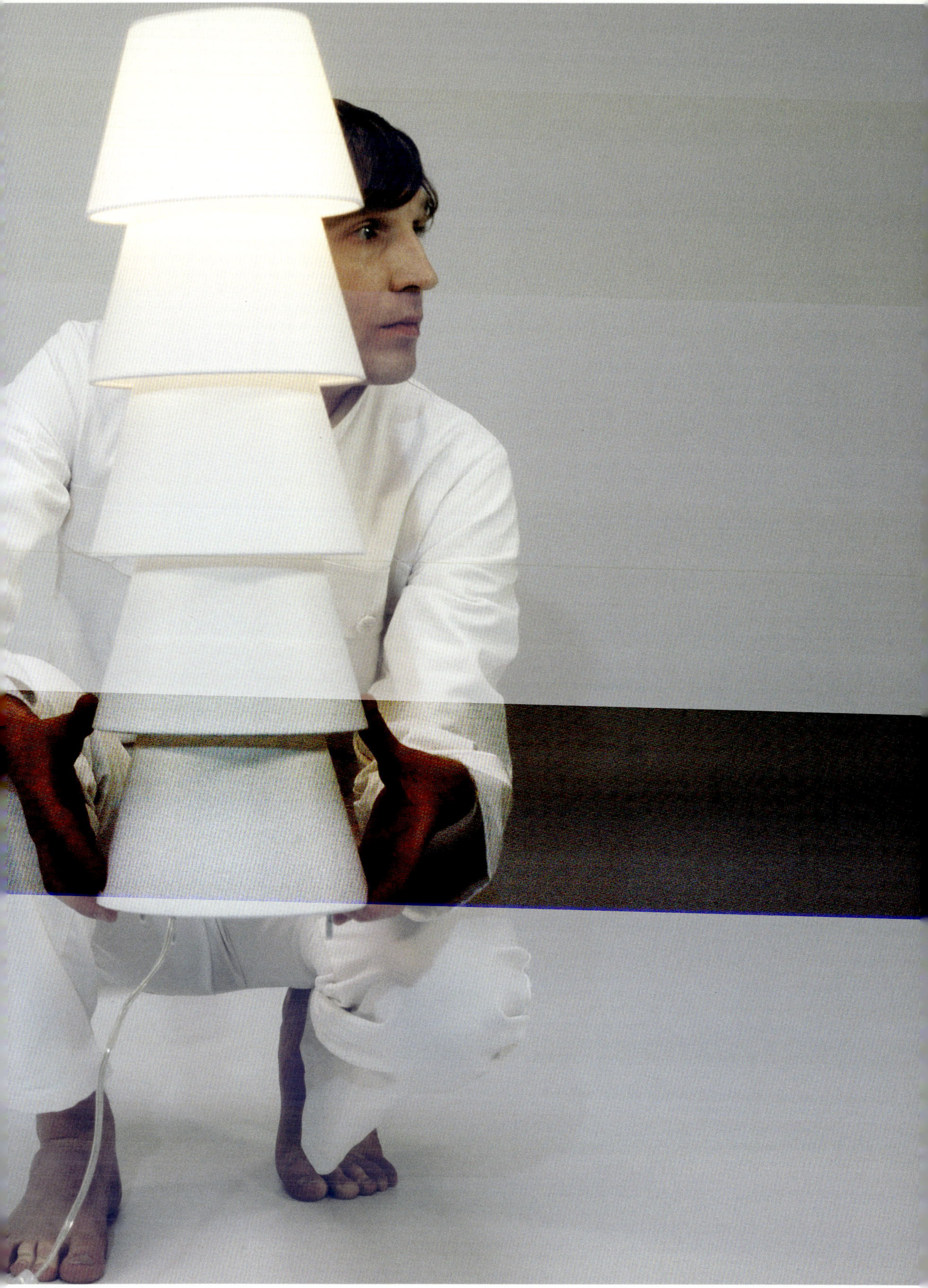

coll.nr. 074 00
Tree-trunk bench
Jurgen Bey, 1999
3 bronze casts of chair backs
various sizes

A fallen tree can serve as a seat. The addition of bronze classical chair backs makes it a proper piece of furniture, a crossing between nature and culture. Jurgen Bey makes clear that it is ridiculous to transport trees when they are locally available. Therefore only the chair backs are for sale.

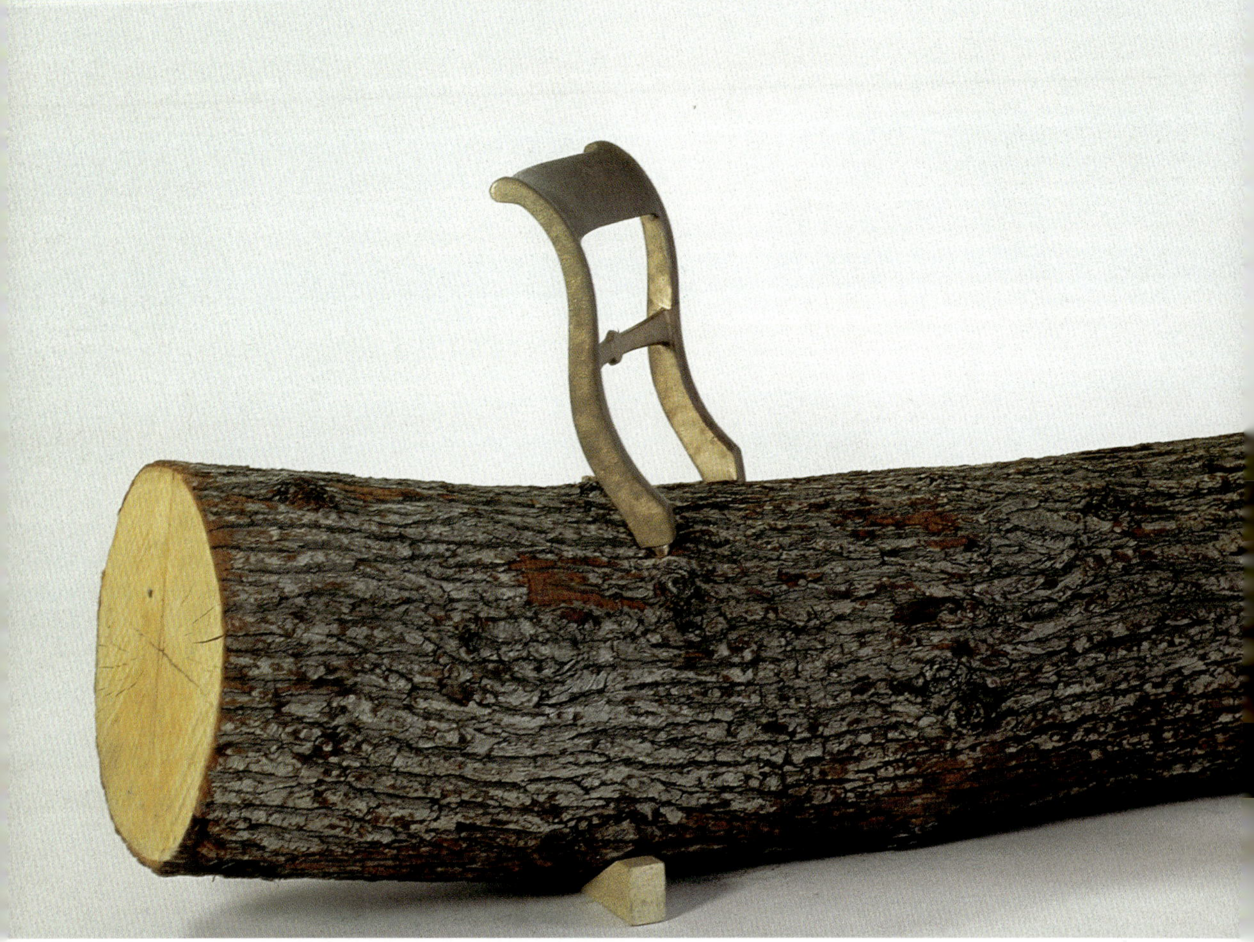

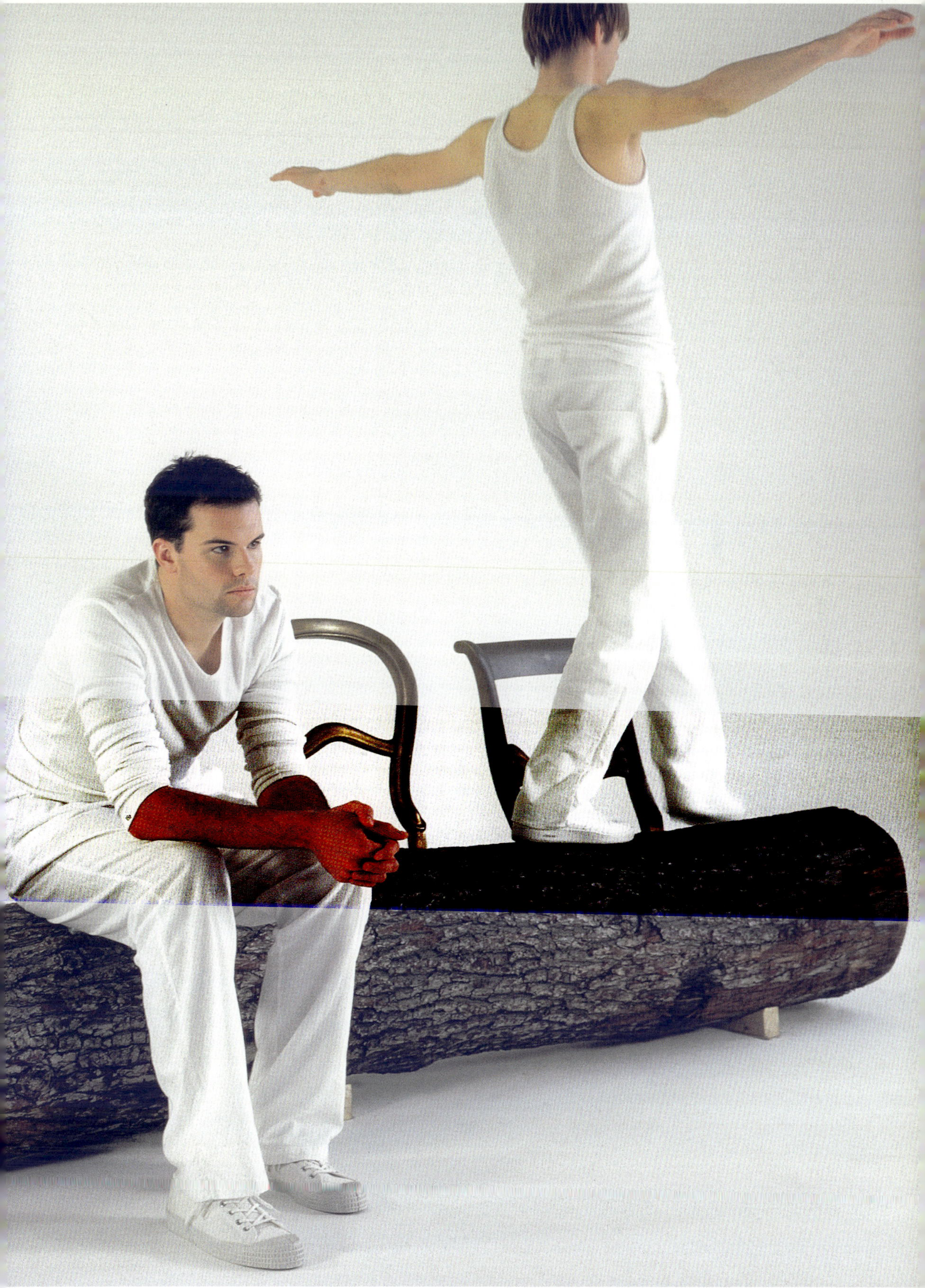

coll.nr. 137 01
Hare
doormat
Ed Annink, 2002
coir, PVC
191 x 94 cm

coll.nr. 137 02
Hippo
doormat
Ed Annink, 2002
coir, PVC
145 x 69 cm

Ed Annink has made use of the fact that Gerd Arntz's statistic pictograms are free of copyright and put them into a different context.

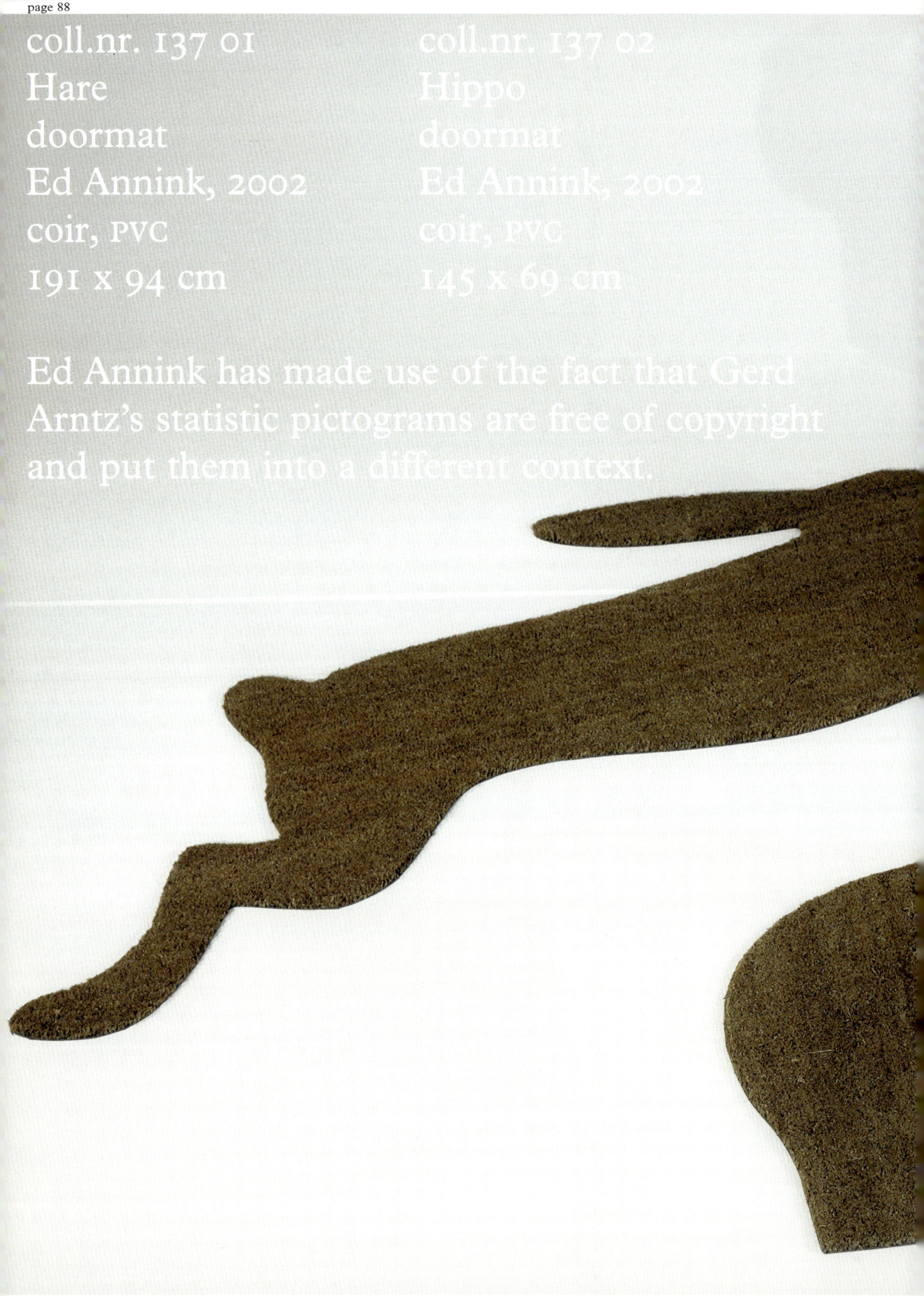

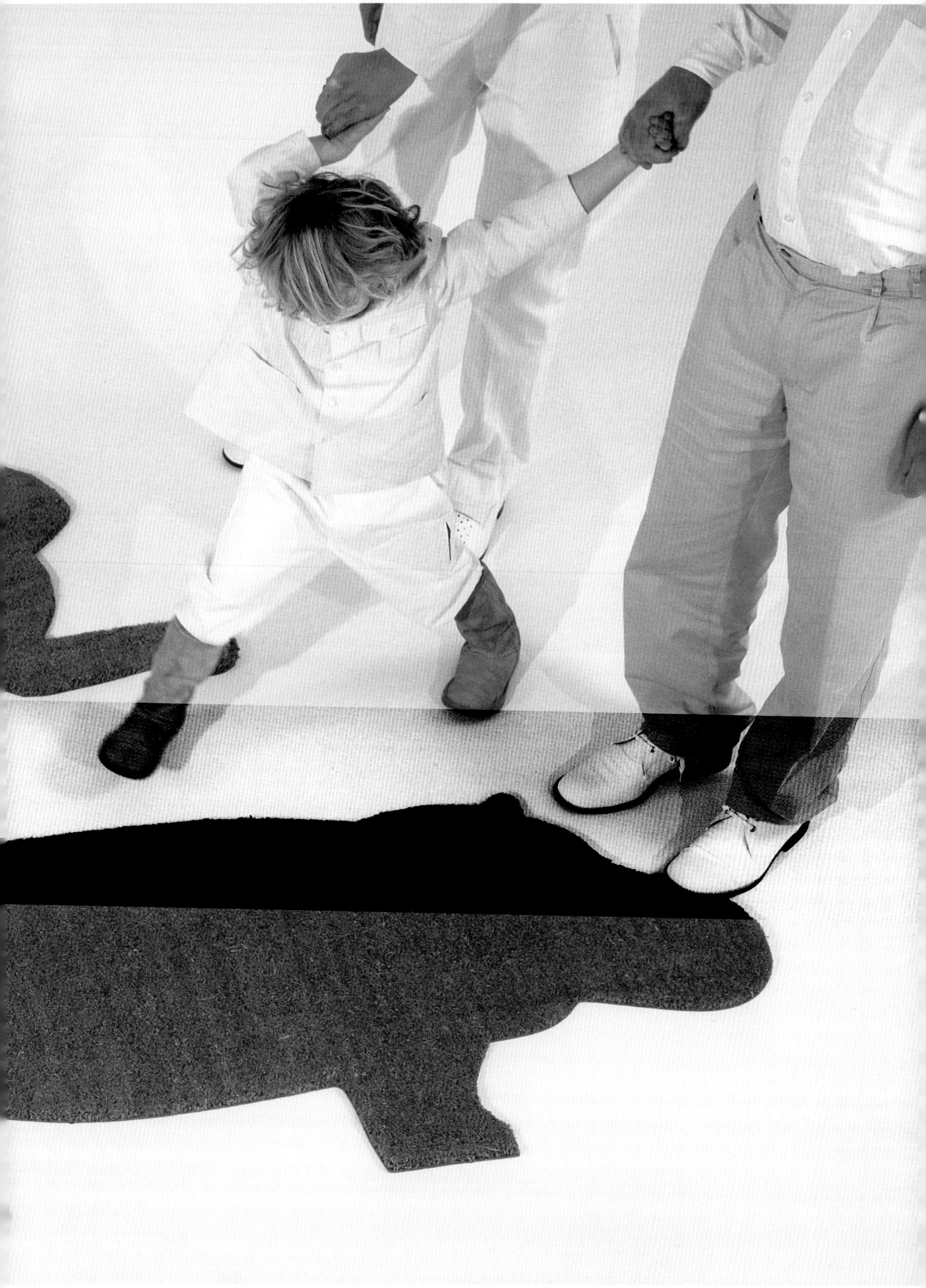

coll.nr. 130 00
Sticky lamp
Chris Kabel, 2002
[illegible] 15w bulb
[illegible] 25 x 7 cm

This design brings a new functionality to packaging. The plastic which would normally be discarded has become the casing. The self-adhesive fixing offers endless possibilities. You can stick it wherever you want, on the ceiling, the door, wall or floor.

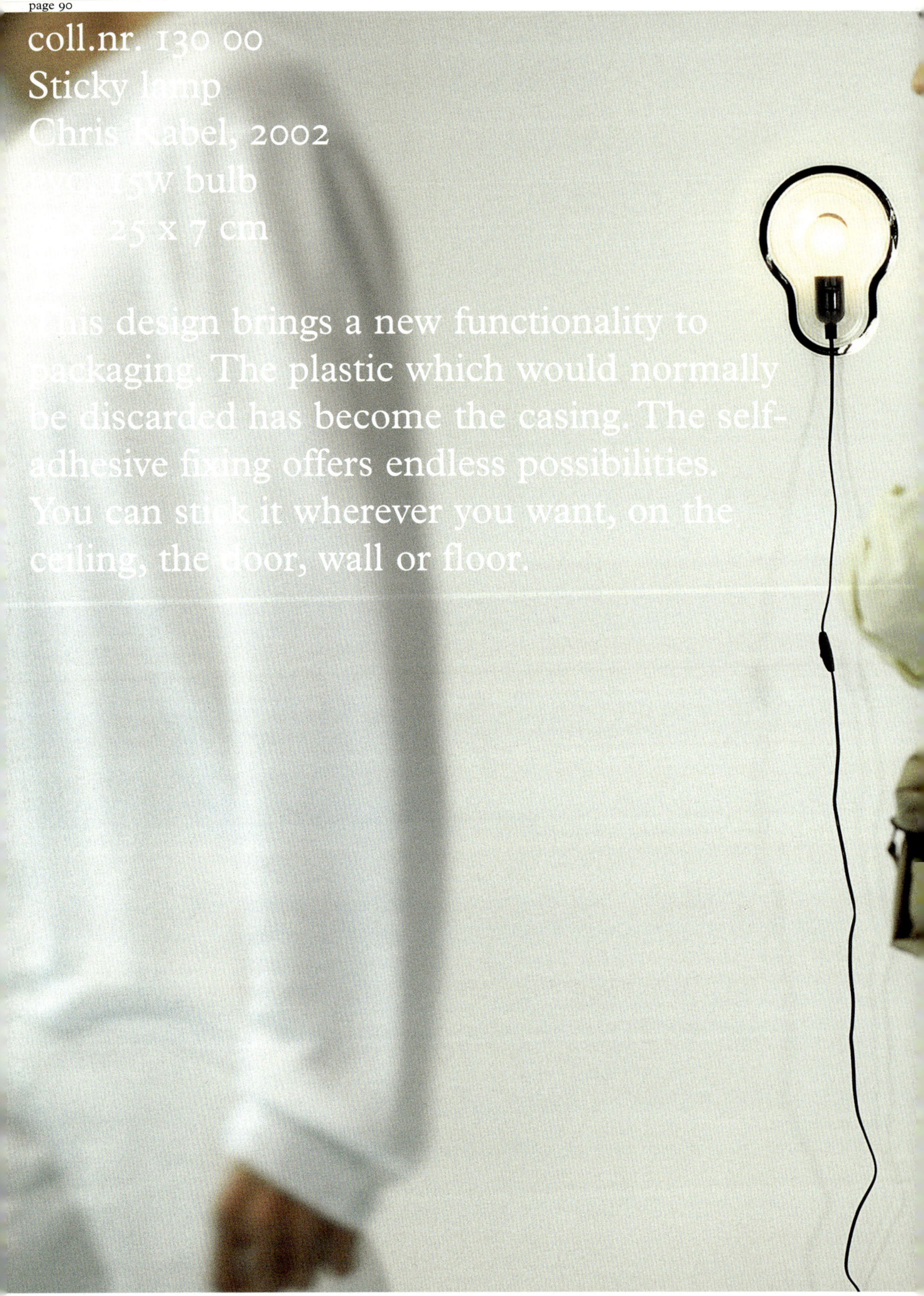

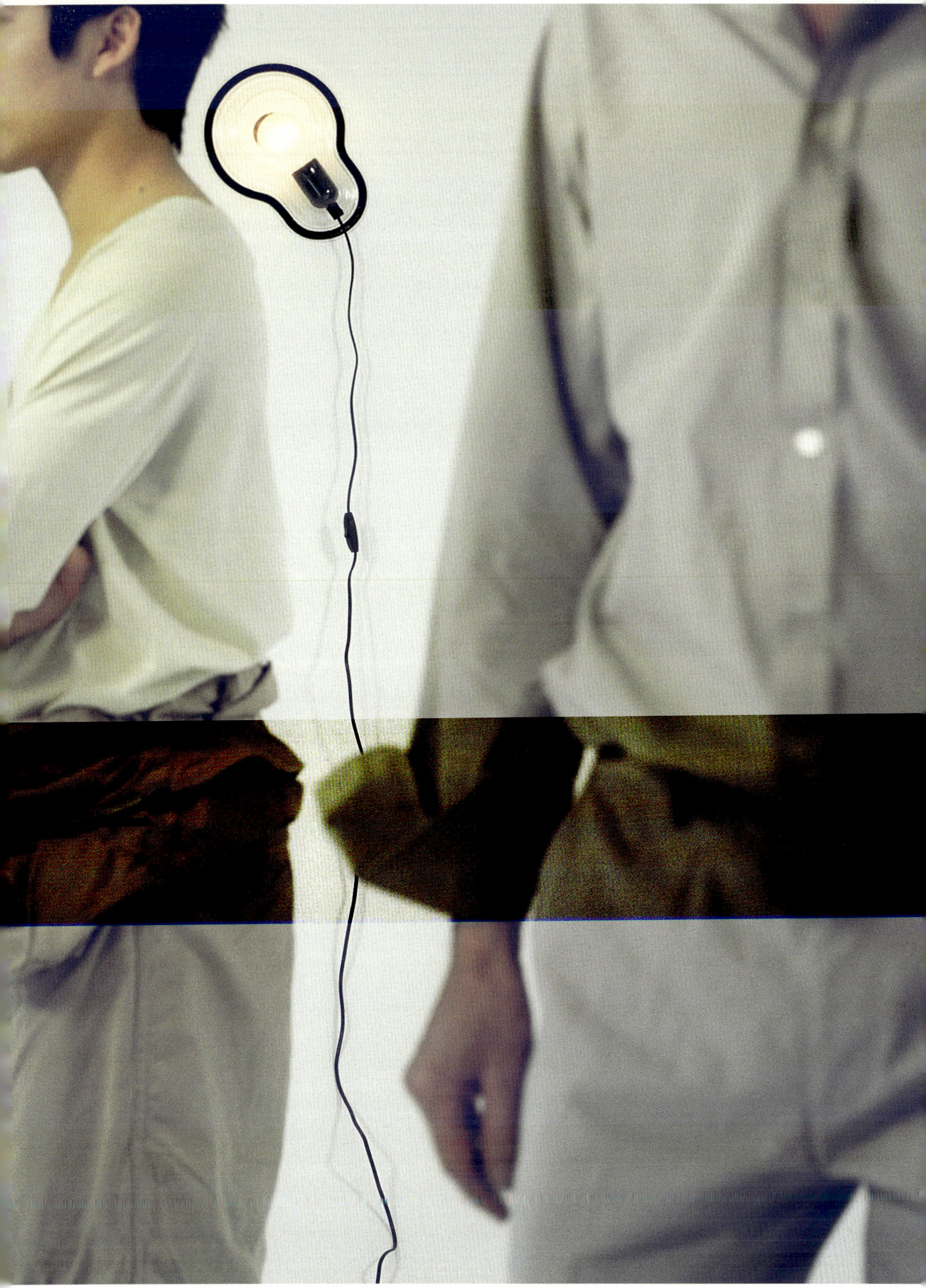

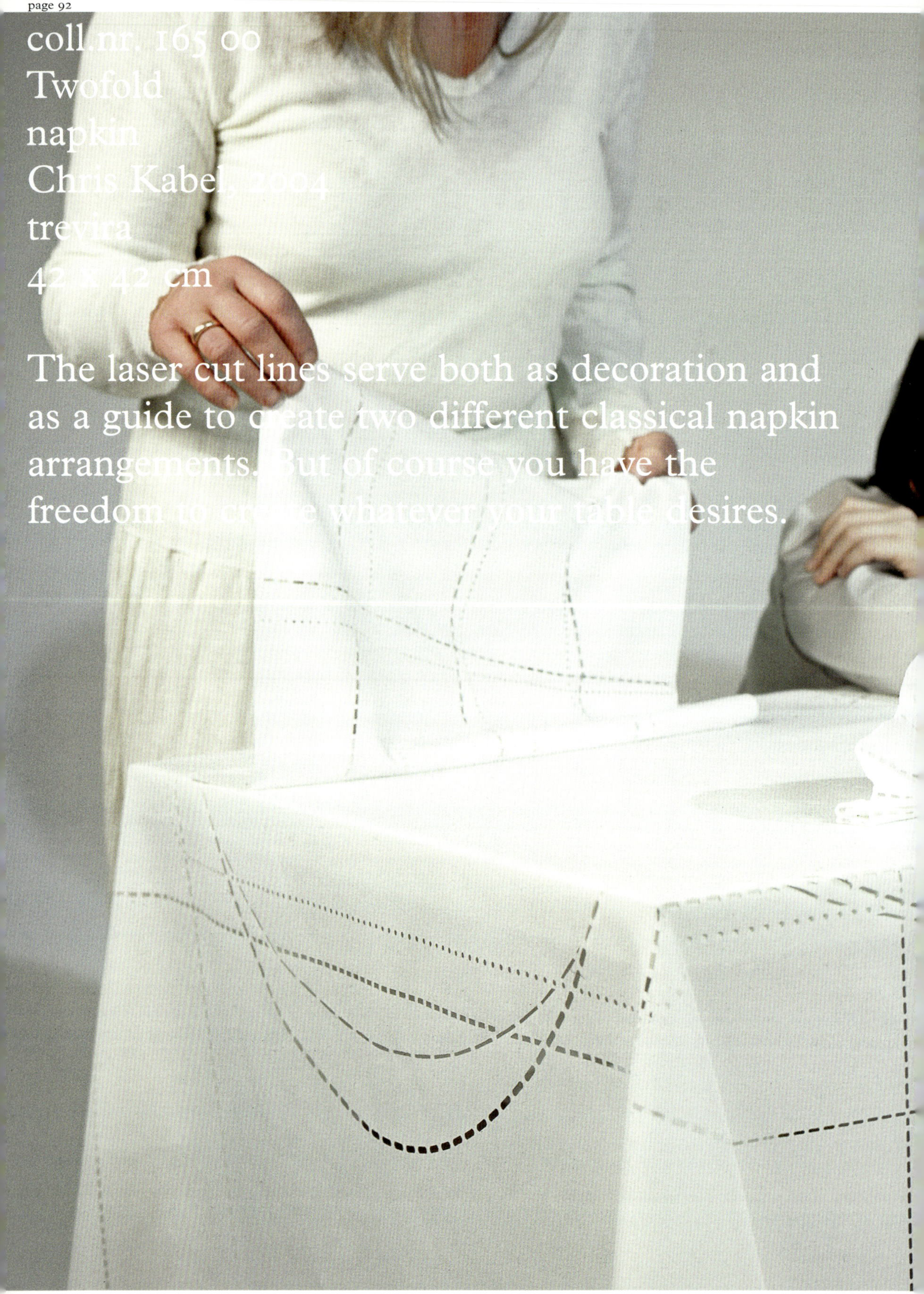

coll.nr. 165 00
Twofold
napkin
Chris Kabel, 2004
trevira
42 x 42 cm

The laser cut lines serve both as decoration and as a guide to create two different classical napkin arrangements. But of course you have the freedom to create whatever your table desires.

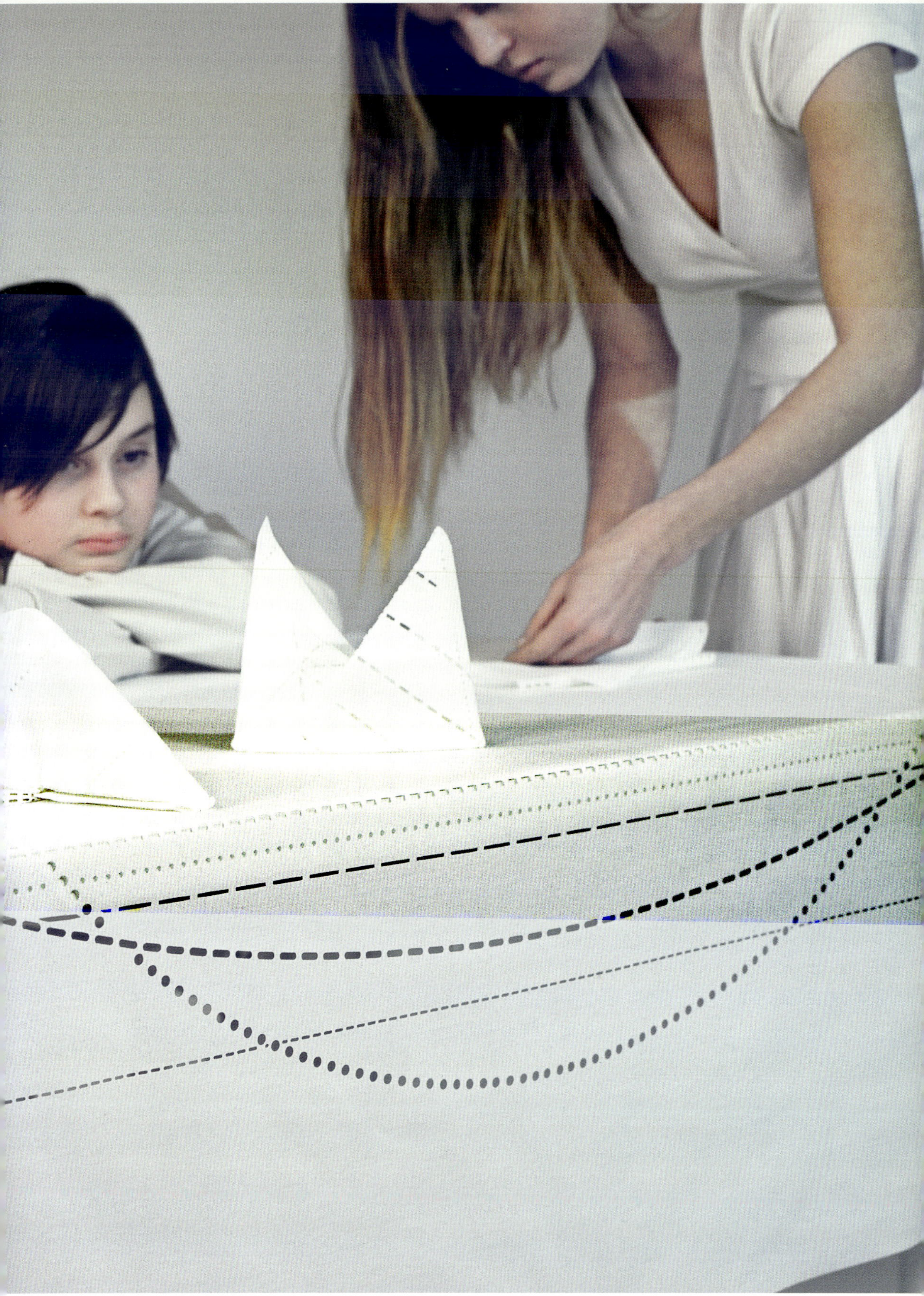

coll.nr. 033 00
Stool
Richard Hutten, 1994
beech, soft foam, PVC coating
50 x 50 x 40 cm

This stool requires interaction to discover its hidden properties. It only becomes apparent that the seat is soft when a certain pressure is applied. This quality means that it can double as a side-table.

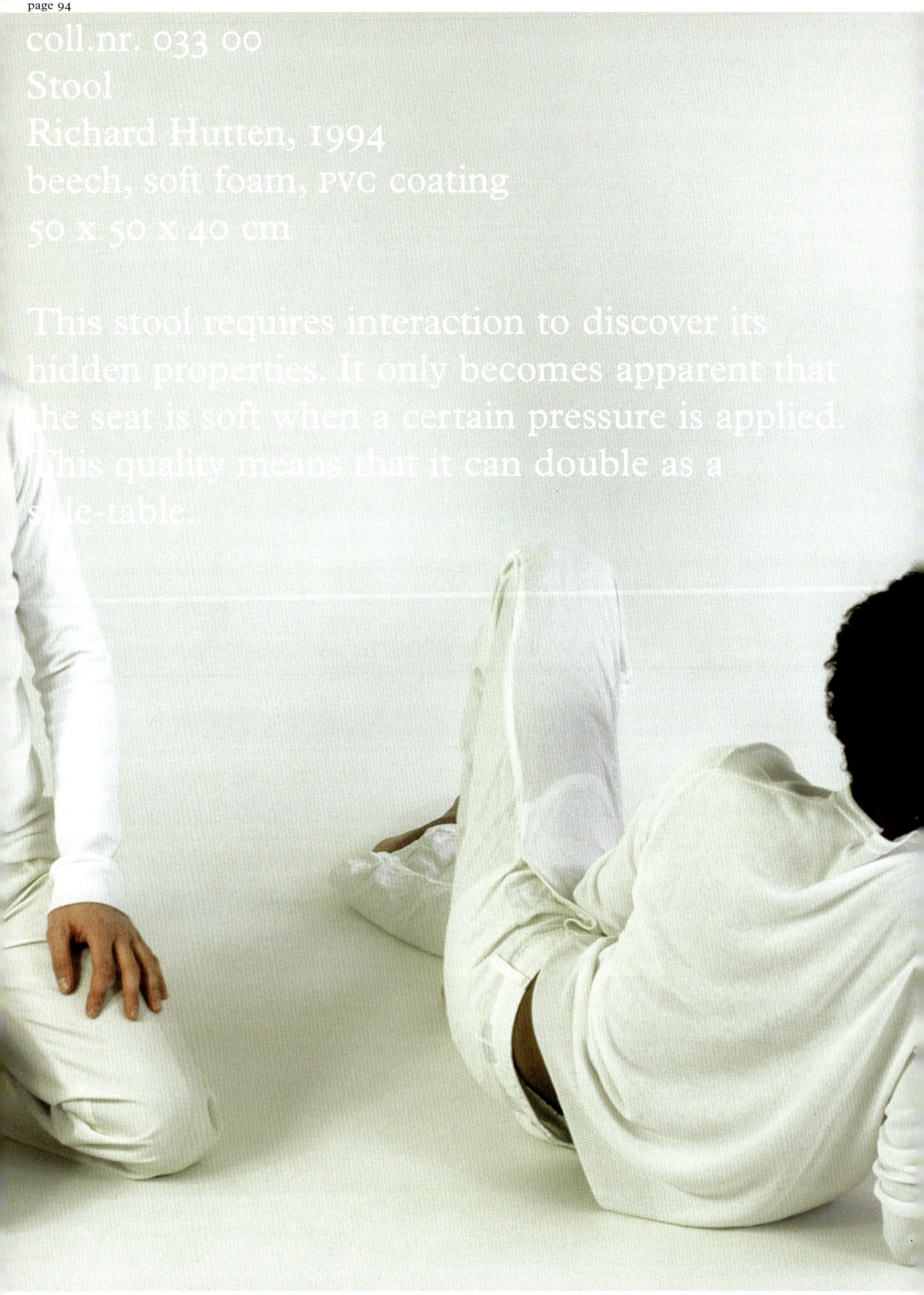

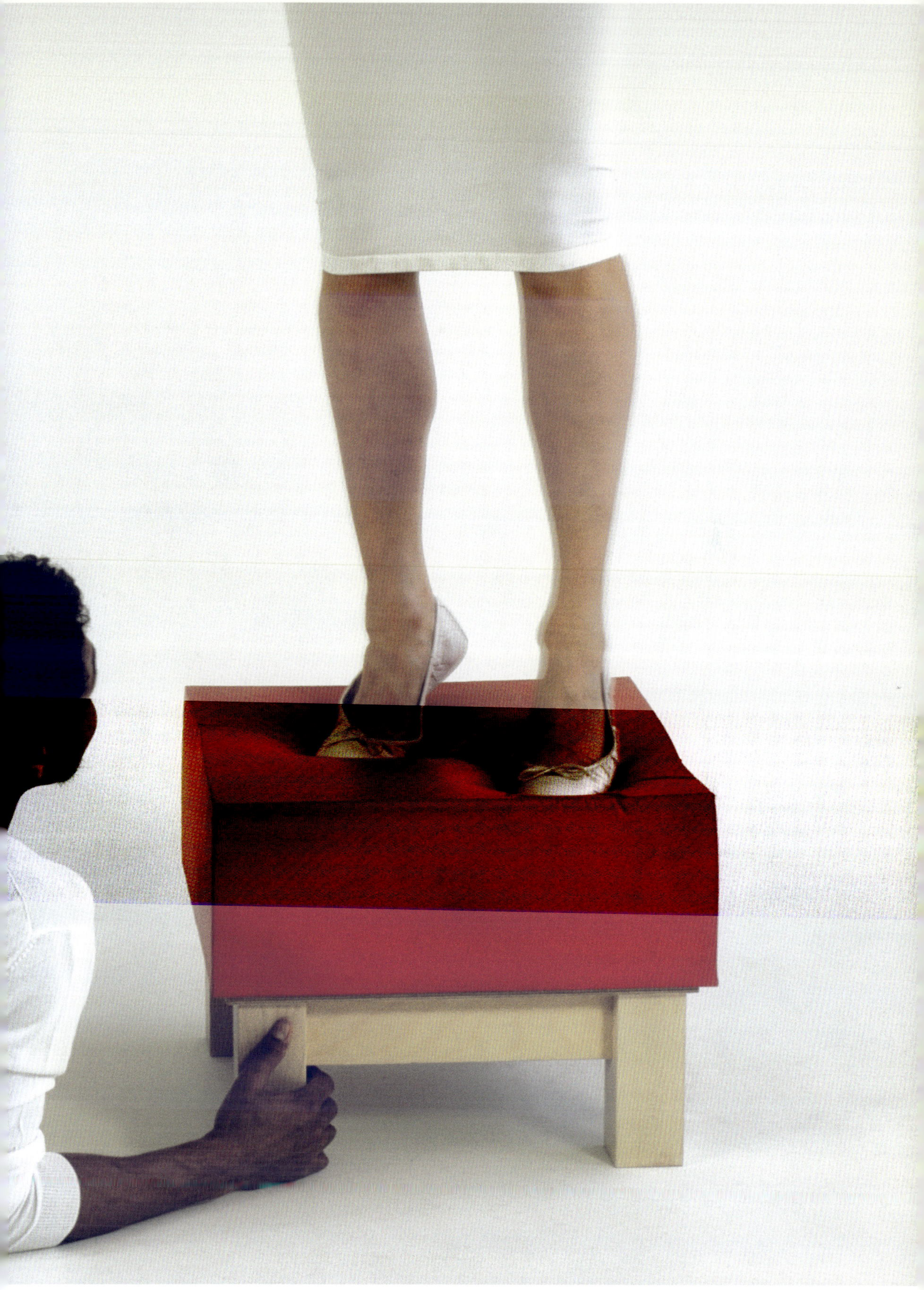

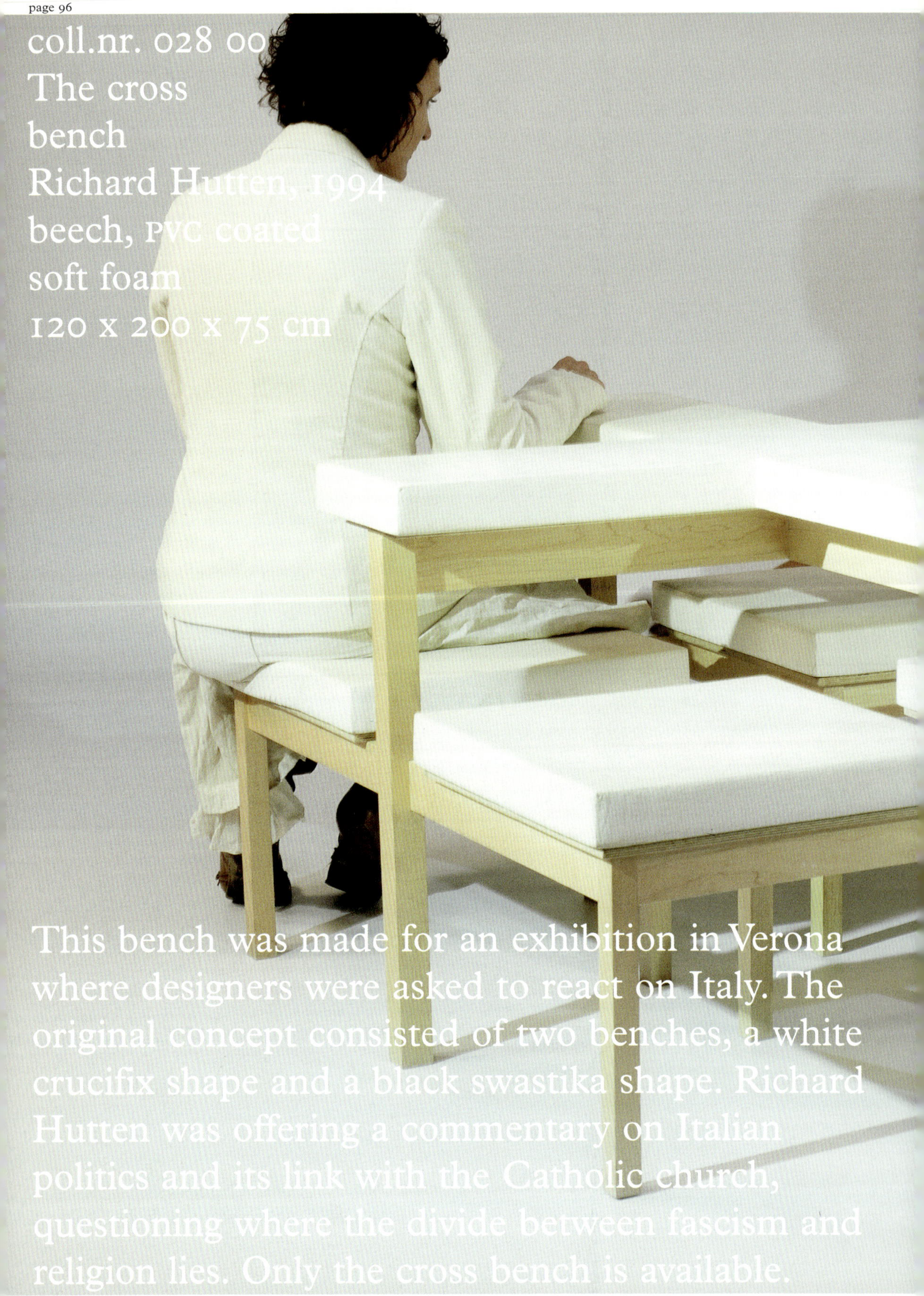

coll.nr. 028 00
The cross
bench
Richard Hutten, 1994
beech, PVC coated
soft foam
120 x 200 x 75 cm

This bench was made for an exhibition in Verona where designers were asked to react on Italy. The original concept consisted of two benches, a white crucifix shape and a black swastika shape. Richard Hutten was offering a commentary on Italian politics and its link with the Catholic church, questioning where the divide between fascism and religion lies. Only the cross bench is available.

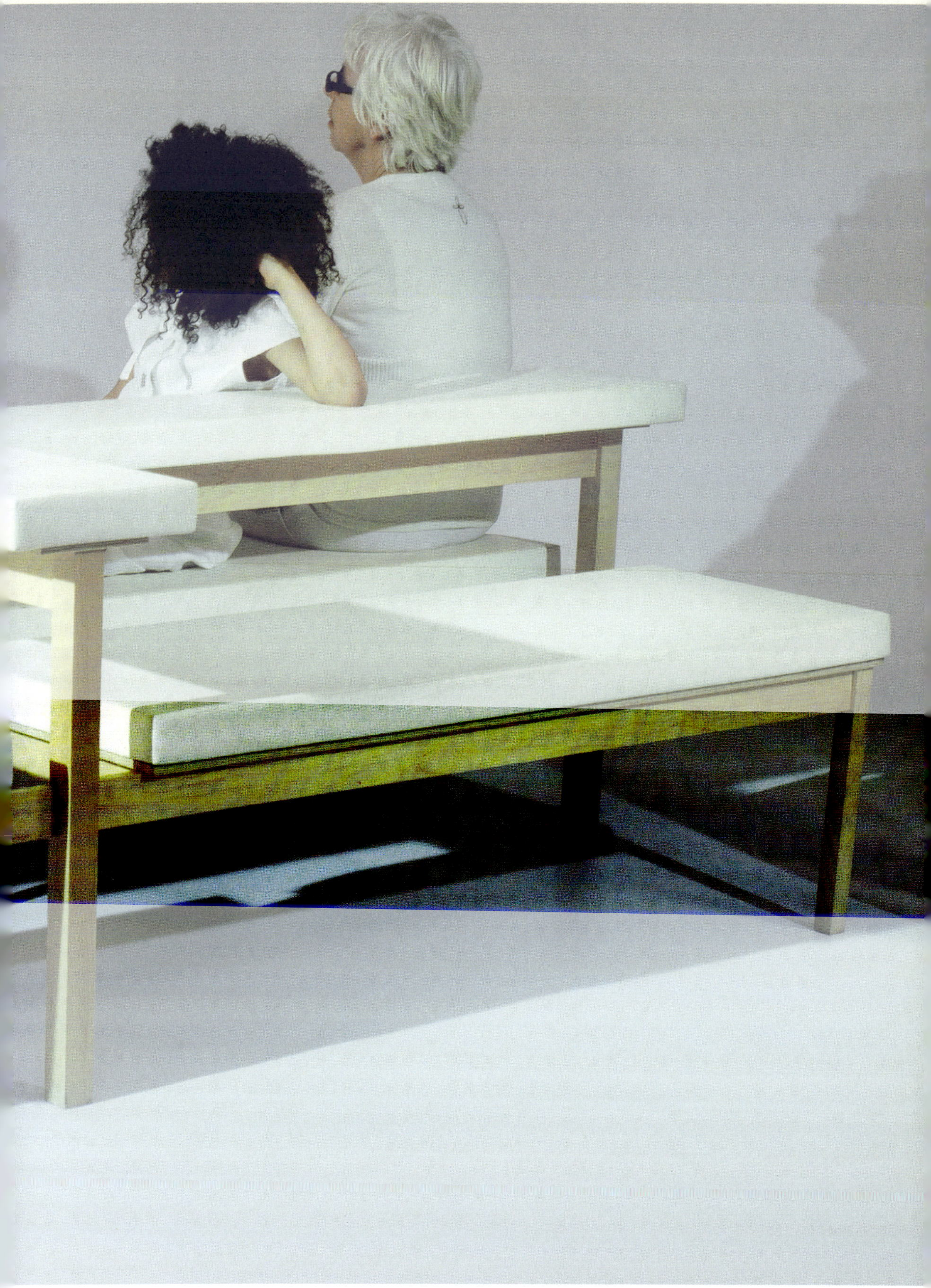

coll.nr. 089 00
Do frame
tape
Martí Guixé, 2000
self adhesive vinyl tape
5 cm, 25 m roll

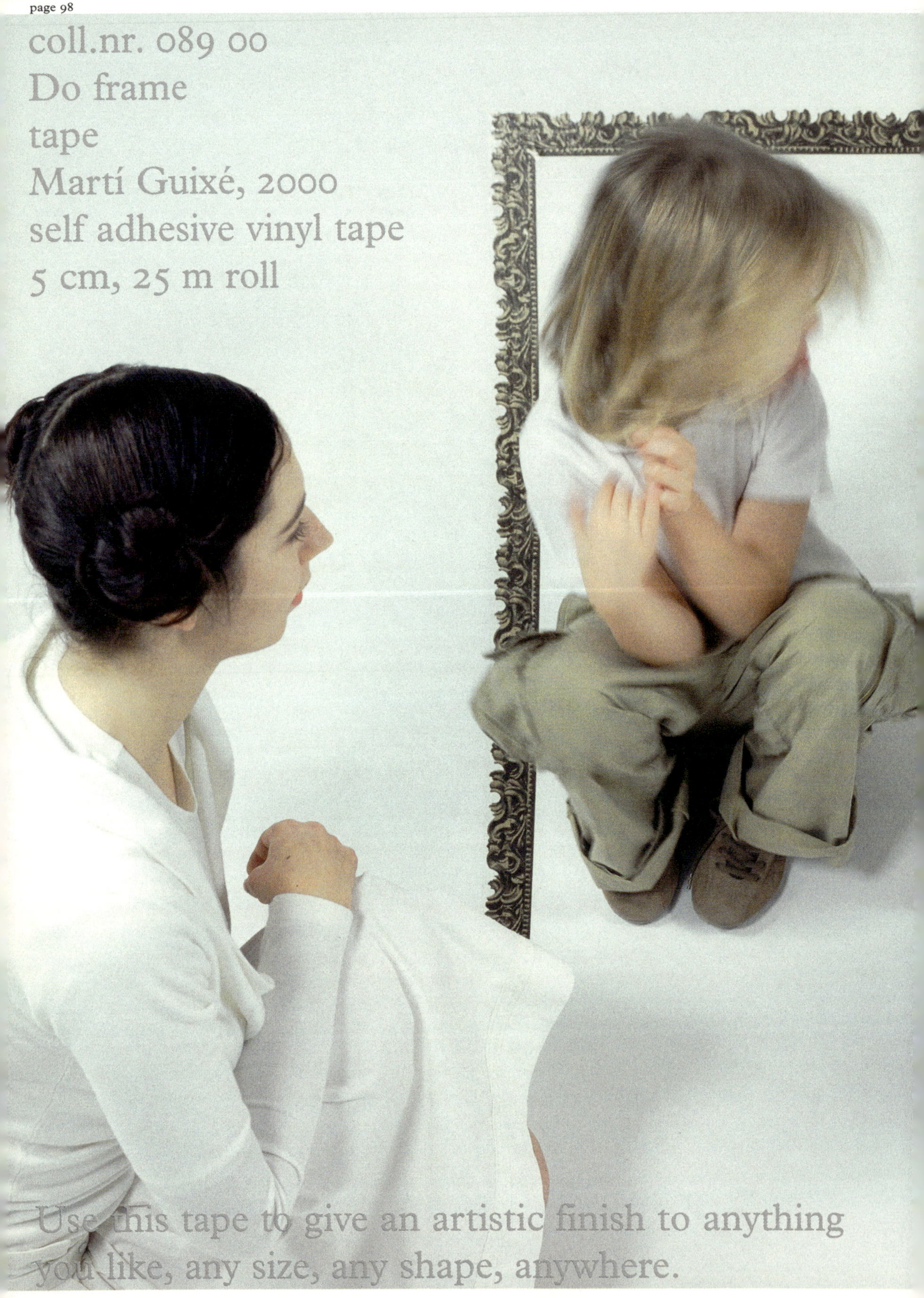

Use this tape to give an artistic finish to anything you like, any size, any shape, anywhere.

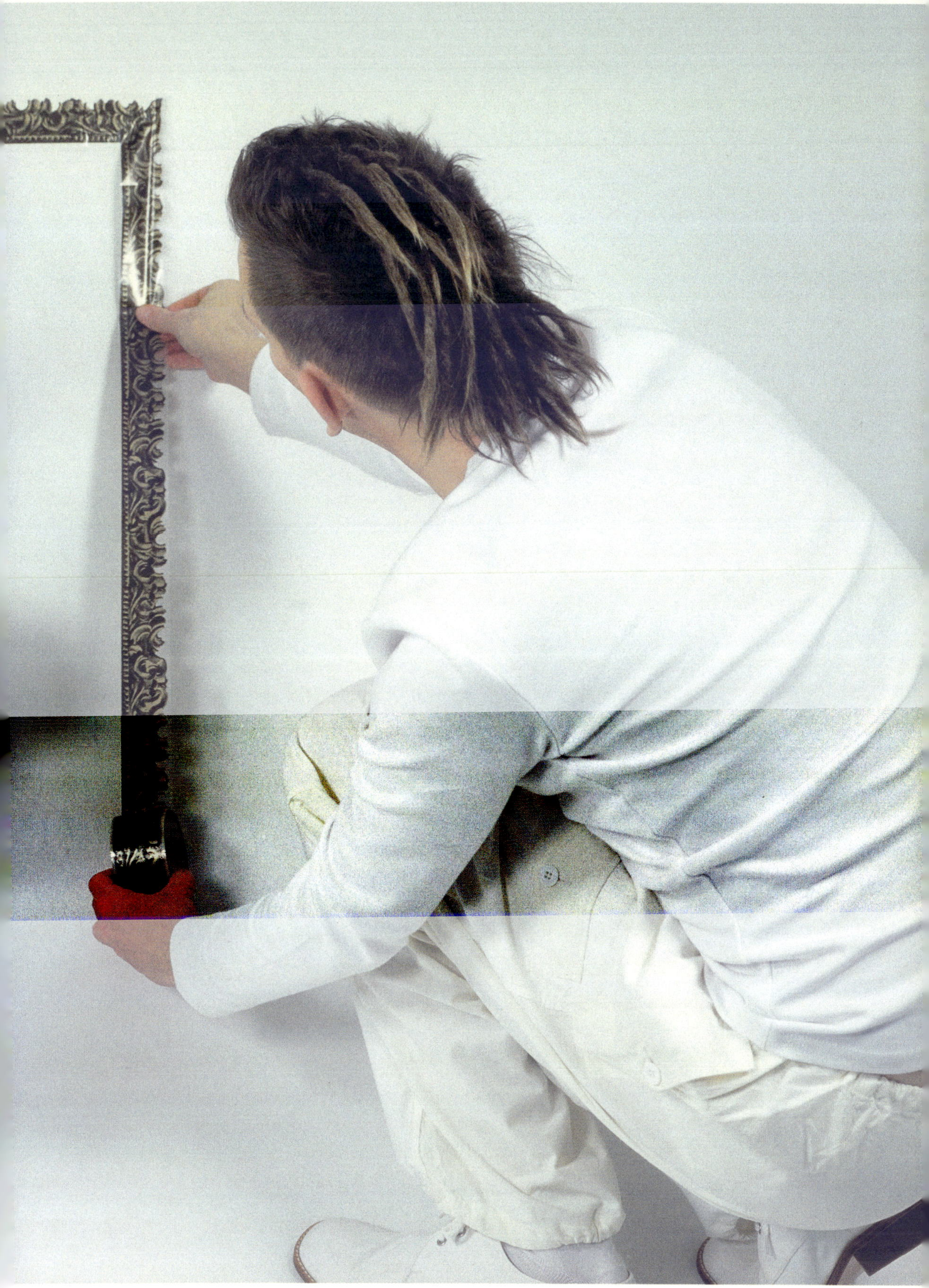

coll.nr. 191 00
Red blue lego chair
Mario Minale, 2004
lego bricks
60 x 60 x 90 cm
limited edition of 5

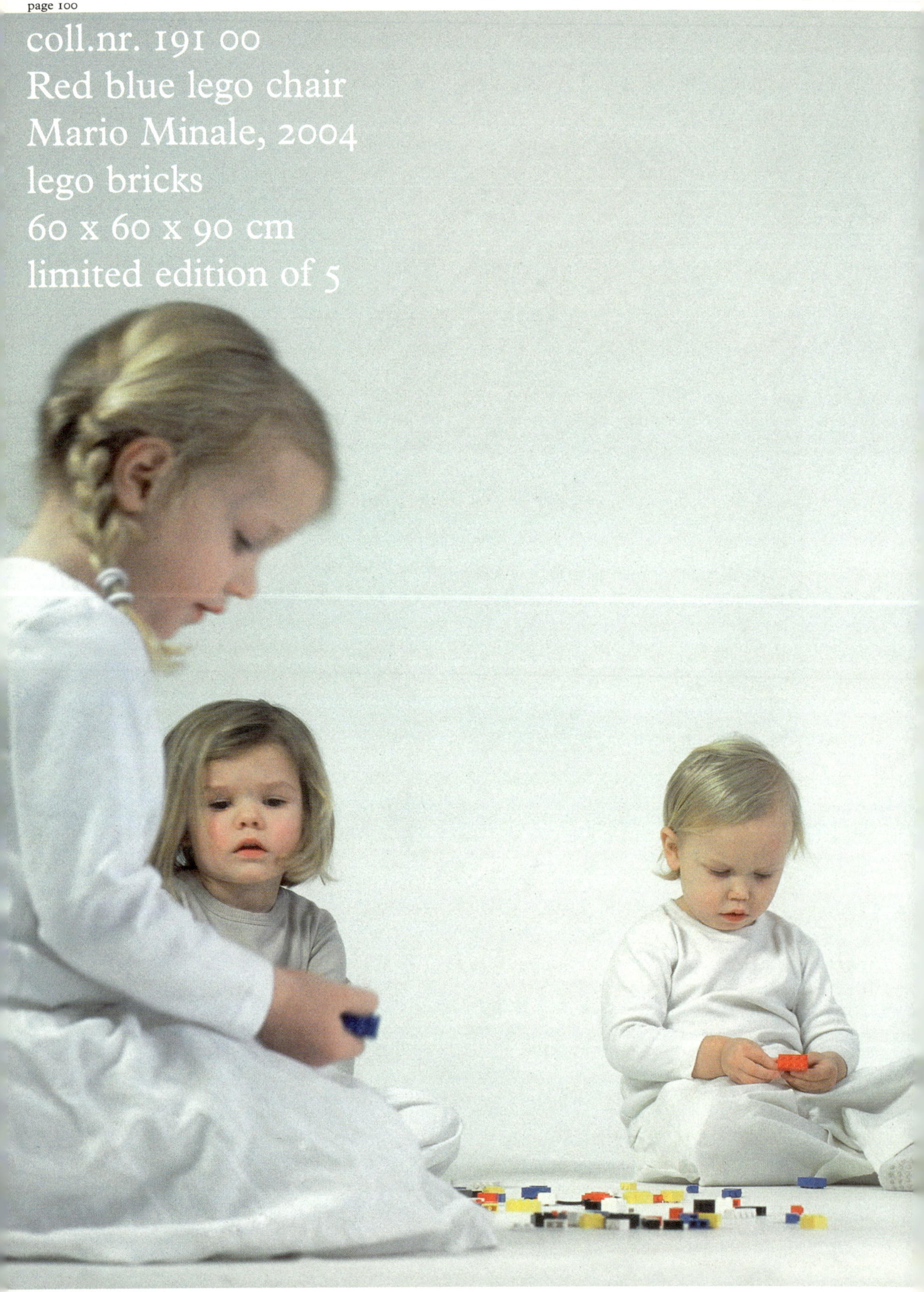

This design aims to make the iconic Red-blue chair by Gerrit Rietveld commercially accessible by building it from lego. It is 6% larger than the original due the size of the bricks. Unfortunately, because of copyright this chair is only available in a small edition as an art project but provides an interesting thought of how we can create classic products by our own means.

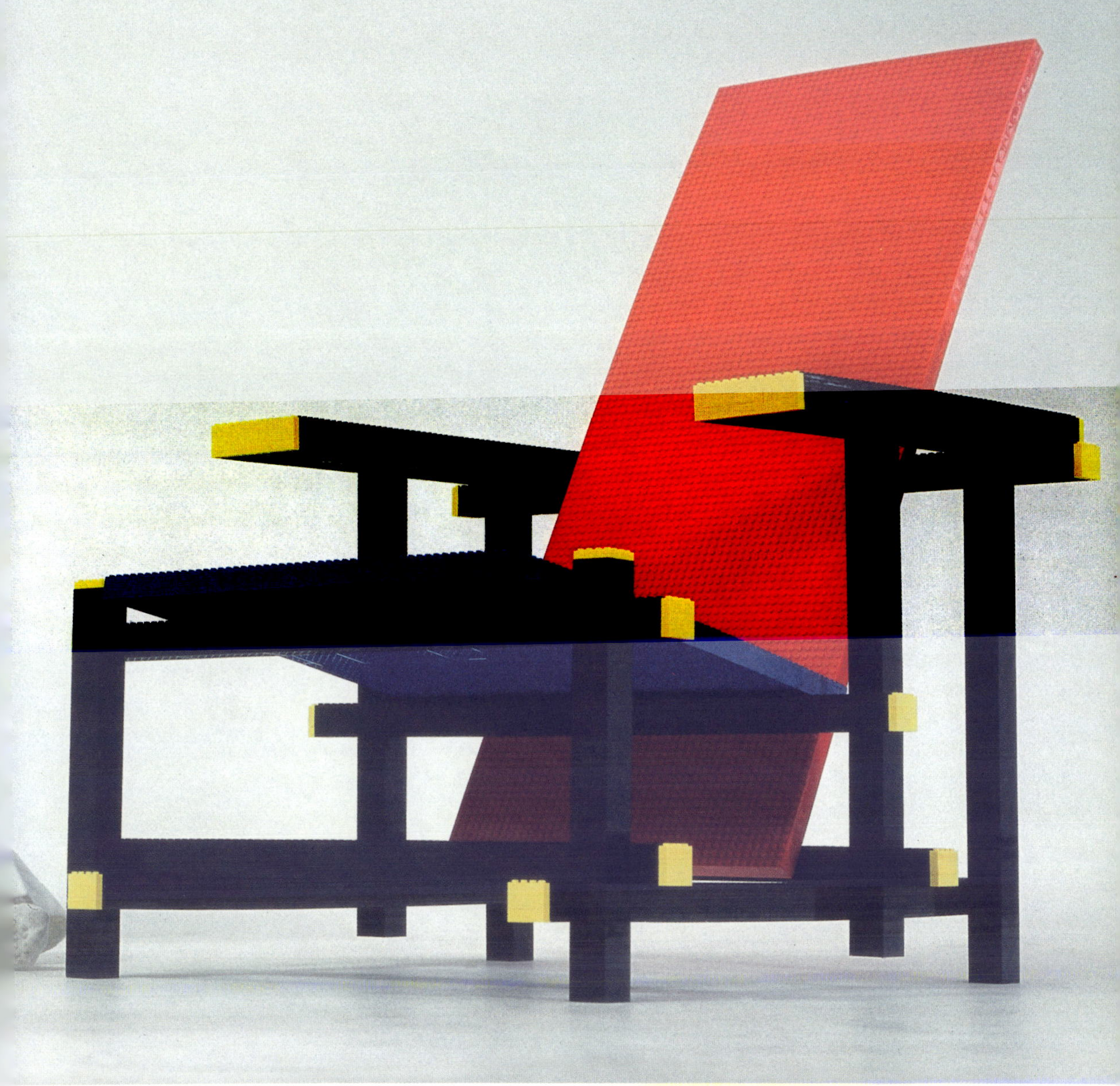

coll.nr. 135 00
Bowls plus
Michelle Huang, 2002
melamine, various colours
set of 3 different bowls

The shape of these bowls originate from Chinese rituals. In Chinese culture it is polite not to eat all the food that the host is offering, as if to say, “You gave me plenty”. Michelle Huang noticed that the younger Chinese generation living outside of China is loosing touch with these traditions. She has now re-invented them for everyone.

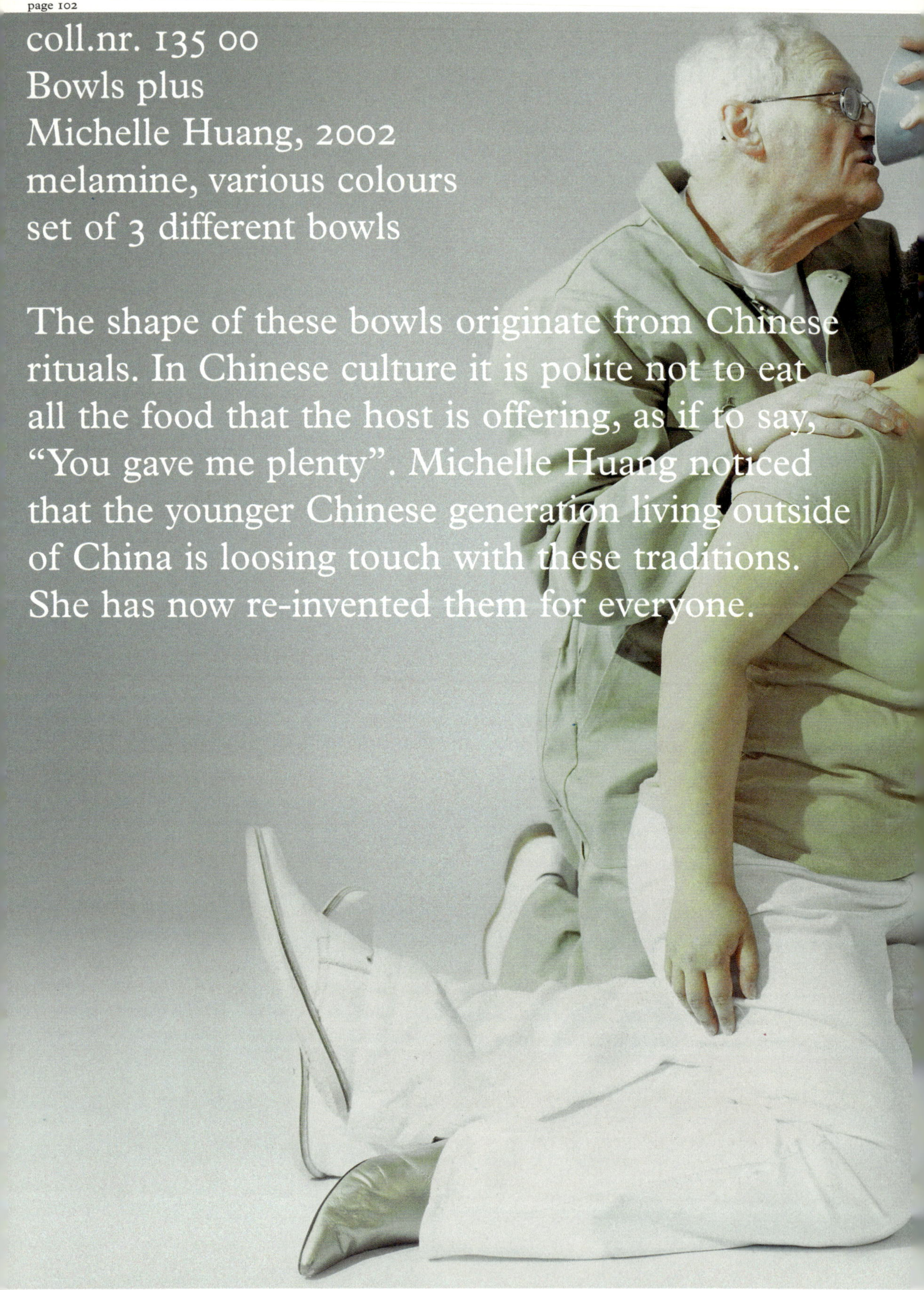

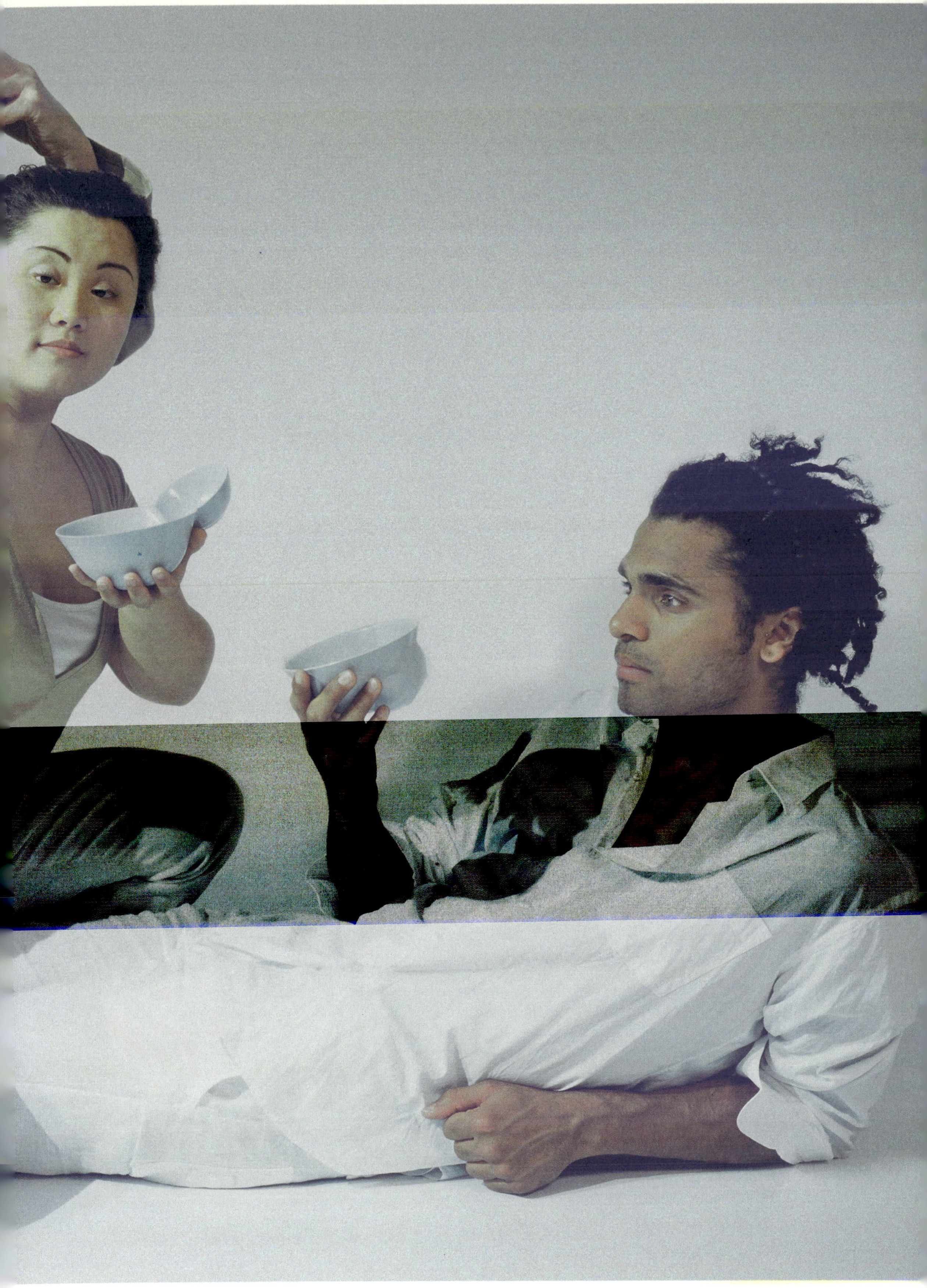

coll.nr. 113 00
Come a little bit closer
bench
Nina Farkache, 2001
stainless steel, glass marbles, painted MDF
3-seater: 56 x 230 x 43 cm
5-seater: 68 x 406 x 43 cm

This bench creates a unique, almost unexplainable kind of atmosphere between people. The seats sliding across the marbles combined with the sound of rolling glass mean it's hard not to have fun and the experience unites you with your neighbour, even when you are not moving at all.

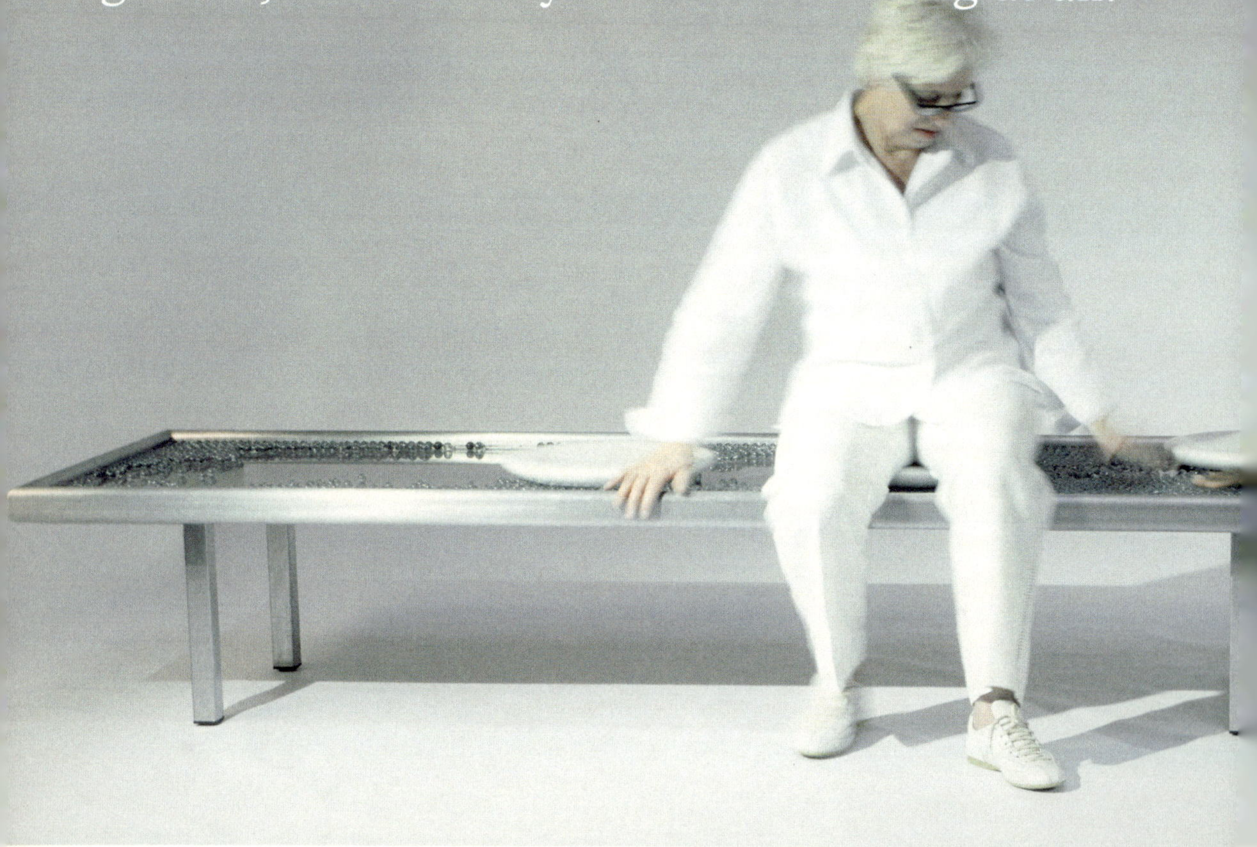

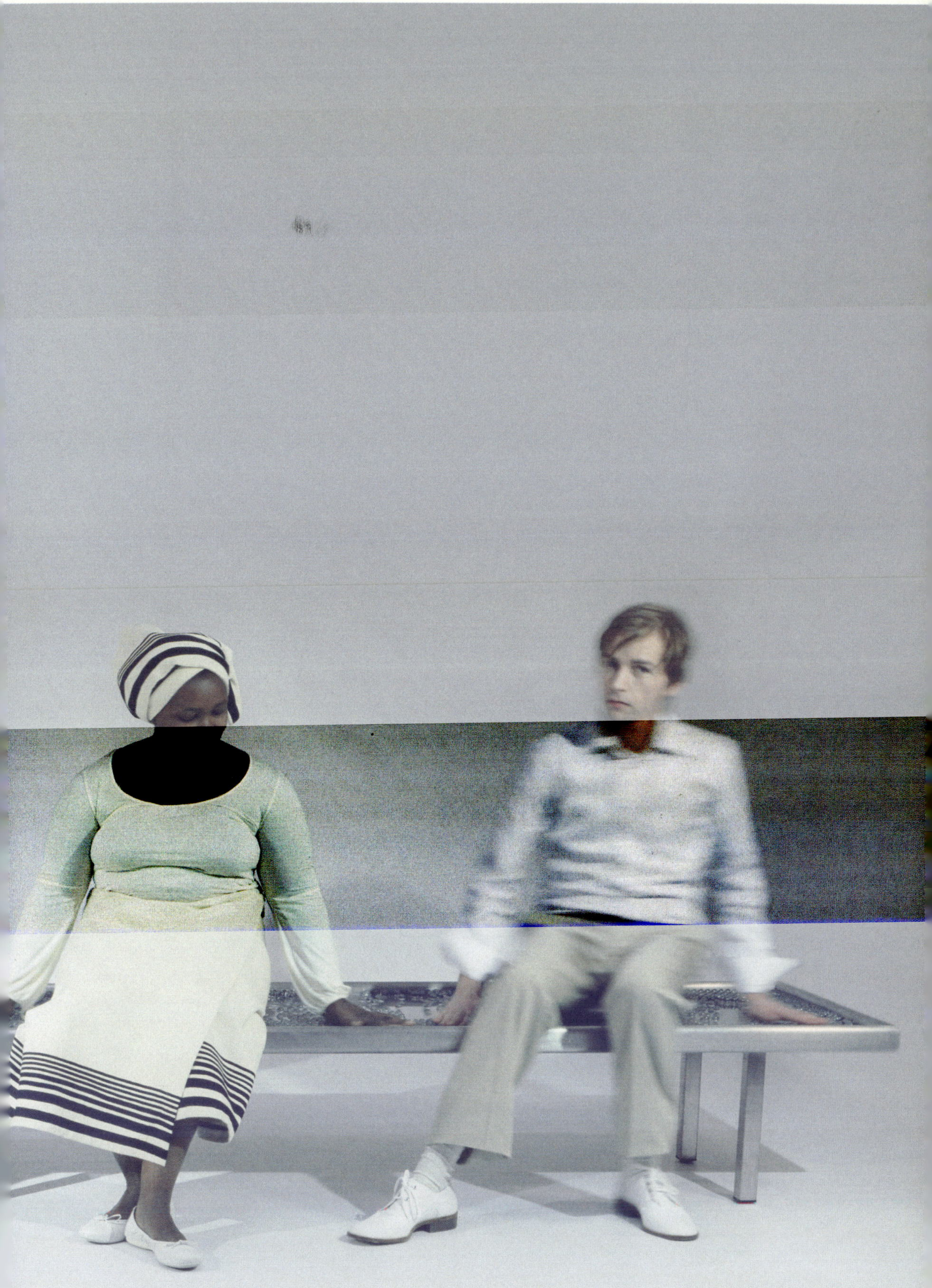

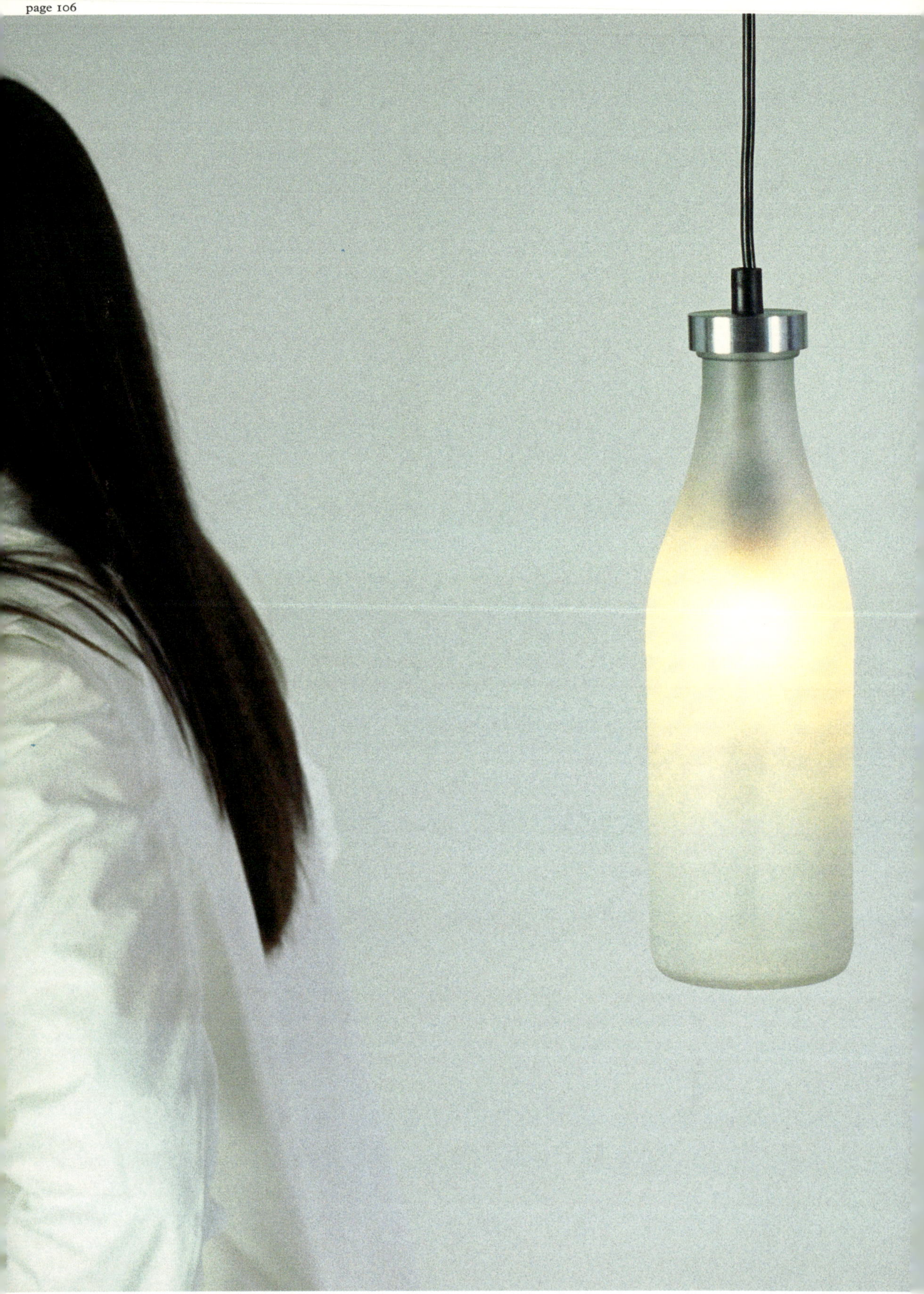

coll.nr. 011 01
Milk bottle lamp (single)
Tejo Remy, 1991
milk bottle, 15W bulb
ø 8.5 x 310 cm

This lamp functions in the same way as its counterpart the Milk bottle lamp, except this one hangs independently.

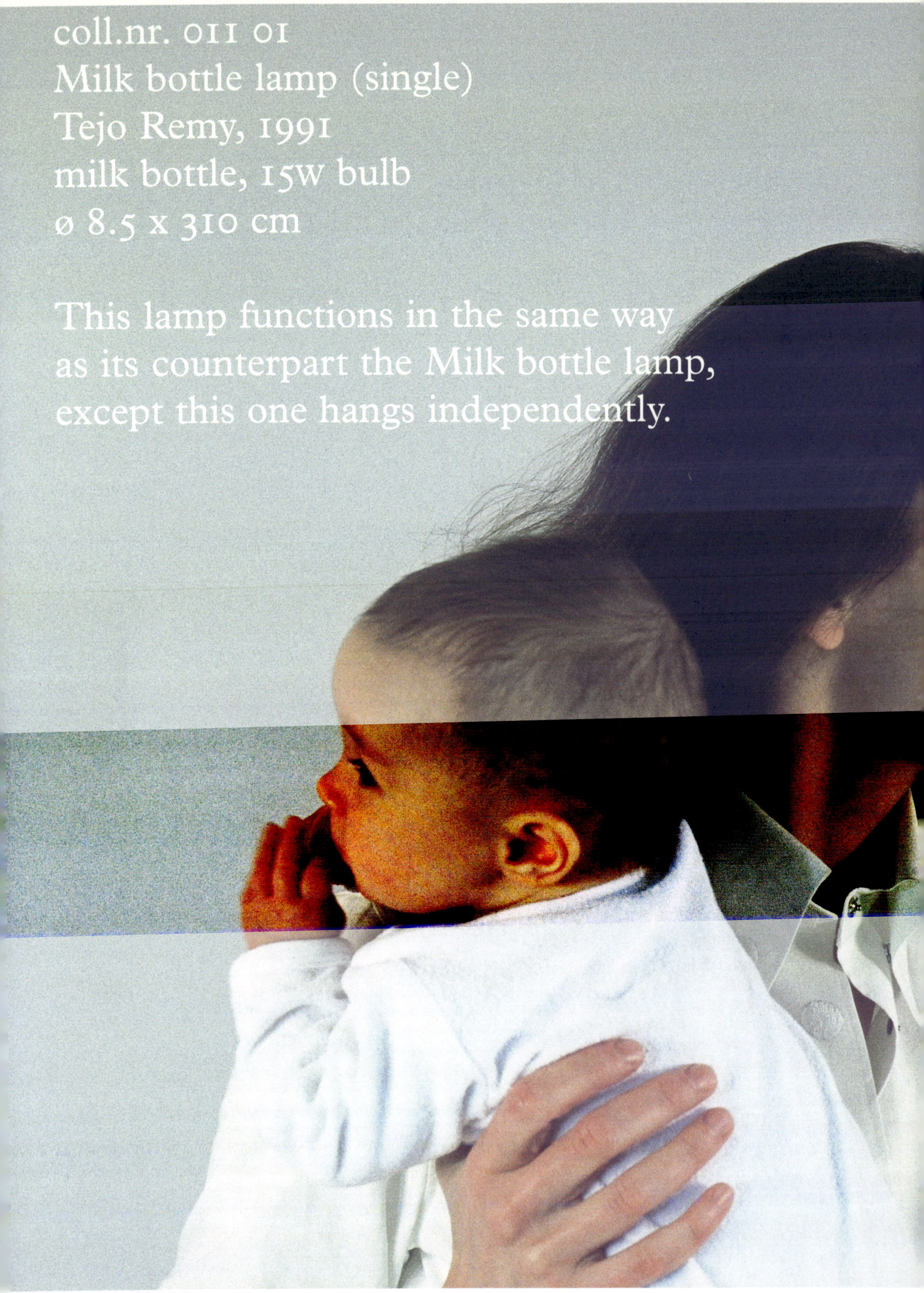

coll.nr. 067 00
Kokon furniture table-chair
Jurgen Bey, 1997/99
PVC covering, existing furniture
various models and colours

Here old furniture is combined and disguised to produce new forms, functions and identities. By using the so-called spider's web technique, desolate furniture is wrapped with synthetic fibres creating a smooth, elastic skin. The Kokon furniture range was a result of Droog's 1997 Dry Tech project.

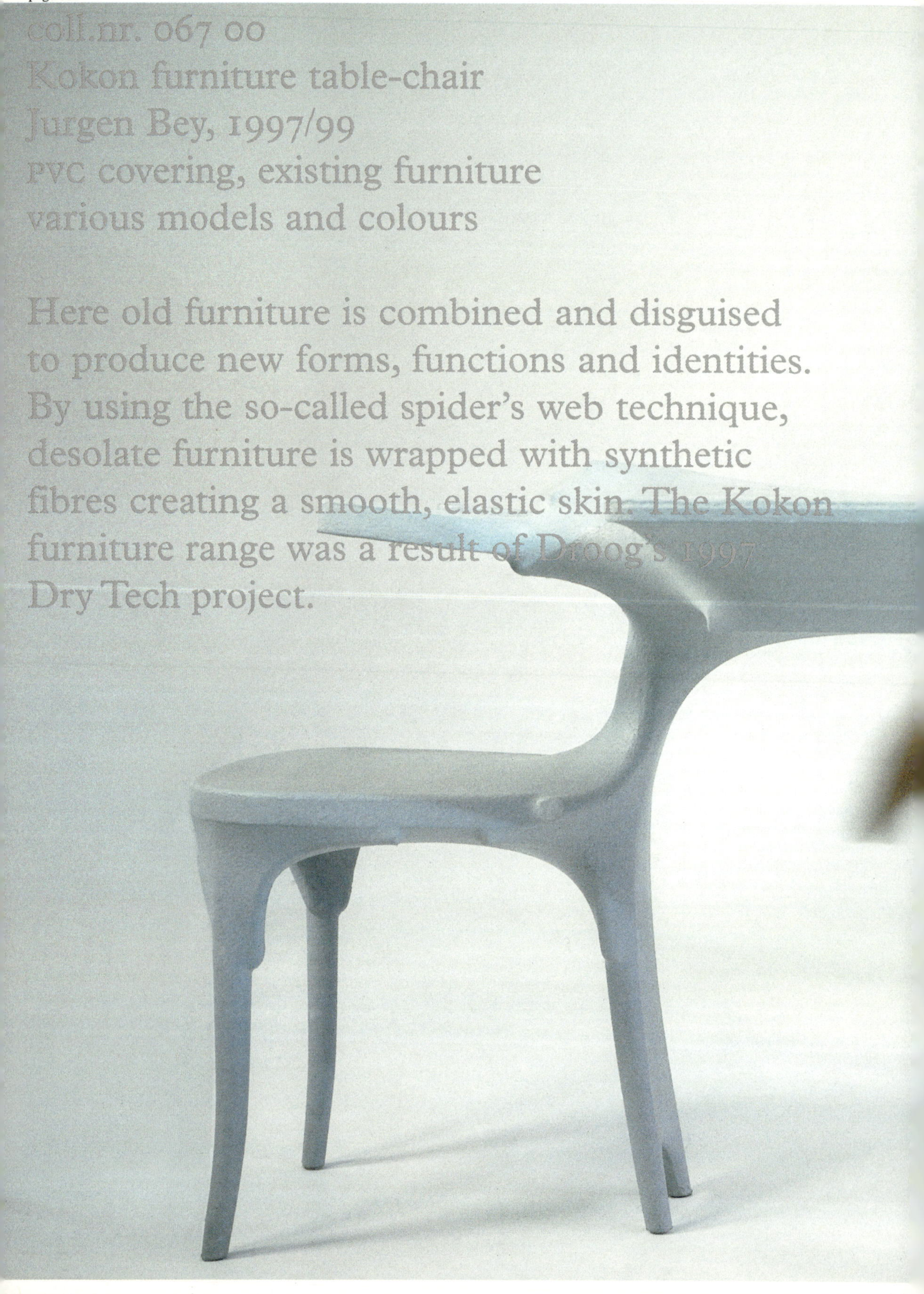

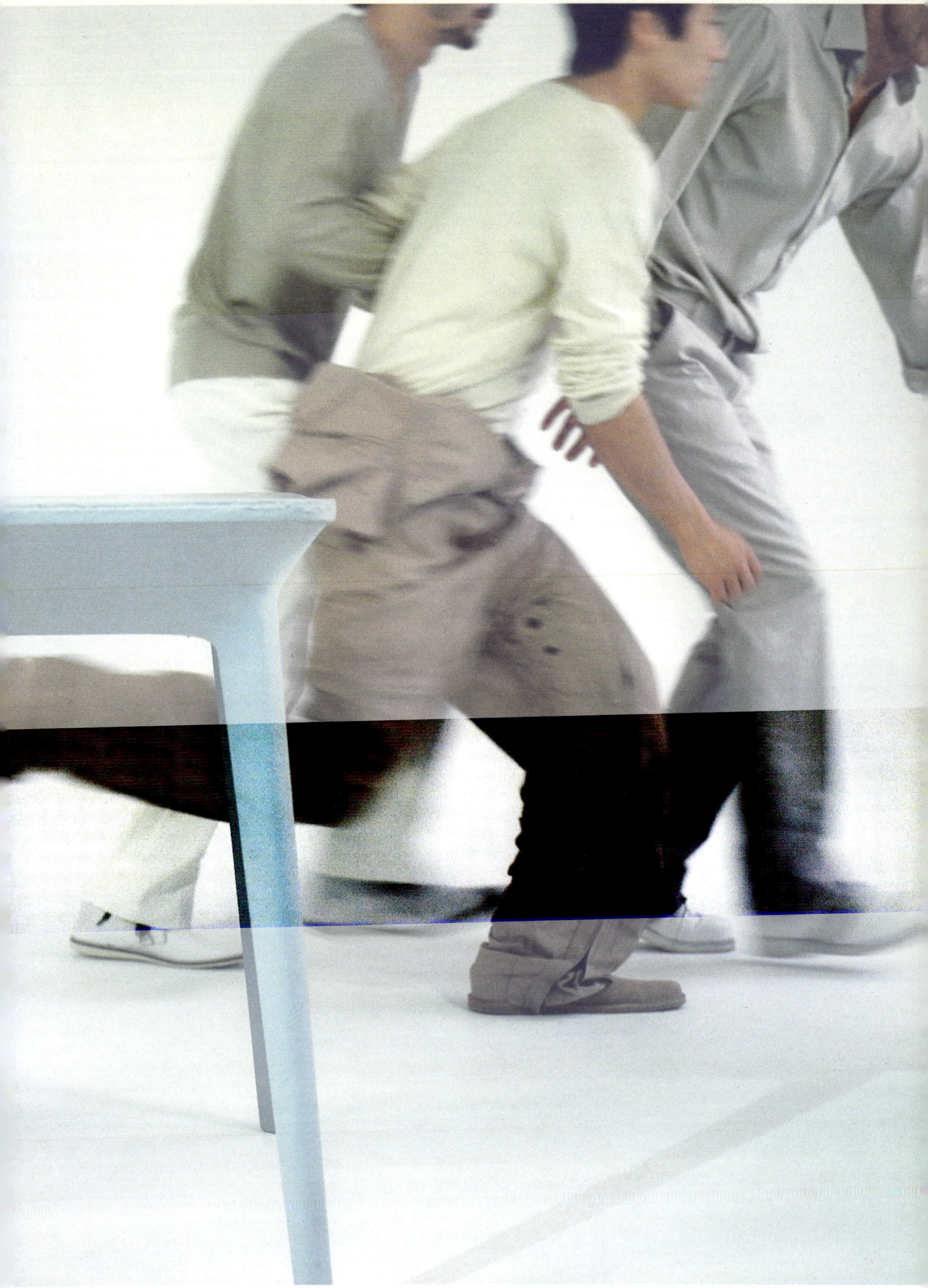

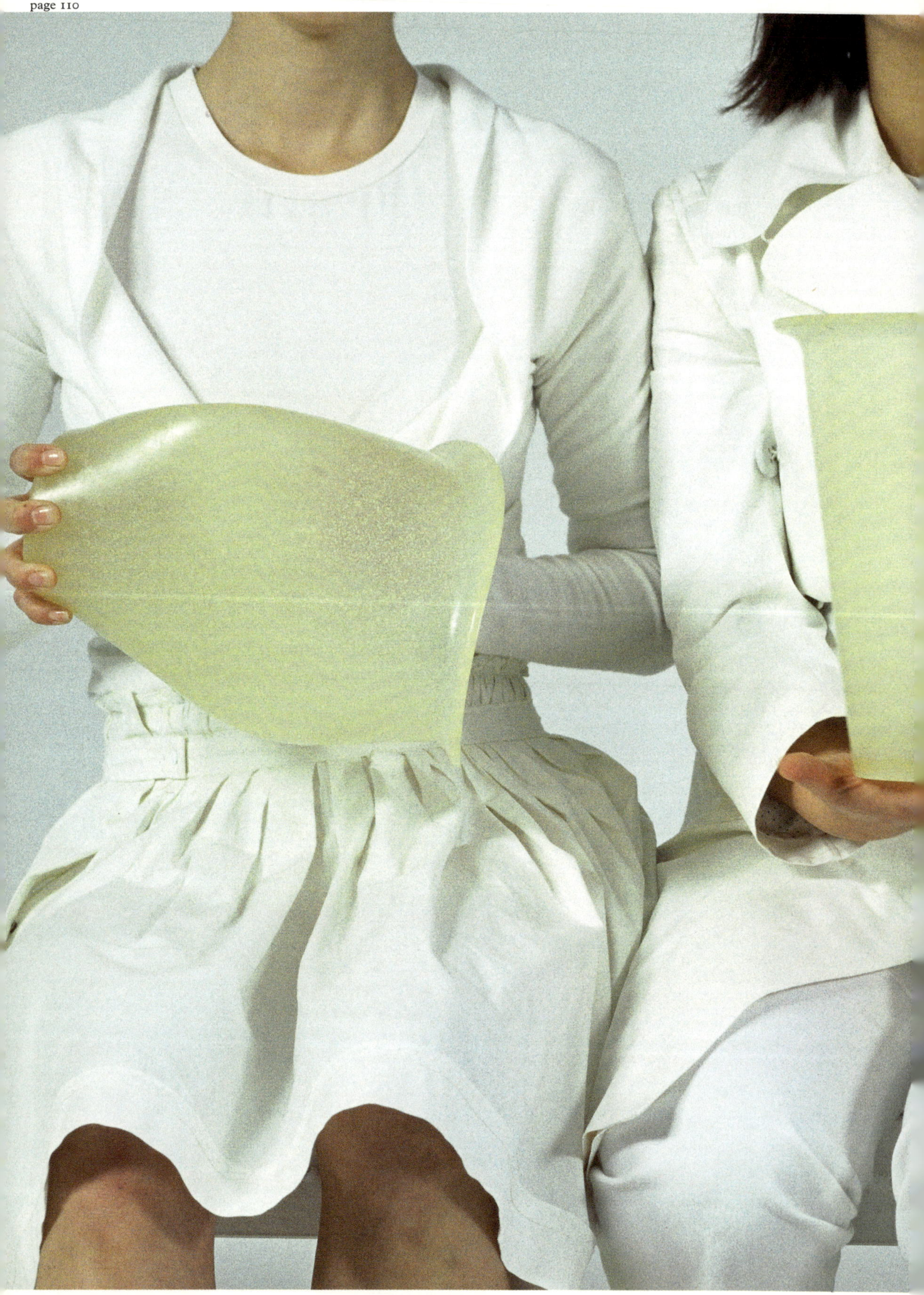

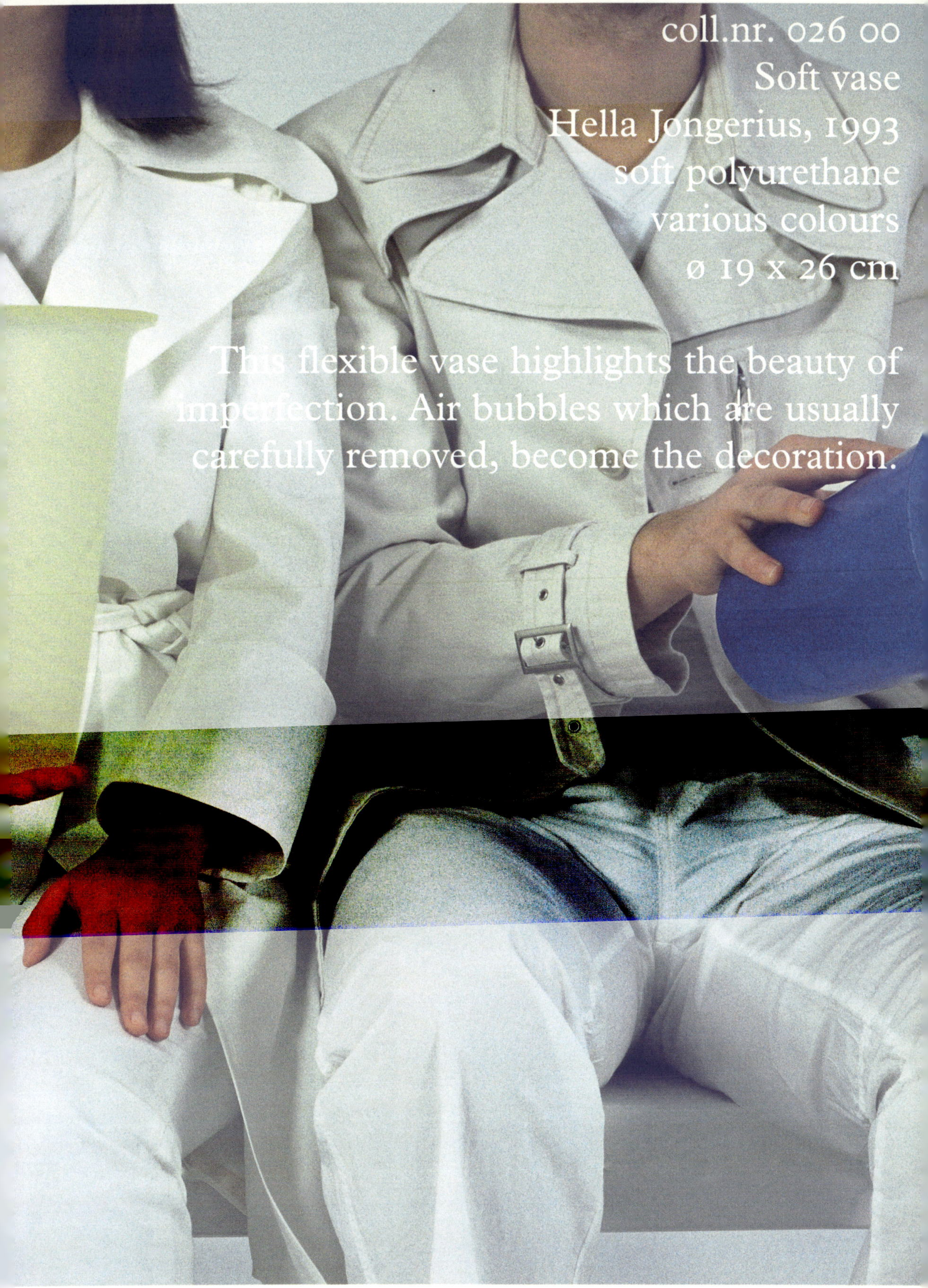

coll.nr. 026 00
Soft vase
Hella Jongerius, 1993
soft polyurethane
various colours
ø 19 x 26 cm

This flexible vase highlights the beauty of imperfection. Air bubbles which are usually carefully removed, become the decoration.

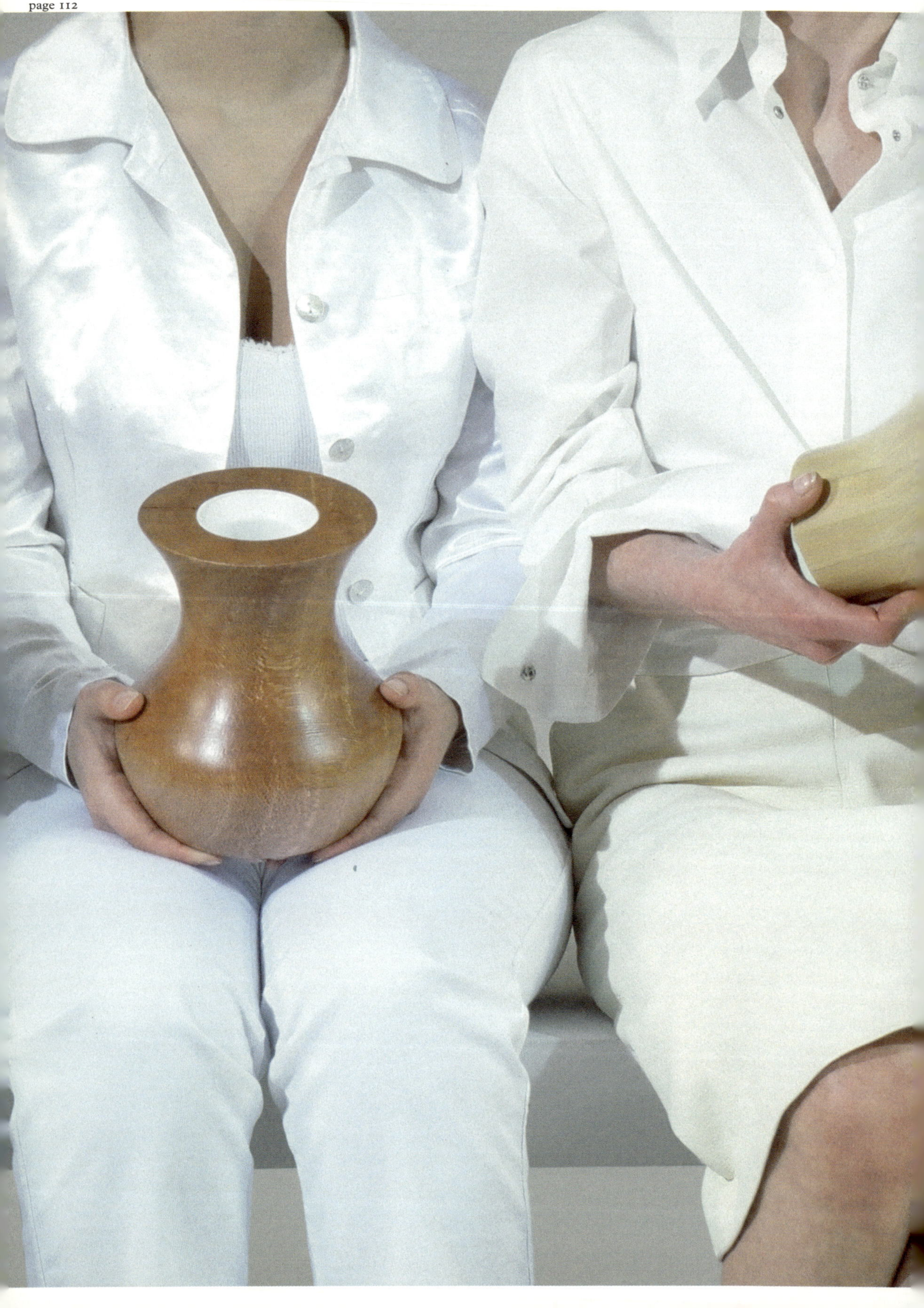

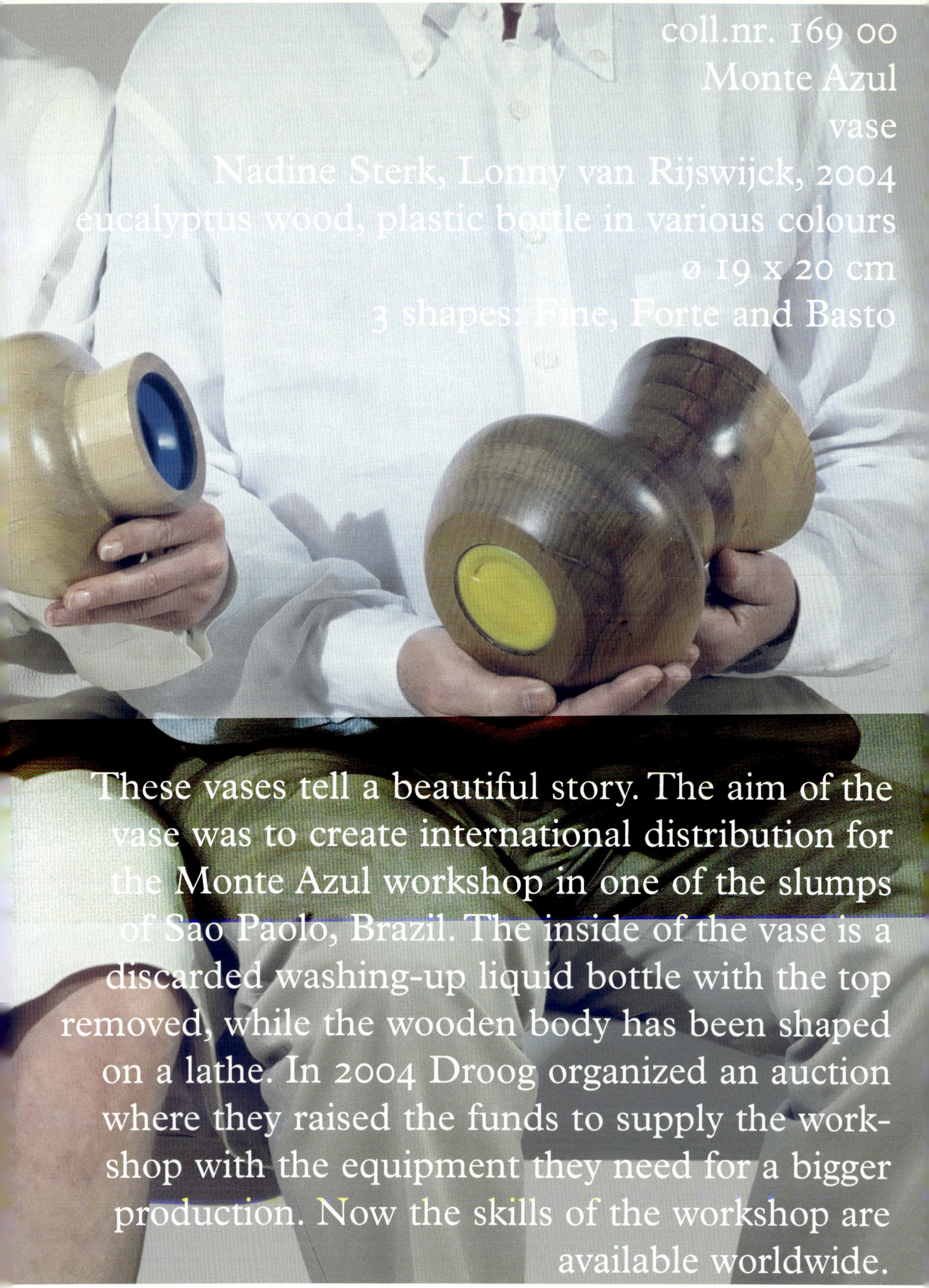

coll.nr. 169 00
Monte Azul
vase
Nadine Sterk, Lonny van Rijswijck, 2004
eucalyptus wood, plastic bottle in various colours
ø 19 x 20 cm
3 shapes: Fine, Forte and Basto

These vases tell a beautiful story. The aim of the vase was to create international distribution for the Monte Azul workshop in one of the slumps of Sao Paolo, Brazil. The inside of the vase is a discarded washing-up liquid bottle with the top removed, while the wooden body has been shaped on a lathe. In 2004 Droog organized an auction where they raised the funds to supply the workshop with the equipment they need for a bigger production. Now the skills of the workshop are available worldwide.

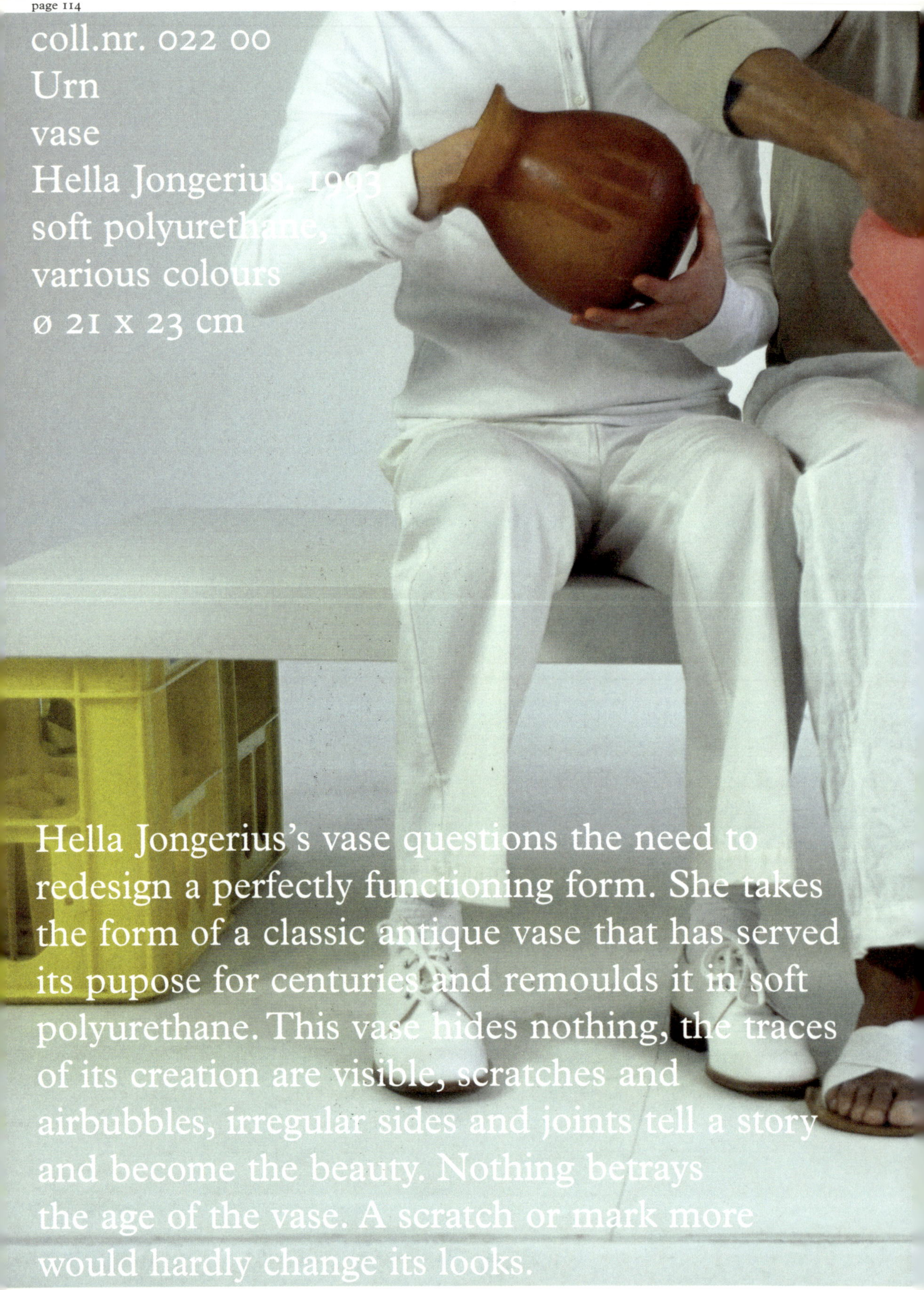

coll.nr. 022 00
Urn
vase
Hella Jongerius, 1993
soft polyurethane,
various colours
ø 21 x 23 cm

Hella Jongerius's vase questions the need to redesign a perfectly functioning form. She takes the form of a classic antique vase that has served its pupose for centuries and remoulds it in soft polyurethane. This vase hides nothing, the traces of its creation are visible, scratches and airbubbles, irregular sides and joints tell a story and become the beauty. Nothing betrays the age of the vase. A scratch or mark more would hardly change its looks.

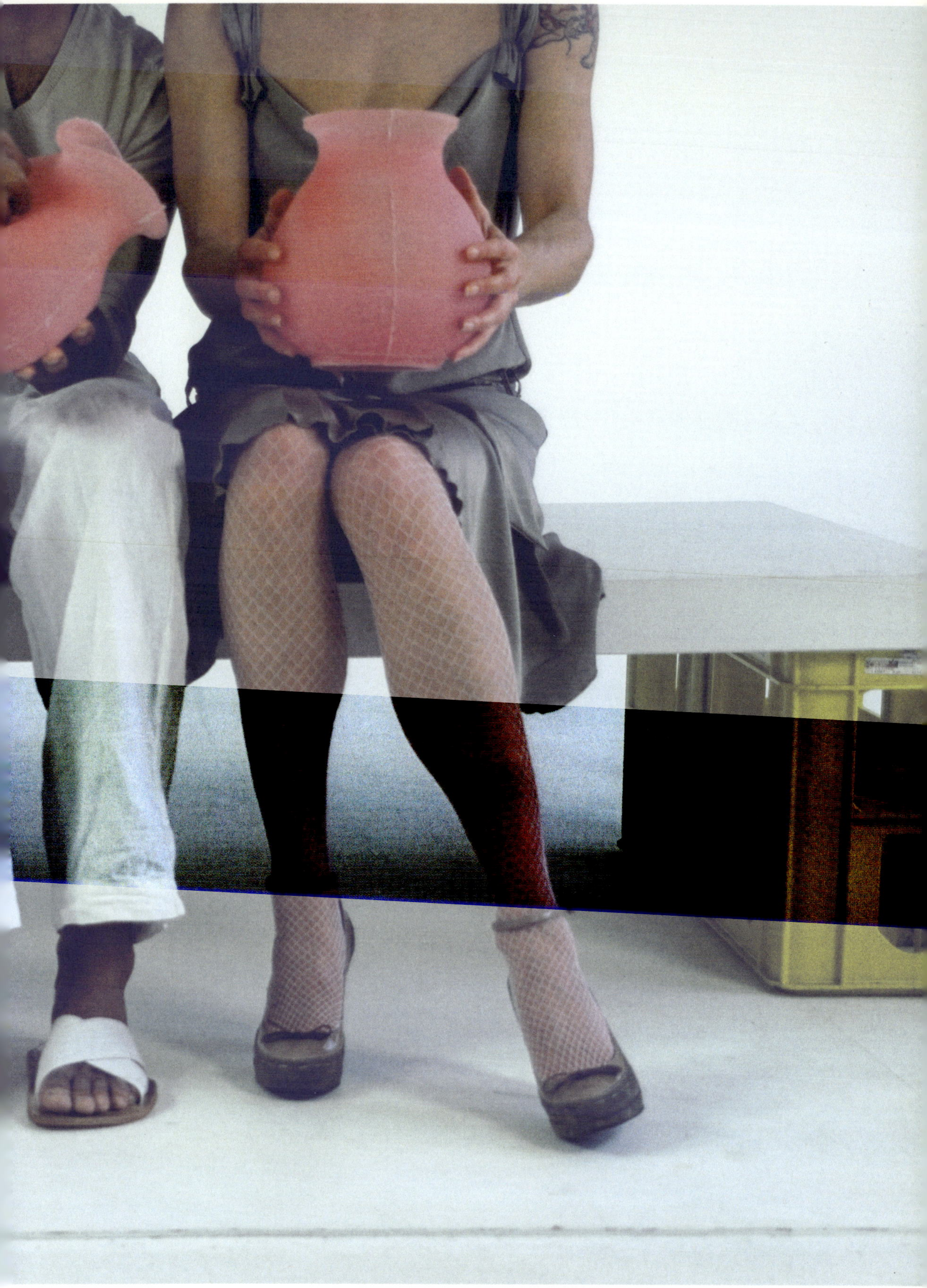

coll.nr. 177 00
Flexlamp
Sam Hecht, 2004
silicone, 11W energy saving bulb
ø 33 x 22 cm

The material of this lampshade may look rigid from a distance but is in fact flexible enough to be twisted and squeezed. The light casing is combined with the shade to look like one but it can be easily removed to fit an energy saving bulb.

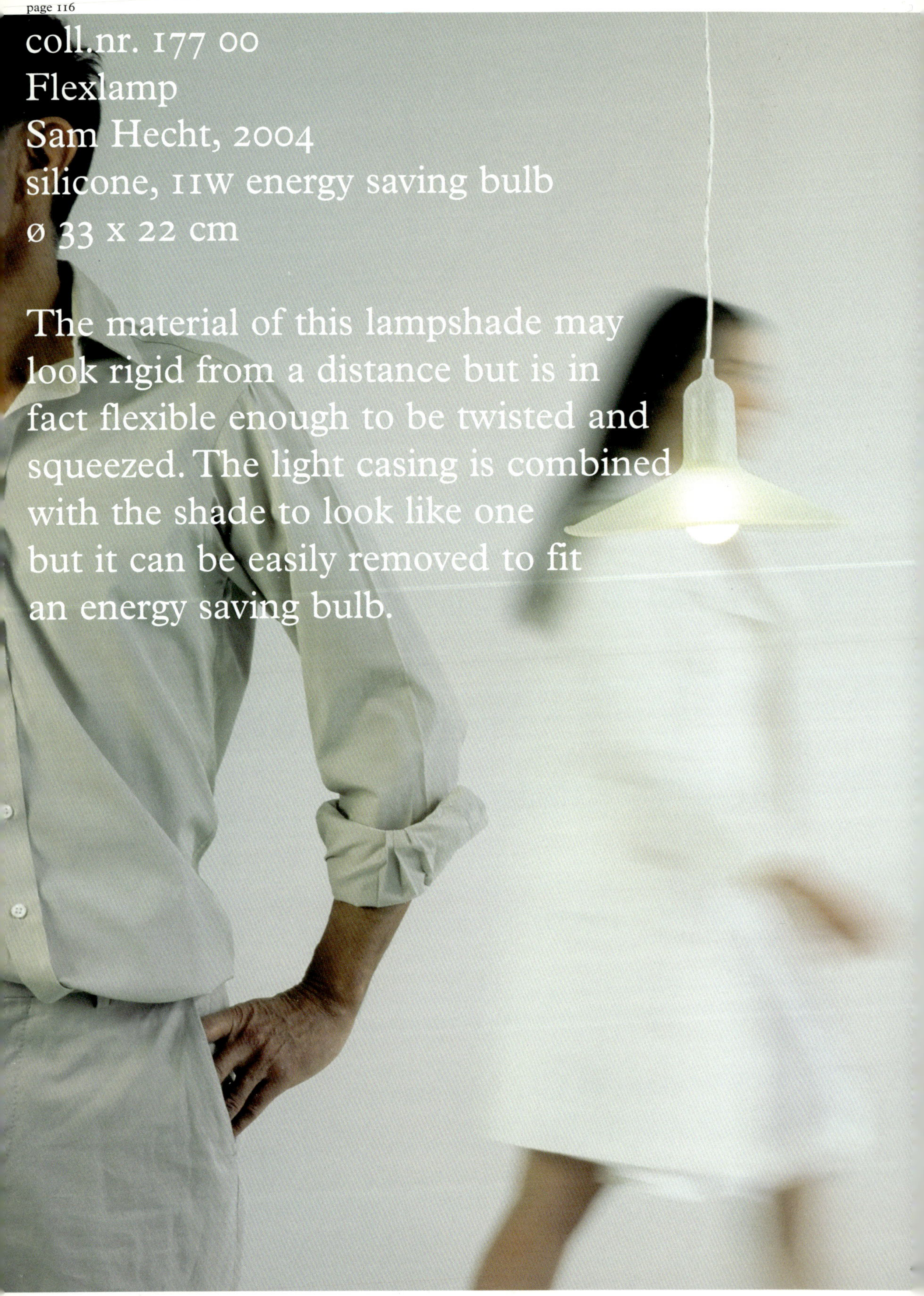

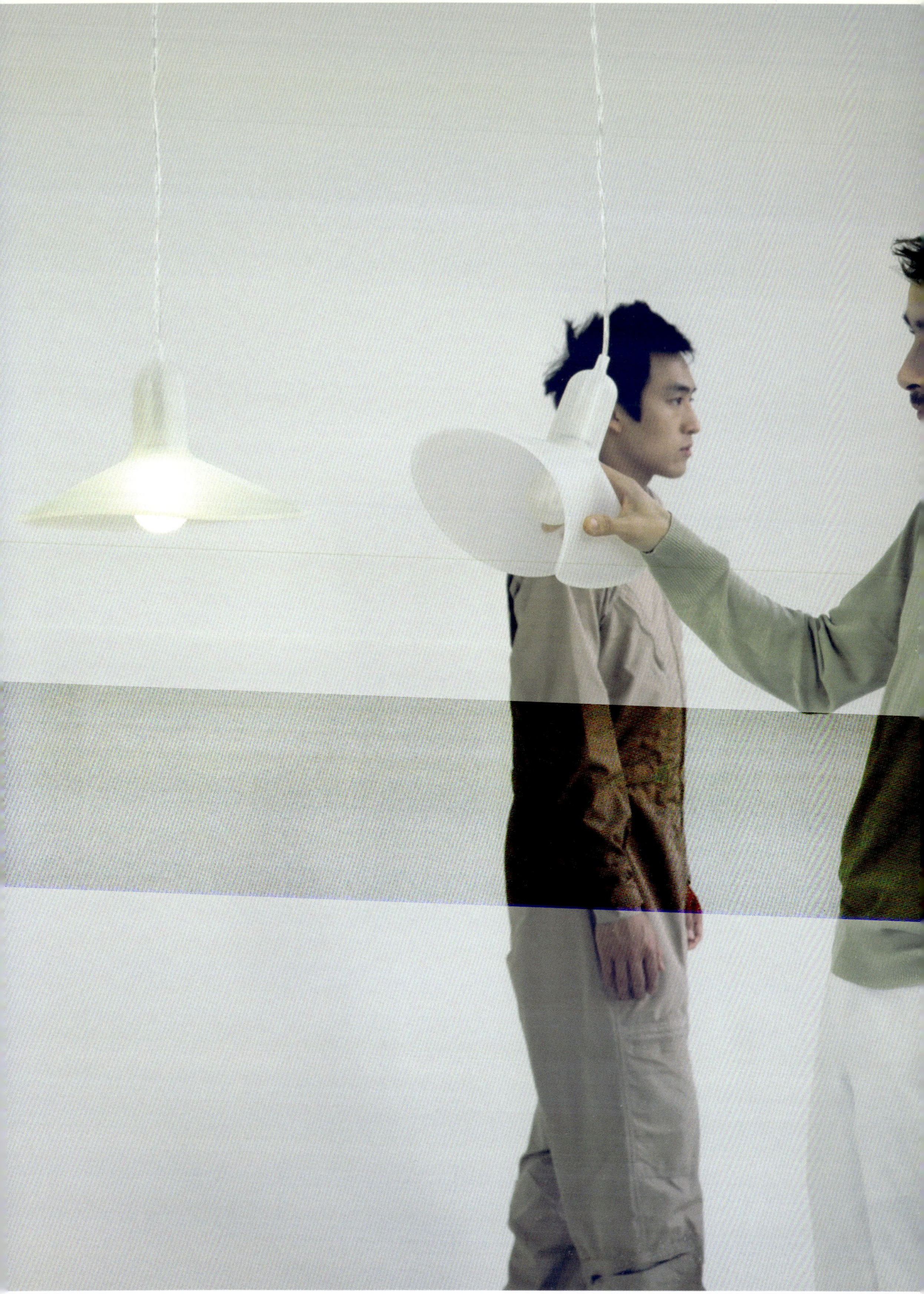

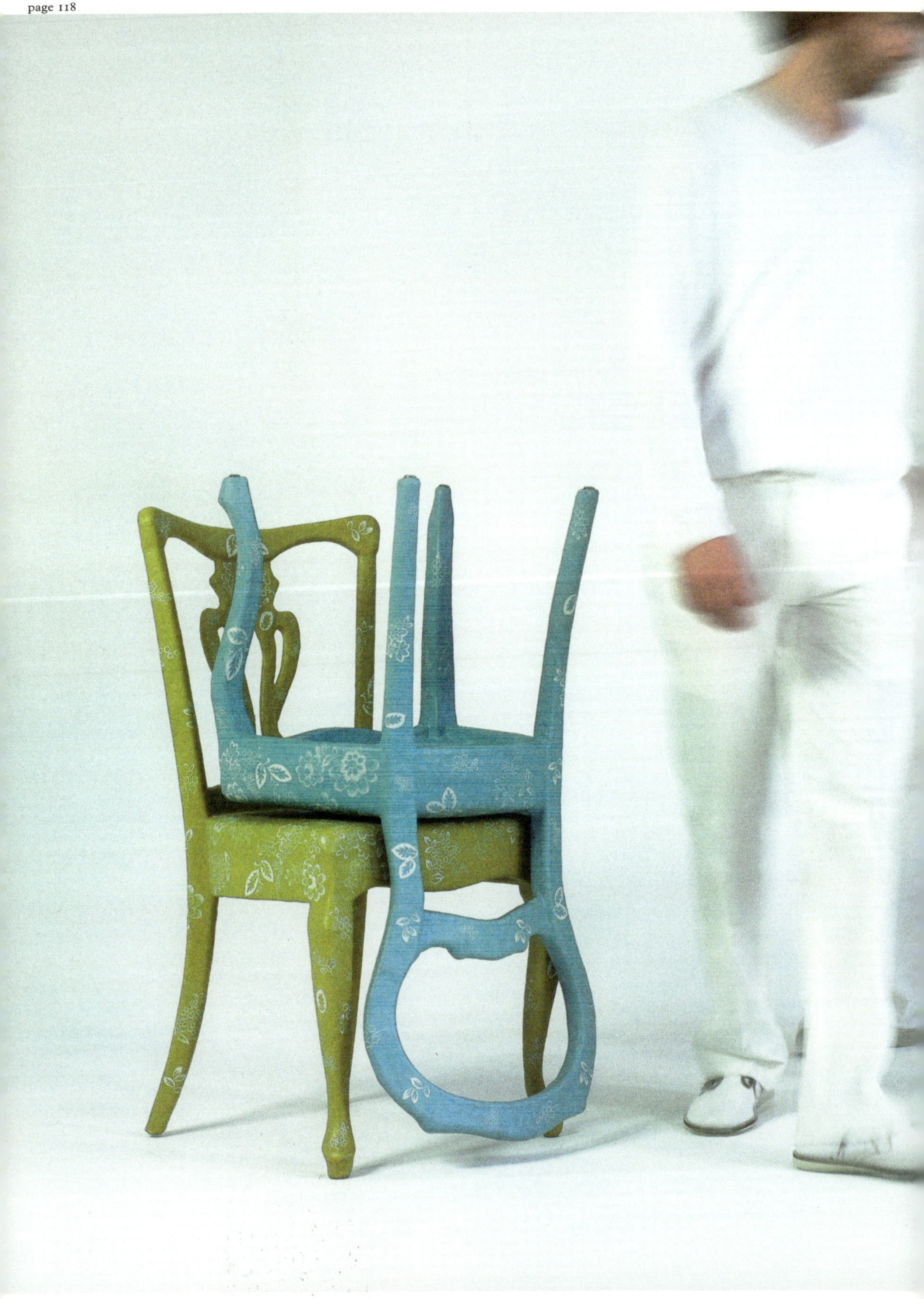

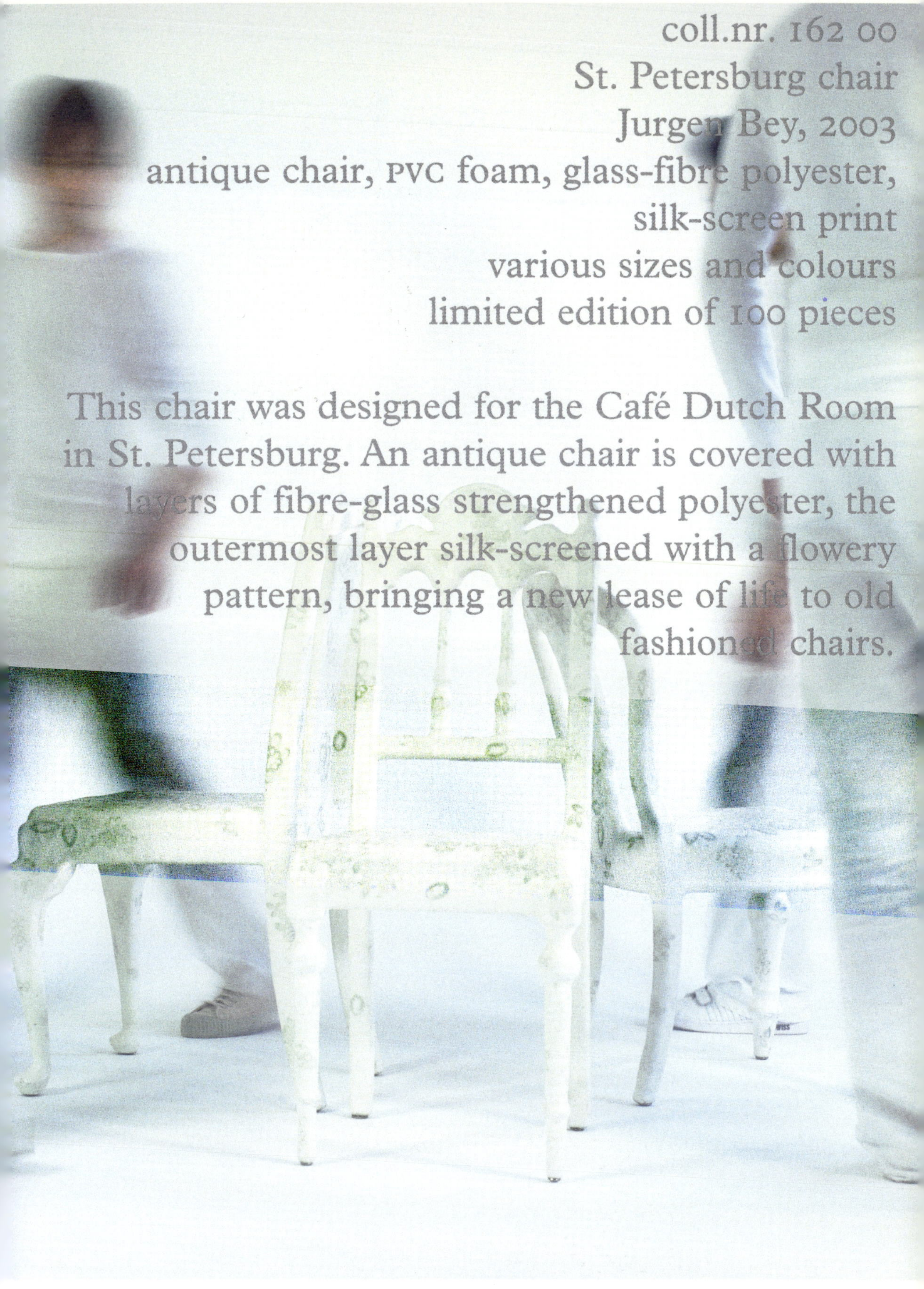

coll.nr. 162 00
St. Petersburg chair
Jurgen Bey, 2003
antique chair, PVC foam, glass-fibre polyester,
silk-screen print
various sizes and colours
limited edition of 100 pieces

This chair was designed for the Café Dutch Room in St. Petersburg. An antique chair is covered with layers of fibre-glass strengthened polyester, the outermost layer silk-screened with a flowery pattern, bringing a new lease of life to old fashioned chairs.

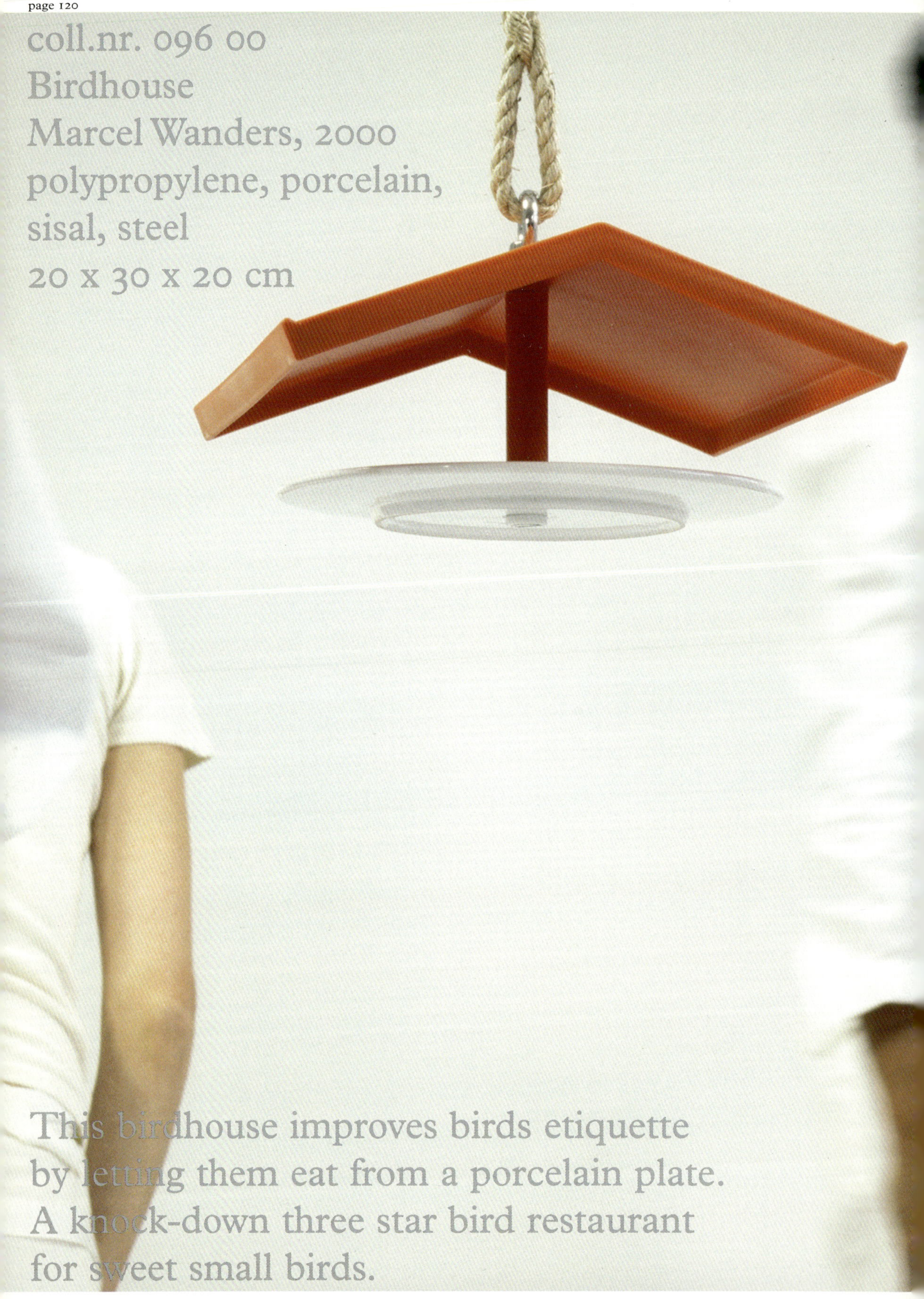

coll.nr. 096 00
Birdhouse
Marcel Wanders, 2000
polypropylene, porcelain,
sisal, steel
20 x 30 x 20 cm

This birdhouse improves birds etiquette by letting them eat from a porcelain plate. A knock-down three star bird restaurant for sweet small birds.

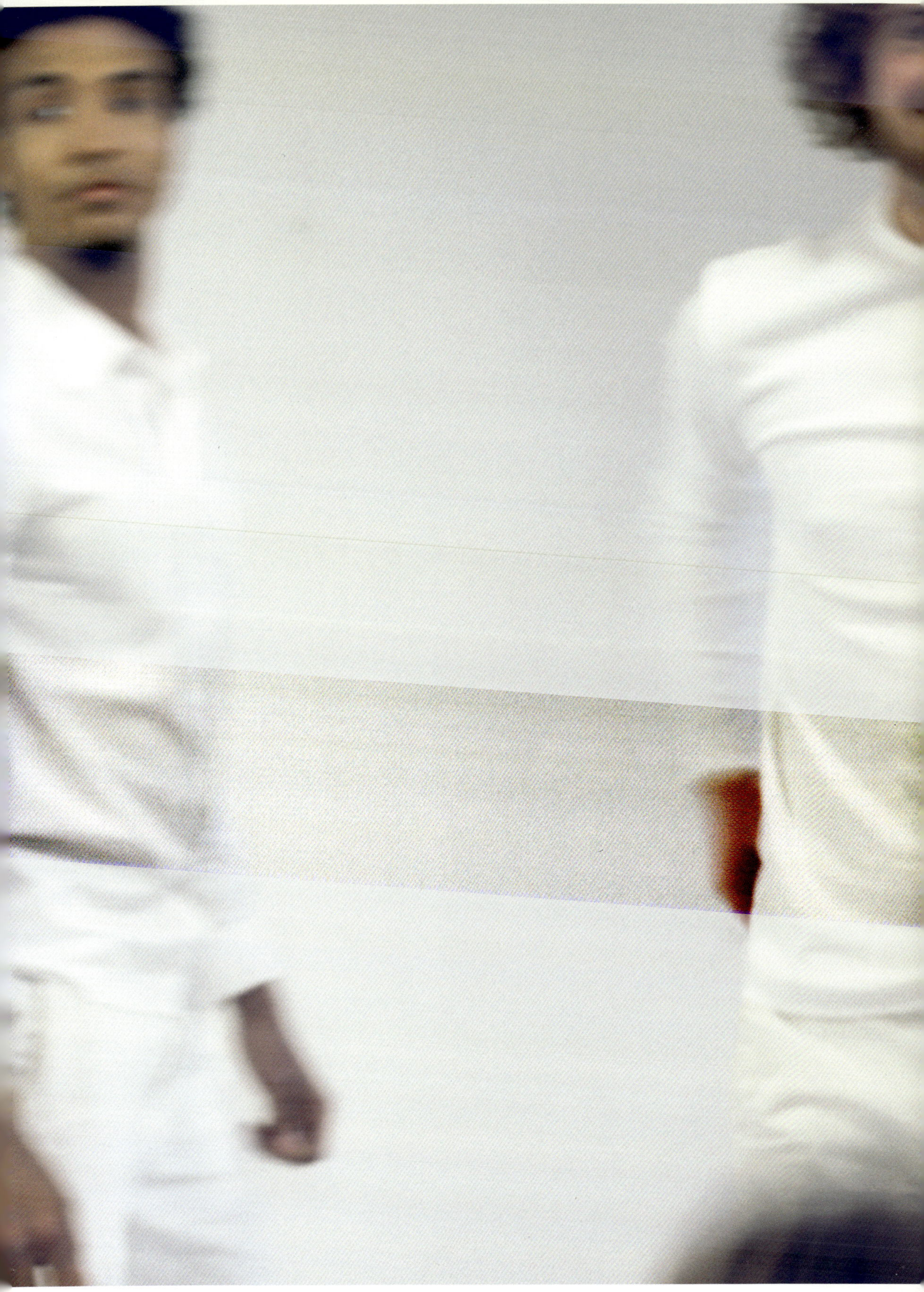

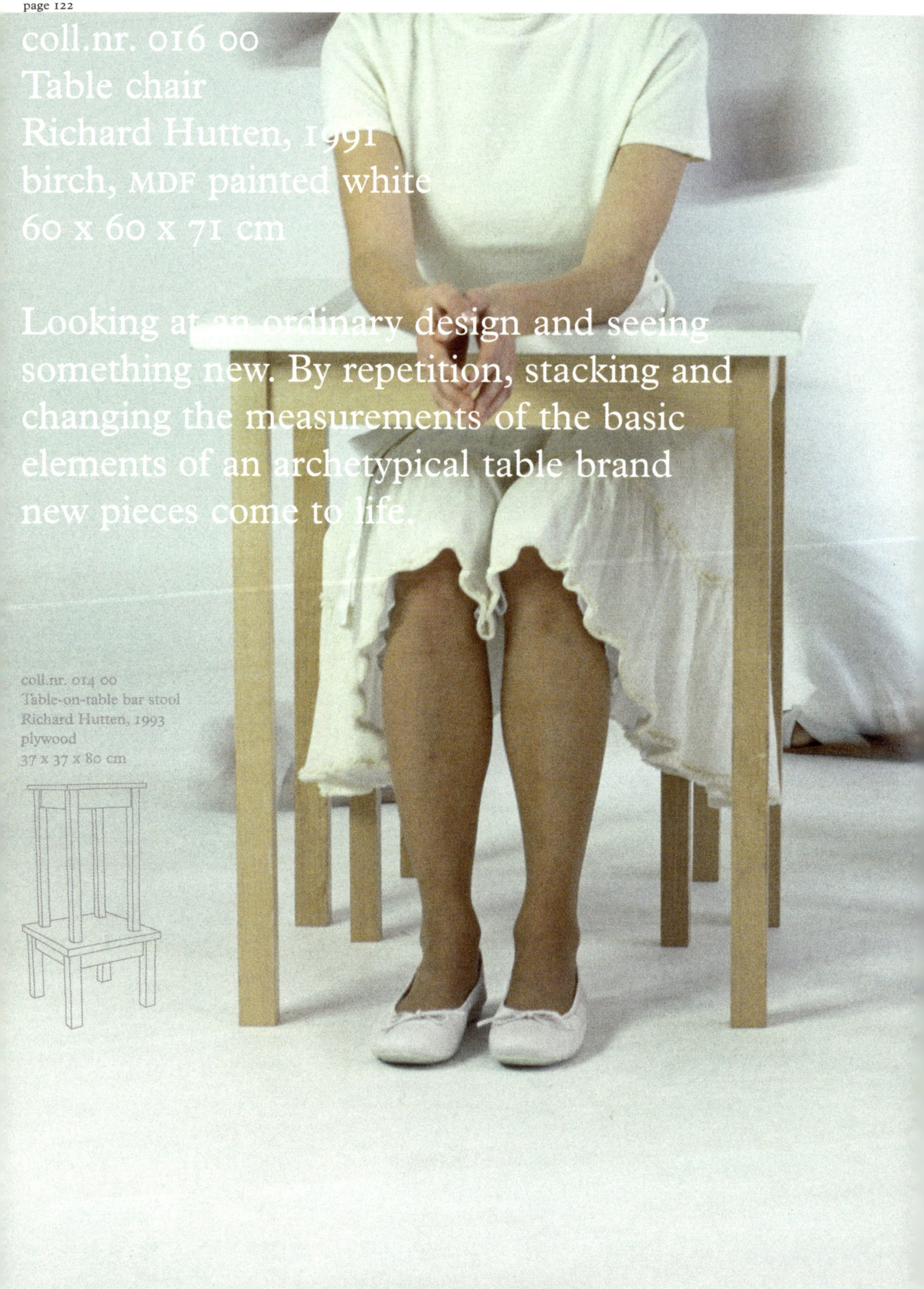

coll.nr. 016 00
Table chair
Richard Hutten, 1991
birch, MDF painted white
60 x 60 x 71 cm

Looking at an ordinary design and seeing something new. By repetition, stacking and changing the measurements of the basic elements of an archetypical table brand new pieces come to life.

coll.nr. 014 00
Table-on-table bar stool
Richard Hutten, 1993
plywood
37 x 37 x 80 cm

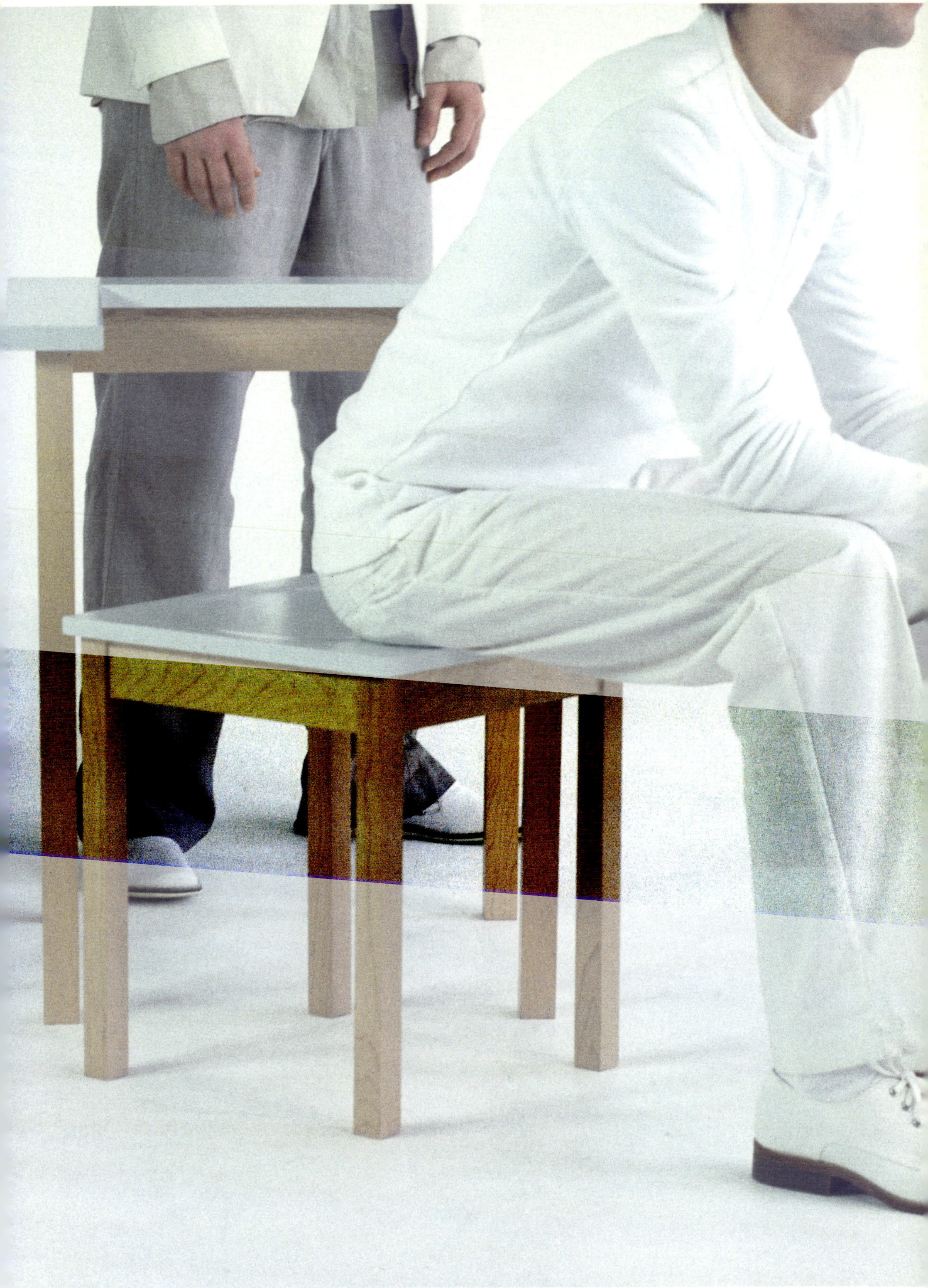

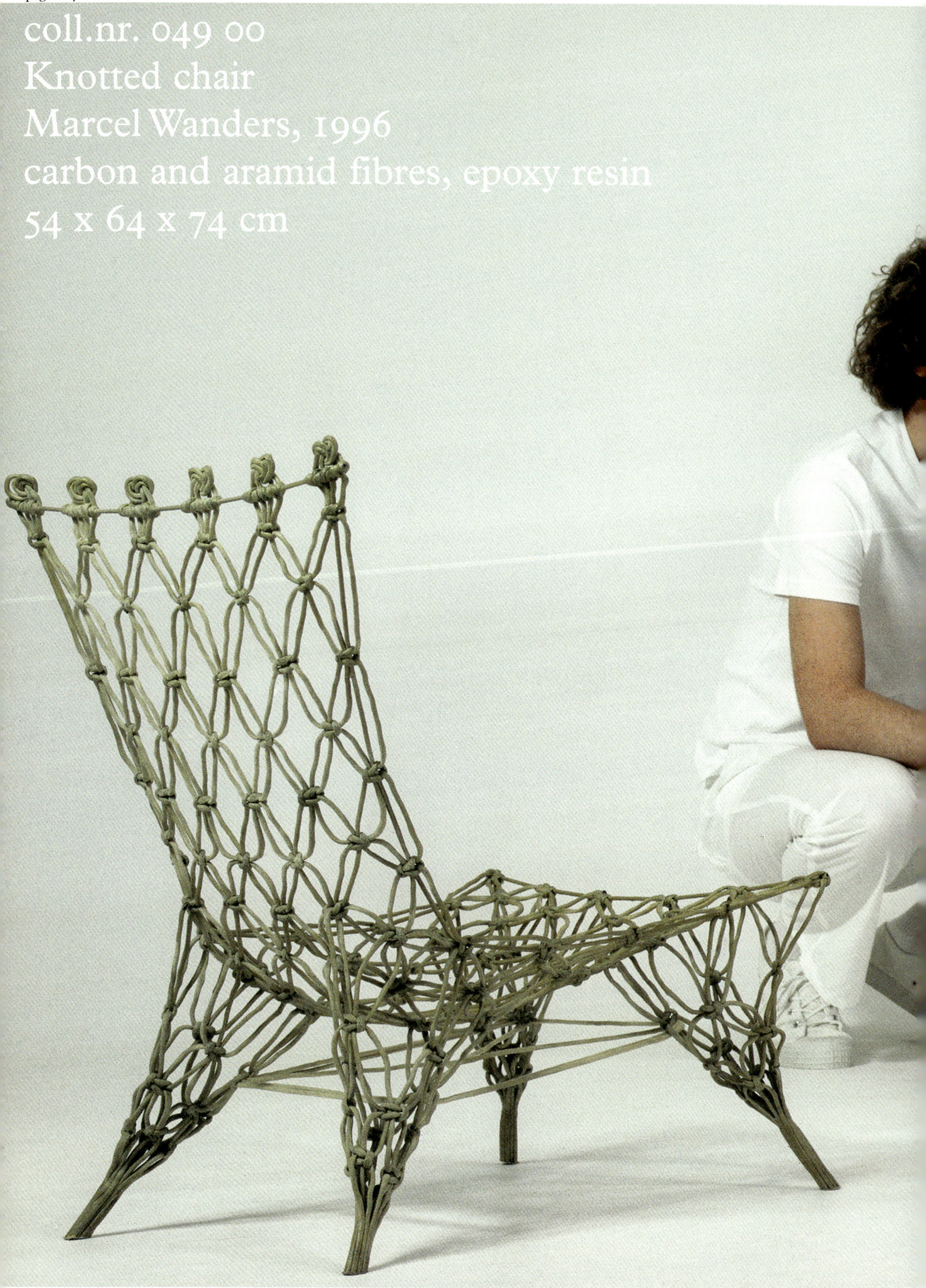

coll.nr. 049 00
Knotted chair
Marcel Wanders, 1996
carbon and aramid fibres, epoxy resin
54 x 64 x 74 cm

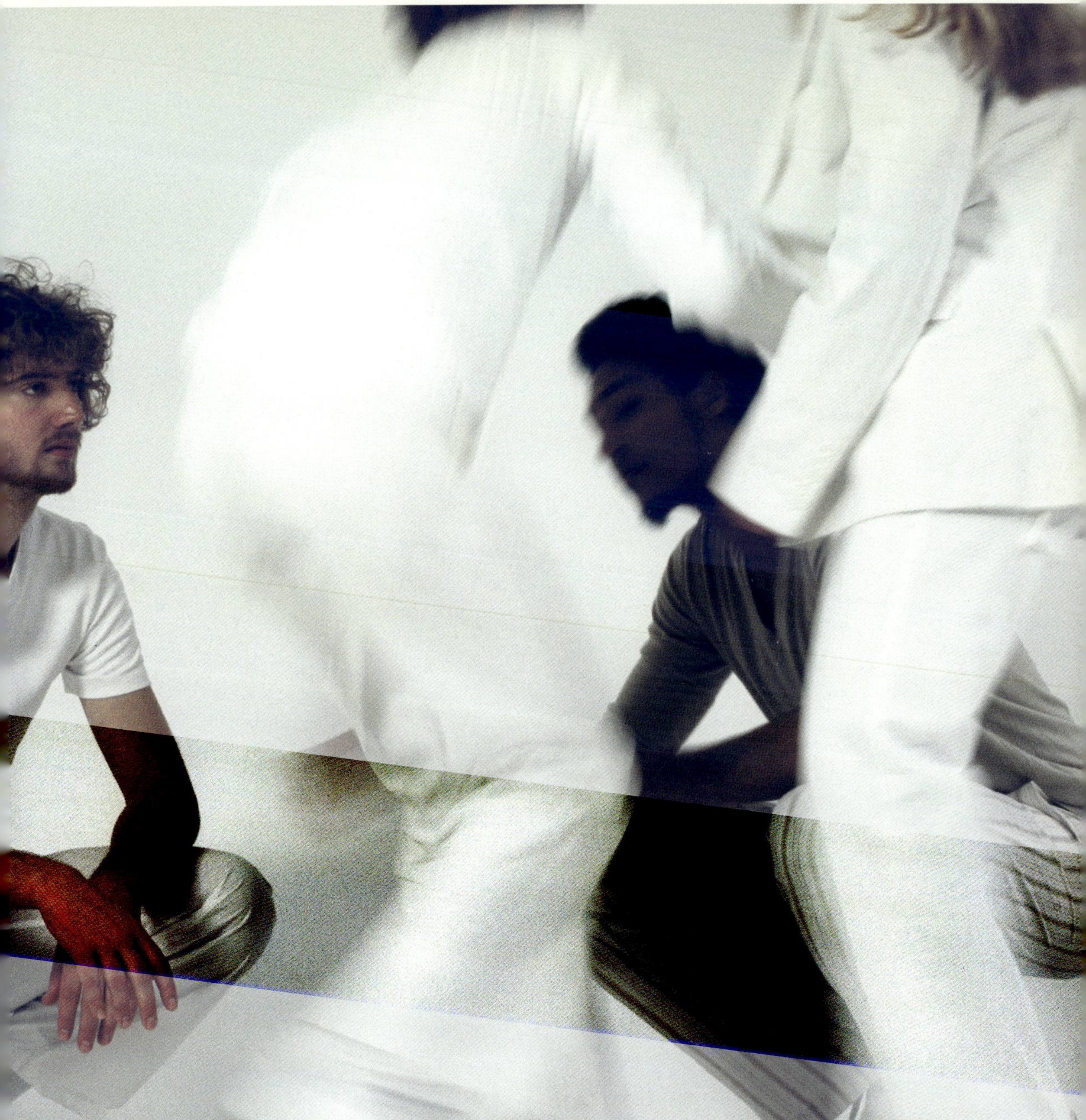

This lightweight chair combines industrial techniques and handcrafting. A thread constructed of aramid and carbon fibres, is knotted into the shape of a chair and then impregnated with epoxy resin and hung in a frame to dry, leaving the final form in the hands of gravity. The Knotted chair was a result of Droog's 1996 Dry Tech project.

coll.nr. 158 00
Heat wave
electric radiator
Joris Laarman, 2003
aluminum, polyurethane, 1600W
210 x 95 x 5 cm

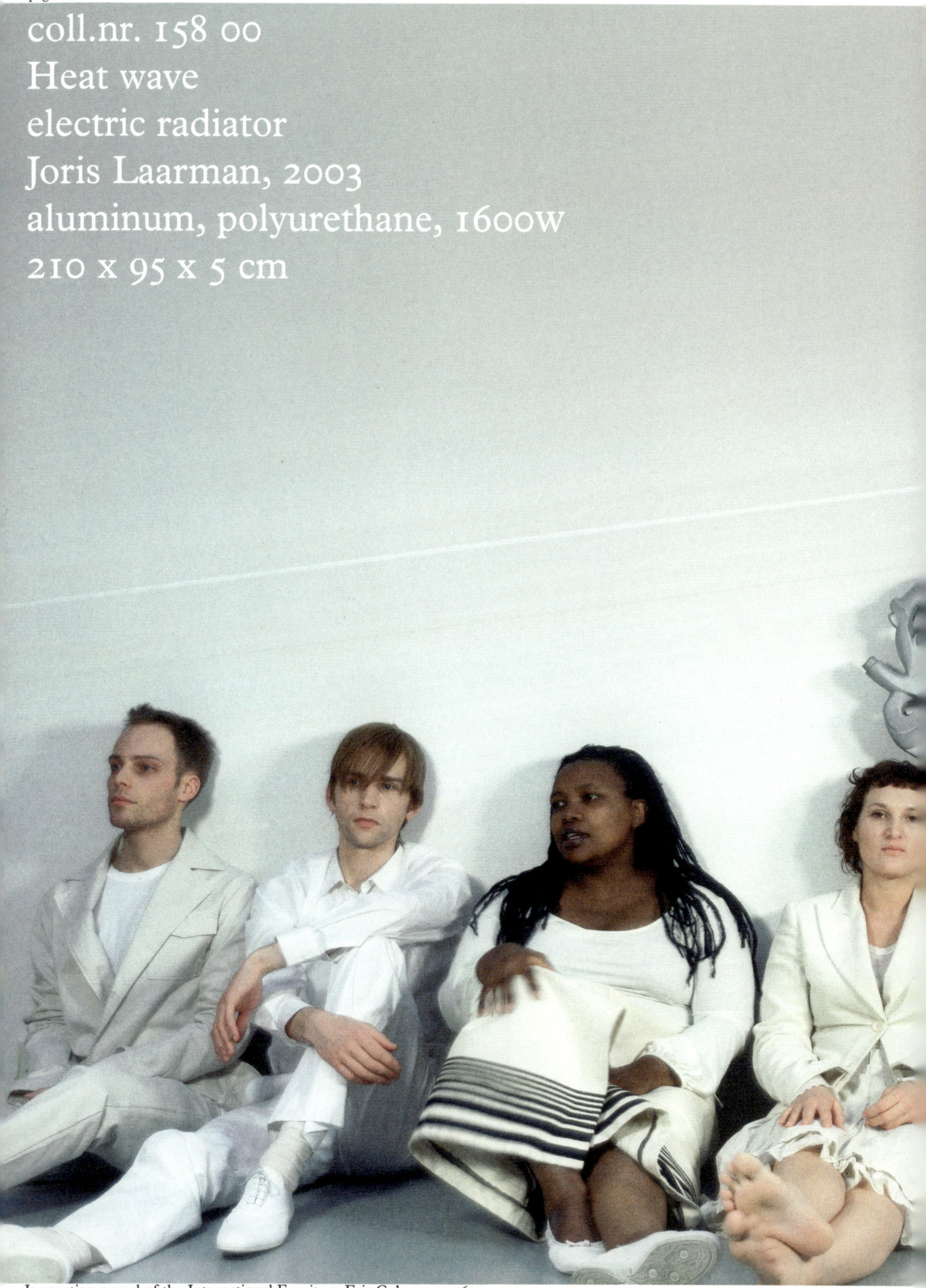

Innovation award of the International Furniture Fair Cologne 2006

This design approaches the radiator with a new mindset. Its original shape discards the old radiator design and makes it into a decorative piece that you no longer want to hide. The decoration works also as the function as the increased surface area provides more radiation of heat. And if you look at the pattern very closely you may discover hidden details.

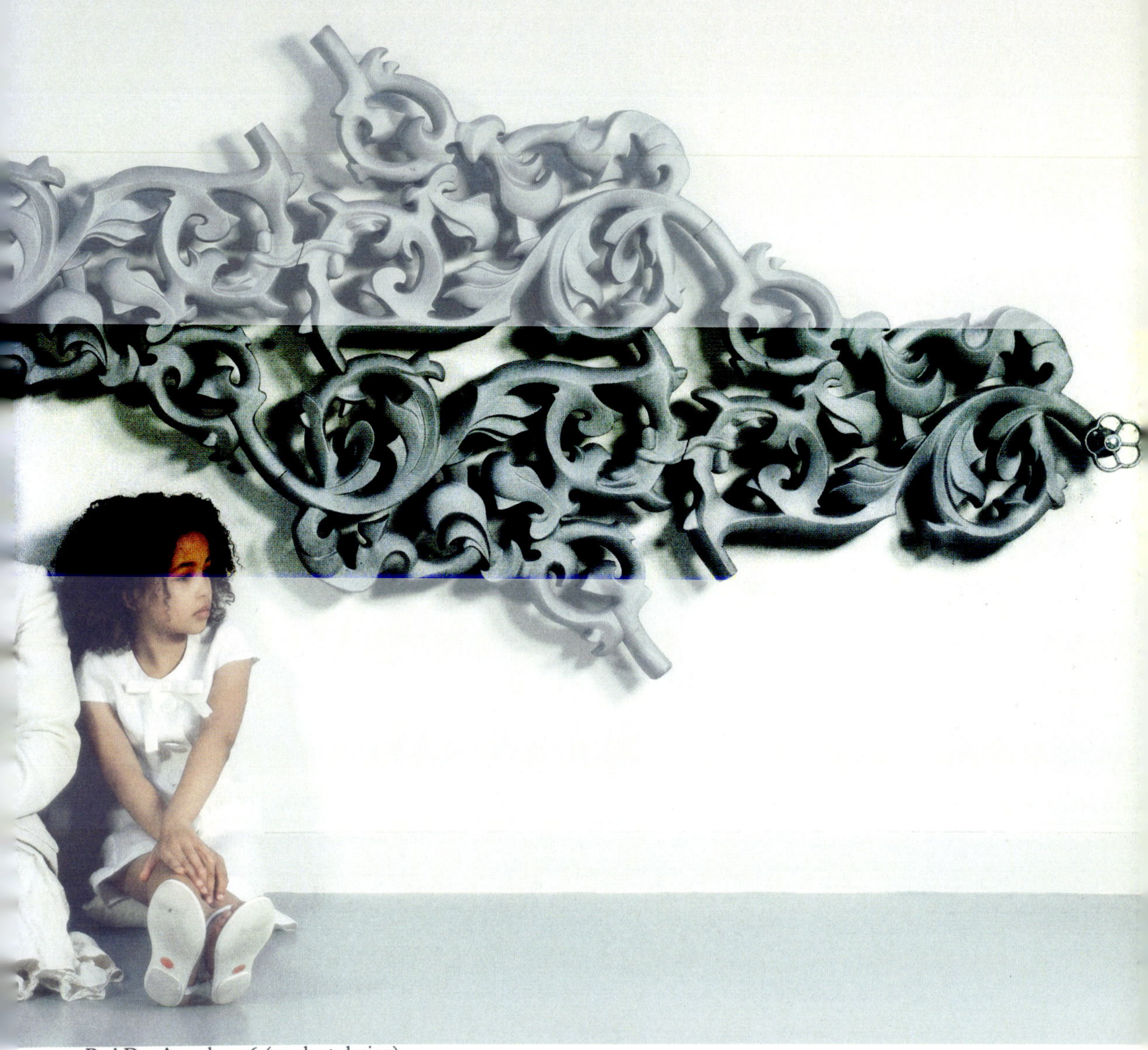

Red Dot Award 2006 (product design)

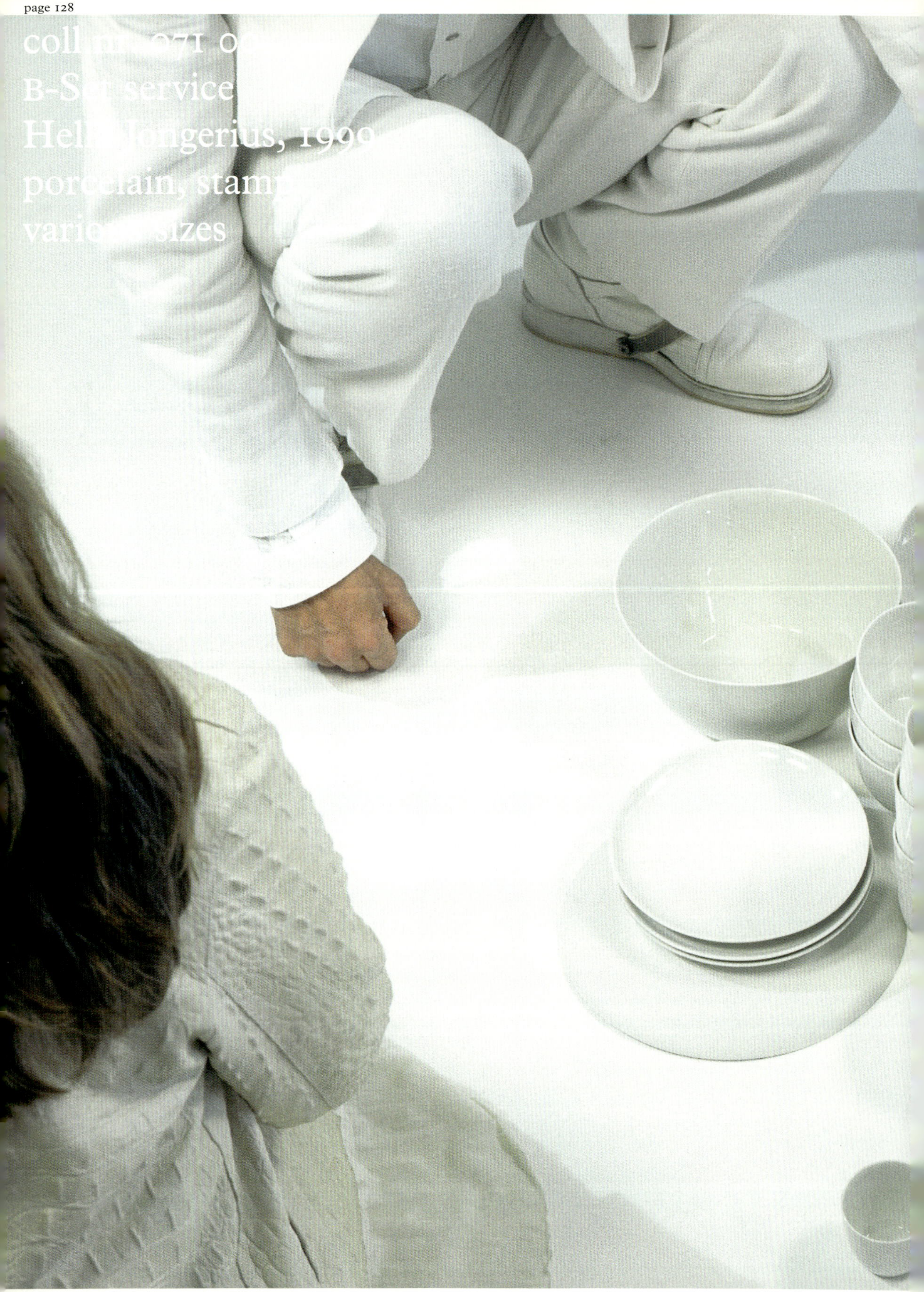

coll nr. 071 0

B-Set service

Hella Jongerius, 1999

porcelain, stamp

various sizes

Different kiln temperatures result in slighty but characteristic and unpredictable shapes.

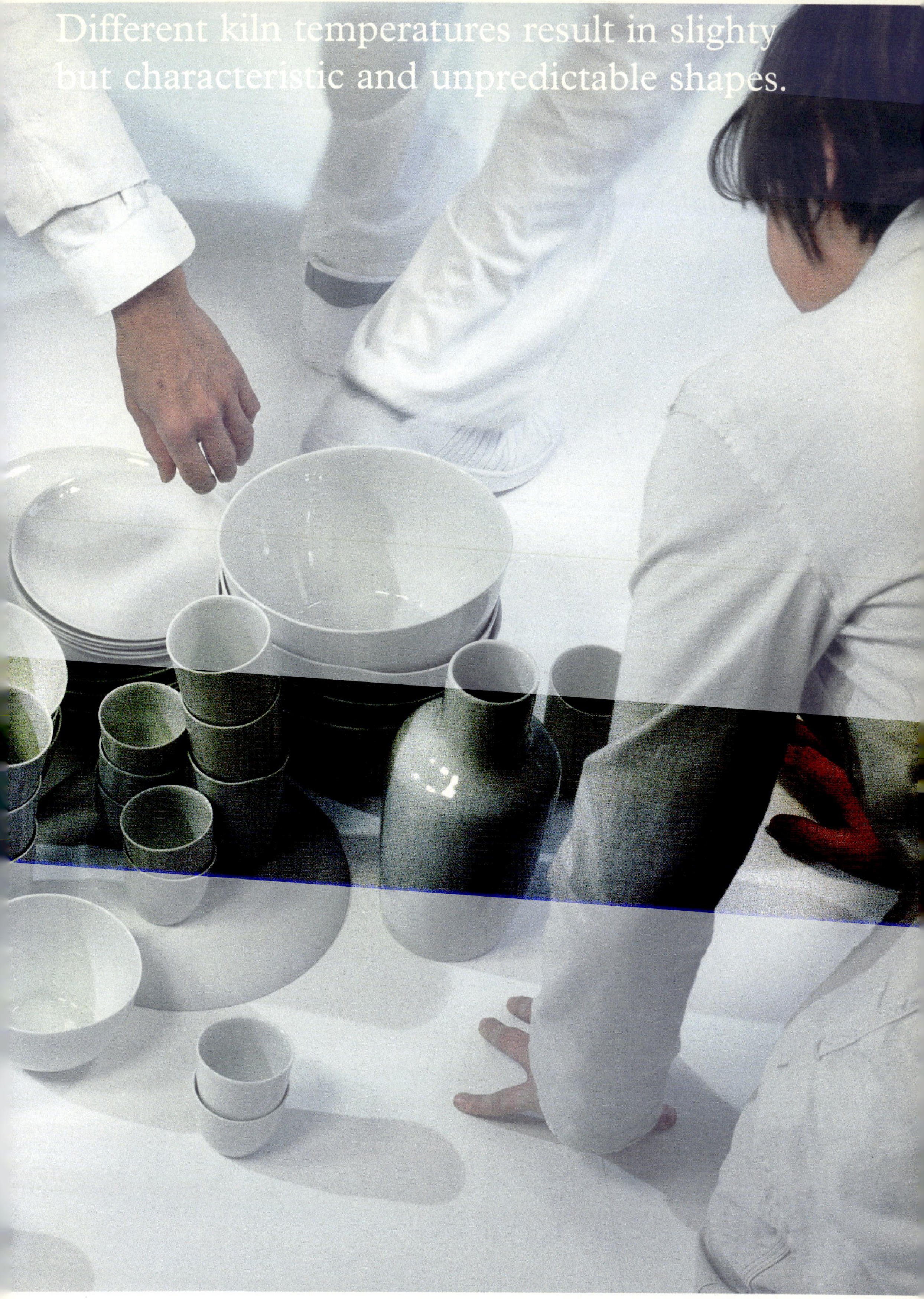

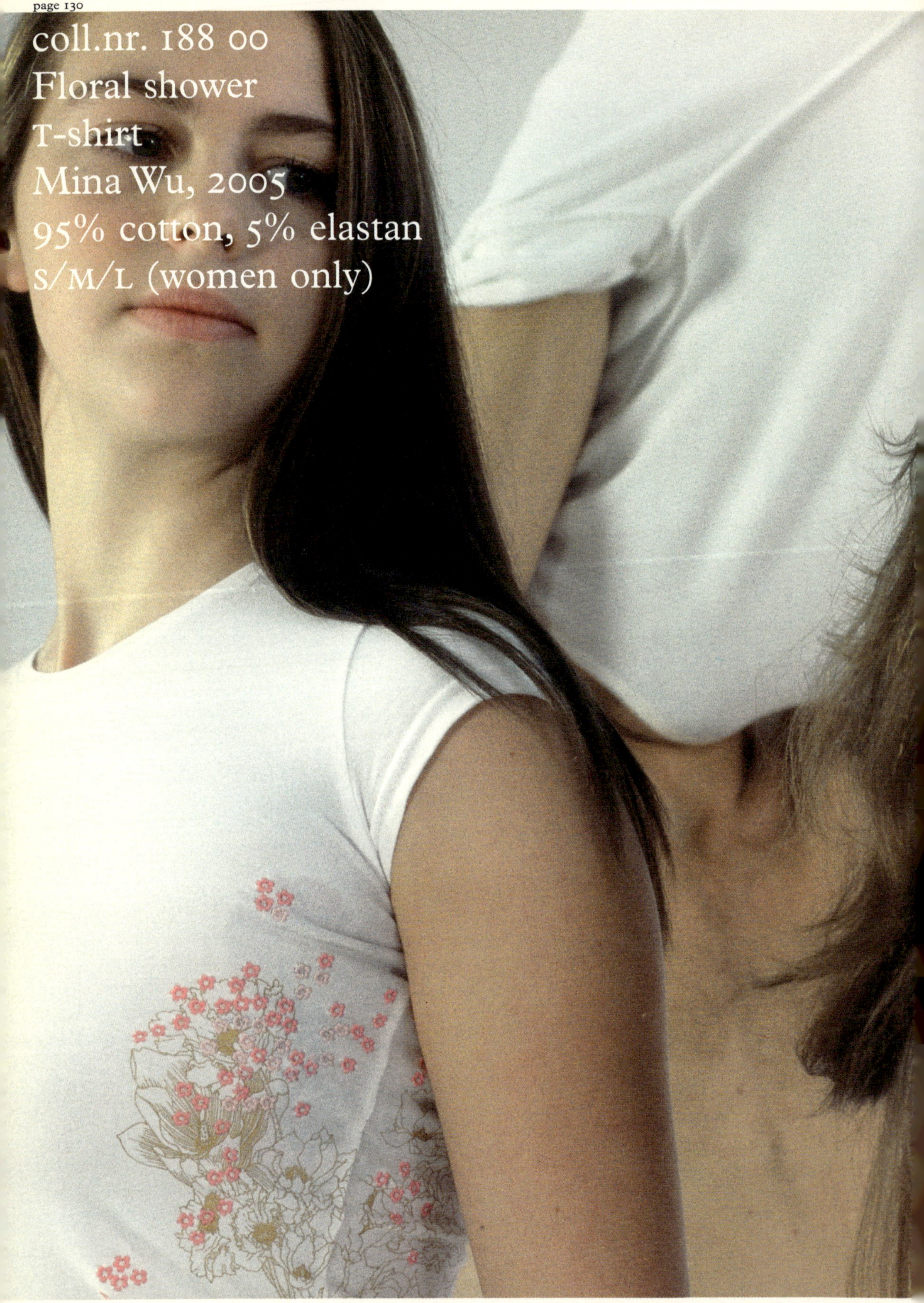
coll.nr. 188 00
Floral shower
T-shirt
Mina Wu, 2005
95% cotton, 5% elastan
S/M/L (women only)

This T-shirt celebrates the usually neglected part of a garment, the armpit. Mina Wu turns it into something positive with a decorative print of flowers, both on the inside and outside. Over the top of the outer print she has added embroidery.

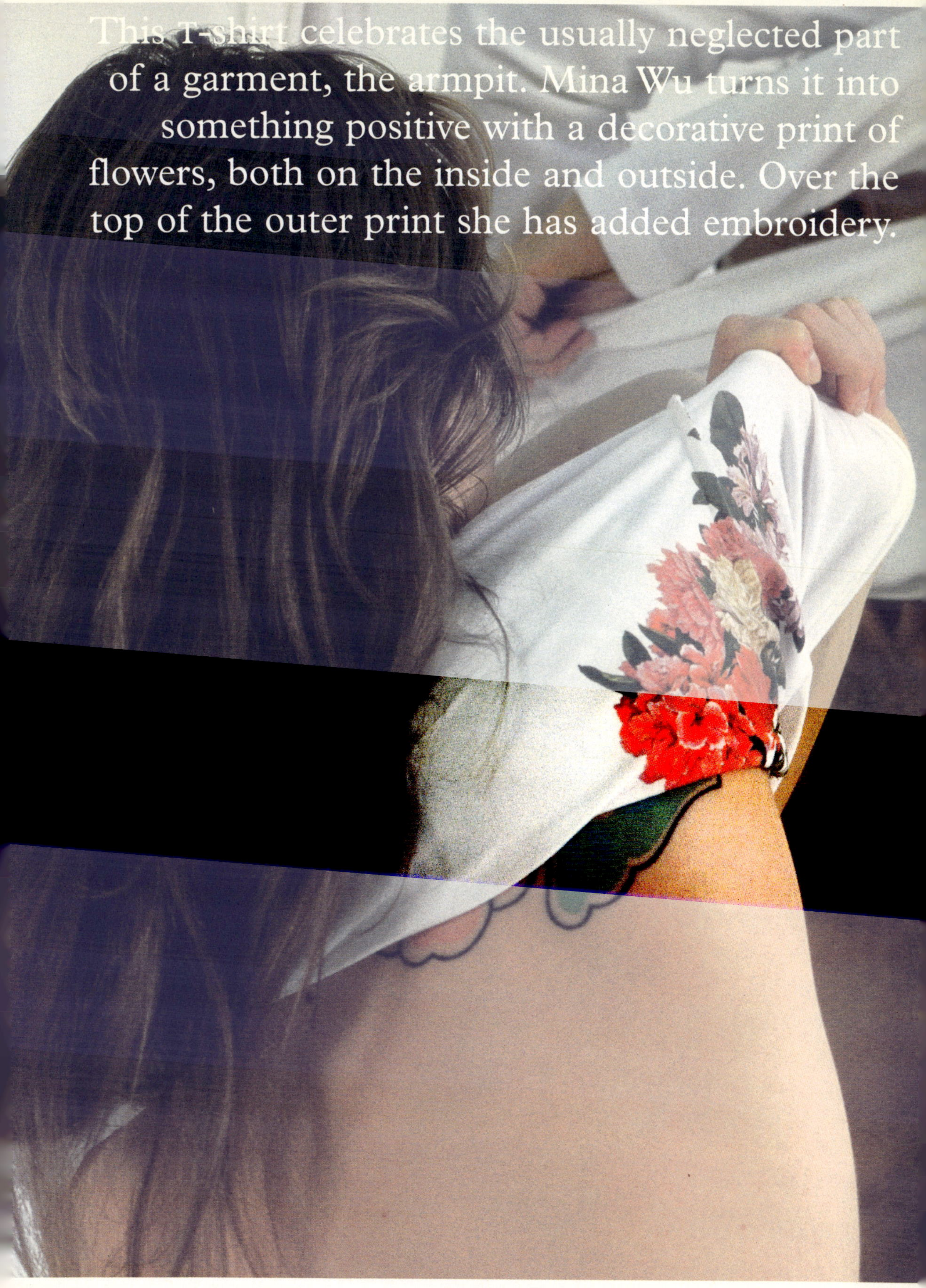

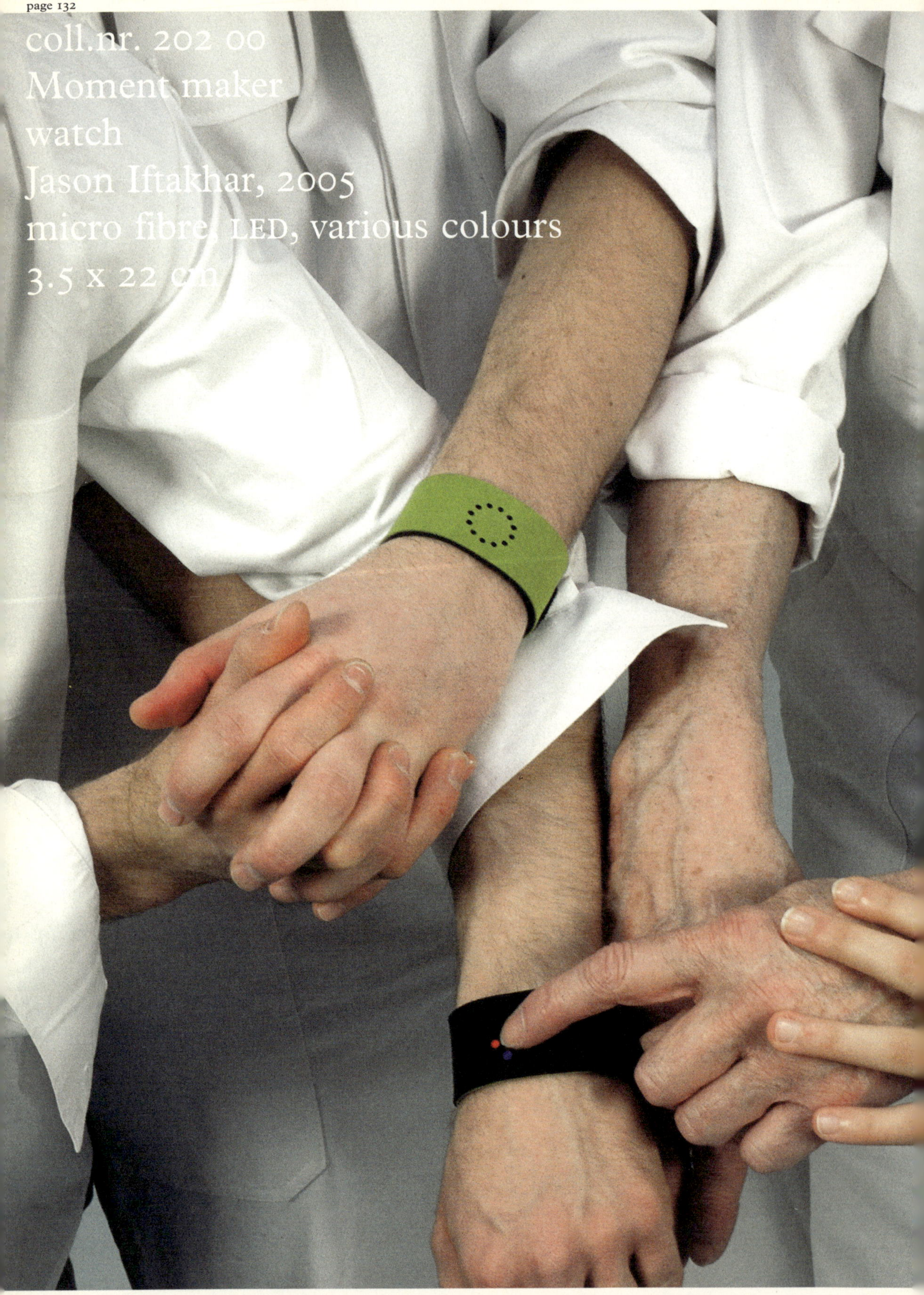

coll.nr. 202 00
Moment maker
watch
Jason Iftakhar, 2005
micro fibre, LED, various colours
3.5 x 22 cm

Moment maker is an innovative design that escapes from the over complexity of time telling, by condensing it into two pinpricks of light. The wristband only shows its identity as a watch when the hidden button is pressed and two coloured LED's are briefly illuminated, indicating the time with an accuracy of five minutes and highlighting a small moment in your day.

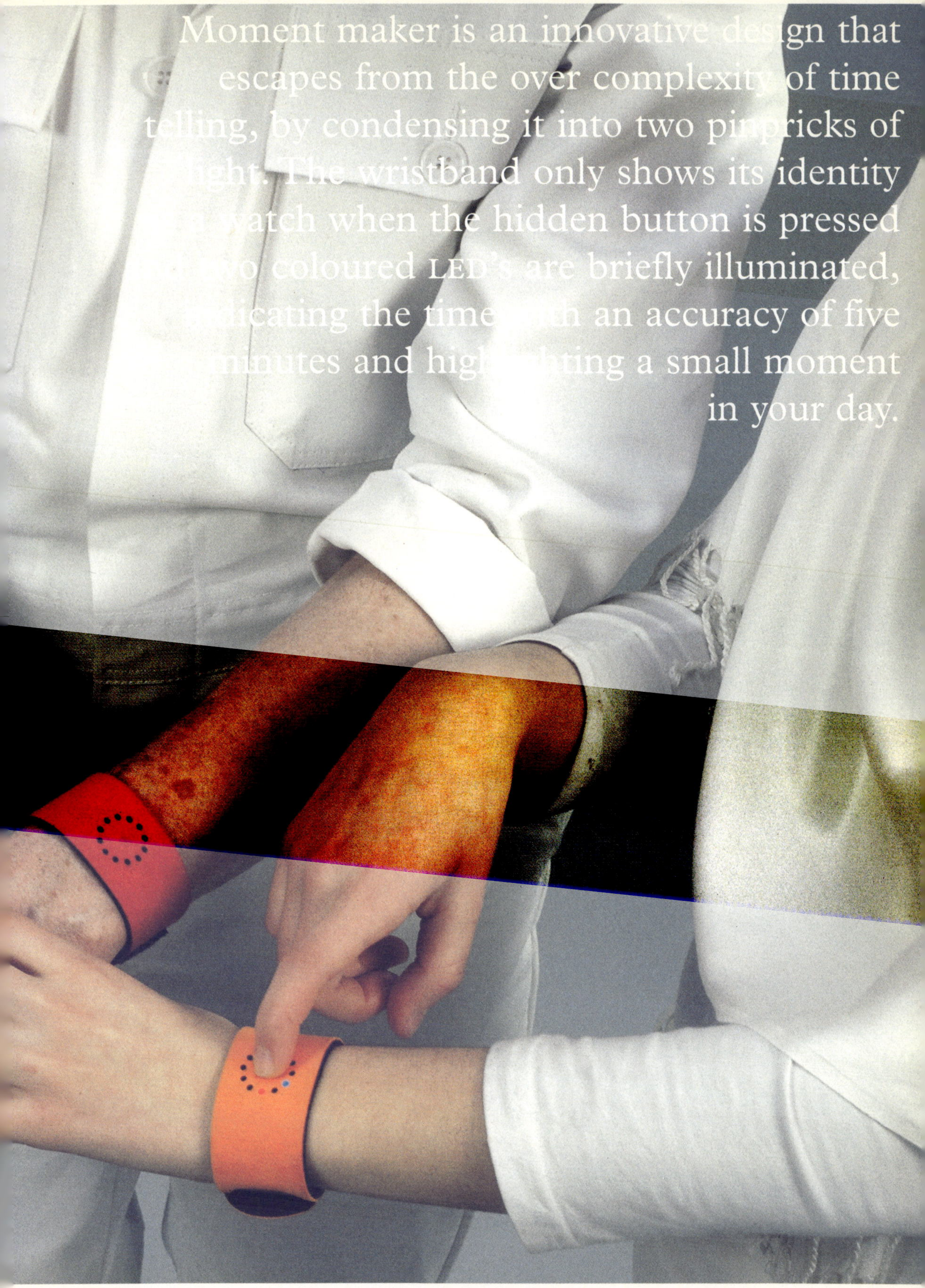

coll.nr. 066 00
Porcelain lamp
Dick van Hoff, 1997
porcelain, max. 60w
ø 23.5 x 16 cm

Porcelain is most commonly connected to tableware and in the context of lighting it is usually referred to the technical aspects. Here it takes on a new role.

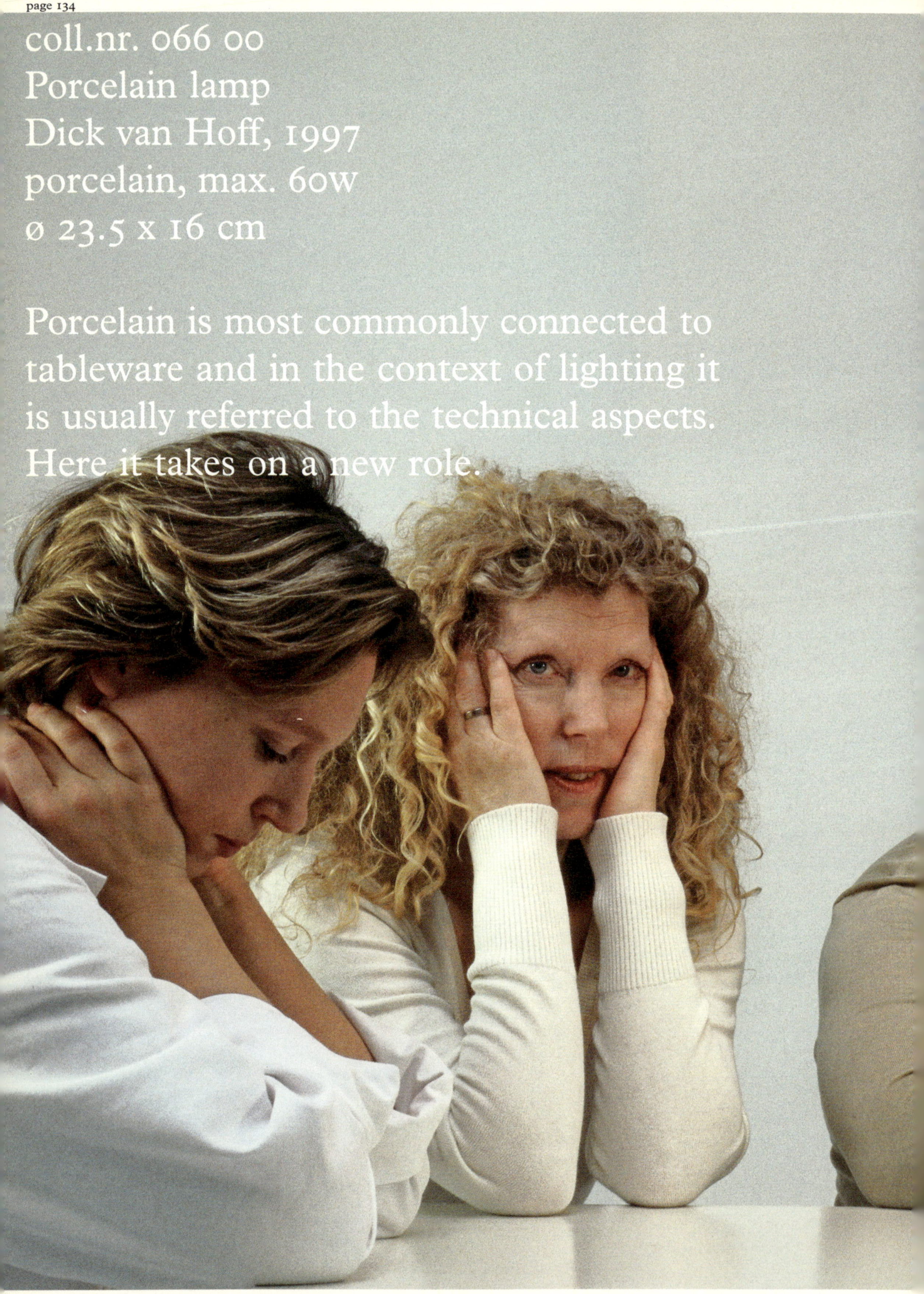

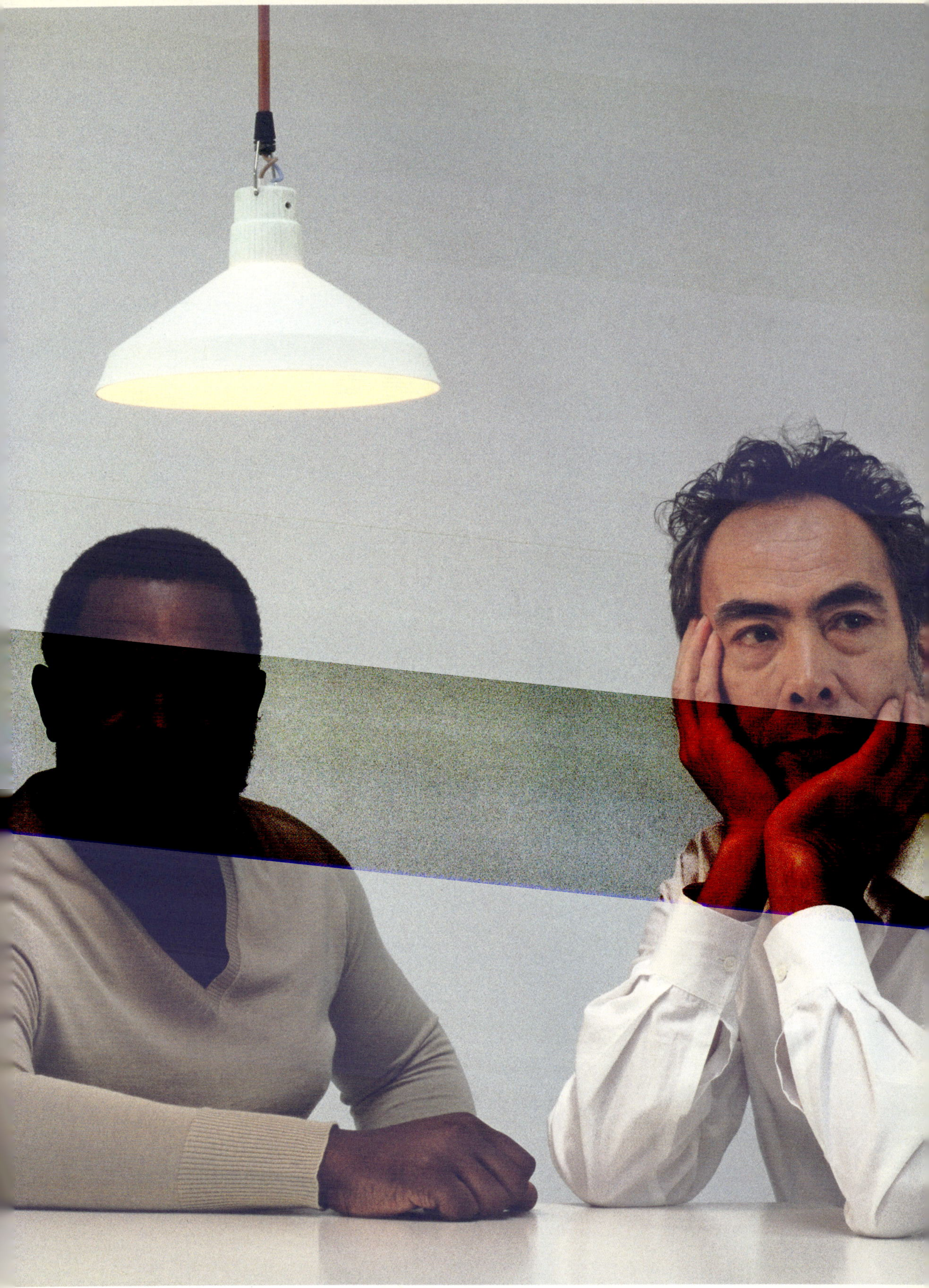

coll.nr. 002 00
Chair with holes
Gijs Bakker, 1989
maple
44 x 43 x 78 cm
numbered edition of 50 pieces

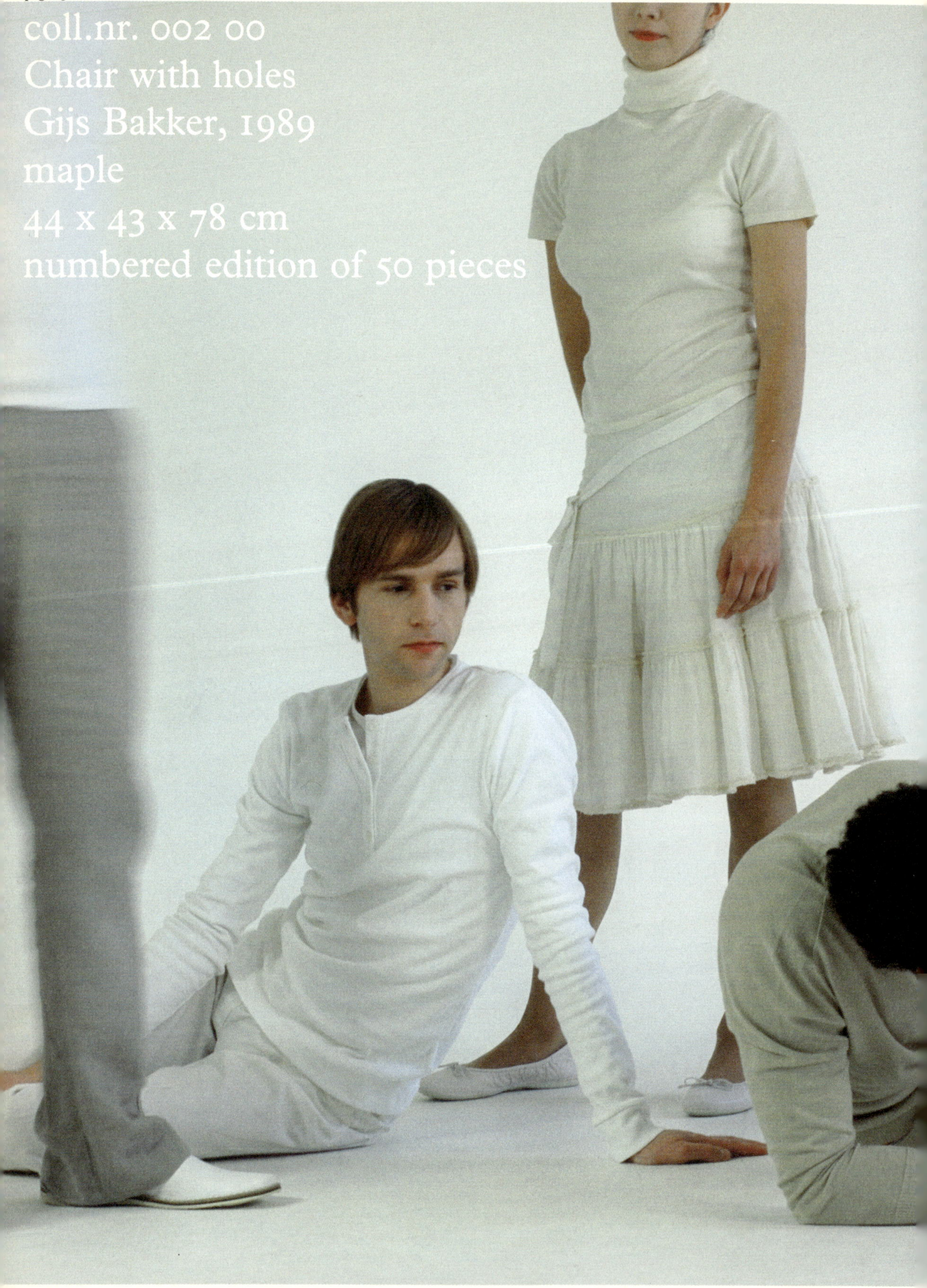

By drilling holes in a given chair it has been made lighter, both visually and physically. The bigger the demands on the construction the smaller the holes. The chair looses almost a third of its weight that way.

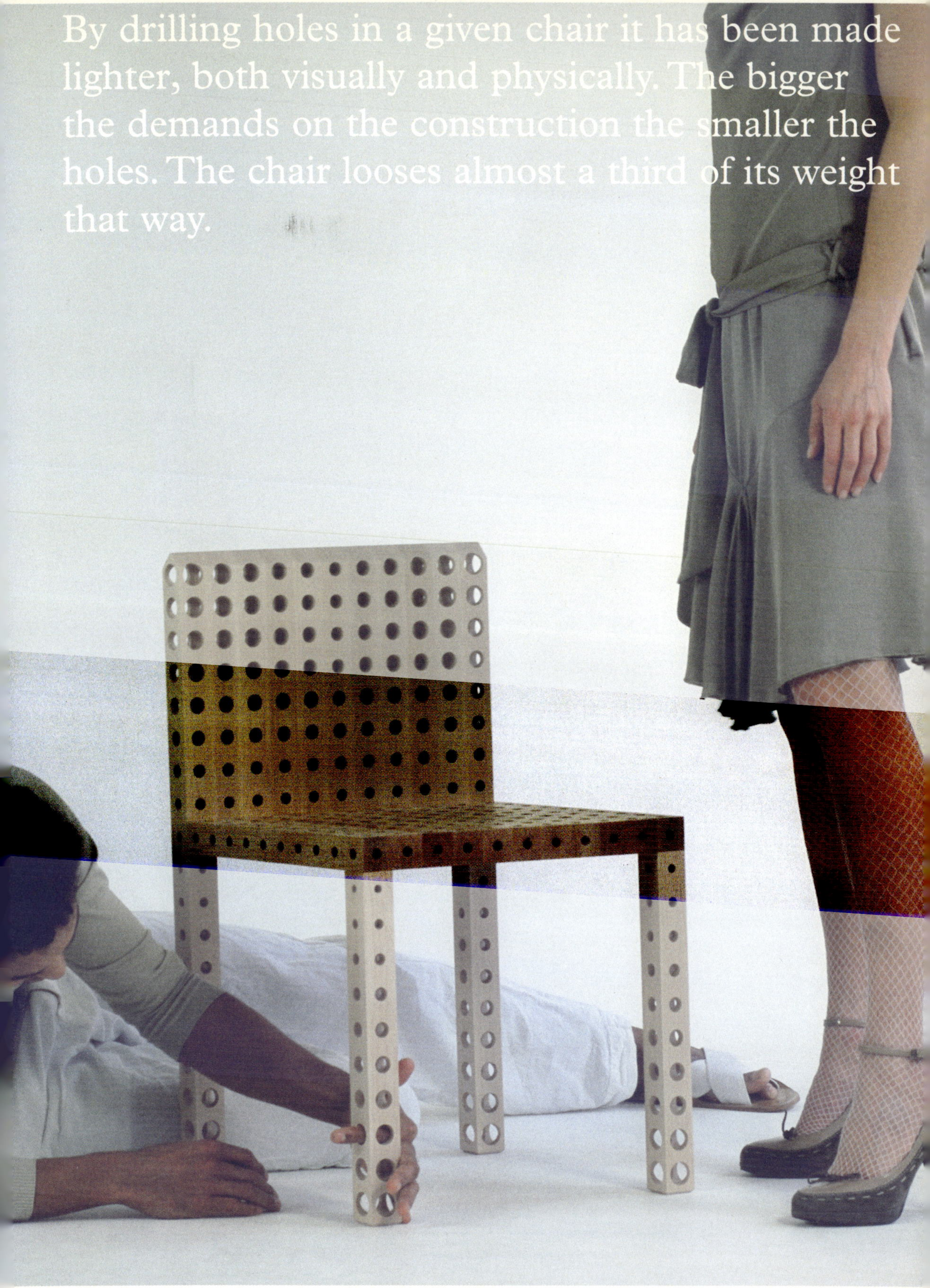

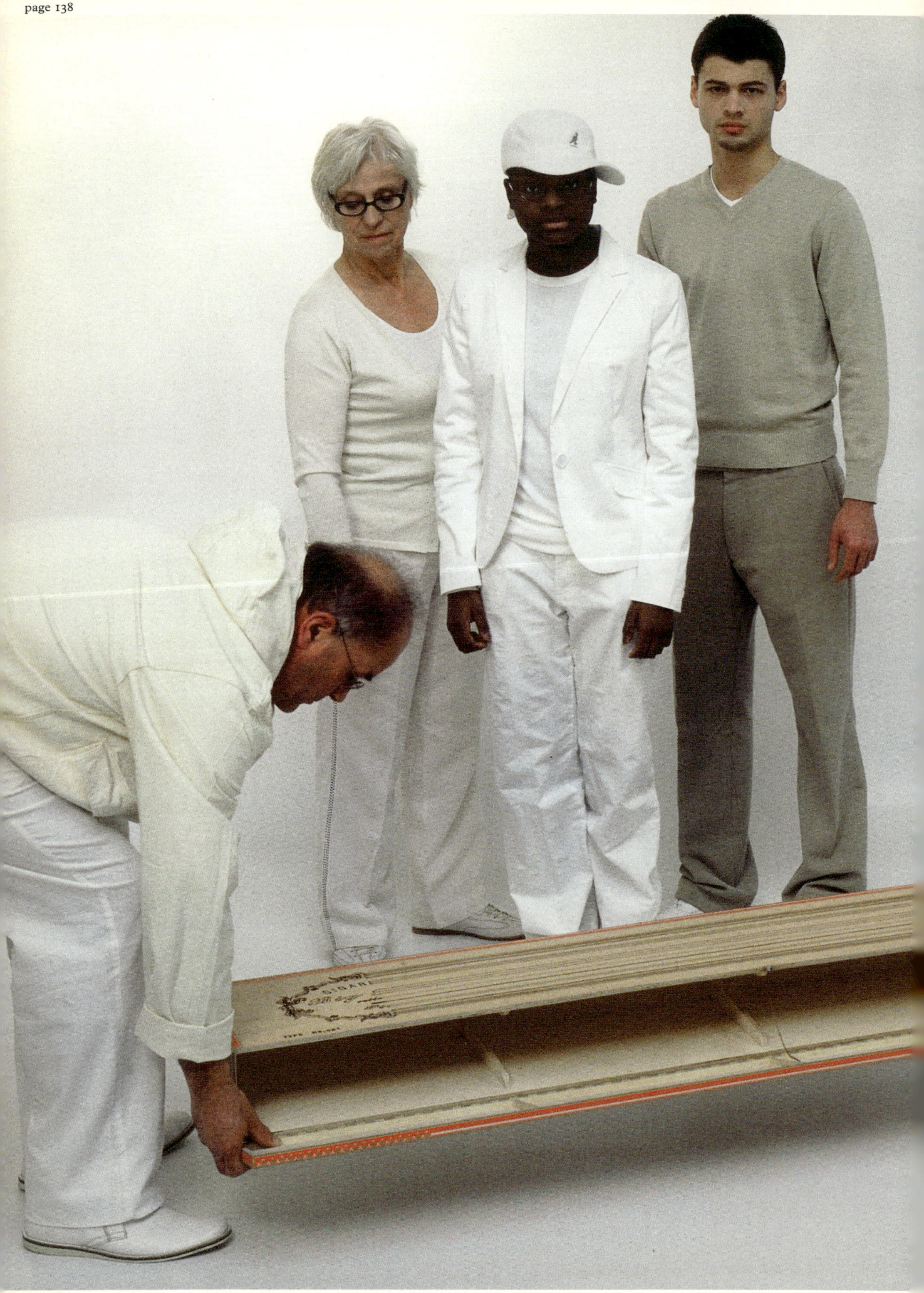

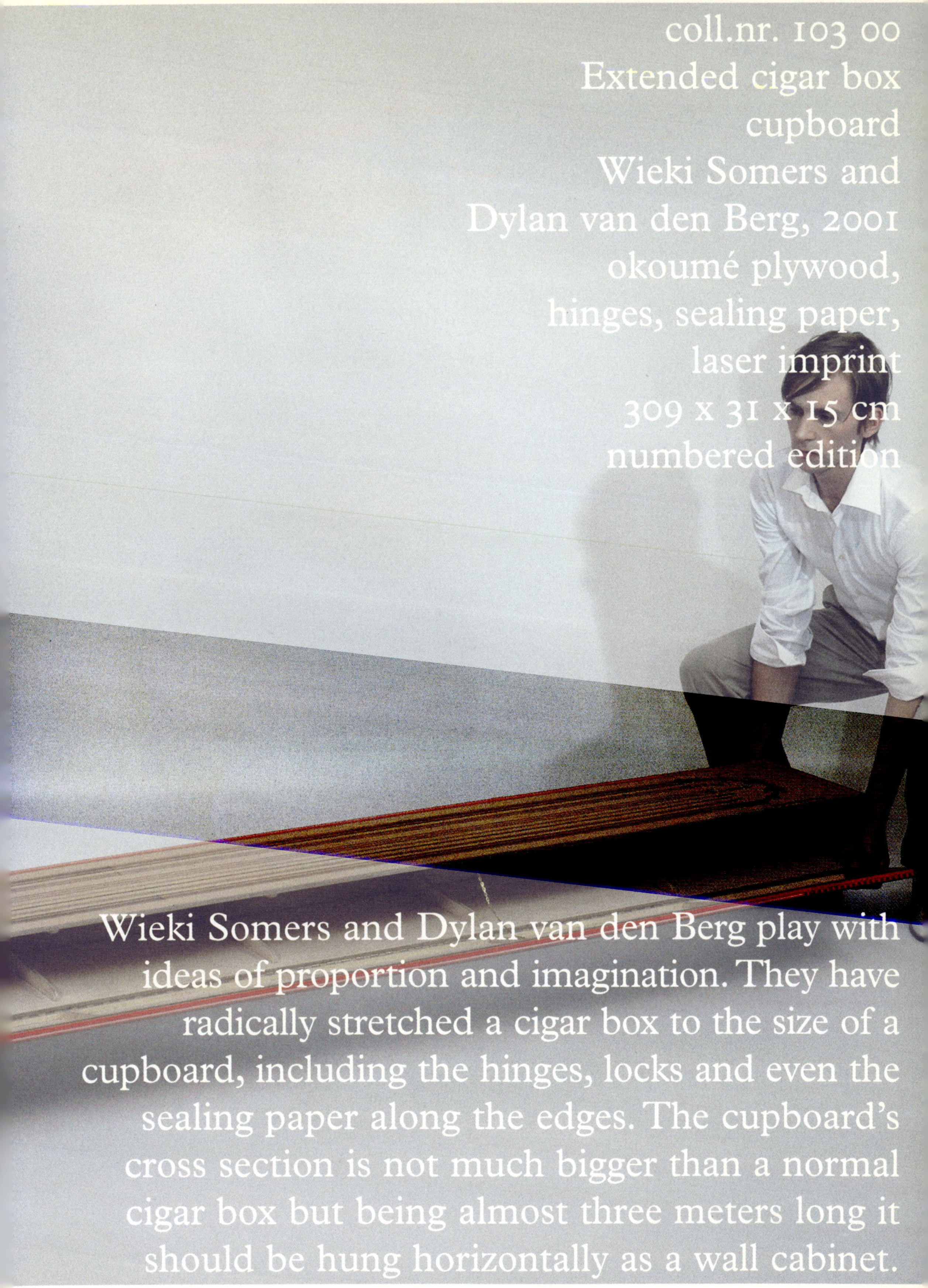

coll.nr. 103 00
Extended cigar box cupboard
Wieki Somers and Dylan van den Berg, 2001
okoumé plywood, hinges, sealing paper, laser imprint
309 x 31 x 15 cm
numbered edition

Wieki Somers and Dylan van den Berg play with ideas of proportion and imagination. They have radically stretched a cigar box to the size of a cupboard, including the hinges, locks and even the sealing paper along the edges. The cupboard's cross section is not much bigger than a normal cigar box but being almost three meters long it should be hung horizontally as a wall cabinet.

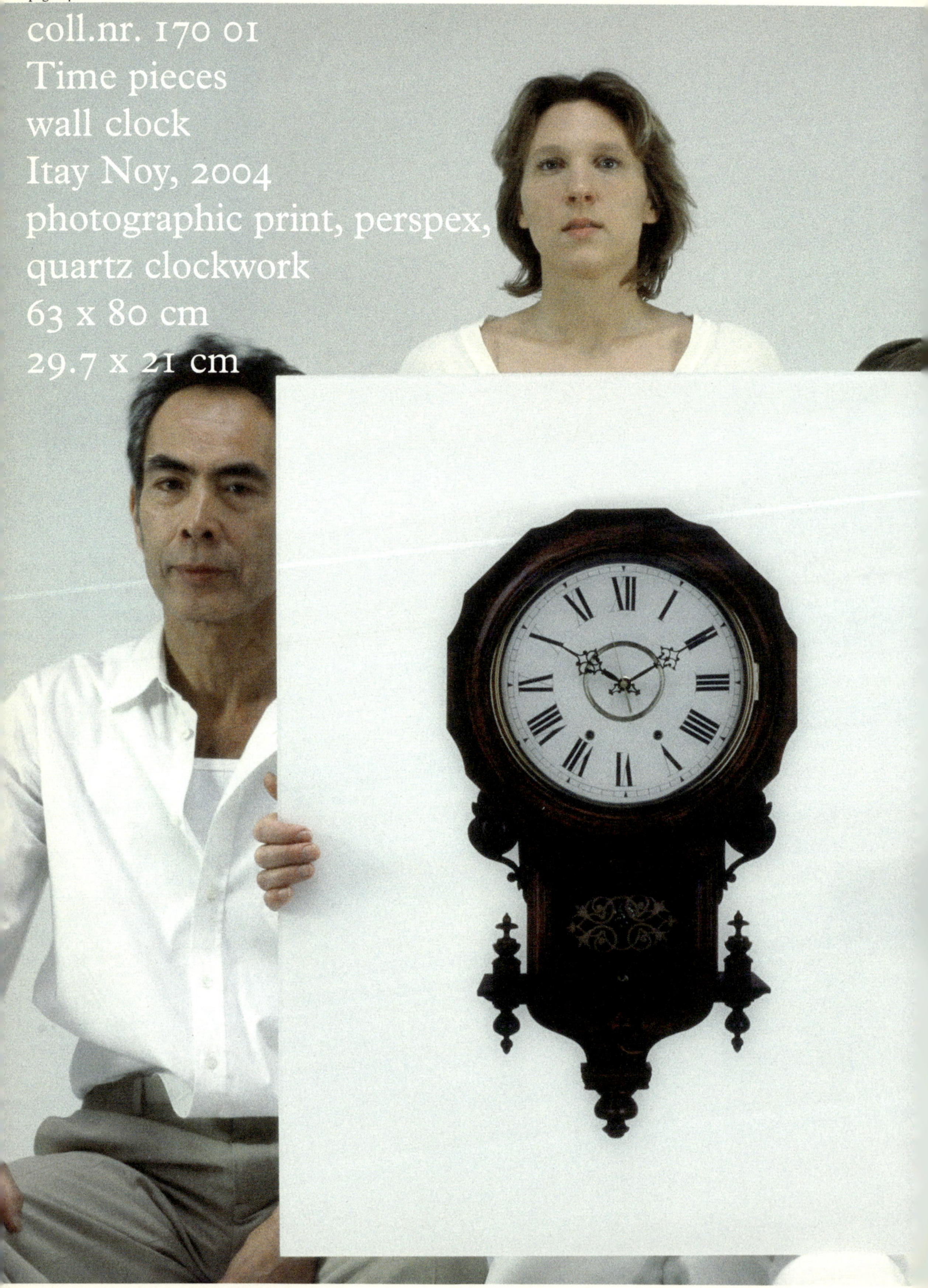
coll.nr. 170 01
Time pieces
wall clock
Itay Noy, 2004
photographic print, perspex,
quartz clockwork
63 x 80 cm
29.7 x 21 cm

Here a new clock is created with the ghost of an old one. Antique wall clocks have been photographed, scaled to their original size and fitted with new mechanisms. The larger version chimes every 15 minutes as a constant reminder of the original.

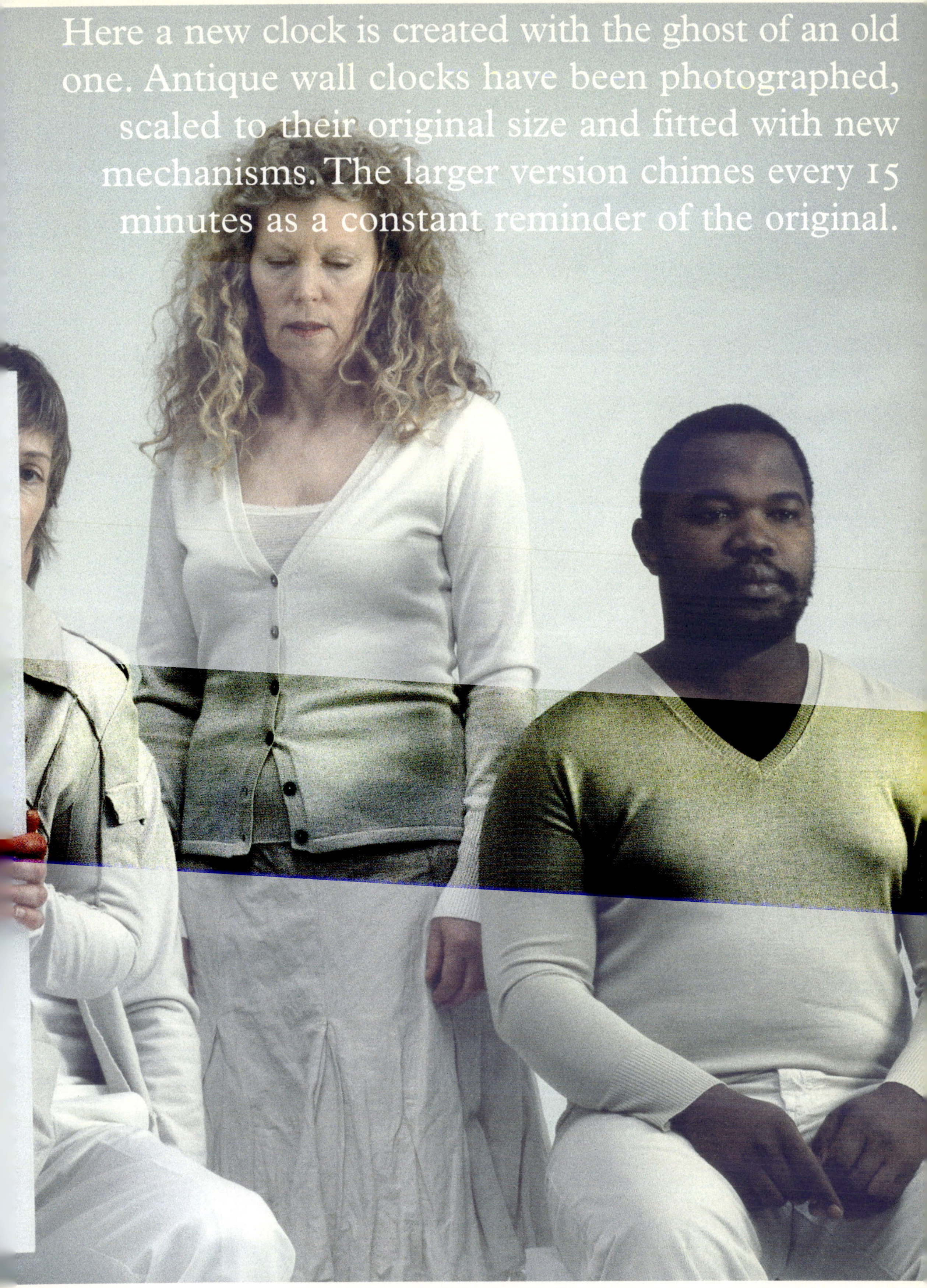

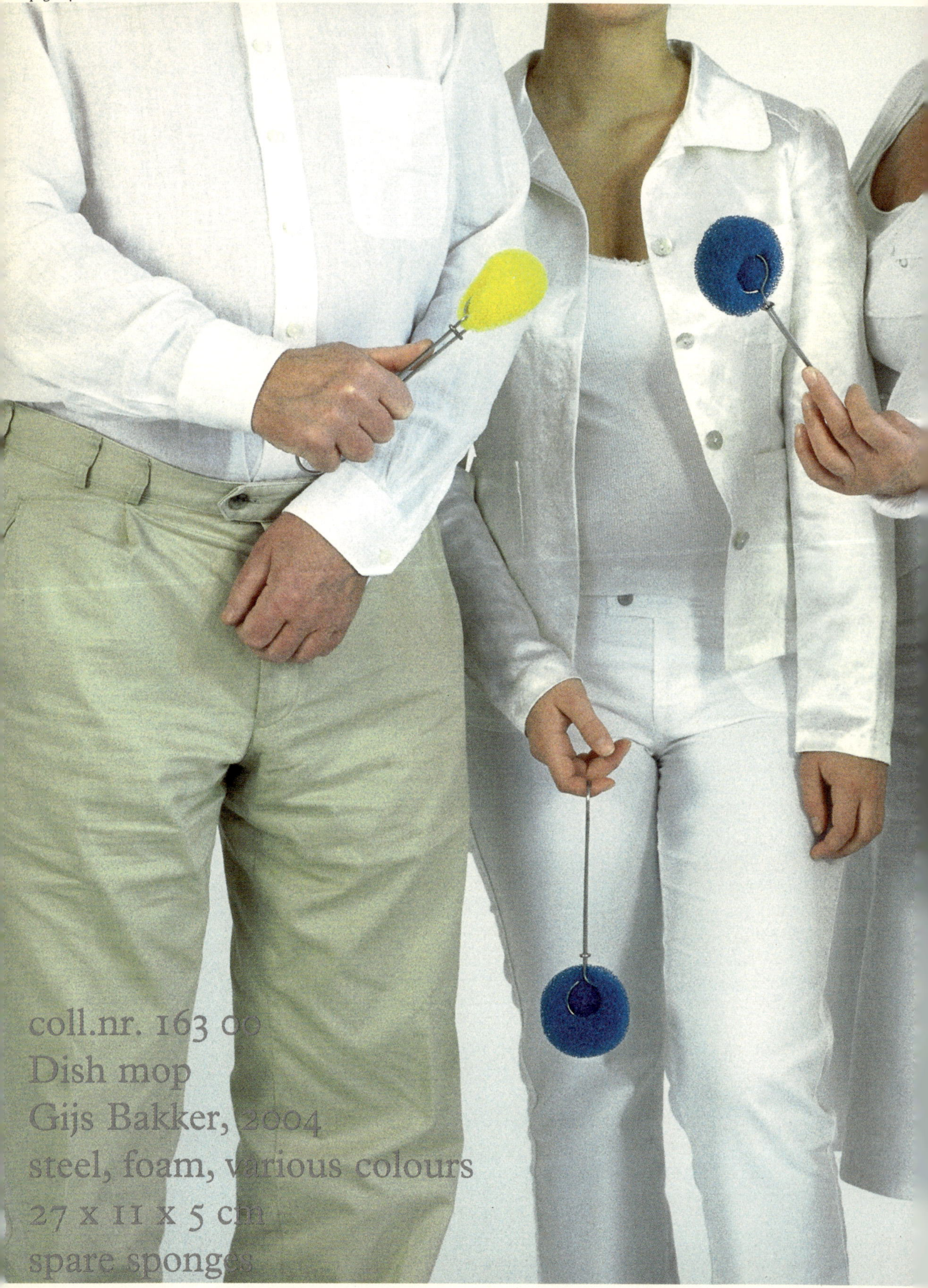

coll.nr. 163 00
Dish mop
Gijs Bakker, 2004
steel, foam, various colours
27 x 11 x 5 cm
spare sponges

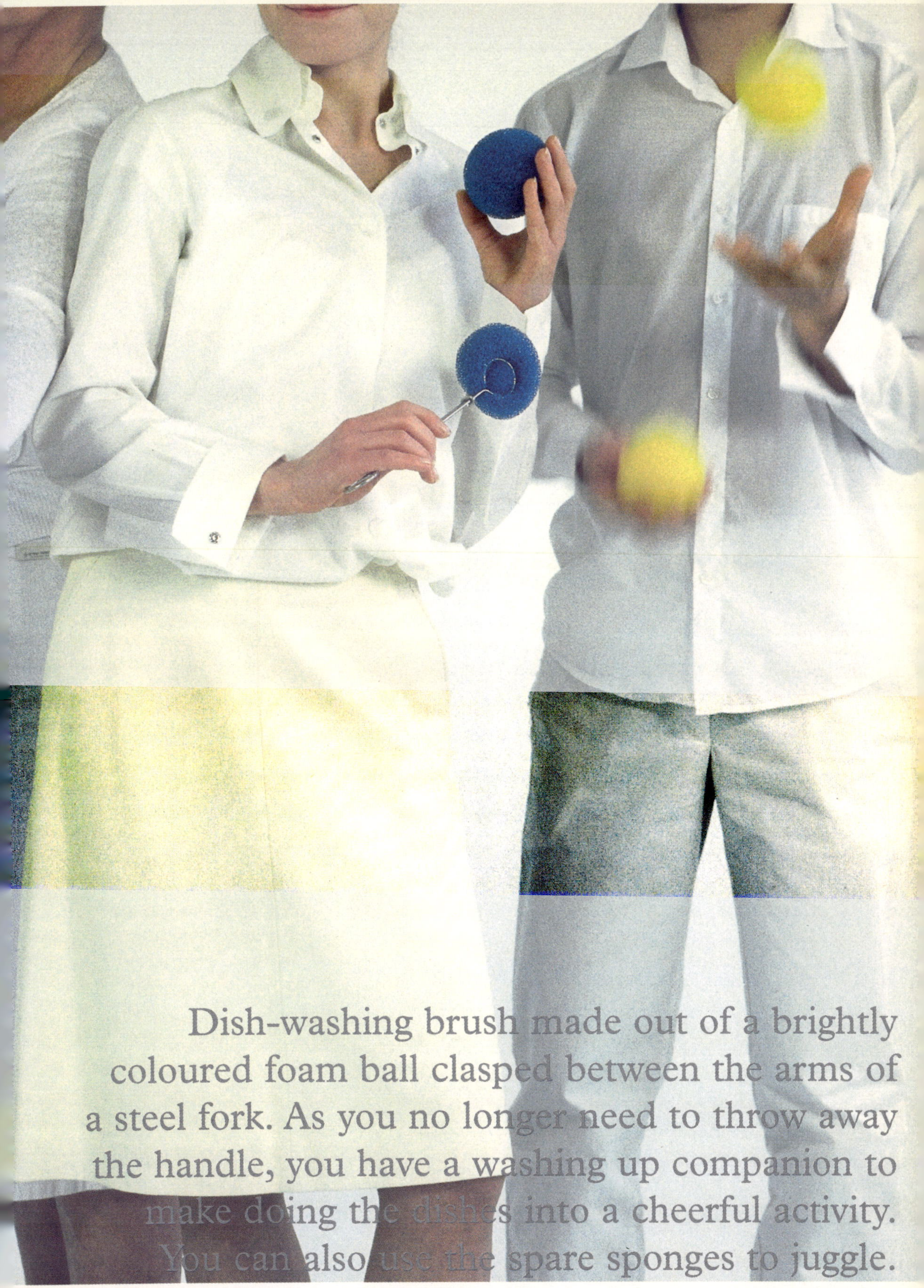

Dish-washing brush made out of a brightly coloured foam ball clasped between the arms of a steel fork. As you no longer need to throw away the handle, you have a washing up companion to make doing the dishes into a cheerful activity. You can also use the spare sponges to juggle.

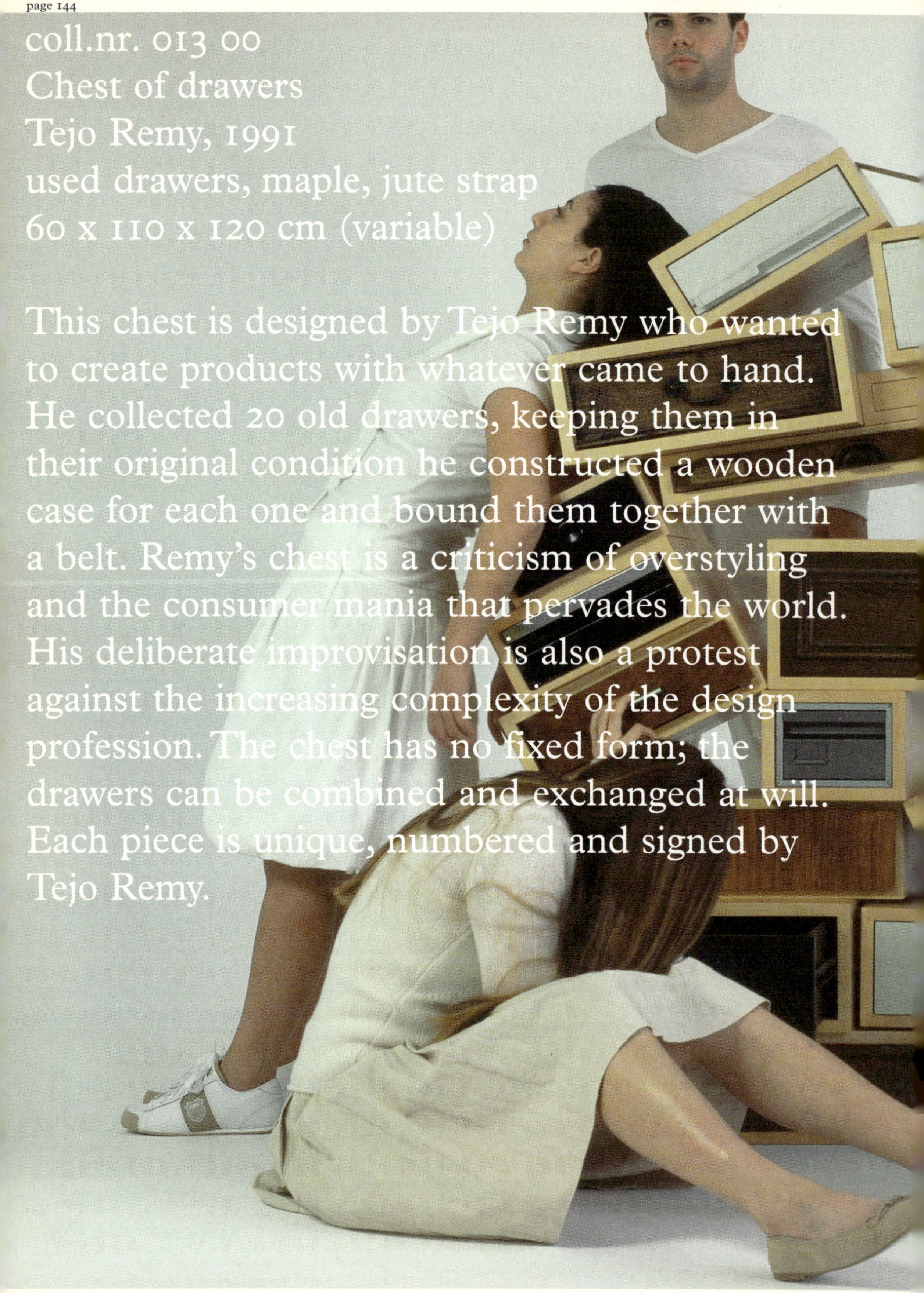

coll.nr. 013 00
Chest of drawers
Tejo Remy, 1991
used drawers, maple, jute strap
60 x 110 x 120 cm (variable)

This chest is designed by Tejo Remy who wanted to create products with whatever came to hand. He collected 20 old drawers, keeping them in their original condition he constructed a wooden case for each one and bound them together with a belt. Remy's chest is a criticism of overstyling and the consumer mania that pervades the world. His deliberate improvisation is also a protest against the increasing complexity of the design profession. The chest has no fixed form; the drawers can be combined and exchanged at will. Each piece is unique, numbered and signed by Tejo Remy.

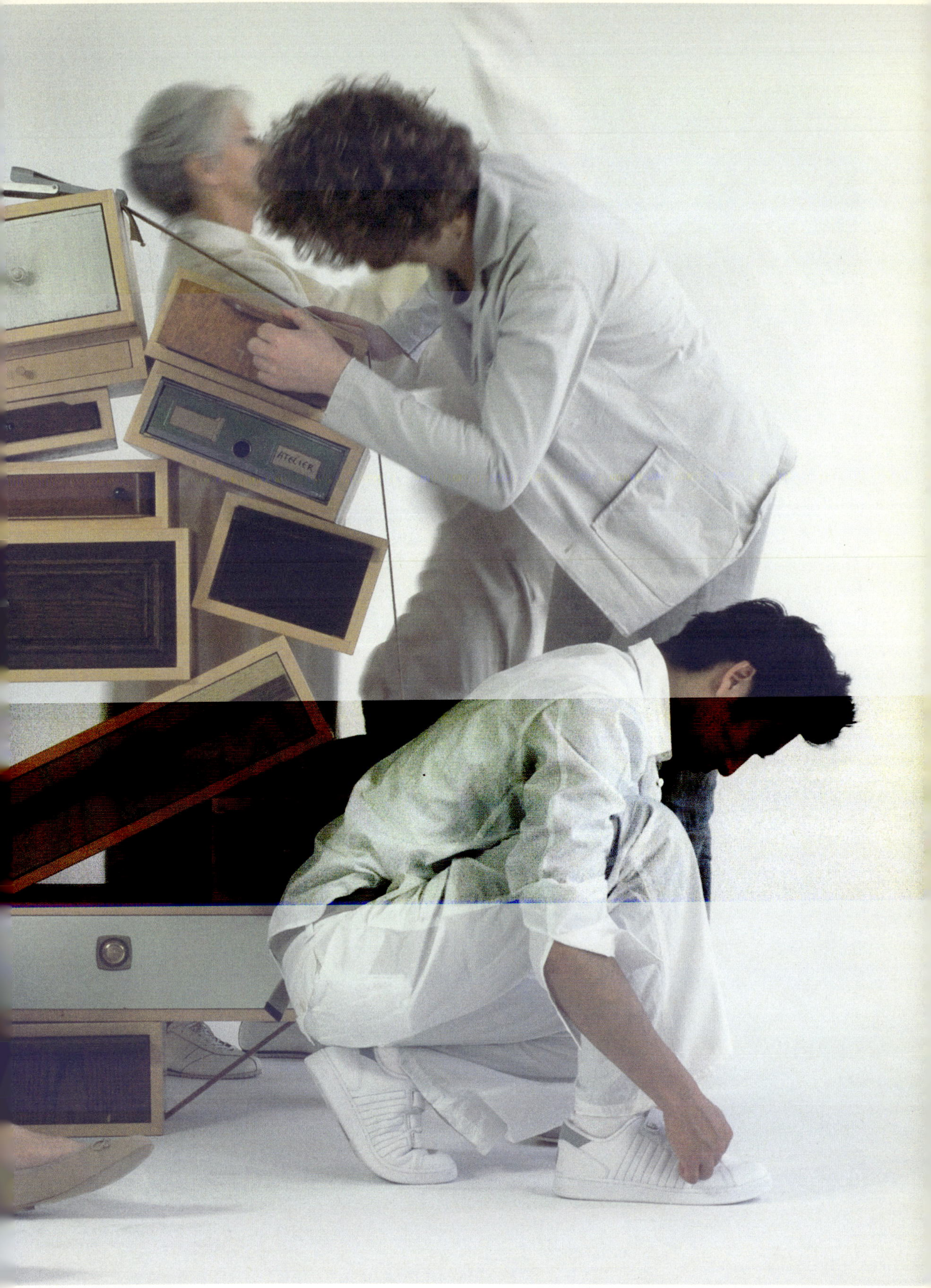
ATELIER

coll.nr. 073 00
Gardening bench
Jurgen Bey, 1999
hay, resin
200 x 72 x 78 cm

This bench starts and ends with nature. Natural waste is compressed with resin and cut at the desired length. The identity of the material is not lost in the process and nature dictates the lifespan of the bench.

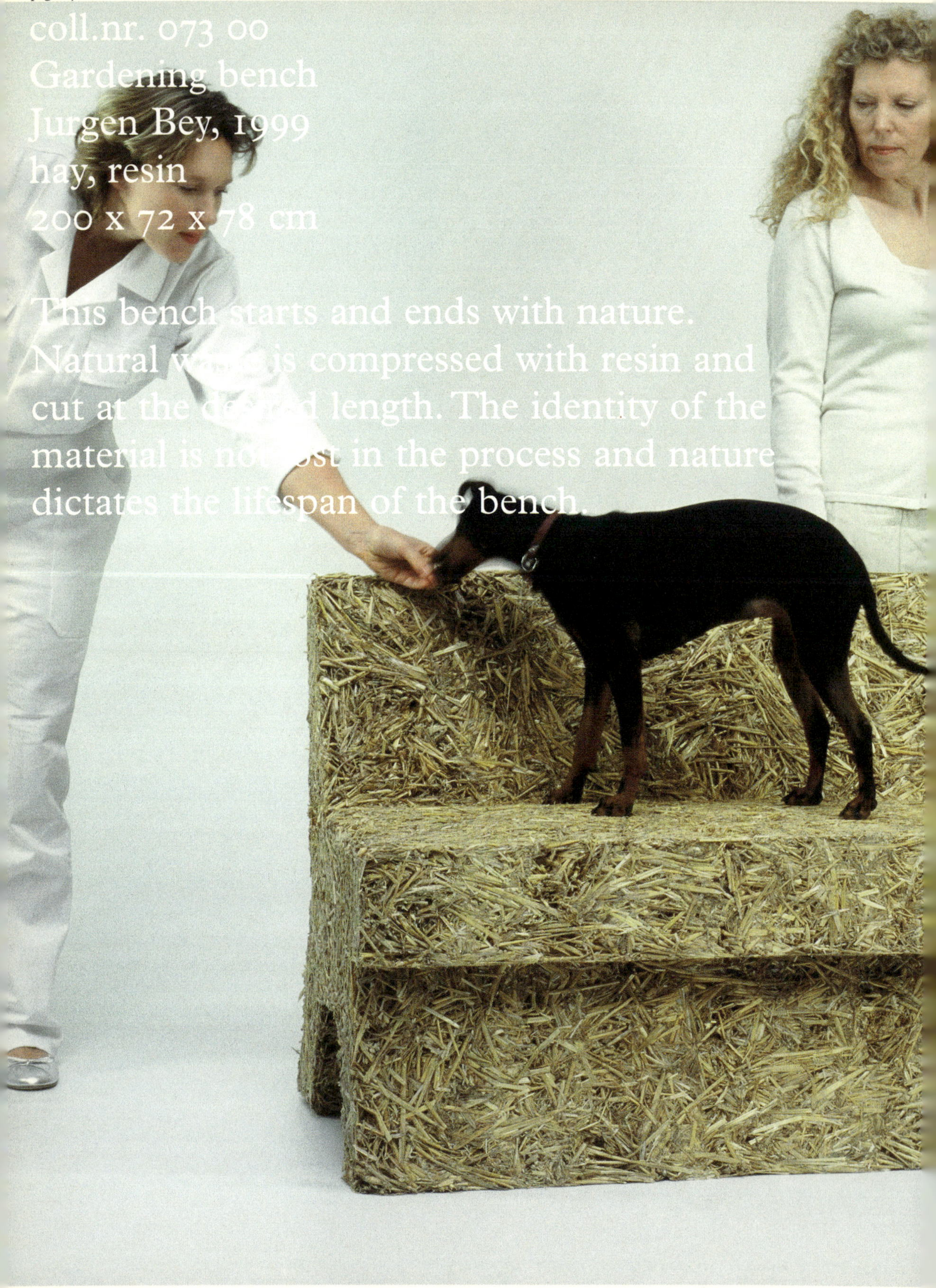

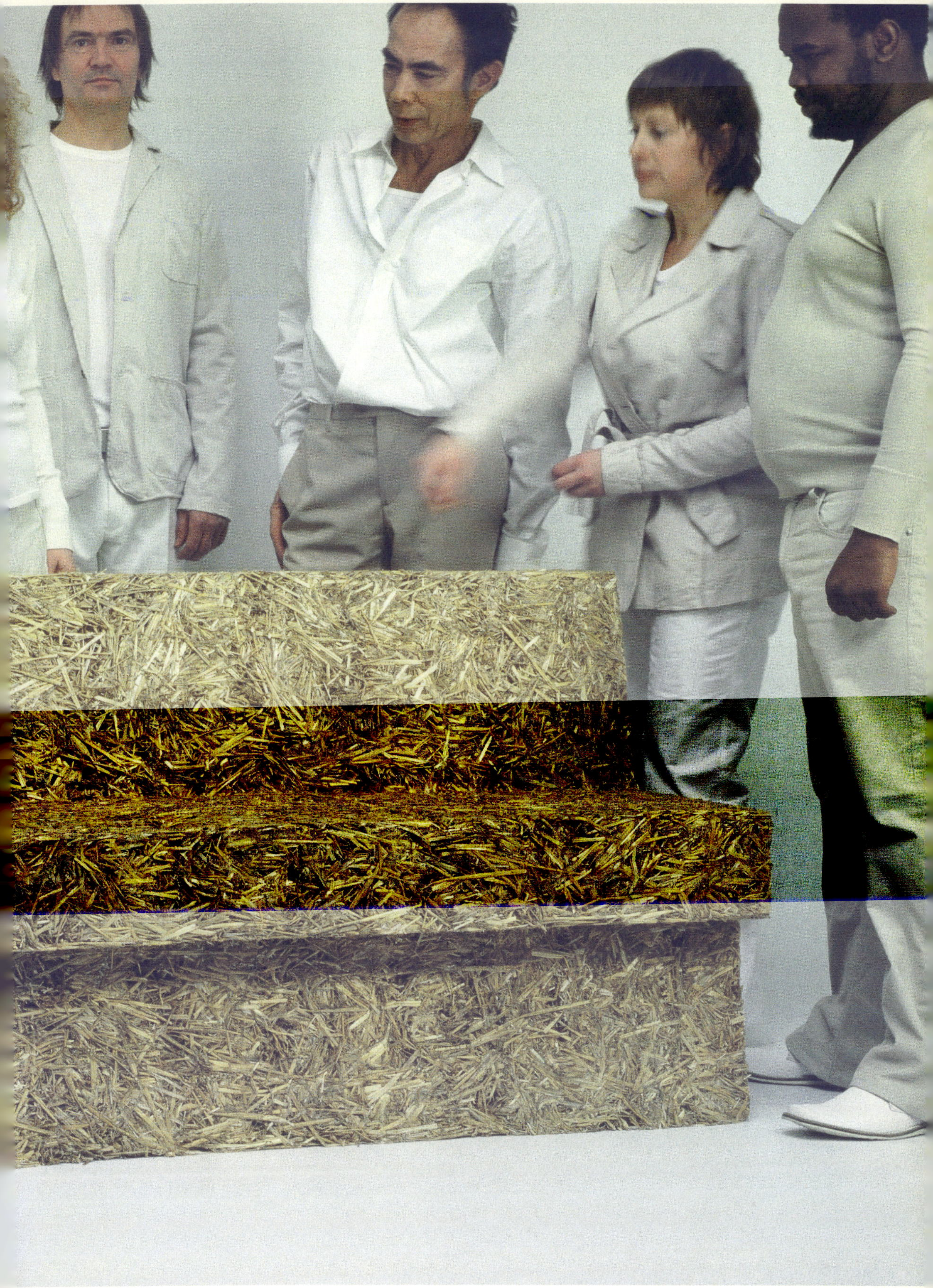

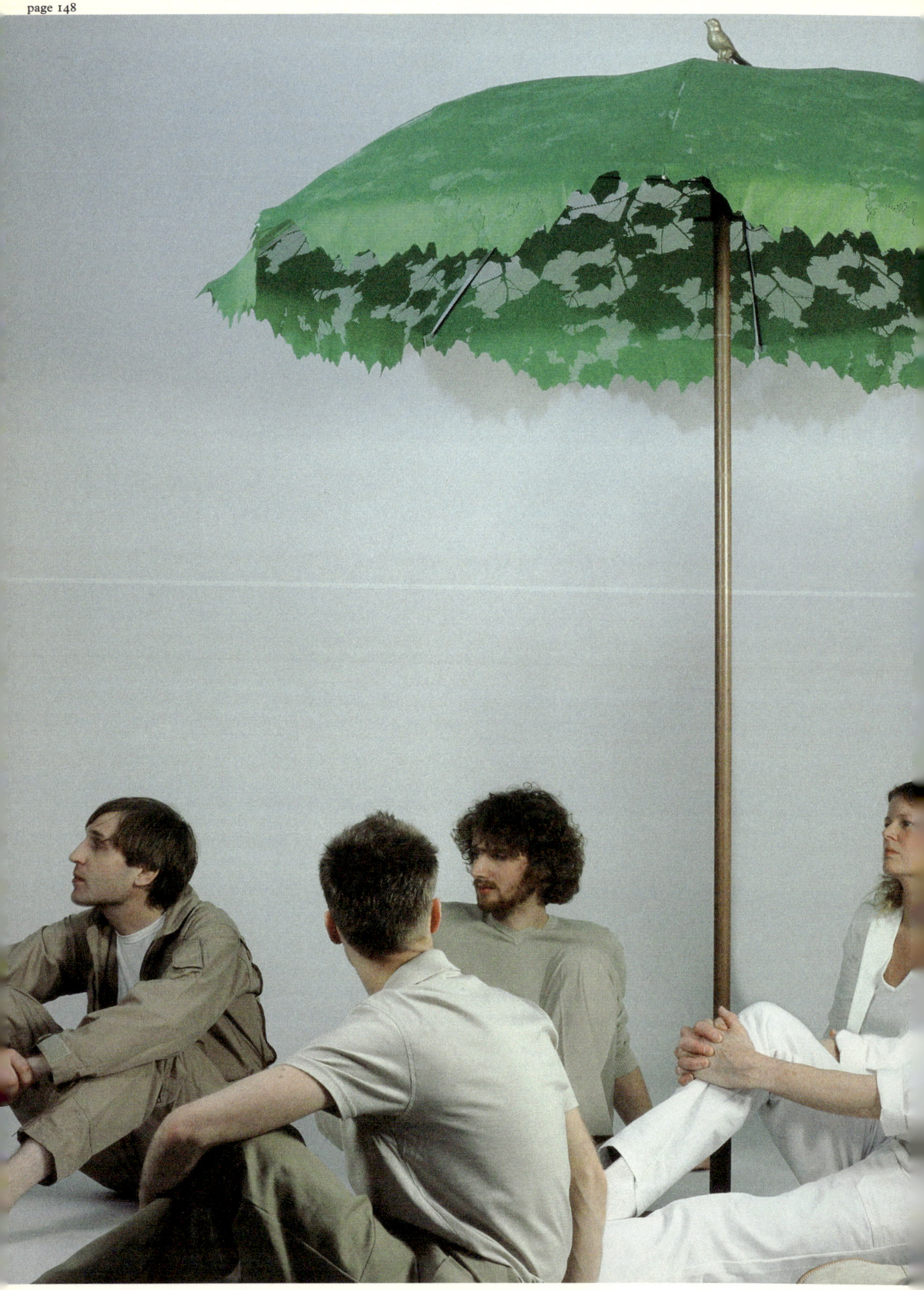

coll.nr. 182 00
Shadylace
parasol
Chris Kabel, 2004
green polyester, wood, resin (gold)
white polyester, aluminum, resin (silver)
ø 210 x 235 cm

This parasol allows just a little sun to shine through, creating a dappled shade. It comes complete with a small bird perched on top.

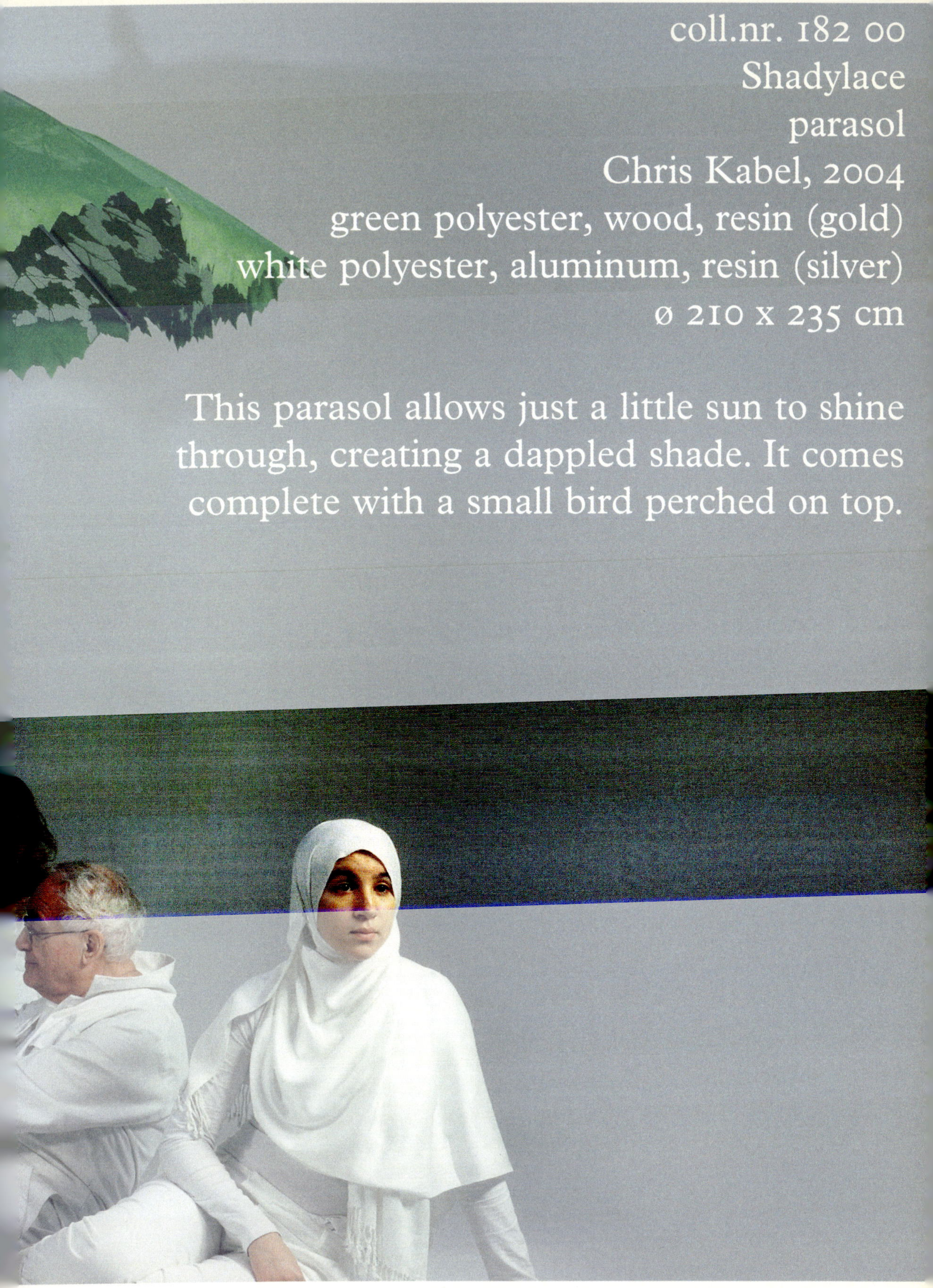

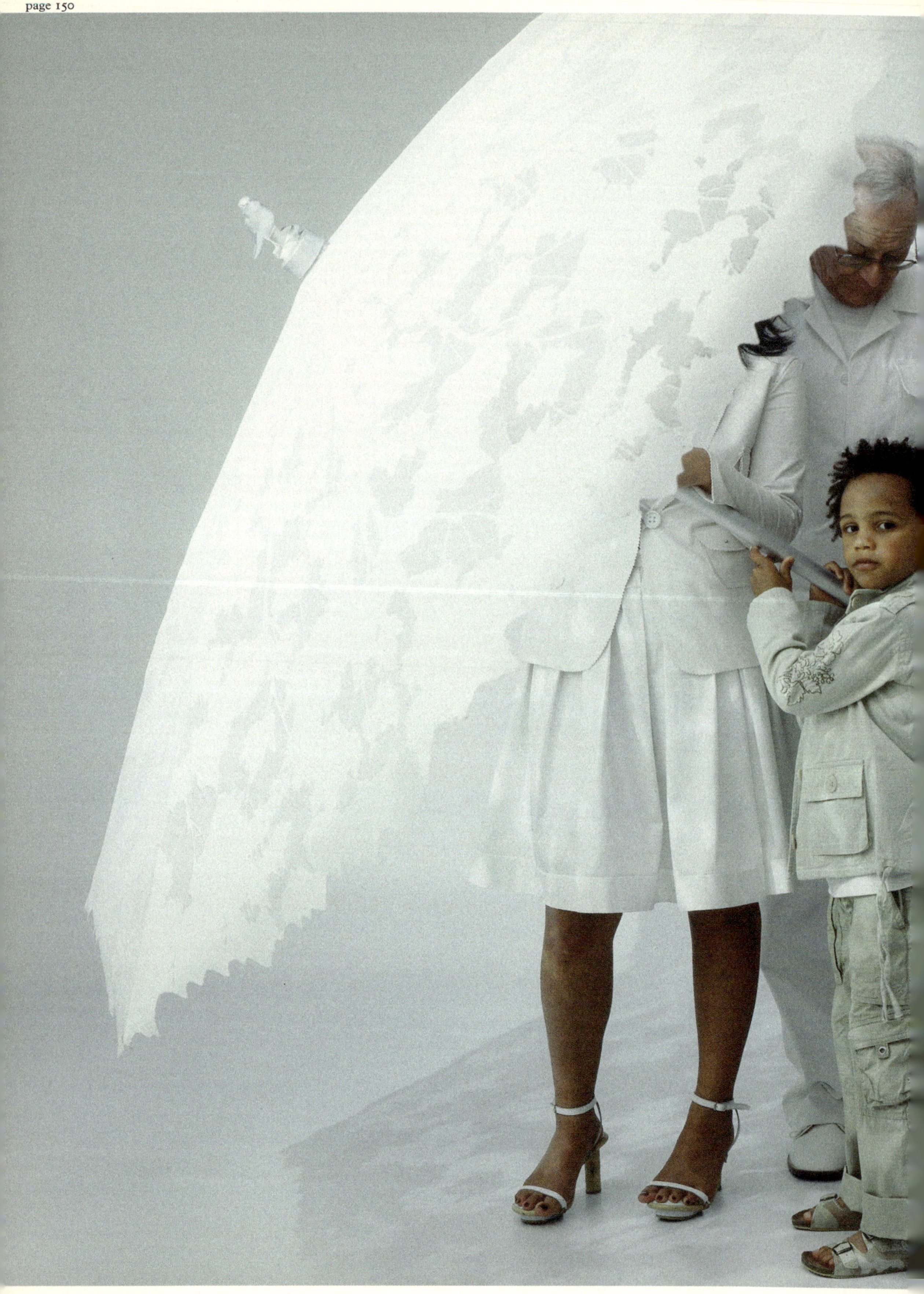

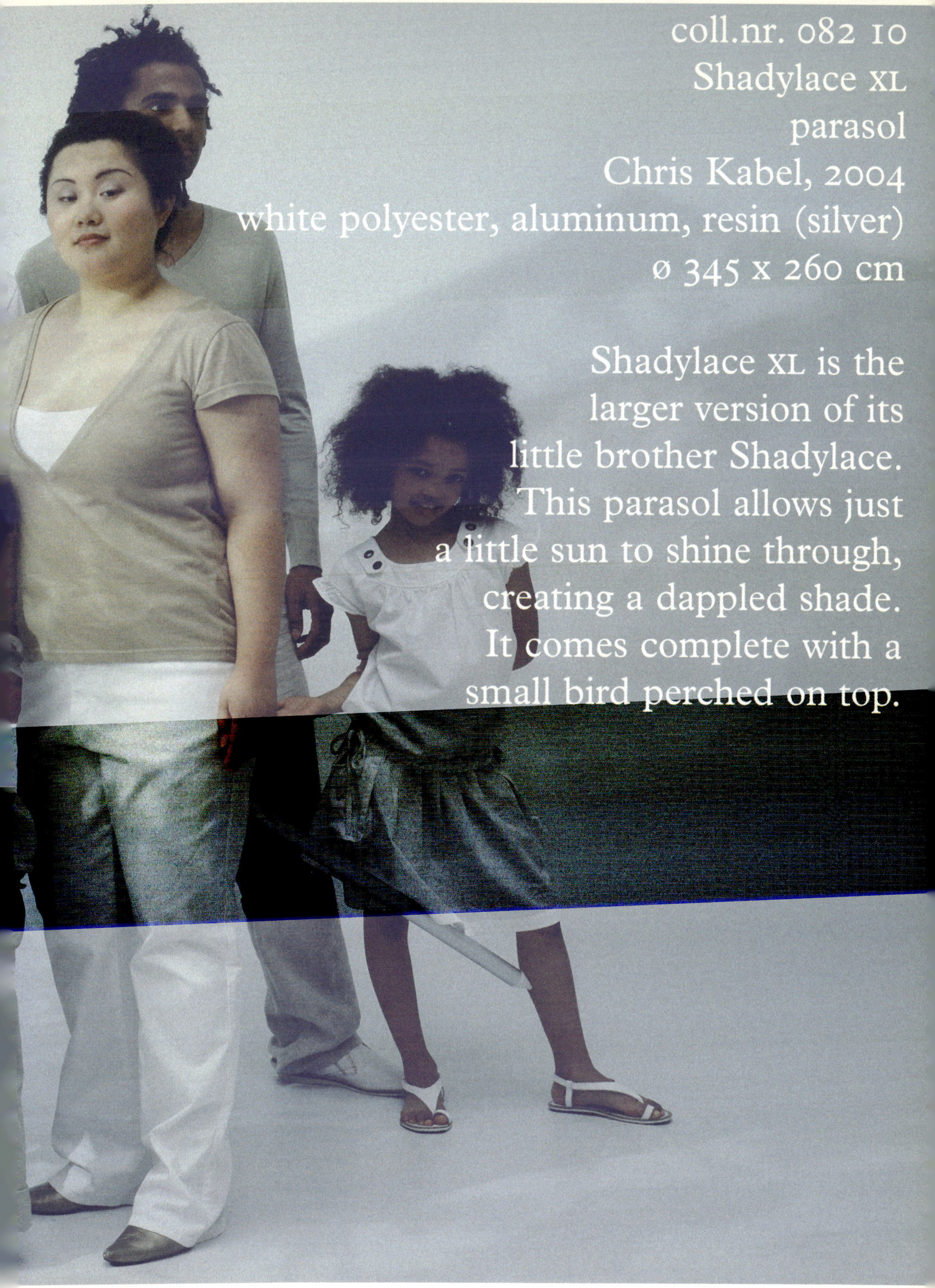

coll.nr. 082 10
Shadylace XL
parasol
Chris Kabel, 2004
white polyester, aluminum, resin (silver)
ø 345 x 260 cm

Shadylace XL is the larger version of its little brother Shadylace. This parasol allows just a little sun to shine through, creating a dappled shade. It comes complete with a small bird perched on top.

coll.nr. 219 00
Swing with the plants
Marcel Wanders, 2000
polyethylene, nylon rope
75 x 23 x 10 cm

The seat of the swing can be filled with soil and seeds planted inside. As the vines grow up the ropes, it becomes a poetic resting place for either your garden or your living room.

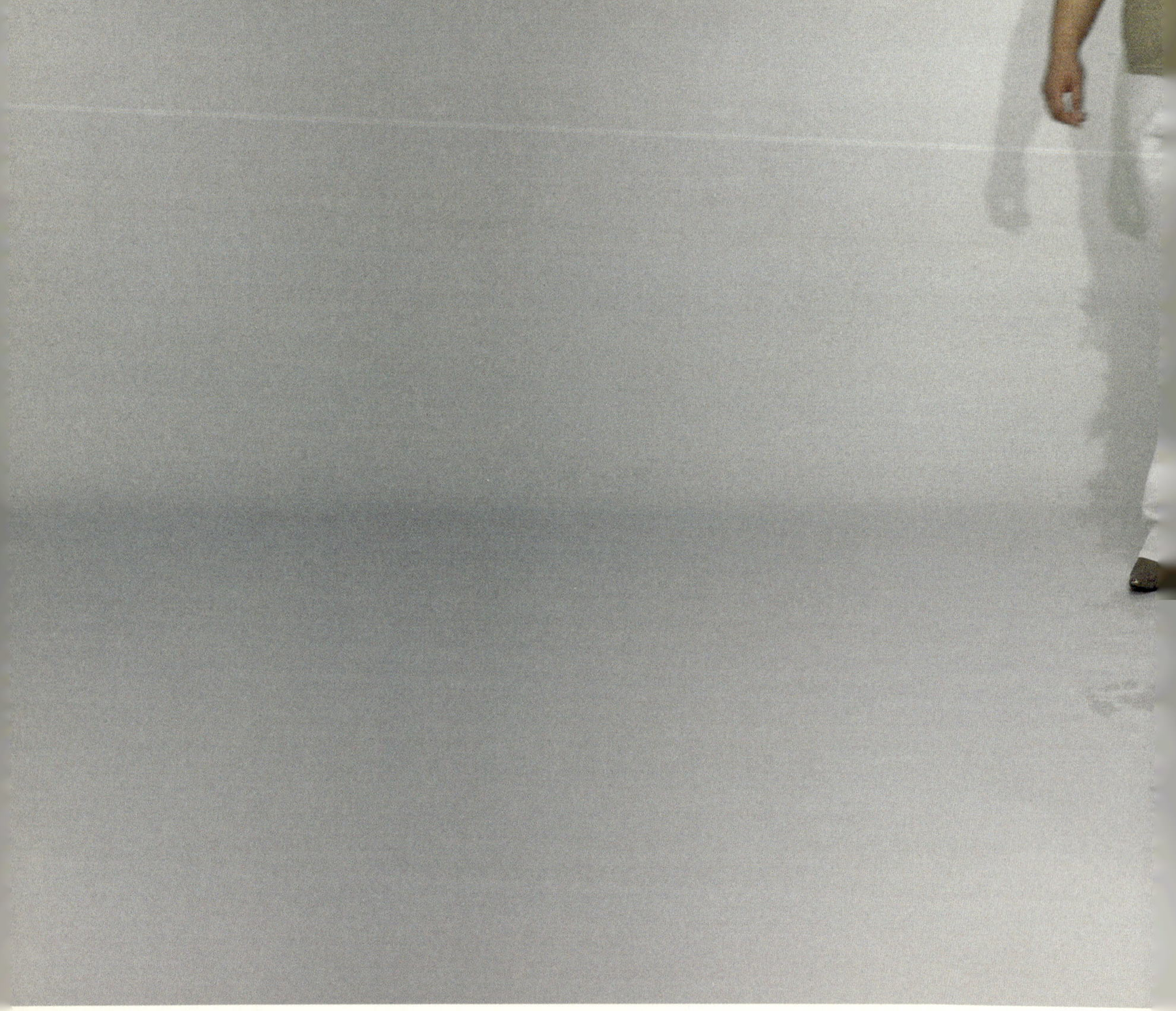

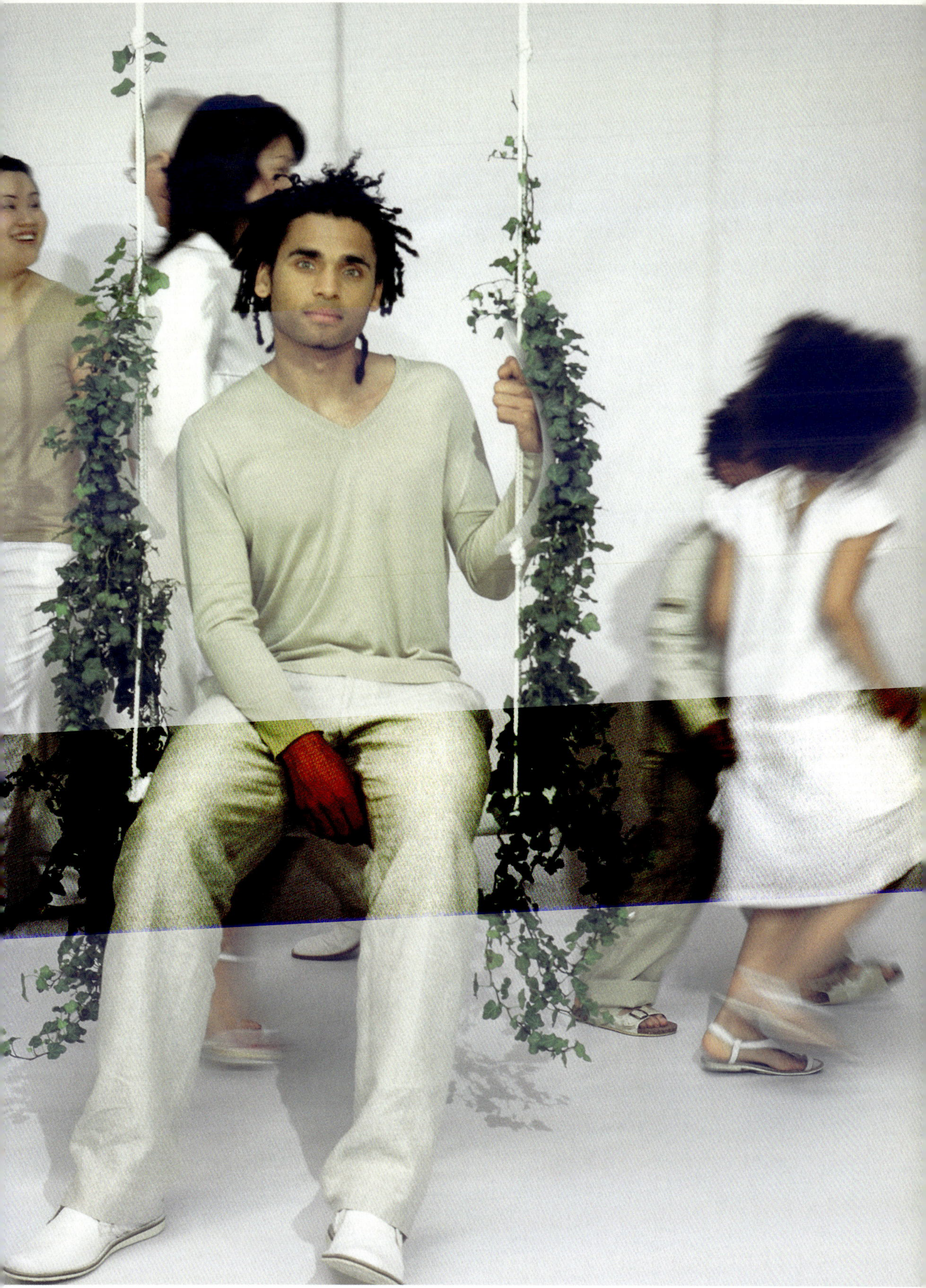

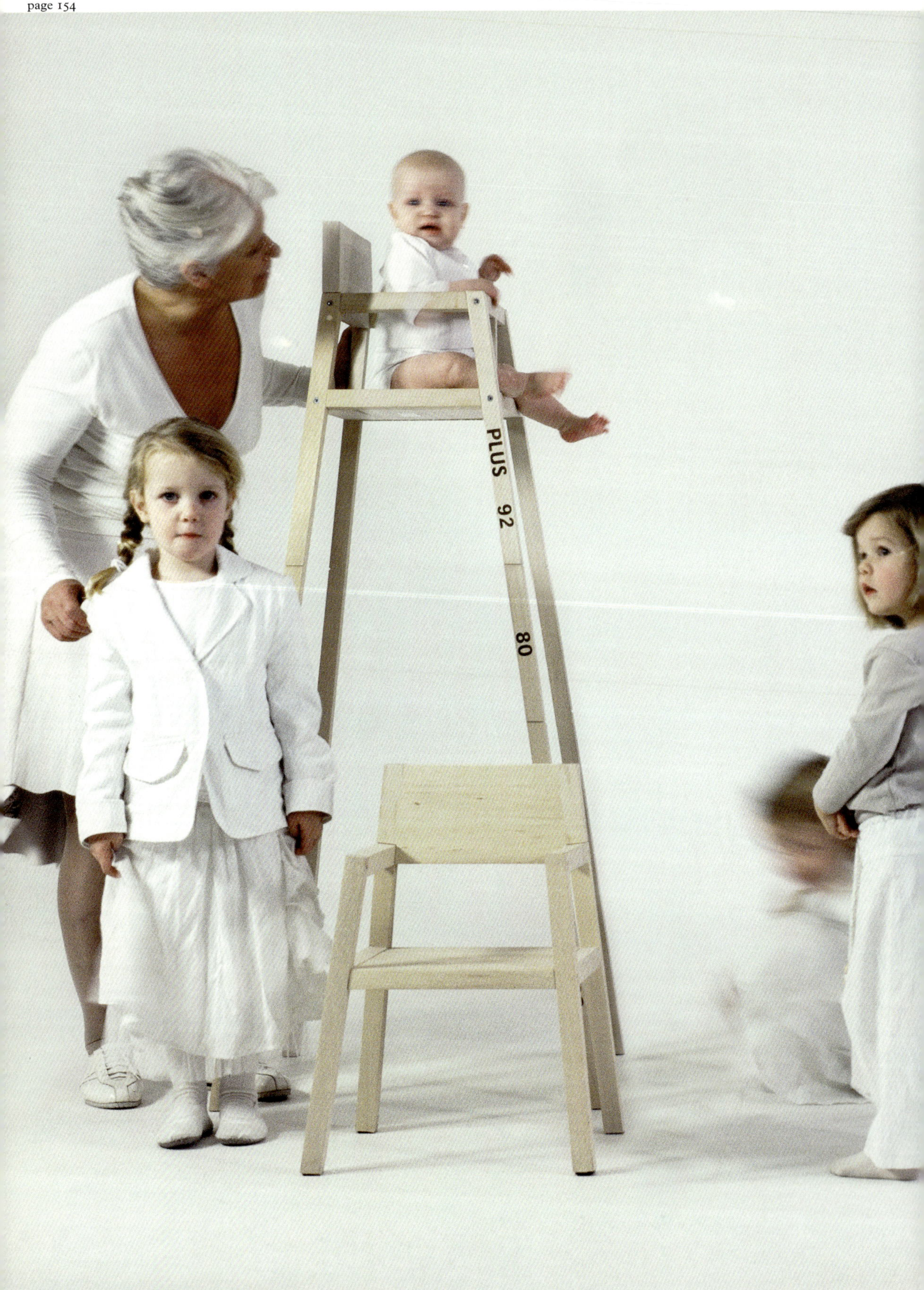

Red Dot Award 2006 (product design)

coll.nr. 146 00
Highchair
Maartje Steenkamp, 2003
white beech
60 x 60 x 145 cm

This chair is a companion through childhood, as the child grows the chair diminishes. The notches on the legs indicate each stage of the chair. So when you feel it is time, you can saw off what is not needed any more.

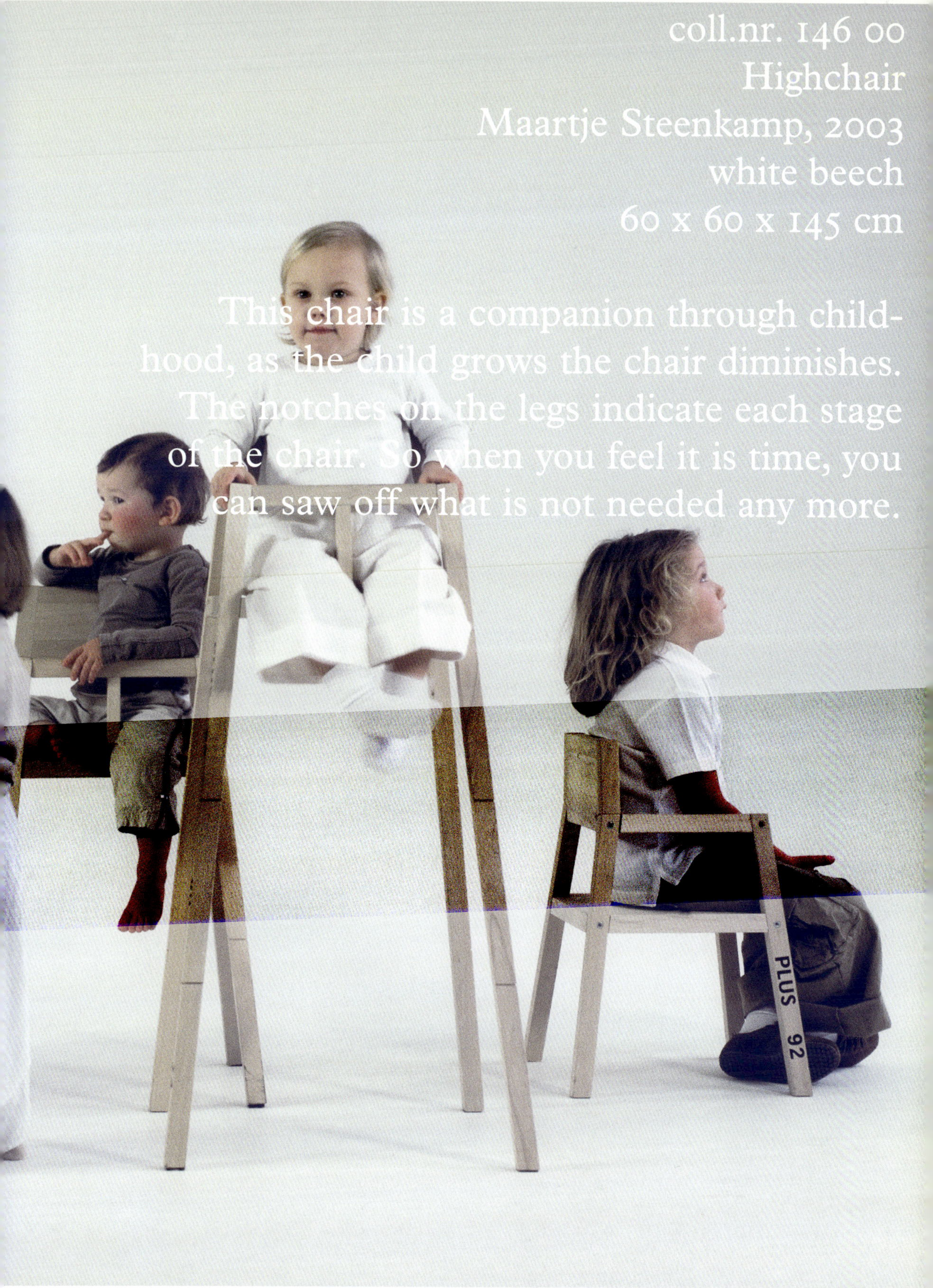

coll.nr. 186 00
Tableau
tablecloth
Maurice Scheltens, 2005
cotton, print
6 settings: 212 x 140 cm
8 settings: 278 x 142 cm

Using photogram technique, this tablecloth is decorated with the silhouettes of the aftermath of a dinner party. The shadows tell the story.

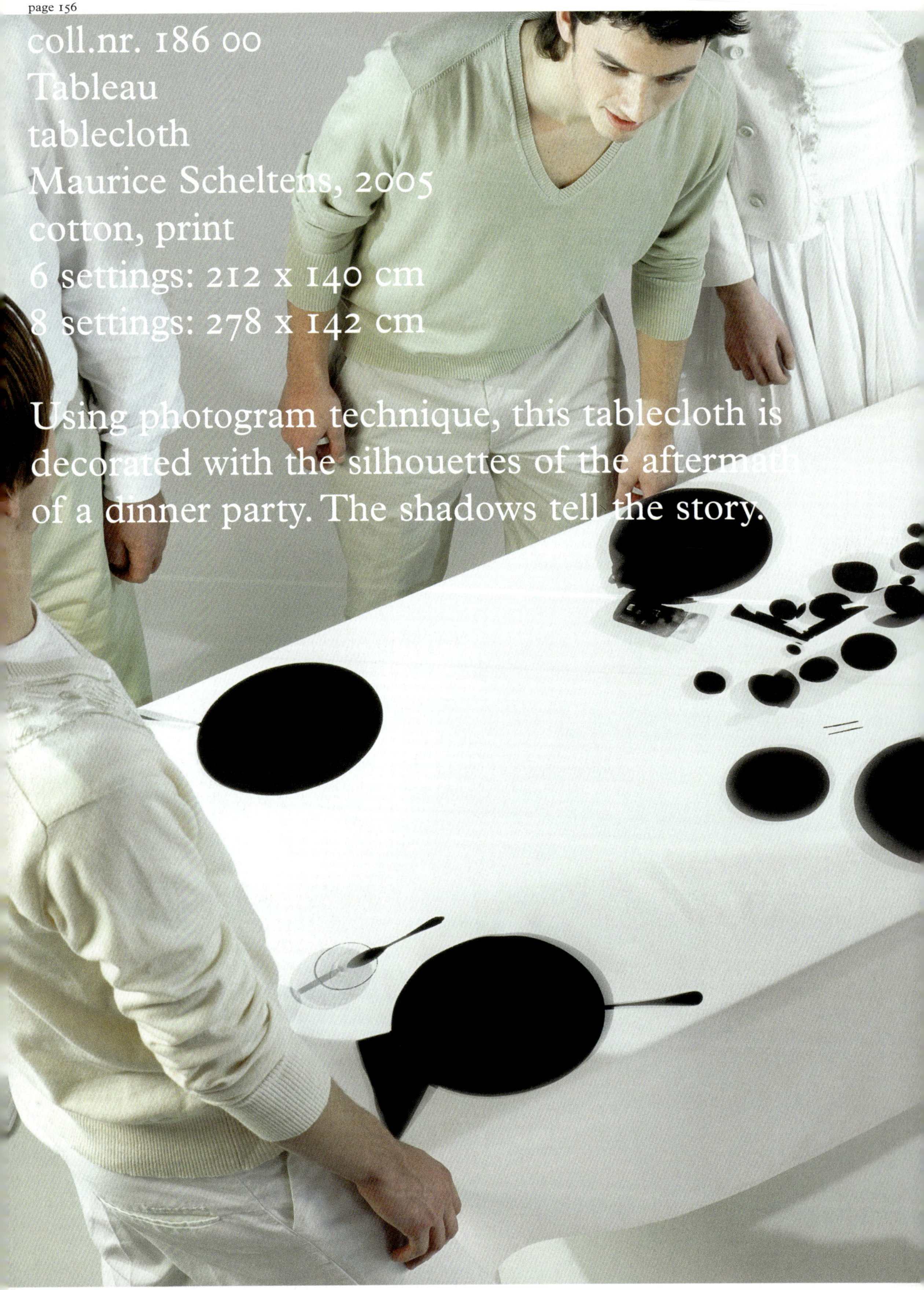

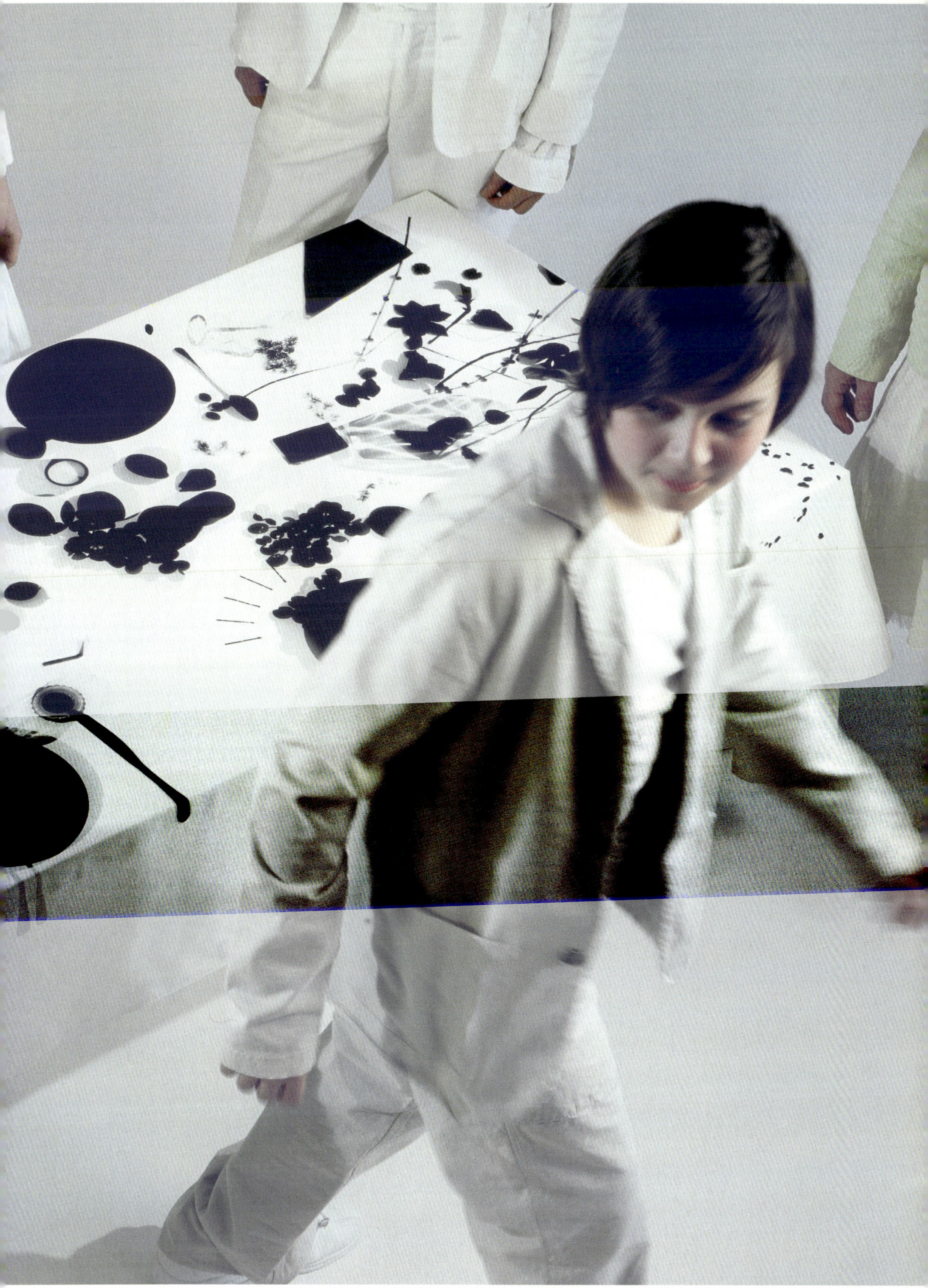

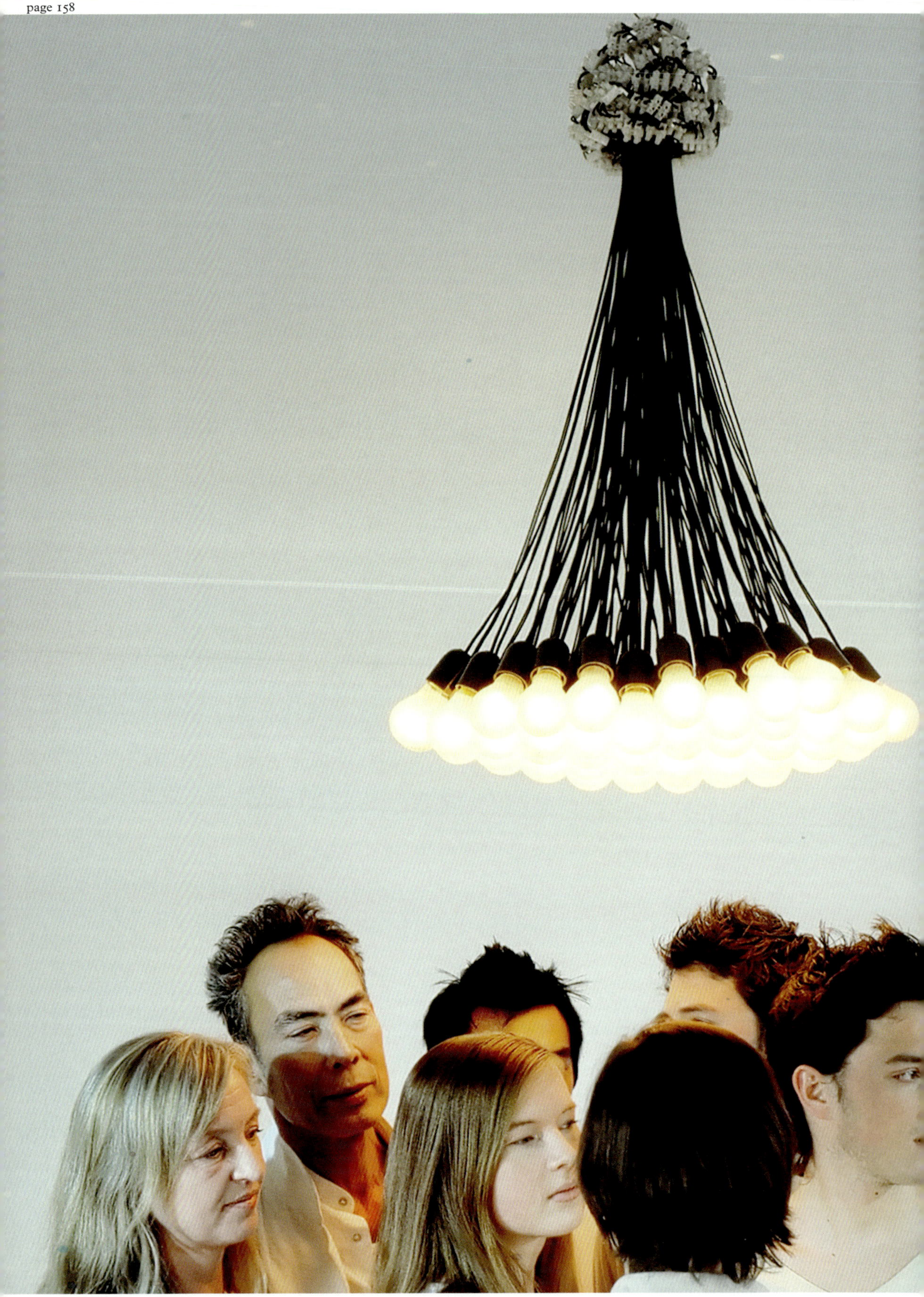

coll.nr. 021 00
85 Lamps
Rody Graumans, 1993
85 bulbs 7w/15w, standard fittings
ø 70 x 110 cm

This lamp uses only what is necessary to create light. By multiplying these essential elements an opulent chandelier is created. Less and more united in a single product.

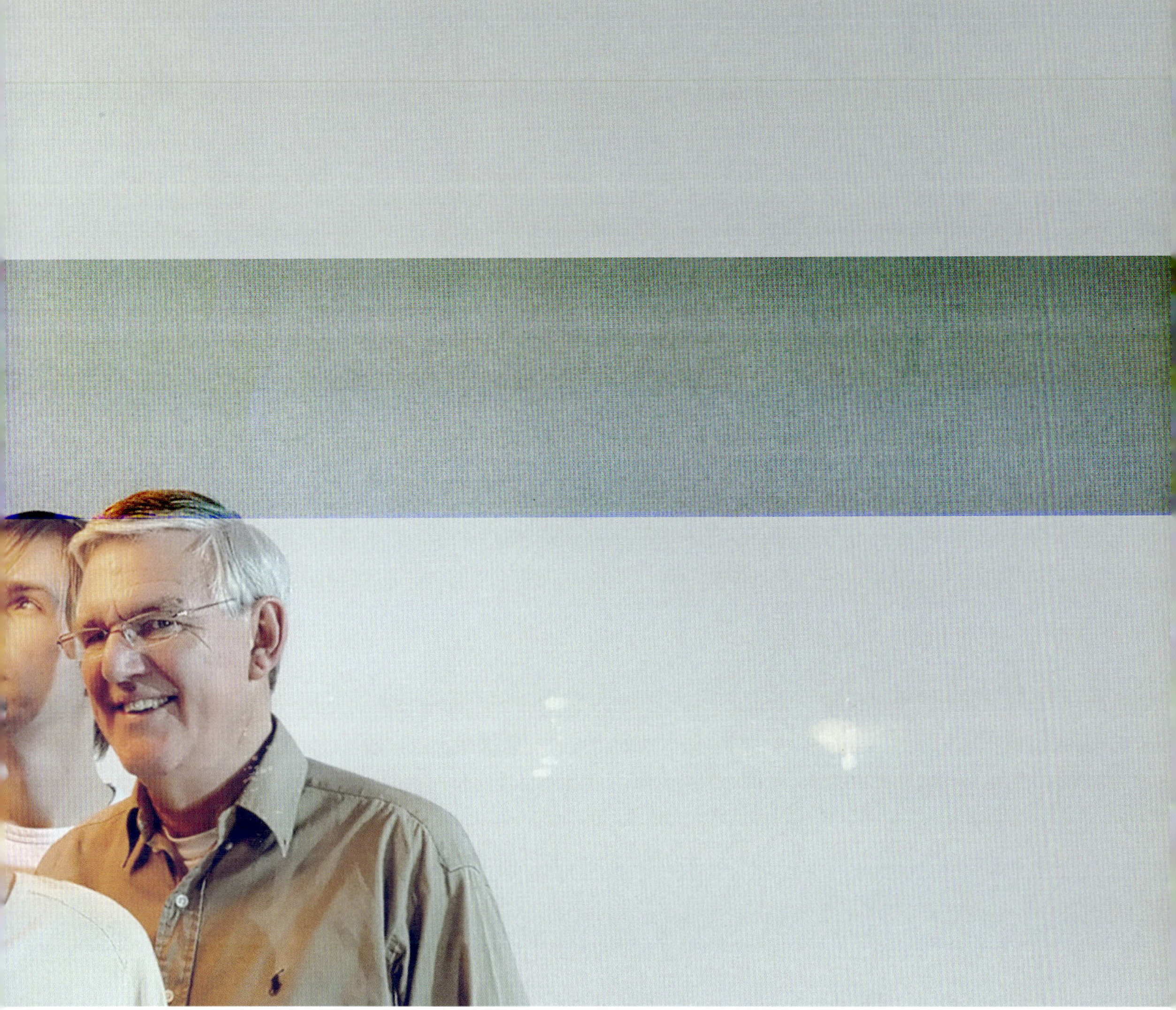

coll.nr. 187 00
Blooming over cup
Mina Wu, Jan B., 2005
porcelain, transfer print
ø 5.5 x 9 cm

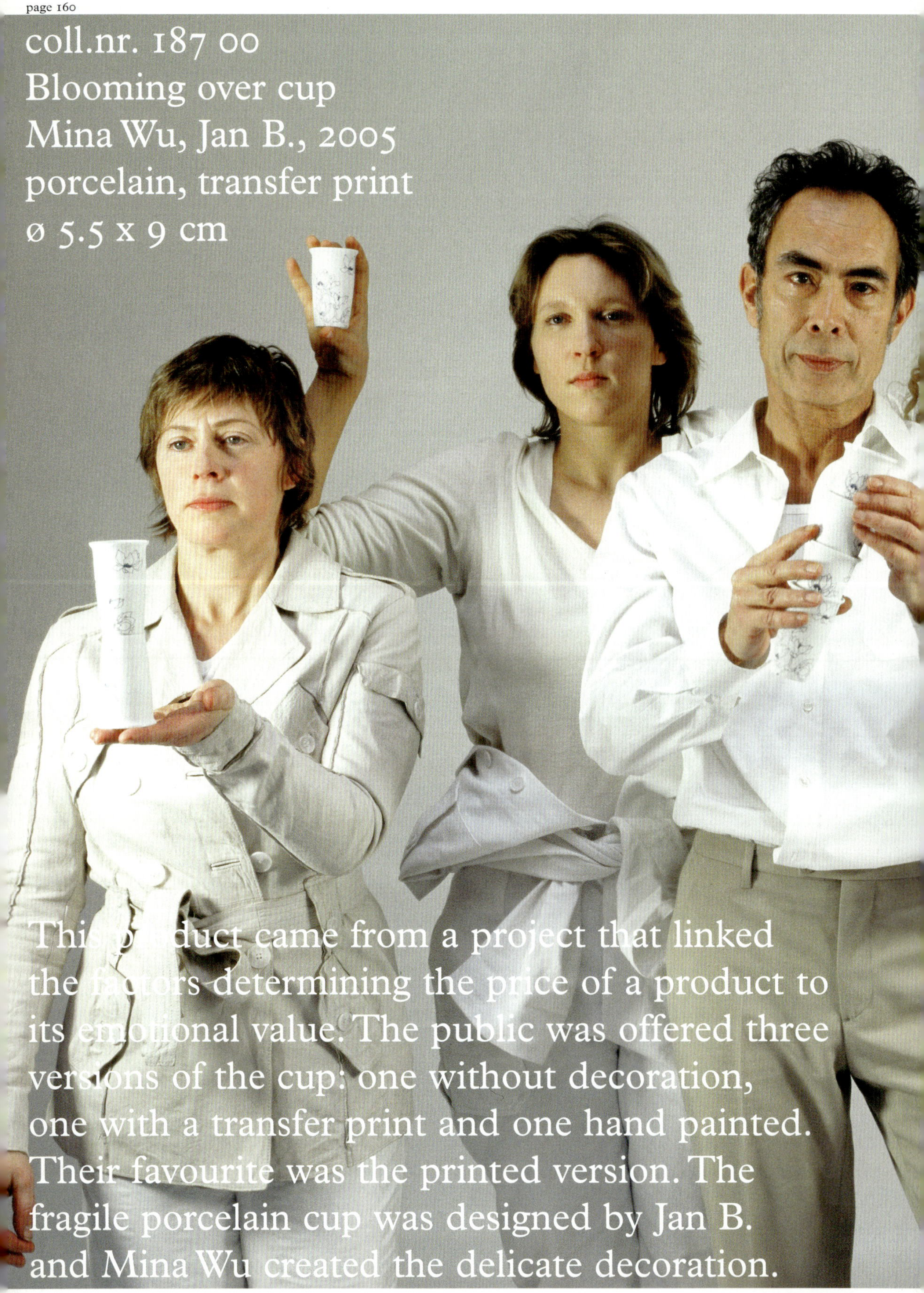

This product came from a project that linked the factors determining the price of a product to its emotional value. The public was offered three versions of the cup: one without decoration, one with a transfer print and one hand painted. Their favourite was the printed version. The fragile porcelain cup was designed by Jan B. and Mina Wu created the delicate decoration.

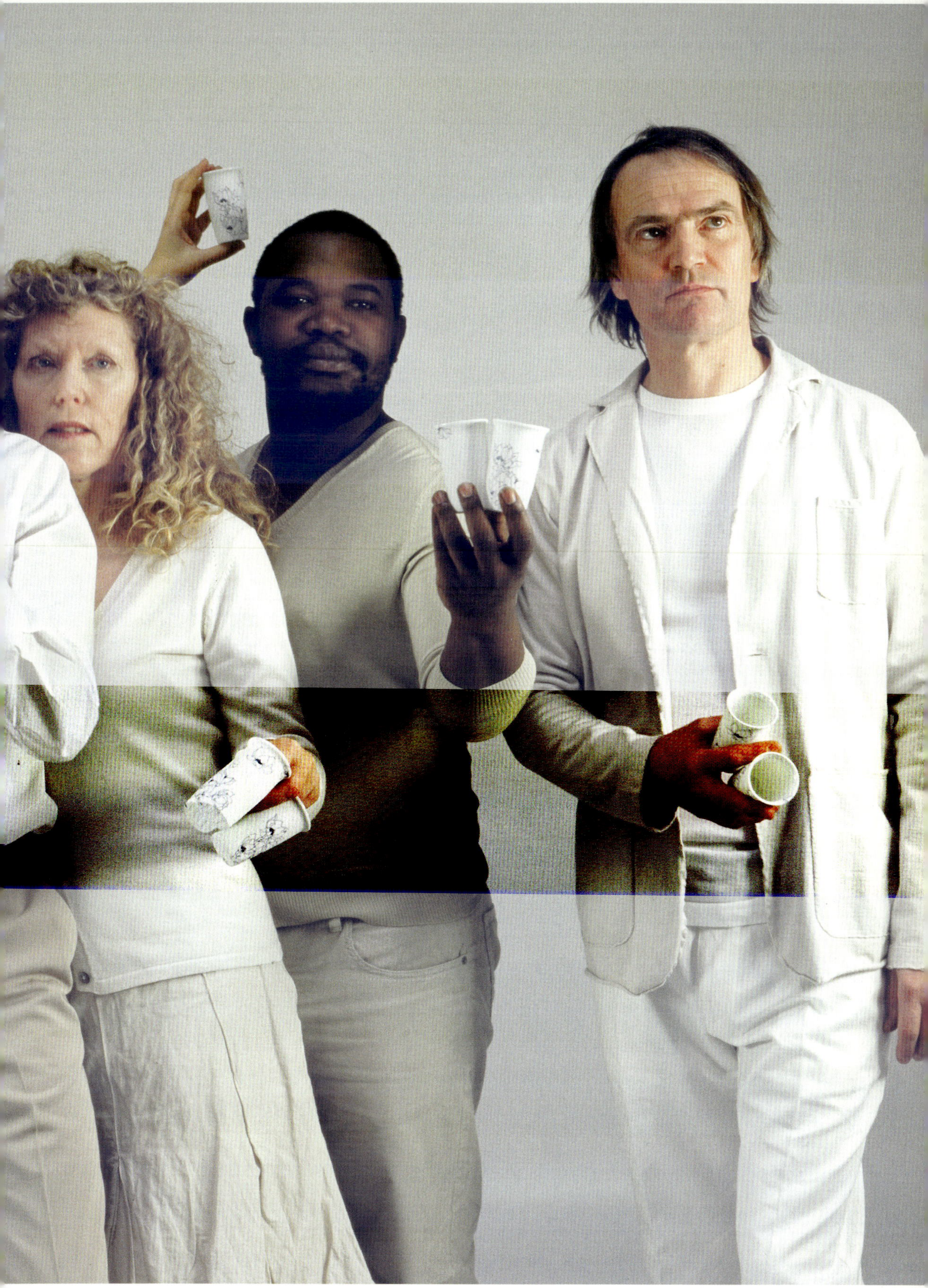

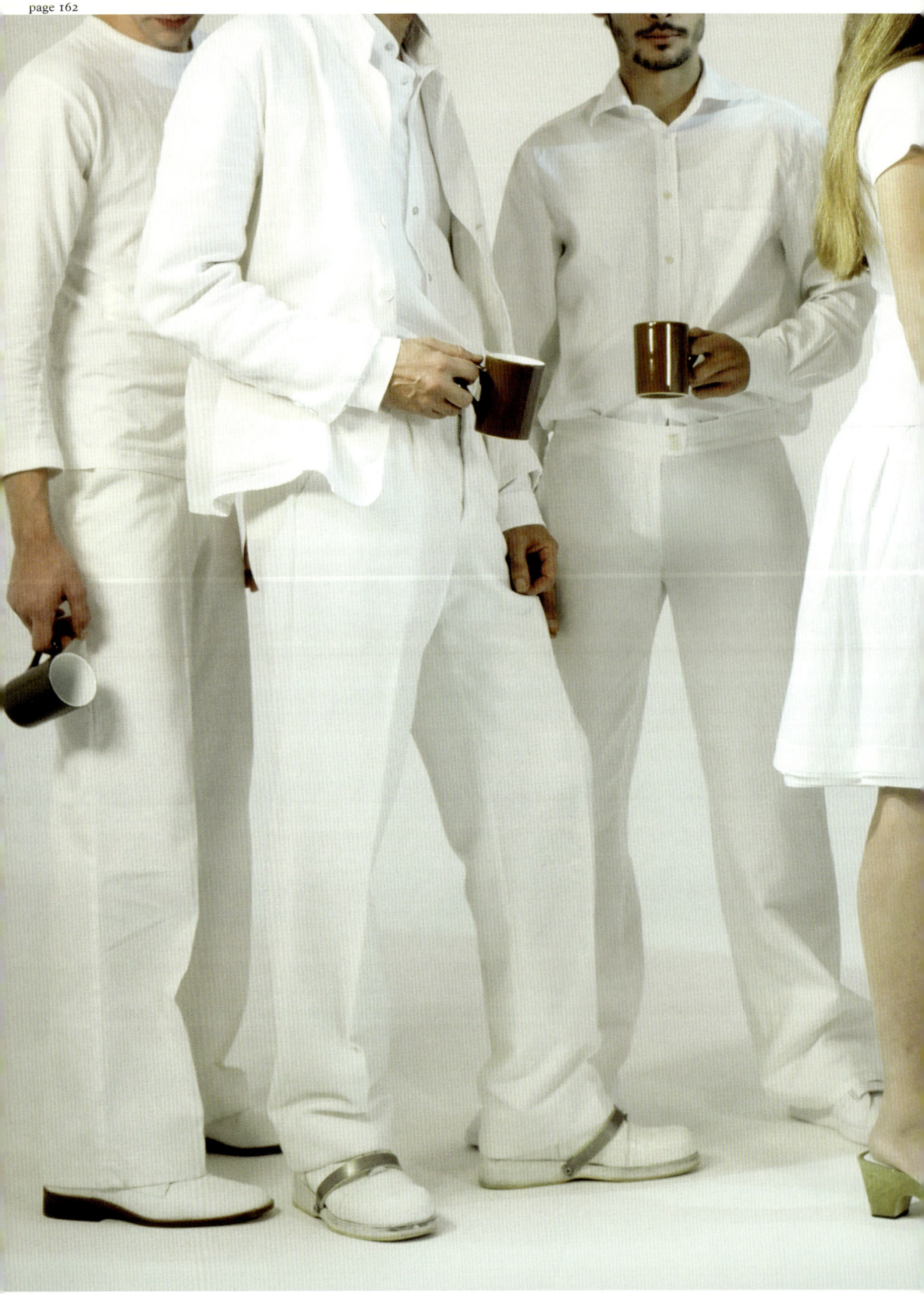

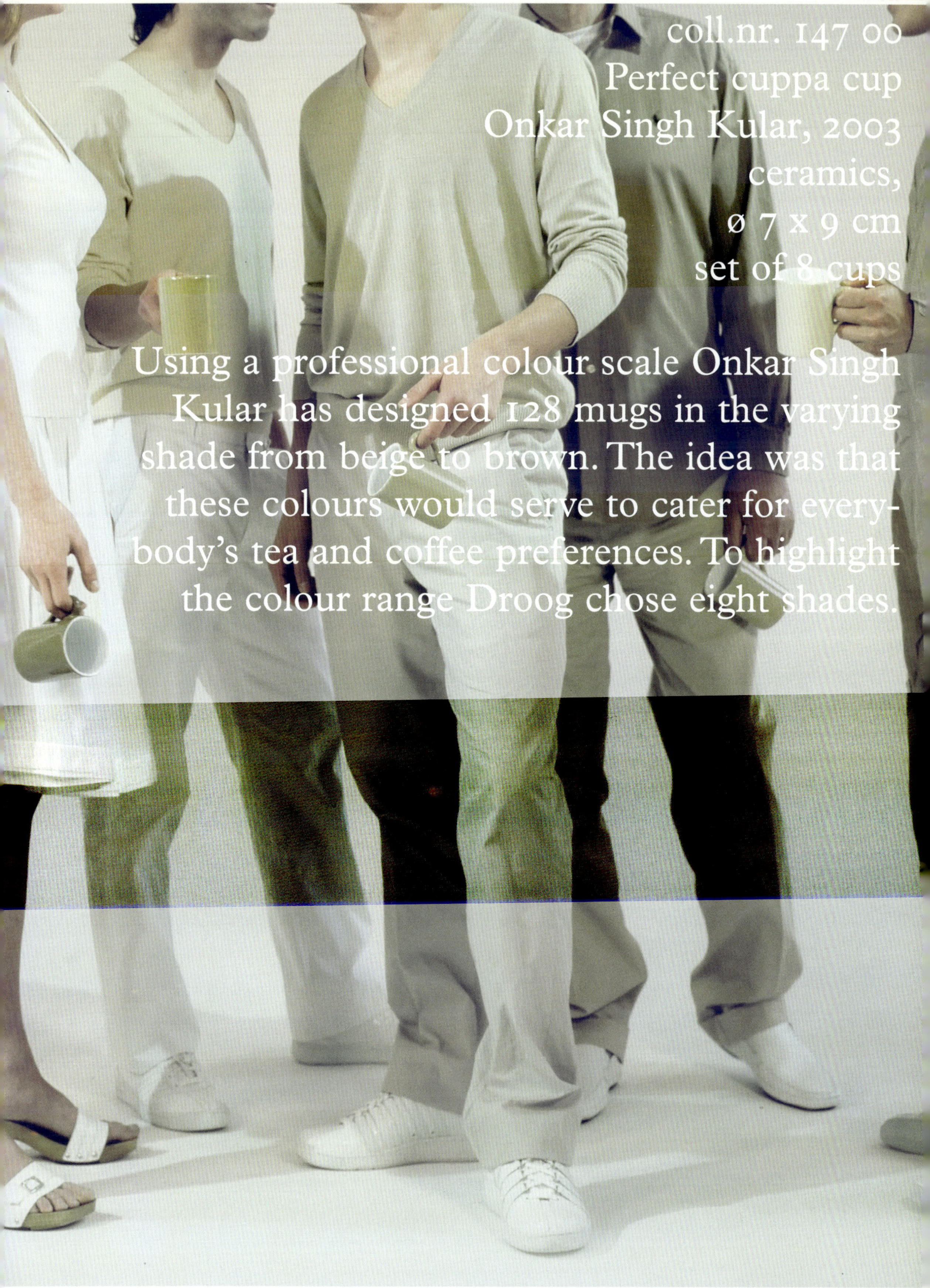

coll.nr. 147 00
Perfect cuppa cup
Onkar Singh Kular, 2003
ceramics,
ø 7 x 9 cm
set of 8 cups

Using a professional colour scale Onkar Singh Kular has designed 128 mugs in the varying shade from beige to brown. The idea was that these colours would serve to cater for everybody's tea and coffee preferences. To highlight the colour range Droog chose eight shades.

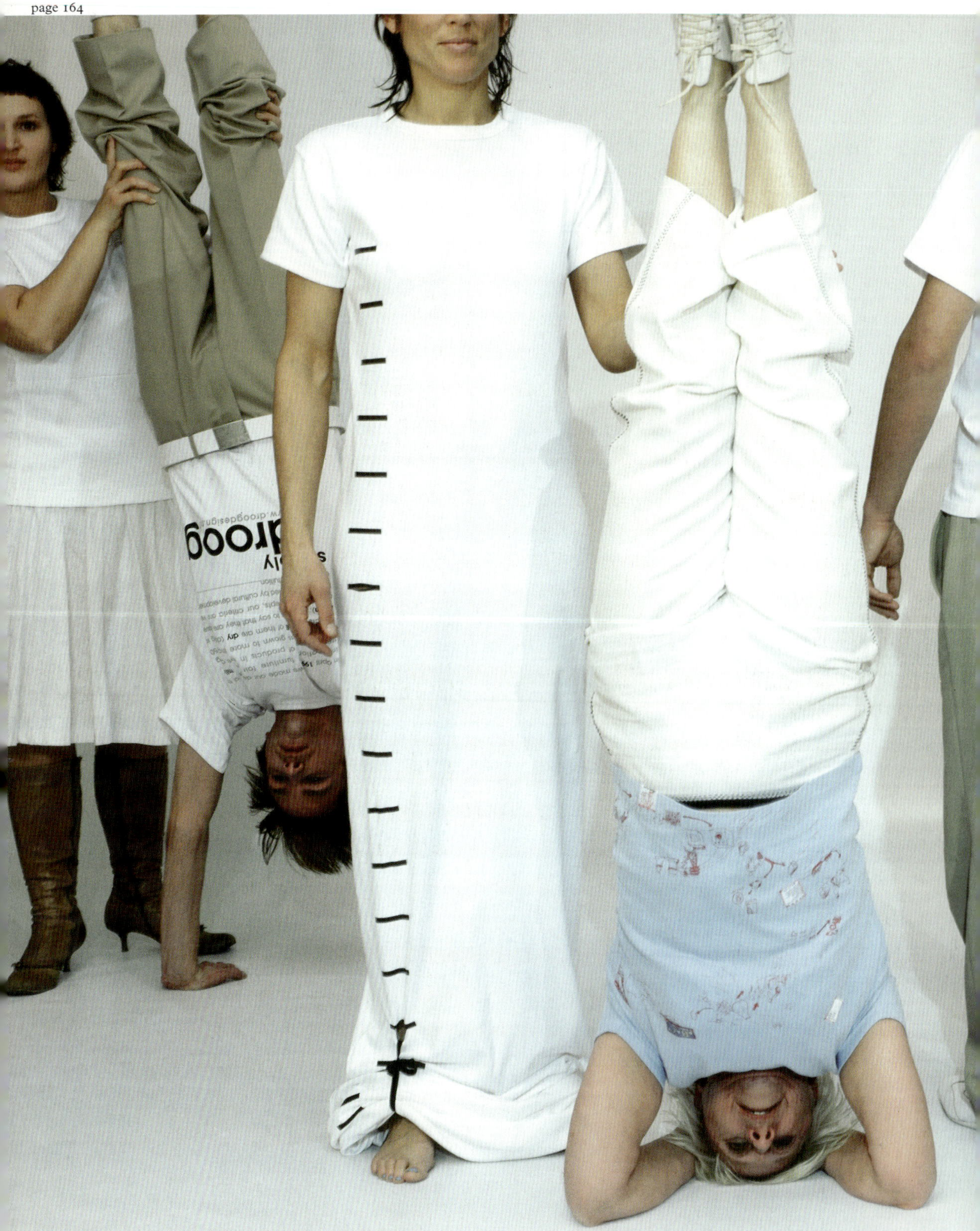

No Iron T-shirt
Helena Seget

Simply Droog
Cherif Morsi

Number one 'The Tallest Man' by Sarah Dorkenwald and Ruth Spitzer (Canada) was made to the measurements of the world's tallest man but can be adjusted to your desired length.

Number two 'This T-shirt tells its own story' by Arlene Birt (U.S.A.) illustrates the journey a T-shirt takes from factory to washing machine.

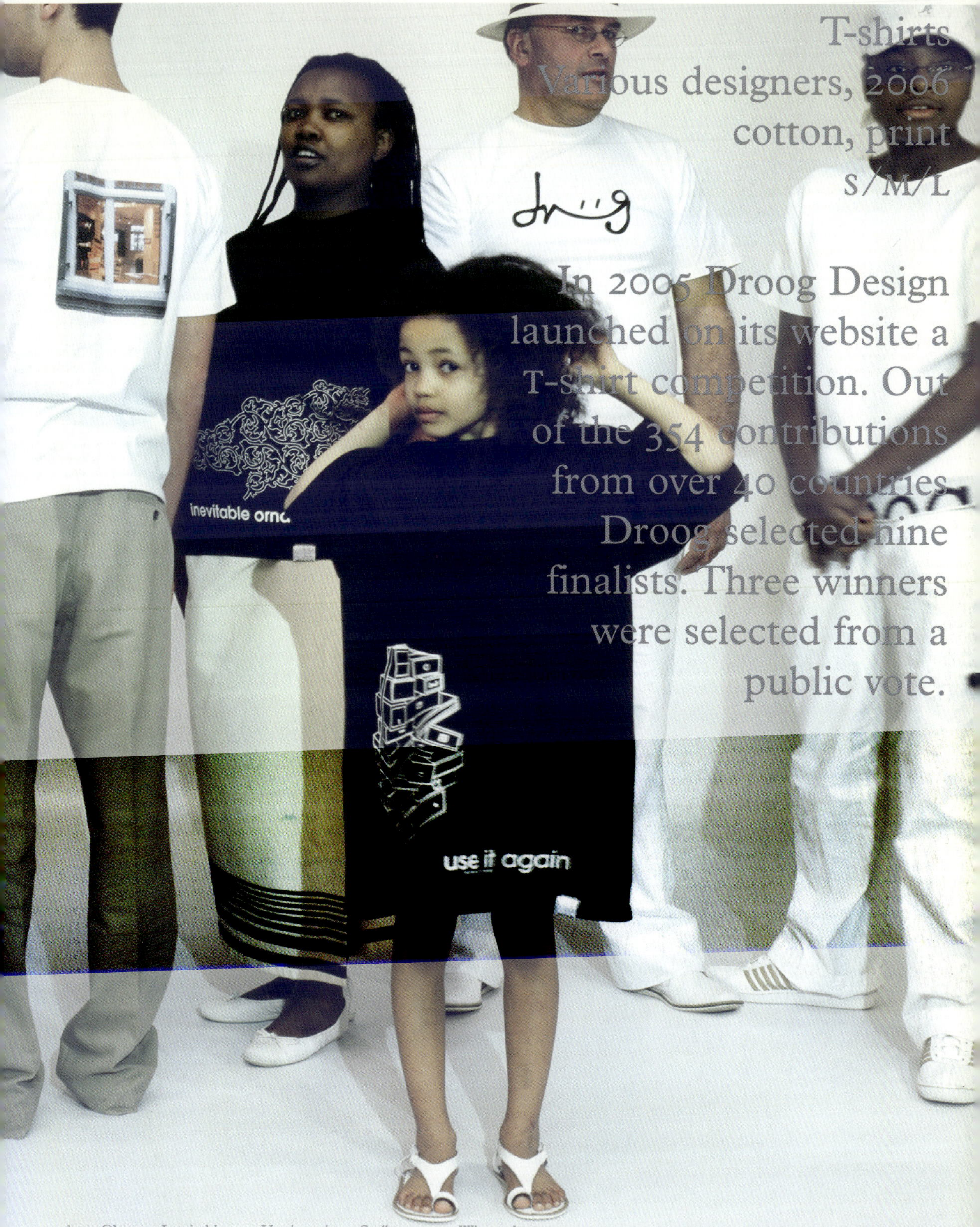

T-shirts

Various designers, 2006
cotton, print
S/M/L

In 2005 Droog Design launched on its website a T-shirt competition. Out of the 354 contributions from over 40 countries Droog selected nine finalists. Three winners were selected from a public vote.

droog@home
Yoya Yoshika

Inevitable ornament
Martijn Schönfeld

Use it again,
Martijn Schönfeld

Scribe
Junjie Koh

Winter droog
Aleksandra Adamczyk

Number three the 'Sweat shop shirt' by Drus Dryden (New Zealand) highlights the humanitarian issues surrounding sweatshop labour. By assembling the T-shirt yourself you save three cents, the wage of a sweatshop worker. (not in photo)

Designers

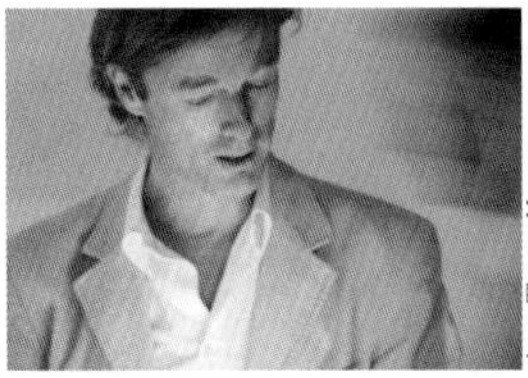

Ed Annink
pages 18, 42, 88

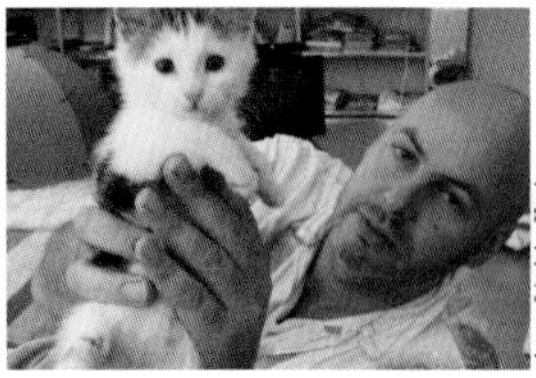

Jan B.
page 160

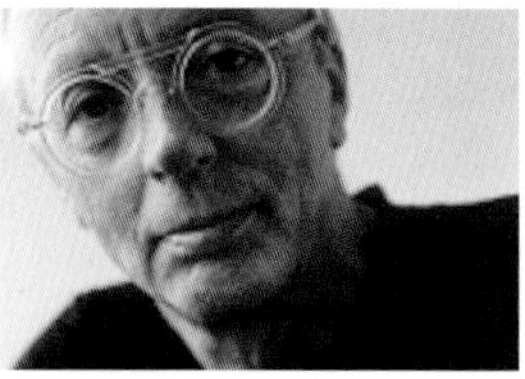

Gijs Bakker
pages 20, 136, 142

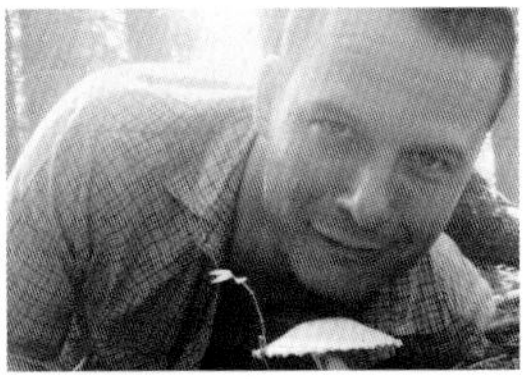

Dylan van den Berg
pages 48, 138

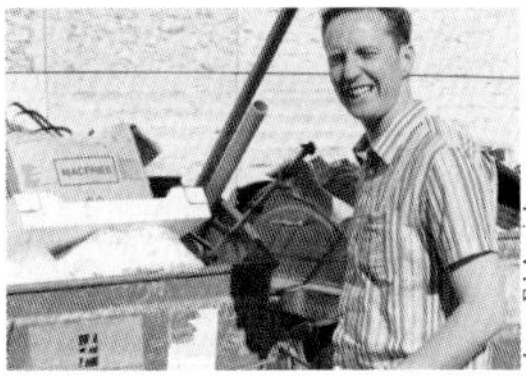

Jurgen Bey
pages 60, 86, 108, 118, 146

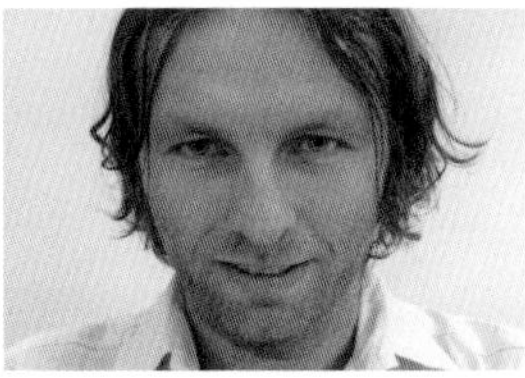

Arian Brekveld
page 76

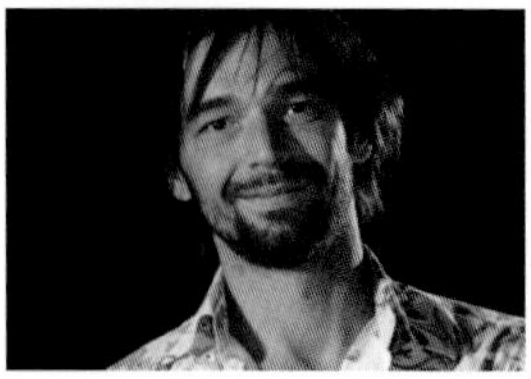

Niels van Eijk
page 24

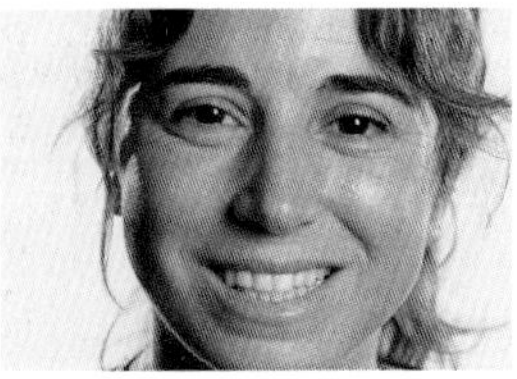

Nina Farkache
page 104

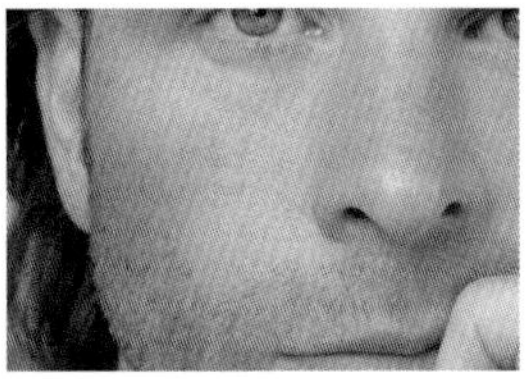

Rody Graumans
page 158

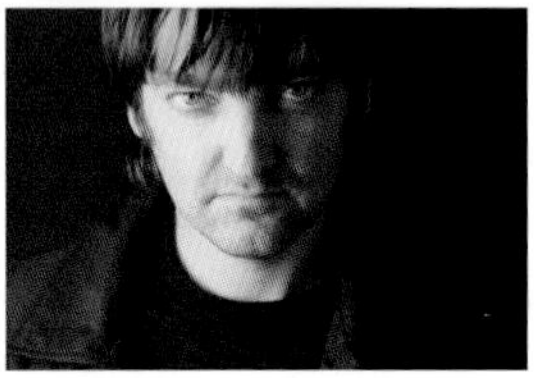

Martí Guixé
pages 30, 58, 80, 98

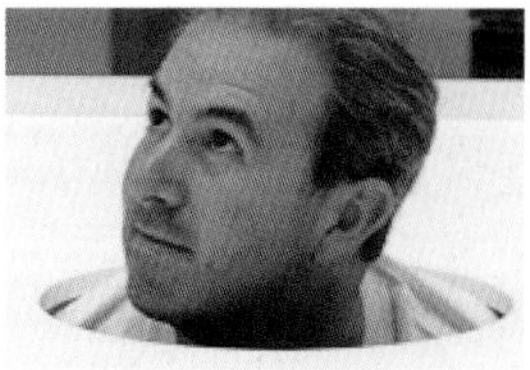

Sam Hecht
page 116

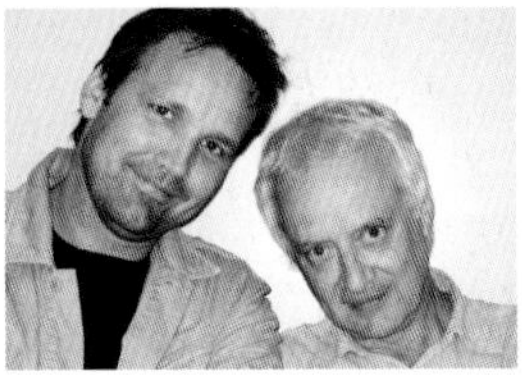

Jan Hoekstra, Leon Ramakers
page 32

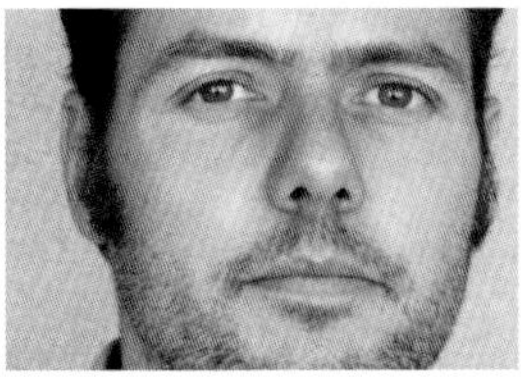

Dick van Hoff
page 134

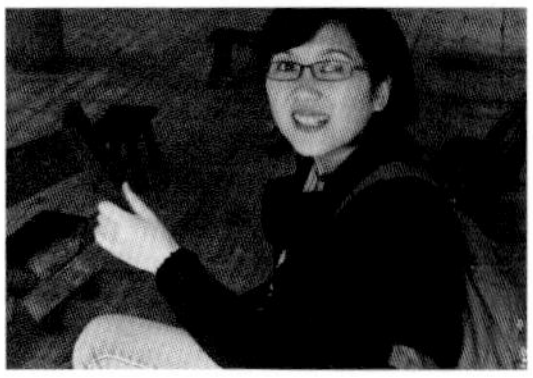

Michelle Huang
page 102

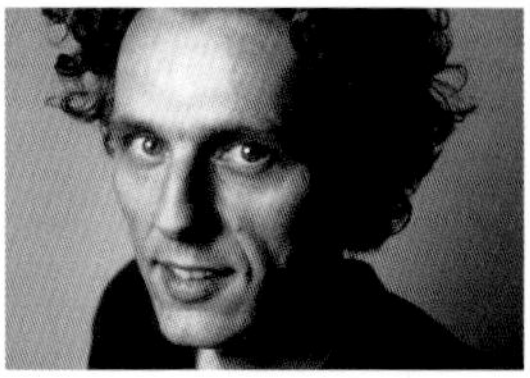

Richard Hutten
pages 28, 29, 94, 96, 122

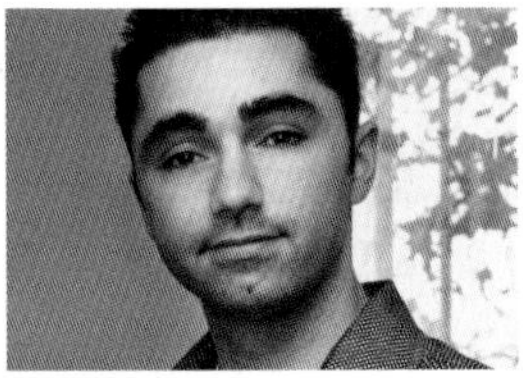

Jason Iftakhar
page 132

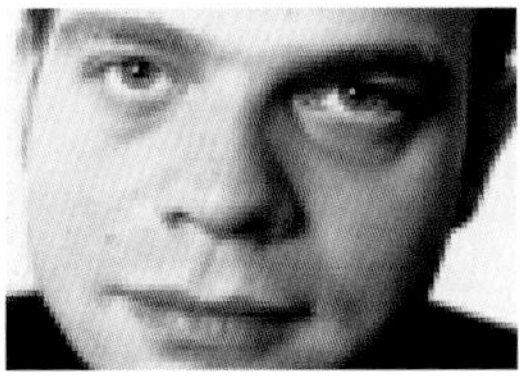

Peter van der Jagt
pages 62, 74

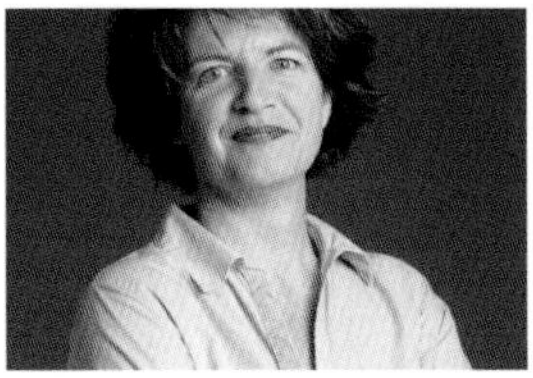

Hella Jongerius
pages 12, 70, 72, 110, 114, 128

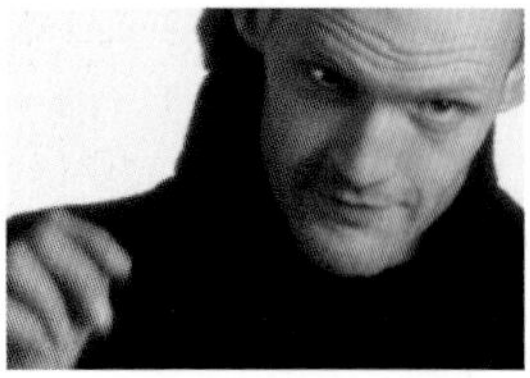

Chris Kabel
pages 14, 22, 90, 92, 148, 150

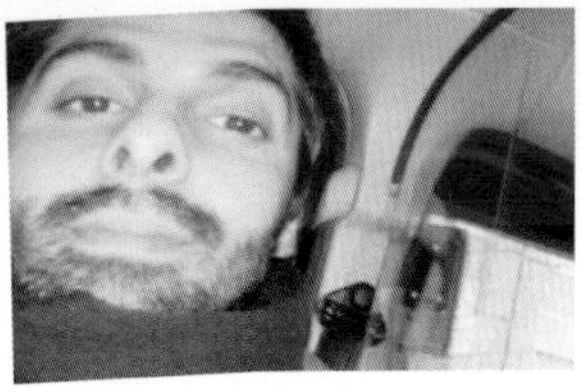
Onkar Singh Kular
page 162

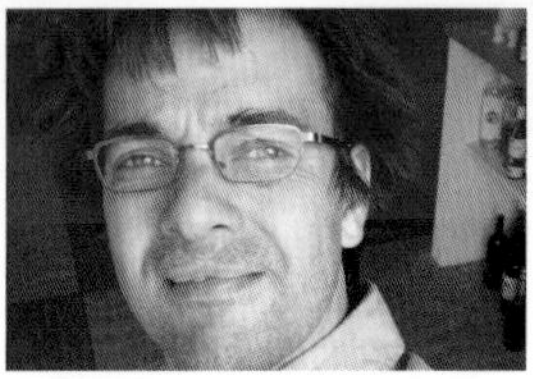
Erik Jan Kwakkel
page 74

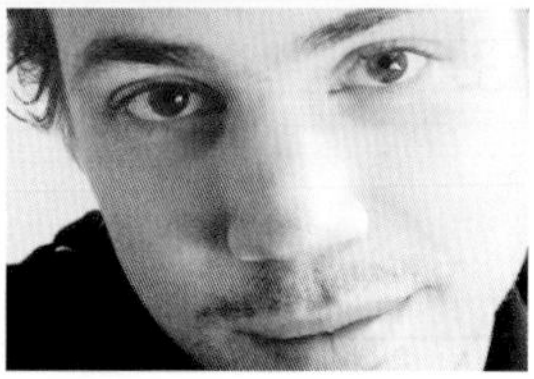
Joris Laarman
page 126

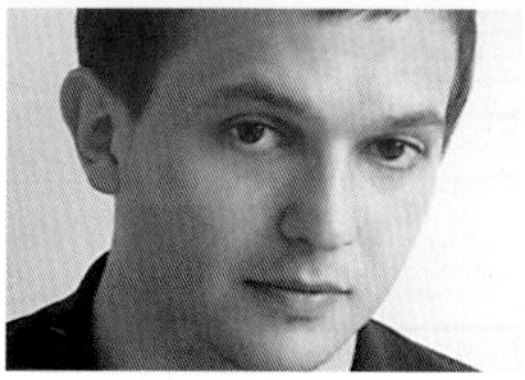
Mario Minale
page 100

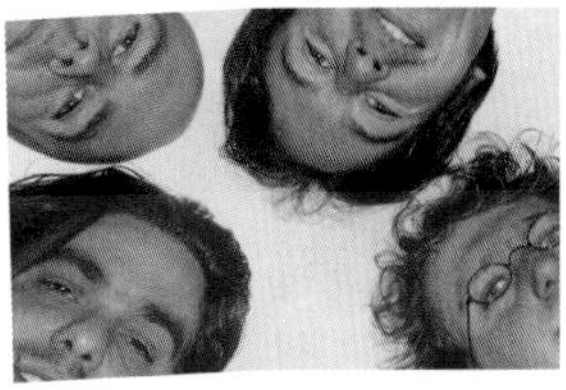
NEXT Architects
page 46

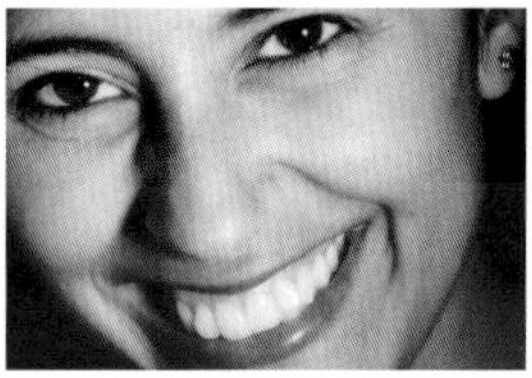
Aura Luz Melis
page 46

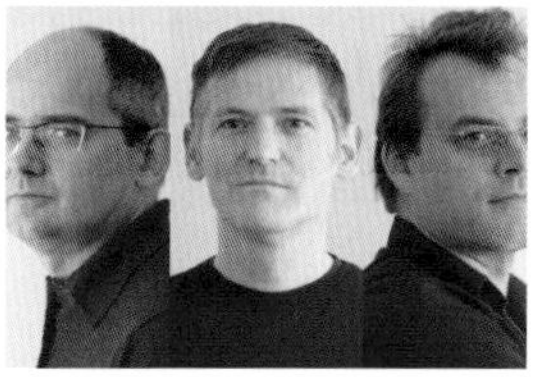
NL Architects
page 78

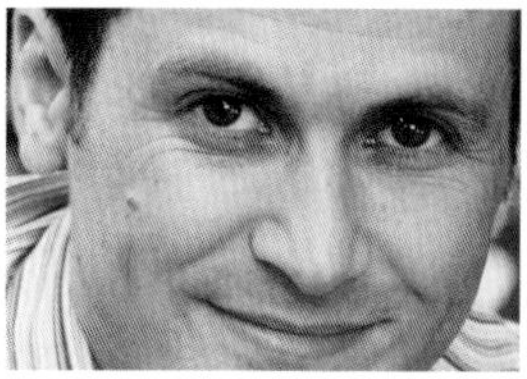
Itay Noy
page 140

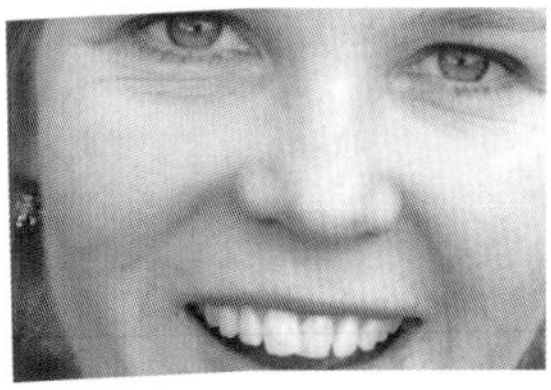
Saar Oosterhof
page 68

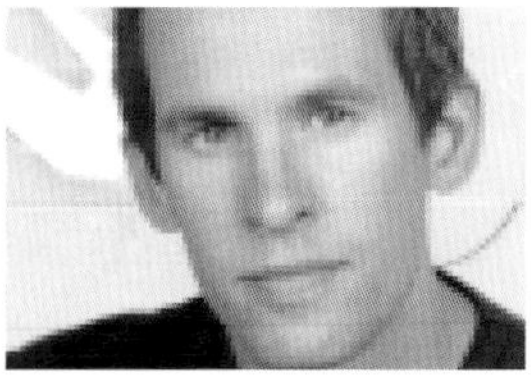
Marijn van der Poll
page 66

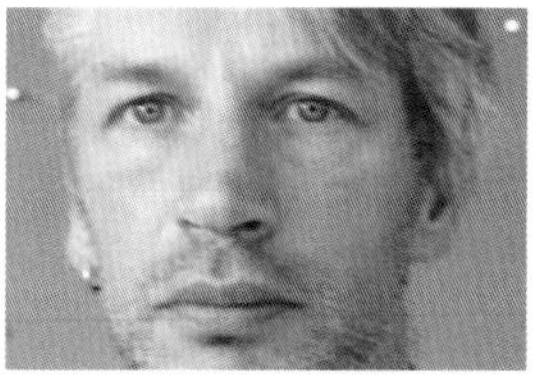
Tejo Remy
pages 26, 50, 106, 144

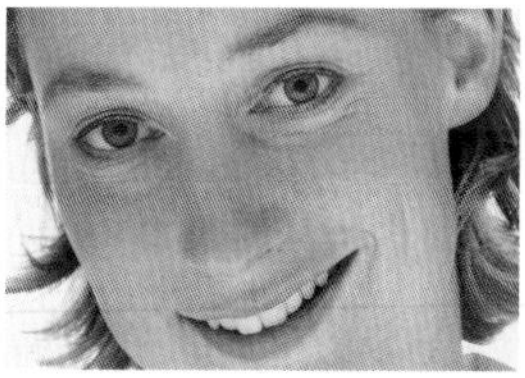
Lonny van Rijswijck
page 112

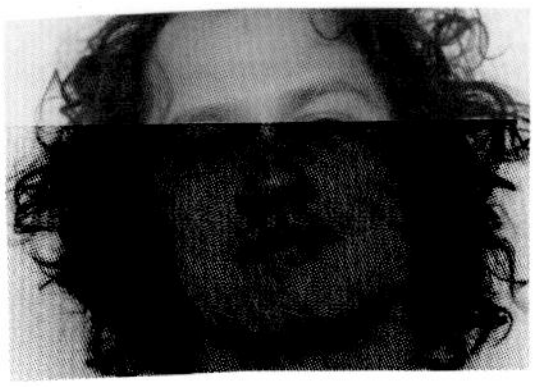
Maurice Scheltens
page 156

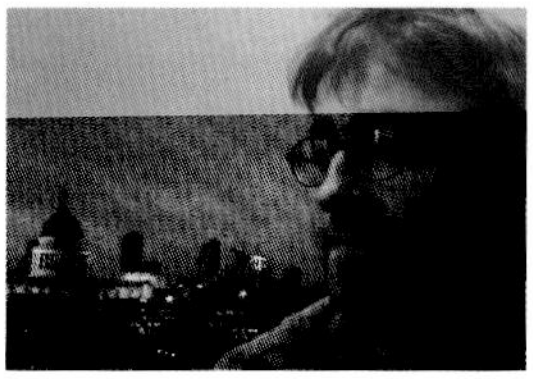
Hector Serrano
page 44

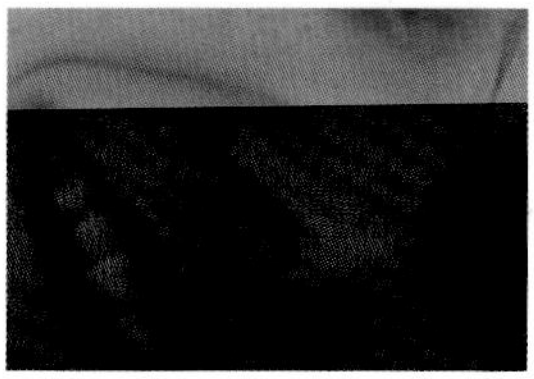
Wieki Somers
pages 48, 138

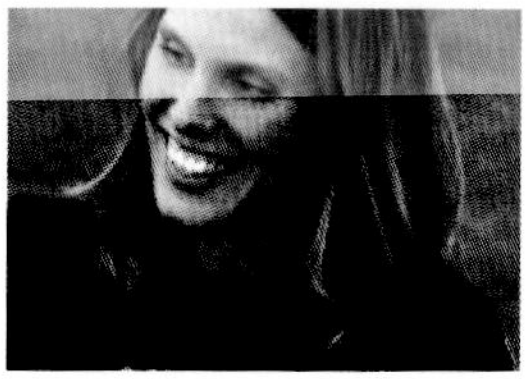
Maartje Steenkamp
page 154

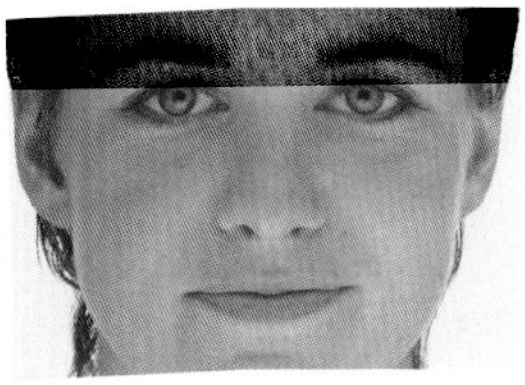
Nadine Sterk
page 112

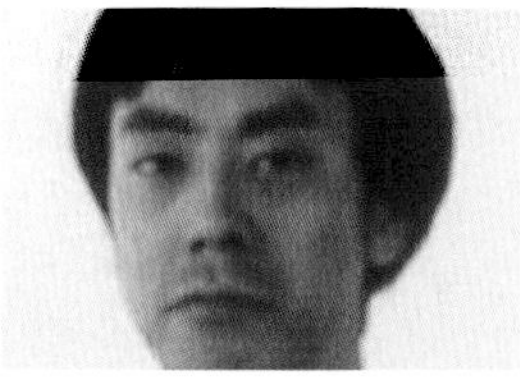
Tadaaki Narita
page 82

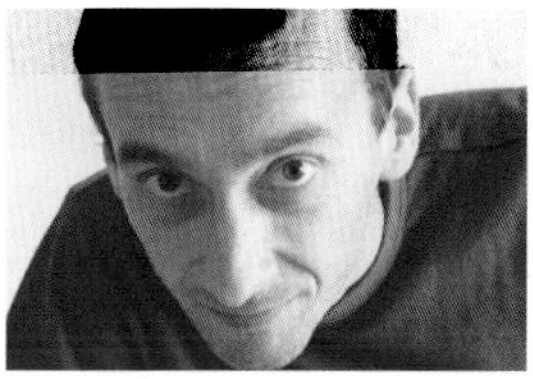
Paolo Ulian
page 54

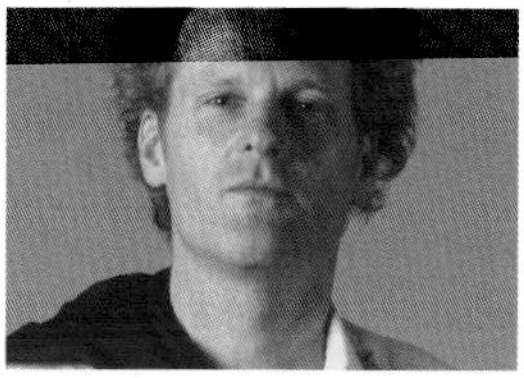
Bas van Tol
page 34

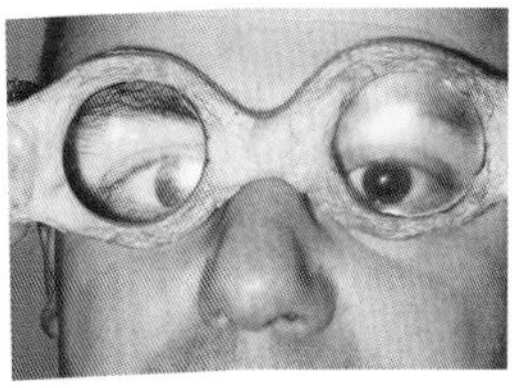
Arnout Visser
pages 34, 36, 38, 40, 52, 56, 74

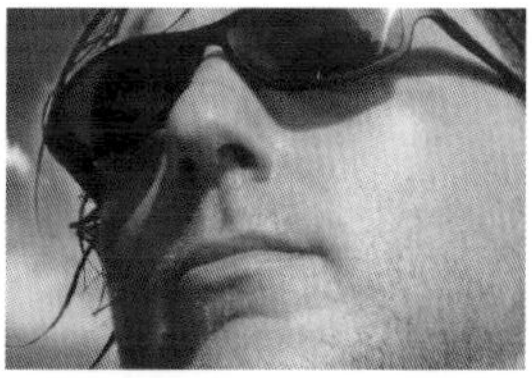
Marcel Wanders
pages 84, 120, 124, 152

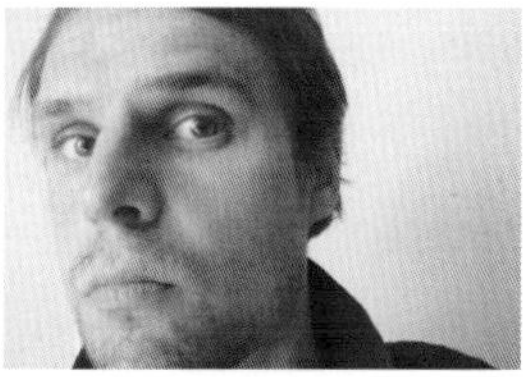
Bas Warmoeskerken
page 64

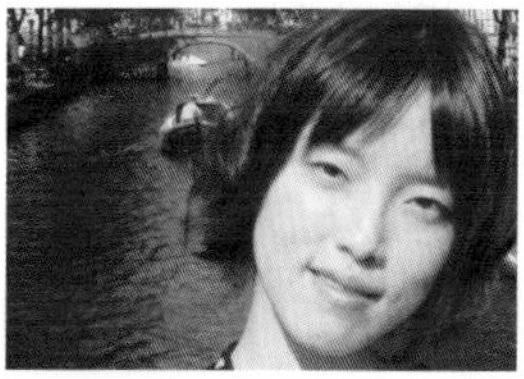
Mina Wu
page 16, 130, 160

Credits

Editing: Renny Ramakers
Introduction: Renny Ramakers
Captions: Sarah Hoyle, Anneke Moors
Translation: Michael Gibbs, Sarah Hoyle
Production: Sabine Gouw, Anneke Moors
Design: Irma Boom
Printing and lithography: Drukkerij Rosbeek

Publisher: Droog, Amsterdam
www.droogdesign.nl

ISBN-10: 90-808574-3-2
ISBN-13: 978-90-808574-3-8

Photography

Photography: Robaard/Theuwkens
Styling director: Marjo Kranenborg (CMK)
Creative assistant: Christel Duijs (CMK)
Styling assistant: Wilma van Pomeren
Make up: Fabiënne Jansen, Liselotte van Saarloos
@House of Orange

Models:
Lamia Abbassi, hond Theo van Adrichem, Victor Alling, Wendel ten Arve, Mea Bavinck, J.P. Bastos, Nisrine Benmerieme, Renate de Boer, Lina Brian, Wolf van de Bos, Honkie Chan, Nico Dekker, Rene Dekker, Noorah van Doornewaard, Saarah van Doornewaard, Luukas van Doornewaard, Yara van Doornewaard, Aaf van Essen, John Fournier, Helen Frik, Sabine Gouw, Jeen Hammink, Machteld Hammink, Khanyi van der Heide, Langa van der Heide, Nandy van der Heide, Flean Holdert, Hans Hovy, hond Hans Hovy, Mel Huang, Alice Jagtenberg, Germaine Jagtenberg, Julie Jagtenberg, Jan Jongejans, Eelis Kiviniemi, Jukka Kiviniemi, Iris Kramer, Maria Klok, Josine Lamberts, Max Lammertse, Moshekwa Langa, Djuro Leideritz, Hester Lenstra, Michael Leung, Padraig McKee, Bas Medik, Melanie Milan, Brian Nijboer, Carmen Nitzer, Phaedra Nitzer, Charlotte Rijkenberg, Martijn Schönfeld, Nora Schuit, Efrem Stein, D.J. Tesselaar, Mireille Verkolf, Jan Verschure, Amber van Vogelpoel, Tjeerd van Waijenburg, Barbara Wijnveld, Jordi Wildschut, Nicky Wildschut, Jeremy Zijlstra

Credits clothing:
Benetton, Cinderella, Day, DNA Collection, Expresso, Fred de la Bretoniere, Jan Jansen for Orson + Bodil, K-Swiss, Lady Day, Mads Nørgaard, Naja Lauf, Noon, O Collection, Orson + Bodil, Pilar Chica, Queen mum, Ramirez, ScapaScapa Kids, Sisley, Stella Nova, The English Hatter, The People of the Labyrinth

Thanks to:
Staff and co-workers Droog Design
Studio Pindakaas

This publication is made to celebrate the travelling exhibition 'A Human Touch' and has been made possible by the means of The Netherlands Culture Fund, The Netherlands Ministry of Foreign Affairs and The Netherlands Ministry of Education, Culture & Science.

Buitenlandse Zaken